21003

GW00417593

bus

FINANCE CAPITALISM UNVEILED

FINANCE CAPITALISM UNVEILED

BANKS AND THE GERMAN POLITICAL ECONOMY

Richard Deeg

Ann Arbor
THE UNIVERSITY OF MICHIGAN PRESS

Copyright © by the University of Michigan 1999
All rights reserved
Published in the United States of America by
The University of Michigan Press
Manufactured in the United States of America
♾ Printed on acid-free paper

2002 2001 2000 1999   4 3 2 1

No part of this publication may be reproduced, stored in a retrieval system,
or transmitted in any form or by any means, electronic, mechanical, or
otherwise, without the written permission of the publisher.

A CIP catalog record for this book is available from the British Library.

Library of Congress Cataloging-in-Publication Data

Deeg, Richard, 1961–
    Finance capitalism unveiled : banks and the German political
economy / Richard Deeg.
      p. cm.
   Includes bibliographical references and index.
   ISBN 0-472-10936-7 (acid-free paper)
   1. Finance—Germany.   2. Banks and banking—Germany.
   3. Germany—Economic conditions—1990–   I. Title.
HG186.G3 D364   1998
332.1′0943—ddc21   98-25519
                                         CIP

To my family

Contents

Tables and Figures

Tables

Figures

Preface

In this book I have set out to accomplish two main goals. The first is to provide a much more comprehensive and nuanced analysis of the German banking system and its broader role in the German political economy than one presently finds in the literature. The popular and scholarly focus (sometimes bordering on obsession) on the three big German commercial banks has unfortunately obscured the crucial role of the savings and cooperative banks in Germany. While a number of scholars in Germany have studied these other banks, these banks have received only superficial attention in English language studies of Germany. I have sought to redress this imbalance by providing an analysis of the historical evolution and organization of the German banking sector that incorporates all three major types of banks. My account of the banking system rejects simple functionalist explanations of its organizational development and instead provides a more historical and constructivist explanation which argues that the key institutions of the system emerged out of particular political struggles among groups to protect their social and economic position. This broader depiction of the banking system, in turn, leads to a recasted understanding of the relationships between German banks, industry, and the state.

The second goal of this book is to show how the banks and German political economy have adapted to the recent era of regional and global economic integration. As I will argue, there has been considerable change in Germany as a result of these external pressures. Perhaps most prominent are the push to develop an Anglo-Saxon style securities sector and the weakening ability of large banks to influence industry. On the whole, however, this book suggests that the key institutions of the German political economy have been incrementally adapted to accommodate such pressures while preserving the key characteristics that make them distinct. Thus, German capitalism is still significantly different from "Anglo-Saxon" capitalism, even as the two have become more similar in several respects.

This project began in the late 1980s while I was in graduate school at MIT. I still remember distinctly the day when, sitting in Chuck Sabel's office, Chuck suggested I pursue the all-important yet untold story of German banks. The subject struck a chord with me right away and I set off to Germany to learn this story. As Chuck surmised, there was indeed an important and relatively unknown story to be told about the German banks—even though it wasn't quite the story he thought it would be. For Chuck's "hot tip" and long years of guidance, I am greatly indebted to him. I would also like to express gratitude to my two other advisers at MIT, Suzanne Berger and Dick Samuels, for their probing questions and immense patience.

This project has benefited immeasurably over the years from the support of many institutions and individuals. I would like to start by thanking the Landeskreditbank of Baden-Württemberg and its former president, Rolf Schoeck, for the opportunity they provided me to learn about German public banking from the inside. I am especially indebted to Wilfried Heger of the Landeskreditbank who spent endless hours with me discussing German banking and opened the doors to countless interviews in the German banking community. I am also pleased to say that he has become an enduring friend. I would like to thank Fred Peemöller of the Deutsche Bank who shared much of his knowledge about German banks with me and arranged several important interviews within the bank. I wish also to express gratitude to David Soskice and the Wissenschaftszentrum Berlin for their substantial financial, technical, and intellectual support over many years. The penultimate version of this book was written while I was in residence at the Max-Planck-Institute for the Study of Societies (Cologne) during 1995. The generous support of the Institute and its directors—Renate Mayntz, Fritz Scharpf, and Wolfgang Streeck—and the intellectual stimulation provided by my many fine colleagues there greatly advanced this project toward completion. I would especially like to thank Susanne Lütz of the Institute for her key role in bringing me there and, more importantly, for the fruitful scholarly relationship we have begun.

Parts of chapter 3 have been previously published and I wish to acknowledge the permission granted by the original publishers to include portions of these articles in this book. These include Carfax Publishing Limited for "Banks and Industrial Finance in the 1990s," *Industry and Innovation* 4, no. 1 (June 1997): 53–73; Frank Cass and Company for "The State, Banks, and Economic Governance in Germany," *German Politics* 2, no. 2 (August 1993): 149–76; and Kluwer Academic Publishers for "What Makes German Banks Different," *Small Business Economics* 10, no. 2 (1998): 93–101.

I am also indebted to several individuals who, by reading parts or all of my manuscript or through many discussions with me, greatly shaped my thinking; these are Chris Allen, Steve Casper, John Griffin, Margaret Levi, Bernard Mennis, and Gary Mucciaroni. A special note of thanks goes to Sigurts Vitols— my "soulmate" in matters of German banking. After so many years of collaboration it has sometimes become difficult to know where Sigurts' ideas end and my own begin—I trust he will forgive any unwitting transgressions. Last, but far from least, I would like to thank my wife, Rebecca Evans, and my family whose love and support have made my life as rich as it is and given me what I needed to make this book happen.

List of Acronyms

BAKred	Bundesaufsichtsamt für das Kreditwesen
	(Federal Banking Supervisory Office)
BAWe	Bundesaufsichtsamt für den Wertpapierhandel
	(Federal Supervisory Office for Securities Trading)
BVR	Bundesverband der deutschen Volks- und Raiffeisenbanken
	(Federal Association of German Volks- and Raiffeisenbanken)
BDI	Bundesverband der deutschen Industrie
	(Federal Association of German Industry)
BW-Bank	Baden-Württembergische Bank
DtA	Deutsche Ausgleichsbank
	(German Equalization Bank)
DG Bank	DG Bank Deutsche Genossenschaftsbank
	(DG Bank German Cooperative Bank)
DGZ Bank	Deutsche Girozentrale–Deutsche Kommunalbank
	(German Girozentrale–German Communal Bank)
DQP	diversified quality production
DSGV	Deutscher Sparkassen- und Giroverband
	(German Savings Bank and Giro Association)
ERP	European Recovery Program
GA	Gemeinschaftsaufgabe, "Verbesserung der regionalen Wirtschaftsstruktur"
	(Joint Task for the Improvement of Regional Infrastructure)
HELABA	Hessische Landesbank
KBG	Kapitalbeteiligungsgesellschaft
	(equity participation company)
KfW	Kreditanstalt für Wiederaufbau
	(Loan Corporation for Reconstruction)

KWG	Kreditwesengesetz
	(Banking Act)
L-Bank	Landeskreditbank Baden-Württemberg
(also LKB)	(State Credit Bank of Baden-Württemberg)
LfA	Bayerische Landesanstalt für Aufbaufinanzierung
	(Bavarian State Corporation for Reconstruction Finance)
LGK	Landesgirokasse Stuttgart
MBG	Mittelständische Beteiligungsgesellschaft
	Baden-Württemberg
	(Mittelstand Equity Participation Corporation
	of Baden-Württemberg)
NordLB	Norddeutsche Landesbank
RAG	Ruhrkohle AG
SüdwestLB	Südwestdeutsche Landesbank
WestLB	Westdeutsche Landesbank

CHAPTER 1

Financial Systems and Models of Capitalism

It has become virtually axiomatic that global economic integration—especially the integration of financial markets—severely curtails the ability of states to pursue autonomous macroeconomic policies. In a world of high capital mobility, any nation that deviates too far from the desires of the international currency and capital markets is immediately punished by them. The consequence of globalization is thus widely seen as pressure toward economic policy convergence. Moreover, this is widely depicted as convergence to neoliberal economic policy in which national governments—regardless of partisan makeup—are promoting market forces through privatization, deregulation, and a general reduction of state economic intervention (Andrews 1994; Keohane and Milner 1996; Kurzer 1993; Notermans 1993).[1] In Europe, the pattern of economic integration and policies of the European Union appear to be reinforcing this general direction of change.

Economic globalization is also regarded as promoting convergence in the organization and production strategies of firms and industries, that is, in the very structure of national economies.[2] Capitalist systems have been typically divided into two broad types. First, there are "coordinated" or "communitarian" market economies, which are characterized by a higher degree of coordinated activity across firms and a capacity for collective action by firms. This model is best represented by Germany and Japan. Second, there are "liberal" or "individualist" market-based economies, which are characterized by a low degree of interfirm coordination and low capacity for collective action by firms. This model is best represented by the United States and Britain (Albert 1993; Thurow 1992). Convergence arguments are premised on the hypothesis that distinct national models of capitalism cannot coexist in their current form in the globalized economy.

At least three broad convergence mechanisms are at work—competitive selection, imitation, and harmonization. Competitive selection will weed out inferior types of organization and strategies, unless firms adopt the more competitive strategies of their international competitors (or receive protection). This mechanism is closely related to the second, in which firms, workers, and policymakers consciously imitate the strategies and institutional arrangements viewed as "best practice." Finally, because national economies are organized around different rules and institutions that create structural advantages or disadvantages for their firms in international competition, firms in one nation will push for a "level playing field" leading to harmonization of economic policy, regulation, and, ultimately, economic structures. Thus globalization raises not only the specter of policy convergence, but also that of convergence in national economic structures. In both cases, markets as a form of economic governance are widely seen to be displacing the state and other institutional mechanisms for governing economic activity.

Even for those who may not subscribe to this radical convergence thesis, it is undeniable that there has already been substantial change and at least some convergence among national financial systems. The financial system is widely regarded as one of the key institutions that distinguish coordinated from market-based capitalist systems, and it has been widely used as a major independent variable for explaining the industrial strategies and success of different national economies. In theory, coordinated market economies rely much more heavily on bank finance of corporate investment. Banks also typically own shares in industrial firms and place their representatives on numerous corporate boards. Through this combination of financial dependence on banks and extensive bank representation in corporate governance, banks, it is argued, promote a long-term perspective in corporate strategy. They also provide critical institutional capacity for coordinating collective action by business. Thus these systems are often said to be characterized by coordinated or negotiated adjustment, because firms adjust to market challenges through a combination of individual and collective responses. Market-based economies, in contrast, rely heavily on securities markets for corporate finance. Banks do not hold extensive stakes in industry and play little or no role in corporate strategizing. Firms adjust individually to market pressures. In effect, they sink or swim on their own.

The thesis of convergence in financial markets, then, rests on the argument that national financial sectors and their state regulators are engaged in a competitive struggle to capture the rapidly growing trading volume in international markets. Market integration and competition among London, New York, Frankfurt, Tokyo, and other financial centers are forcing convergence toward a model of financial market regulation (and ultimately structure) that emphasizes the securities-based finance mechanisms characteristic of liberal market economies (Moran 1991). In other words, the argument suggests that the bank-based industrial finance characteristic of coordinated market economies will ultimately converge toward the securities-market-based system of industrial finance. This, in turn, means that the close bank-firm relationship characteristic of bank-based systems will erode. Declining bank influence and increased securities market financing will bring about an Anglo-American style of corporate governance in which firm management is beholden to the short-term whims of the stock market. With this change, the capacity for collective action and long-term planning—the key comparative institutional advantages of coordinated market economies—would presumably be lost, or at least significantly circumscribed. Thus convergence in financial systems will exert strong pressure toward broader structural economic convergence.

Is such convergence in capitalist systems inevitable? Are financial systems losing their distinct institutional character? If so, does it follow that the organization of production in other sectors of the economy will converge toward that of other capitalist countries? Are firms in coordinated systems being untied from their collective moorings? Finally, what does this mean for the state in terms of the pressures and capacity to intervene in industrial change?

This book provides one set of answers to these questions through examination of the German economy. Germany is the focus of this book because it represents the foremost economy in Europe and the prime European example of a coordinated market economy. Thus if our concern is the robustness of this model of capitalism under conditions of growing global economic integration, Germany serves as an excellent critical case study. The German financial system is the central subject of the book because its particular institutional character is central to the German model of capitalism. The banking system shapes both firm behavior and the possibilities and incentives for state economic intervention. Moreover, the integration of financial markets is quite advanced, and thus it represents a sector where we can expect to find globalization-induced sectoral changes.

The argument of this book, briefly stated, is that despite financial market integration and considerable convergence (harmonization) in the regulation of financial markets, the traditional structure and broader economic functions of national financial systems are not inevitably undermined. The German financial system and its role in shaping industrial adjustment and state economic policy remain empirically and theoretically distinct from those of other major industrial countries. There is still a notable capacity for collective action by business.

Adjustment by firms and sectors to new economic challenges still involves extensive cooperation and negotiation over the pace and direction of change. Organizational and production strategies of German firms and sectors continue to follow the principles of their traditional emphasis on customized, high-quality products.

But before we can talk about convergence, there are many enduring and widely held misconceptions about the German financial system and its economic role that must be dispelled. In brief, the importance of the major commercial banks for German industry is generally overestimated in the political economy literature, while the critical functions of savings and cooperative banks have been consistently overlooked. This book redresses this imbalance by examining the respective roles of each of these major bank types in the German political economy. Moreover, it would be equally erroneous to argue that the German financial system and its functions are exactly the same as those Shonfield (1965) characterized some 30 years ago in his seminal treatise on national economic models. Since the late 1960s, the German financial system has undergone significant changes as a result of both domestic and international pressures, with attendant consequences for the adjustment pattern of the German economy and the nature of state economic intervention. Arguments about three sets of changes are advanced in this book. German reunification and the transformation of the eastern German economy have reinforced all three. First, the capacity of large banks to influence, and thus coordinate, the actions of large nonfinancial corporations has eroded significantly since the 1960s. The role of banks in coordinating collective action by business is overestimated. The collective action capacity of business resides primarily within industrial sectors themselves, though this capacity has also diminished—partly as a result of waning bank power. It is in the relationship between banks and large nonfinancial corporations where we find the greatest convergence with the liberal market economies model. These changes could very well—but will not necessarily—lead to more dramatic change in the broader organization of the German economy.

The second set of changes results in part from the first: the state's role in promoting and coordinating economic adjustment has grown as the banks' role has declined. The state and quasi-public institutions are increasingly important for facilitating adjustment by individual firms and facilitating or mediating coordination among firms. The state is therefore partially, but only partially, compensating for the declining self-coordination capacity of business. This also suggests that globalization does not necessarily lead to the disengagement of the state from economic intervention. Rather, it is associated with changes in the form of state intervention. Markets are not necessarily displacing the state. Rather, the interplay of states and markets continues to play a central role in governing economic activity.

The third change is that the German system for financing small and medium-sized enterprises has developed along a trajectory in which traditional institutions are adapted in a manner that promotes successful adjustment among such firms. The importance of banks for financing and promoting adjustment by smaller firms has grown in the face of international financial market integration. This apparent paradox will be explained by analyzing the interaction of the specific manner in which the banking system is organized, the nature of competition in the banking industry, and a series of state regulations, policies, and interventions. This change shows that collective action is still possible and can produce a positive-sum outcome even as markets become more important.

The German case suggests that simple notions of convergence among models of capitalism are overdrawn. Instead, national economies are following a process of parallel adjustment to common economic changes. Primarily because of path-dependence, national economies refract common international pressures differently. Even under intense convergence pressures, institutional change is still predominantly incremental. National economies can adapt successfully without losing their distinctive institutional character and systemic logic. This is possible because the functions of existing institutions can be changed or new institutions can be established that maintain traditional systemic functions in a manner consistent with current conditions of international competition. Thus the pattern of institutional adjustment examined in the book contributes to our understanding of the origins of institutions and the sources of change and stability in institutions.

The Institutional Basis of Capitalist Systems

The institutions that compose distinct national economies must be understood because they create identifiable incentives and constraints on the behavior of economic actors. Such institutions generally have their origins in the initial process of industrialization in a given country. They evolve over time, but they continue to bear the mark of their origins. Thus each national economy is distinguished from others by the structure of its institutions. Three institutions are commonly viewed as most central to determining national economic distinctiveness. These include the financial system (including the system of corporate governance), the labor markets and labor relations system, and the character of the state, that is, the state's capacity to influence adjustment through rule making (laws and regulations) and allocating resources (Hall 1986; Soskice 1991; Zysman 1994).

The existence of institutionally distinct national economies, or national institutional frameworks, has several implications. The first is that these lead to different patterns in the organization of production and product market strategies (Kitschelt 1991; Streeck 1996; Zysman 1994). While firms are theoretically free to choose their production strategies, each type of strategy is associated with certain requirements or preconditions. Such requirements may include particular forms of employee relations, relations to owners, and relations to other firms. Because of these requirements, each strategy is better supported by some institutional frameworks than others. For example, the German institutional framework lends itself well to incremental innovation in high-quality manufacturing and customized production. This is so because customized production requires long-term commitments and cooperation between the firm and its employees, owners, and suppliers—commitments facilitated in various ways by the German institutional framework. The American framework, in contrast, lends itself well to radical technological innovation and price-competitive standardized production. This strategy is facilitated by the American framework's emphasis on the rapid reallocation of resources. From this it follows that similar sectors in different countries are nonetheless likely to pursue different organization and product strategies, and different sectors in the same country will exhibit similarities in their organization and strategies because they are all subject to the same institutional environment.

Distinct national institutional frameworks have also been linked to nationally specific patterns of industrial development and adjustment. Zysman, for example, distinguishes three forms: state-led adjustment, in which the state sets developmental objectives and manipulates markets toward those objectives; negotiated adjustment, in which there are explicit bargains among economic interest group elites over the pace and direction of economic change; and company-led adjustment, in which the market decides winners and losers while the state serves chiefly as the regulator of market competition (1983; 1994, 257). Finally, national institutional differences have also been associated with different national patterns in innovation and the character and extent of national economic growth (Katzenstein 1989; Kitschelt 1991; Soskice 1995; Zysman 1994).

The literature on national models of capitalism emphasizes the important interaction effects of these key institutions. Thus the distinctive pattern of organizing production and economic development of a given country is not the result of a specific institution, but a result of the "logic" created by its particular mix of institutions.[3] One of the problems with this approach, however, is that it typically overlooks the critical role of regional and sectoral institutions—both economic and noneconomic—within nations that shape firm behavior. This set of institutions has been given greater attention by the governance literature (Cawson 1985; Hollingsworth, Schmitter, and Streeck 1994; Streeck and Schmitter 1985).

The Meso Perspective

Indeed, there are important differences in the organization of economic activity across sectors within a given nation. For example, the U.S. agriculture industry is characterized by corporatism and strong state intervention, thus corresponding to Zysman's negotiated adjustment model. Other U.S. sectors, however, are dominated by market competition and a minimal state role, corresponding to the company-led adjustment model (Campbell, Hollingsworth, and Lindberg 1991). The governance literature explains differences in organization and strategies among sectors using the particular history of that sector, but also by sectoral properties such as the nature of technologies used, products made, and product markets.[4] Thus within a given country, some sectors may be dominated by large, hierarchic corporations, while others may be characterized by a prevalence of small firms producing goods through extensive cooperative relations.

Building on its contributions to understanding the role of regional and sectoral institutions, the governance literature has recently begun to incorporate national institutions into its analytical framework. "Differences in governance within sectors are often recognizable as national differences in that they follow a similar logic across sectors" (Hollingsworth, Schmitter, and Streeck 1994, 272). The national context affects sectoral governance in three ways: (1) through common rules of behavior that shape all sectors of the national economy, for example through national company law; (2) through factual conditions or institutional parameters confronted by all economic actors in a country, for example national differences in the organization of the financial system and corporate finance, or national training systems; and (3) through common cultural and political resources that define incentives and constraints for individual and collective action. The two literatures have thus moved to a more common ground, acknowledging the importance of institutions at different levels.[5] The general conclusion, then, is that sectors within a given country will differ significantly from each other in their governance structures. But taken as a group and compared to a second country, the sectors of the first country are likely to exhibit common features that distinguish them from sectors in the second country.

Like the national capitalisms literature, the governance literature is also concerned with the effects of international economic competition on sectoral governance structures and national institutional frameworks.

> As noneconomic domestic institutions are increasingly recognized as important sources of success and failure in world markets, economic competition turns into social system competition, and competitive pressures for economic rationalization become pressures for general social change. A country whose system of industrial order [i.e., national institutional framework]—under given "terms of trade" (i.e., given institutionalized criteria of success and failure in the international "market")—provides firms in a particular sector with competitive advantage is likely to turn into a principal location for production in that sector. As a result, its share in global sectoral output and capacity will increase. The country will also be able to retain its system of governance, including its preferred performance standards. Conversely, a country whose industrial order disadvantages firms under given conditions of international competition will either experience sectoral deindustrialization, or will have to rebuild its institutions and adjust its performance preferences. The latter will as a rule be accompanied by redistribution of political power and economic advantage, between as well as within sectors. Competition between industrial orders may thus cut deeply into a country's social and political fabric. (Hollingsworth and Streeck 1994, 283)

What, then, are the specific sources of transformative (and convergence) pressures on national institutional frameworks? One set of pressures is associated with the process of internationalization, such as the growth of product markets and product market competition beyond national boundaries. Internationalization also includes the internationalization of supplier relations and production chains through global sourcing or international alliances in production, marketing, etc.; the internationalization of financial markets; the internationalization of labor markets; and the internationalization of corporations through the creation and integration of subsidiaries in multiple nations (Hollingsworth and Streeck 1994, 289). Firms and sectors are also adjusting to a common technical revolution in telecommunications and microelectronics. Finally, many firms and sectors are under pressure to adopt the concepts of lean production—team work, just-in-time, decentralization of responsibility, and reintegration of design, engineering, and production. These organizational principles involve changes in intra- and interfirm relations and inevitably affect sectoral governance.

Thus the economic challenge for firms and sectors is structural adjustment to take advantage of new technologies and more flexible methods of organizing work and other economic transactions (Hall 1995). But firms do not operate in a vacuum; as argued earlier, the costs and feasibility of various adjustment strategies are heavily shaped by the institutional environment in which firms operate. Firm adjustment involves various problem-solving tasks, and institutions—national, regional, and sectoral—help determine the solutions to individual and collective sectoral problems. But many of these institutions themselves are under strong pressure to change. Thus an important question becomes, how are the essential national framework institutions—hereafter to be understood as incorporating national, regional, and sectoral institutions— changing? And how does this affect individual firm and sectoral behavior, that is, their adjustment strategies and governance patterns?

Governance and Adjustment: Markets versus Banks

One of the central institutional features that distinguishes liberal market capitalism and coordinated market capitalism, or national institutional frameworks in general, is the system of corporate finance. In somewhat stylized terms, coordinated market economies have a bank-based system of corporate finance, while liberal market economies have a securities-market-based system. Bank-based systems are most importantly characterized by a relatively high degree of bank debt versus equity as a source of corporate finance. Equity markets are comparatively underdeveloped and also dominated by banks as traders and owners. Thus, in bank-based systems, banks typically are major shareholders in a wide range of corporations. Close relations between banks and firms—cemented by loans and equity holdings—are the hallmark of such systems.

The close relation between the bank and the firm is said to provide the former with an unusual amount of information about the firm that allows the bank to monitor actively firm management and intervene in the firm's affairs to secure the bank's interests. Thus banks are willing to provide long-term, or so-called patient, capital because they are in a strong position to monitor firm management. Furthermore, because of access to inside information about firm clients, the bank is willing to lend more funds (and possibly at better prices) than would occur under an arm's-length market transaction. Banks often play a central role in developing corporate strategy and firm reorganizations. In national economies incorporating this system, adjustments by individual firms and sectors to changing market conditions occur to a significant degree through a process negotiated among and coordinated by major firms and banks (and to some extent governments or labor unions). This capacity is associated with an ability by bank and firm to act in their mutual long-term interests and is viewed as a comparative economic advantage of bank-based systems (Franks and Mayer 1990).

This system is seen as a central and positive element in the long-term success of the German and Japanese economies. In the German case, the bank-based system evolved during initial industrialization in the second half of the nineteenth century. The authoritative historiography (discussed more in chaps. 2 and 3) holds that Germany developed its system of universal banking (i.e., banks are permitted to engage in all financial services), dominated by a handful of large banks, as an efficient solution to the need for large-scale investment required for industrialization (Gerschenkron 1962). By the late nineteenth century, large banks and firms had already become closely entwined. The concentration of economic power and close bank-industry relations enabled this "bank-industrial oligopoly" to collectively—and successfully—steer the course of industrial development. Markets as institutions thus played a secondary role to corporate hierarchies as mechanisms for governing economic change. Finance capitalism, that is, the extensive financial interlocks among banks and industrial firms, became the heart of a broader system of organized capitalism that embodied extensive coordination among firms and a capacity for collective action (Hilferding 1910).

In analyzing the postwar period, Shonfield's (1965, 239–97) still pervasive interpretation of postwar Germany incorporated the central tenets of the organized capitalism model. For Shonfield, three key institutions compose the German national institutional framework. First, there is a high degree of concentration in industry, and cartel-like arrangements are often an integral part of sectoral organization and rationalization. Second, there are centralized, hierarchically ordered trade associations with semipublic status that facilitate coordination among firms. The final and critical linchpin of this institutional framework is the banking system. While the major commercial banks no longer have quite the power over industry that they once did, banks take an overall view of long-term trends in industry and use their substantial influence to press firms to conform with broader sectoral developments. This bank coordination of industry facilitates long-term planning in industry and efficient adjustment to market conditions.

Given the capacity for self-organization by business, direct government economic intervention is largely avoided in favor of providing investment incentives to industry. Even in times of tremendous sectoral crisis, the German state presumably plays a subsidiary role to the private sector, supporting the sectoral rationalization plans worked out by private industry and the major commercial banks (Esser and Fach with Dyson 1983). It consults with, and occasionally pressures, these private sector institutions in the settlement of their affairs but intervenes directly only on an irregular basis. The state also plays an important role in creating the background conditions/regulations (*Rahmenbegingungen*) that make Shonfield's system of "private collective economic management" possible.

In sum, the key institutions of the German national institutional framework interact to produce a systemic logic of negotiated adjustment and pursuit of long-term industrial strategies. The financial system is dominated by banks that have substantial influence in large nonfinancial corporations. Large banks and firms are thus capable, through bank mediation, of extensive collective action. Key industrial adjustments therefore occur most importantly via negotiated or bargained agreements among private economic actors, not via market mechanisms. Long-term bank-firm relations also lead to long-term investment planning and long-term market strategies by management. The industrial relations system creates an important, albeit subordinate, role for organized labor in this system. The state only needs to support private collective economic management through laws, regulations, and the provision of selected resources that facilitate the negotiation of private agreements among capital and labor.

Equity- or market-based systems of corporate finance, in contrast, are ones in which firms rely to a much greater degree on equity markets for finance. Strong secondary markets generally lead to a wide distribution of ownership of publicly traded firms. Banks are less likely to hold significant equity stakes in specific firms, preferring to spread their holdings across a portfolio of firms. Equity investors and banks alike generally prefer to sell their holdings in a firm having difficulties, rather than actively monitor firm management and attempt to exercise influence to alter the firm's course. Thus banks and other outside investors tend to play little or no role in corporate management or governance. Corporate management is primarily monitored indirectly, through the equity markets: poor managers are punished by a declining stock price or outside takeover.

While banks also lend to firms, they, like most equity holders, have more arm's-length relationships to their corporate customers. Banks are less willing to provide long-term loans, preferring short-term financing that reduces their risk exposure. Banks are interested in maximizing their gain from a single transaction or short-term set of transactions, and not in the long-term development of the firm. Because corporations rely on equity markets—notorious for their short-term time horizon—and short-term bank loans, managers are in effect forced to focus on short-term objectives such as quarterly dividends, neglecting in the process the strategic actions required for success in the long run. For a number of analysts, this tendency is an inherent competitive weakness of liberal market economies (e.g., Porter 1990, 1992). The market-based system, however, is commonly seen to have at least one advantage in its superior ability to finance risky investments through venture capital.

In the market-based system, the adjustment of firms and sectors to economic changes is company-led. Firm mergers and takeovers are common adjustment mechanisms facilitated by equity markets. Individual firms devise and pursue strategies with comparatively little external input or control. The primary function of government is generally viewed as ensuring that the rules of market competition are fairly applied. Governments avoid direct intervention into markets. However, in cases where there is an overwhelming political interest in preventing certain market-determined outcomes, government must intervene directly in order to shape this outcome. That is, government cannot tap into a system of collective business action to achieve public goals, as is possible in coordinated market economies such as Germany.

The question that follows from this comparison is, to what extent have financial systems—cornerstones of national institutional frameworks—changed under the condition of global financial market integration? Answering this requires first an examination of the sweeping changes that have occurred in virtually all financial systems over the last two decades.

The Global Financial Markets Revolution

Strongly shaped by the Great Depression and the severe crisis in financial markets associated with it, postwar national financial systems—whether bank-based or market-based—were ruled by regulators' concerns for financial prudence and systemic stability. Like other markets, financial markets became more domestic in their focus, with strict limits or prohibitions on foreign participation. Within domestic markets, financial service firms were corseted by a web of stringent regulations. Most national regulatory systems intentionally restricted competition in financial services in the belief that excess competition was a greater danger than too little. Thus barriers to entry in banking and securities markets were placed quite high, either through law or restrictive practices (e.g., cartels) encouraged by public regulators. There were also limits on price competition, notably through interest rate controls, as well as restrictions on product innovation and changes in the firm population (i.e., restrictions on bank branching or mergers/acquisitions). Stringent regulations and supervision and insulation from foreign markets limited pressures for institutional change.

Since the 1970s, four broad, interrelated changes have radically trans-formed domestic financial markets in nearly all the major industrialized economies (Moran 1991, 10–13; Coleman 1996). First, there have been dramatic increases in price and product competition among financial firms. Second, there has been rapid product innovation—spurred in good part through new information technologies—that has created new financial markets and shifted the relative importance of different financial markets. Third, there have been dramatic changes in ownership structure, with a general trend toward con-centration among financial firms, including the emergence of large, multina-tional financial conglomerates. Finally, there has been a dramatic increase in the integration of national financial markets and a corresponding increase in in-ternational competition among national financial service sectors and their lead-ing financial centers. There is no single cause of these changes. Rather, there are multiple causes, both domestic and international in their origins. Some of these changes were intended by policymakers; others were the unintended con-sequences generated by a dynamic process not subject to the control of any par-ticular actor.

Forces of Change

Certainly the international factors, in particular the globalization of capital flows and connections among financial institutions, are central to the transfor-mation of financial systems. The current period of internationalization essen-tially began in the 1960s when the Eurocurrency, or Euromarkets, became sig-nificant. Euromarkets are offshore markets—essentially operating beyond the purview of national financial regulatory regimes—in which lenders and bor-rowers engage in transactions denominated in foreign currencies. Euromarkets grew dramatically for several reasons, including expanded efforts by banks and other investors (particularly from the United States) to exploit new profit op-portunities or to escape domestic taxes or financial regulations and controls (Moran 1991, 11). States tolerated or even promoted Euromarkets in order to give their international firms greater access to capital (Kapstein 1994, 31–37; Underhill 1991). The internationalization of financial markets was also prompted by the breakdown of the Bretton Woods system and the change from a fixed to a floating exchange rate regime. Volatility in currency markets created new demands and opportunities in international currency trading. Foreign exchange trading grew, and along with it the international interdependence of banking systems, since banks heavily borrowed currency from banks in other countries. The liquidity of international markets was boosted further by petrodollar recycling. The growth in overseas investment by institutional investors—often facilitated by the dismantling of foreign exchange controls—also stimulated the integration of financial markets. Finally, much of this expansion was possible only as a result of the information technology revolution that enabled electronic trading and globally instantaneous information on trading conditions.

There were also domestic factors promoting the broad and sweeping revolution in financial service markets. First, in various nations policymakers began to reduce or eliminate restrictions on competition. This change was pushed in part by new or foreign firms seeking entry into financial markets or facing discrimination in competition. It was also pushed by policymakers interested in improving the position of investors and consumers in the market by stimulating competition among financial service firms.[6] Second, in some cases governments promoted the growth of securities markets to help finance their own debt.[7] In several countries—especially those with limited equity markets, such as Germany and Japan—large financial institutions themselves also began to press in the 1980s for domestic liberalization. These regulatory changes were intended to facilitate the expansion of securities markets, which meant, among other things, opening domestic financial service sectors to greater foreign competition. These financial institutions were motivated by the desire to recapture the business of domestic multinational corporations that were increasingly financing their investment in lower-cost foreign markets or Euromarkets.[8] A final factor behind these changes is negotiated agreements among states to liberalize their financial service markets. The European Union (EU), the Bank for International Settlements (BIS), the General Agreement on Tariffs and Trade (GATT), and the World Trade Organization (WTO) are primary vehicles for such agreements (Underhill 1991).

Patterns of Change

With these changes in financial markets and regulation, national financial systems came under intense pressures for institutional change. Distinctions among national financial systems have been lessening. Three broad structural changes appear common to all leading financial markets, including bank-based and market-based systems. First, in all there is a trend toward concentration among financial firms leading to the growing dominance of large, multinational firms, though the extent of concentration varies considerably across countries because of their vastly different structures. Second, there is a worldwide trend toward securitization, that is, the transformation of financial liabilities into tradable securities. For example, bank loans are increasingly lumped together and sold to institutional investors. Securitization, as the word suggests, increases the role of all kinds of securities markets (as opposed to banks) in financial intermediation processes. A third common trend is that of universalization or desegmentation. Several financial markets, such as the United States, Japan, and the United Kingdom, have traditionally been segmented through regulation. For example, since the Glass-Steagall Act of 1933 in the United States, commercial banks have not been permitted to engage in investment banking activities. Segmentation was partly the product of historical development, but also a product of financial crisis and the desire to limit financial instability by limiting the activities of any given financial institution. Since the 1980s, the United Kingdom, Japan, and the United States have made dramatic steps in removing—or tolerating the erosion of—the barriers that prevent one kind of financial institution from entering into other, previously prohibited financial markets.

There is considerable empirical evidence that suggests that the bank-based model is particularly threatened by these changes and likely to lose its particular institutional logic. Specifically, corporate finance will occur to a high degree through securities markets; banks will gradually lose their corporate monitoring function, even though universal banking will broaden the range of financial market activities in which they are engaged; and the capacity for collective action will erode. This is so first because the trend toward securitization deemphasizes bank loans as a source of corporate finance. Thus a traditional role and basis for close bank-firm relations in the bank-based model is weakened. Banks could continue to own substantial shares in corporations and thus maintain their position of influence in corporate governance. But large holdings by banks (or other investors) run counter to the policy goal and logic of securitization. Well-developed and liquid equity markets—widely seen as necessary for national financial centers to be globally competitive—generally imply that the majority of a company's shares are actively traded and not held long-term by a handful of investors. Moreover, financial regulators in bank-based systems (and the EU) appear increasingly inclined to place more restrictive limits on bank holdings in nonfinancial firms.

Second, although the United States no longer has the international hegemony it once had, it still has unparalleled influence in international negotiations and in shaping international regimes. In financial regulation, the U.S. government and its leading financial firms have had significant success in spreading their ideas about financial systems and regulations into other domestic regulatory regimes and to international regimes, especially in the case of securities markets regulation.[9] Japanese and British regulatory changes in the 1980s were importantly and directly influenced by the United States (Moran 1991, 111; Hall 1993, 98–100). The Basel Accord of 1988 was also largely achieved through the successful application of American influence (Kapstein 1994, 111–19). Finally, the United States has used bilateral and multilateral mechanisms to challenge—on the grounds of restrictive trade practices—the close bank-firm connections common in bank-based systems (e.g., the *keiretsu* in Japan).

Third, quite apart from U.S. pressure or international negotiations, the EU has adopted in its approach to financial regulation a model that embraces universal banking yet emphasizes the expansion of securities markets under mostly U.S.-style regulation (Gonzalez 1993). In the interest of this objective, the EU has placed limits on bank holdings in nonfinancial firms. Most important, however, is that EU regulation seeks to stimulate competition within and across member country financial systems. To the extent that this objective is achieved, it is likely that a handful of large domestic financial institutions will no longer be able to dominate their home markets as in the past, and the influence of banks on nonfinancial firms should weaken. On the other hand, most continental countries have bank-based systems, and banks are likely to be the most important financial institutions for quite some time. Because the EU incorporates both kinds of financial systems within its borders, EU regulation involves a direct—and often pitched—battle between the advocates of the two systems.[10]

Continuity and Change in the German Model

Given these dramatic changes and transformative pressures in financial markets, how has the German financial system changed? What repercussions do changes in the financial system have for nonfinancial firms and the adjustment capacity of nonfinancial sectors? Have changes in the banking system begun to upset the institutional congruence of the German national institutional framework? In other words, what does an altered financial system mean for the other key institutions or subsystems of the German economy whose effectiveness is presumably dependent on a certain type of financial system? Finally, what implications do changes in the financial industry have for state industrial policy? These are the key empirical questions of this book.

Answering these questions is facilitated first by distinguishing fact from fiction. While the German financial system largely fits the stylized bank-based model, there are important deviations from this general model that must be made clear. For example, the dependence of large firms on bank funds was probably never as high as the bank-based and organized capitalism models suggest. Second, the relationship between banks and large firms must be analyzed separately from that between banks and small firms. The relationship between banks and large firms has developed in a manner that deviates most from the logic of the bank-based system. The relationship between banks and small firms, in contrast, has developed in a manner reinforcing the bank-based system. Thus, to a limited extent, there is a bifurcation or emerging dualism in the German finance model. This bifurcation can be explained primarily by the ability of large firms to directly access international capital markets, as well as by the structure of the banking industry itself and the broader institutional environment in which it is embedded.

Banks and Large Firms

One of the principal arguments of this book is that the capacity of the major German banks to influence industry and coordinate its activities has importantly declined over the last two decades. While incidents of direct bank intervention in firms clearly continue, bank intervention and coordination of a broad range of firms are increasingly difficult. This change is attributable first to the growing financial independence of large firms. This results from intensified competition among banks for the business of large firms and the increased ability of large firms to self-finance their investments and access international capital markets, thus bypassing domestic banks. Consequently, traditional bank lending to large firms has decreased dramatically. At the same time, increased domestic and international competitive pressures on the banks have led them to reduce or eliminate many of their industrial shareholdings in order to diversify and minimize their risk exposure. Thus the traditionally close relationship between banks and large firms has loosened significantly.

The big banks in Germany also responded to the decline of large-firm business with three additional strategies. First, they pushed into the market for the *Mittelstand* (small and medium-sized enterprises, or SMEs), where there is still a high demand for traditional bank loans and services. Second, the big banks (and later the savings and cooperative banks) developed a strategy of *Allfinanz*. Pursuing this strategy entailed the expansion or establishment of management consulting companies, investment banks, equity investment companies, and insurance and other companies. The first objective of this strategy is to develop new sources of revenue. The second objective is to serve better the various needs of firms, especially the Mittelstand, which face a growing range of market challenges. In this sense, the Allfinanz strategy complements the first strategy of reorienting the major banks to the Mittelstand. Finally, providing a wider range of financial and other services to firms also was expected to generate information and knowledge about individual firms and sectors that would help the banks to monitor developments better in both and thereby better assess bank risk exposure. Thus, to a certain extent, the major banks hoped that Allfinanz could restore some of their monitoring and coordinating capacity over industry that had been lost through greater large-firm autonomy.

The third response of the banks to the decline of large-firm business, but also an attempt to capture the opportunities for profit afforded by the internationalization of capital markets, is to push for the further development of German securities markets through institutional and regulatory changes. The strengthening of securities markets would enable banks to divest and diversify more readily their equity holdings. More importantly, the German banks want Frankfurt to be a major international financial center, which would position them to gain from the rapid global growth in securities trading activities. For the major German commercial banks, the future lies increasingly in securities trading and investment banking services. To an important degree, this response by the banks is also a reaction to the advent of the European Monetary Union and EU promotion of financial market integration.

The changed relationship between banks and large firms and the push to develop German securities markets have tremendous implications for the traditional German system of (large-firm) corporate governance. That system is clearly in a state of flux. It is unclear whether it will survive the next years with only moderate modifications, or whether in fact the traditional system will evolve toward the type of corporate governance inherent in market-based financial systems. So far the partial retreat of the banks from industrial shareholding and monitoring has been compensated by increased long-term cross-shareholdings among major German firms. This has preserved one of the mechanisms (concentrated ownership) that helps sustain long-term relations among firms and long-term investment. Nonetheless, the foundation for a long-term transformation of the German system of corporate governance is being laid, and this could have substantial consequences for the economic adjustment path of the German economy.

Banks and the Mittelstand

Despite these sweeping changes in bank–large firm relations, the German financial system remains substantially different than market-based financial systems. Because of the unique institutional character of the German banking system itself and the broader institutional context in which banks operate, German banks still perform economic functions to a degree not found in other economies. Most important is that banks provide (1) high levels of long-term financing and (2) market and managerial information, primarily to Mittelstand firms. These first two bank functions contribute importantly to a third function, that is, shaping firm choices in the organization of production. As posited by the national institutional frameworks approach, the institutional structure of the banking industry is therefore significantly correlated with the organizational or governance structure of nonfinancial sectors. These bank functions, though, are only sustainable because of a particular mix of institutional incentives—secured primarily by state policies, regulation, and statutes—that shape bank behavior.

One cannot fully comprehend the real functions of the banks in industrial adjustment without understanding the *federal* structure of the banking system and the principle of group competition. The banking system is characterized by the dominance of three distinct types or groups of banks: private commercial banks, public savings banks, and private cooperative banks. These three banking groups or sectors attempt to compete with each other in what is known as group competition (*Gruppenwettbewerb*). Group competition signifies the fact that savings and cooperative banks generally do not compete with other banks in their own group. Rather, these banks are organized in formal associations and use cooperative arrangements among banks within their respective groups to compete against other bank groups.[11] Historically there was an imperfect but visible division of labor among these banking groups: Commercial banks focused on short-term lending and equity finance for larger firms. Savings banks focused on long-term lending to individuals, small firms, and communal governments. Cooperative banks focused on farmers and small firms organized under Germany's craft sector law. This division of labor began to erode rapidly in the late 1960s as each group sought to engage increasingly in all lines of banking business. This strengthening of competition was importantly the result of market dynamics, but it was also very much promoted and sustained by changes in federal and state (*Länder*) regulation of the industry. These changes encouraged banks to move into nontraditional market segments while preserving the basis for three distinct bank groups. Despite convergence pressures arising from market integration and EU regulation, recent financial market regulatory changes in Germany have been made thus far in a manner that sustains the basis for group competition.

The banking system is federalist because the major national banks and the savings and cooperative bank groups each have either legally or functionally independent operating units in local, regional, national, and international markets. Yet units (be they independent banks or branches) operating at each level are also critically linked, or *inter*dependent, with units operating at other levels of the bank or bank group.[12] The system is federalist, rather than hierarchical, because real autonomy exists to some significant degree at all levels. Another dimension of federalism in the banking system consists of the direct linkages between the savings bank sector and the state: savings banks are controlled by local and state (Land) governments and are viewed by the latter as an important element of political federalism. Group competition and the federalist banking structure are sustained by a combination—with some elements common to all three banking groups, some unique to one group—of market imperatives, institutional histories, and state regulation and laws. In fact, the state (at both the federal and Land level) acted repeatedly and deliberately over the last century to create and sustain group banking in order to achieve various policy goals, including preservation of a strong Mittelstand. Thus a set of national and regional institutions constrains and shapes the nature of bank competition and the organization of the industry in a manner that leads to specific, positive (and politically intended) outcomes.

Consequences of Bank Industry Organization

The existence of three distinct, federalist banking groups and group competition produces several economic outcomes. The first is that it generates increasingly strong competition in all segments of financial markets. Through cooperation between large and small banks within their respective groups, the savings and cooperative banks combine the advantages of decentralization—closeness to the customer—with the scale advantages of larger banking units. This enables small banks to compete effectively in market segments traditionally dominated by large commercial banks, such as export finance. Large commercial banks, through their national branch structure, compete increasingly with savings and cooperative banks in the Mittelstand market. So far European financial market integration reinforces the federalist structure and group competition, since all bank groups face stronger market imperatives to combine more effectively the advantages of organizational decentralization and centralization. Competition is further promoted by the fact that the German banking system is comparatively deconcentrated and the regulatory structure—by purposely sustaining three distinct banking groups—slows considerably concentration trends in the industry. Large commercial banks cannot displace local savings or cooperative banks by buying them; they must compete with them. Thus the sweeping concentration among financial institutions occurring in other financial systems as a result of the financial services revolution is comparatively muted in the German case.

Increased bank competition over the last two decades was one factor facilitating the weakening of close relations between large firms and banks. For the SME market, on the other hand, increased competition strengthened the long-term relationship between banks and SMEs by inducing banks to provide more long-term funds and information to firms. For example, the Allfinanz strategy embodies an explicit attempt to become the external management arm of the small firm by providing a broad array of information services. The adoption and successful implementation of this strategy is also heavily contingent upon the federalist structure and group nature of banking competition: to compete, all banking groups must offer comparable services, and for each group these services can only be offered through successful coordination of local, national, and international units.

Consistent with the precepts of the bank-based model, German SMEs also receive substantial amounts of long-term finance from banks. Adequate long-term finance is assured by three factors—strong bank group competition, the comprehensiveness and competitiveness of savings and cooperative banks, and state regulation and long-term government lending. The savings bank group, which has the largest market share in commercial lending among the three major groups, specializes in long-term financing and uses this to compete with the other banking groups. This places pressure on the other groups to provide long-term funds. Savings and cooperative banks also have unique legal and structural incentives to provide SMEs with adequate long-term funds. Finally, increased long-term financing by federal and Länder development banks over the past two decades expanded the availability of low-cost, long-term funds for SMEs. Since long-term government loans flow to firms via the banks, they help strengthen long-term relations between banks and SMEs. Altogether, the extensive provision of long-term financing and comprehensive business information by banks to firms creates a close, long-term relationship between banks and SMEs. However, strong competition inhibits banks from gaining undue influence over firms.

Banks and Industrial Strategy

As suggested earlier, the banking system must be understood as one central sub-system of the national institutional framework. The German national frame-work is characterized by the predominance of diversified quality production (DQP) as an industrial strategy. This strategy entails the combination of high levels of technology with high levels of skilled labor to produce high-quality goods, typically in relatively small batches. It typically entails extensive coop-eration in development and production among firms, large and small. DQP re-quires a rich set of institutions that create enforceable social constraints on ra-tional market participants and encourage them to restructure toward higher diversity and quality (Streeck 1992).

The banking system is an important institutional element to the German system of DQP. Under DQP, firms require high levels of long-term investment in research and product development and labor force training. By providing long-term loans and stable, long-term relationships to firms, banks enable firms to pursue long-term objectives and the long-term commitment of resources needed for DQP. In this manner, firms avoid or minimize the strong preference for liquidity and short-term profits inherent in market-based finance systems that is unlikely to support all the kinds of investments needed for DQP. Thus the strengthening of bank–small firm ties supports the continuation and adap-tation of the DQP model. While the weakening of bank–large firm ties could be expected to weaken the capacity for long-term investments in the German economy and DQP, large firms have so far found other mechanisms to mini-mize short-term equity market pressures.

Banks and State Industrial Policy

In this book I focus in particular on the relationship between banks and gov-ernments because the capacity of states to intervene in their economies is crit-ically determined by their ability to manipulate the flow of investment capital, either through direct control of financial institutions or more broadly, through monetary and financial regulations.[13] The role of the German state in creating and sustaining a system of long-term industrial finance is greater than com-monly understood. First, many of the largest banks engaged extensively in in-dustrial finance in Germany are under the control of the state and thus often serve as instruments of state intervention. Second, the entire public banking sector accounts for roughly half of bank sector assets, and these banks are subject to significant political influence. Third, industrial credit provision by the state constitutes a substantial portion of all long-term industrial finance (especially for SMEs). While much of this financial aid is targeted toward categories of action by firms (which suggests less purposive intervention), a considerable portion is also used to promote specific industrial objectives of governments (especially of the Länder). Thus the German state is capable of, and indeed pursues, more purposive industrial intervention than is widely believed. This form of state intervention, combined with complementary bank regulations, provides strong incentives for banks to engage themselves in long-term industrial finance (Vitols 1994).

Fourth, as noted above, bank influence over industry alone can no longer be the primary basis for collective business action and the process of negotiated adjustment. This has raised pressure on the state to assume a greater role in facilitating economic adjustment, and it has done so through various actions. State economic policies at both the federal and Länder levels are increasingly microeconomic (or supply-side) oriented—supporting firms with capital and producer services—in the attempt to promote structural adaptation in the economy. Such industrial policies are generally favorable, if not necessary, for the success of DQP. In many cases the implementation of these policies relies heavily on coordination with the banks, especially for Länder governments. Hence, contrary to the finance capitalism model, the banks and state should be viewed not so much as alternative or even competing mechanisms for economic coordination, but as increasingly interdependent or complementary mechanisms. Moreover, the expansion of such policies suggests that states can still influence economic adjustment, even in globalizing economies, by focusing on promoting the development of less mobile forms of capital such as knowledge (technical and managerial), skills, and interfirm networks.[14] Thus, to the extent that Germany has a system of organized *private* enterprise (Zysman 1983, 251–65), it rests on a strong element of *public* power.

Finally, the structure of the financial system and its evolution cannot be explained without examining the critical role of the state in shaping these outcomes. The structure of the financial system importantly reflects state economic policy preferences, as much as it constrains them.[15] In this book I therefore examine—in the context of domestic and international economic changes—both the struggles within the banking industry and the interaction between the state and the industry that are redefining the organization of the banking sector itself, its relations to industry, and its broader economic roles.

Outline of the Book

The book is divided into two parts. Part 1 (chaps. 2 and 3) examines changes in the organization and market strategies of the banking industry and correlates these to changes in bank-firm relations. Chapter 2 is a historical chapter that examines the organizational development of the banking system. The group and federal character of the banking system emerged out of a search for efficient institutional solutions to various economic adjustment problems of the late nineteenth century, as well as political struggles among social groups to preserve their economic position. The state (at the national and subnational levels) played a crucial role, through its rule-making function and direct intervention, in creating and structuring the banking system during the late nineteenth and early twentieth centuries. Decentralization (federalization) in the banking industry was preserved in the postwar period through state action, but also by the logic of group competition that required greater universalization (presence in all financial product markets) of all the banks and by changes in the economy that made Mittelstand firms an increasingly important customer group for all the banks. It is also argued that the emergence and maintenance of a three-sector banking system contributes to the development and persistence of different sectoral and regional patterns of economic governance. Finally, the chapter examines the effects of EU financial regulation on the organization of the German financial system as well as the process of rebuilding the banking sector in eastern Germany.

Chapter 3 examines the changing pattern of industrial finance in Germany and the evolution of bank-industry relations. It examines first the changing relationship between banks and large firms, arguing that there is a declining capacity for bank coordination of industry. The institutions of a bank-based system for large firms are eroding as securities markets and market relationships become increasingly important for both banks and large firms. The chapter then examines the evolving relationship between banks and the Mittelstand. It documents the extension and refinement of the bank-based system for Mittelstand finance and especially the critical role of the state and savings and cooperative banks in this system.

Part 2 of the book (chaps. 4, 5, and 6) focuses on how changes in the organization and strategies of the banking industry combine with government industrial policies to influence the broader process of economic adjustment. Each of the three chapters presents one case study of regional economic adjustment. While each region operates within the same set of national institutions, each differs significantly from the others in the organization of production in regional industries, as well as in the regional and sectoral institutions that shape sectoral governance and the pattern of adjustment. The case studies focus on regional (rather than sectoral) institutions and economic adjustment patterns for several reasons. First, the case studies seek to highlight the key institutions of the German national institutional framework and their interaction effects that influence adjustment in all sectors. The cases focus on the regional (without ignoring national) institutions because production, innovation, and thus adjustment are very much locally rooted, even in the age of globalization. Second, there is significant institutional variation across regional economies in Germany. Thus understanding institutional change and economic adjustment processes requires examination at this level. Indeed, while there is some institutional convergence among regional economies, there remain considerable differences that may in fact contribute to overall national economic competitiveness. Third, despite a growing international orientation of the German banking system, the local and regional levels of the banking system are as important as ever to industrial success. Moreover, these levels of the banking system are increasingly interconnected with other local and regional institutions that influence firms and sectoral adjustment. Thus each case tells a different story about how the German national framework is adjusting to domestic and international economic pressures.

Chapter 4 examines North Rhine–Westphalia. This regional economy epitomizes the organized capitalism model. The region has suffered from long-term structural economic problems, and its economy is still heavily influenced by traditional sectors—energy, steel, and heavy machinery—and its centralized, large-firm industry structure. The chapter utilizes the case of the regional coal and steel industries to show how bank capacity to coordinate adjustment has declined. The chapter further shows how the government of North Rhine–Westphalia became a major actor in regional adjustment processes, in particular using its large Landesbank to intervene extensively in regional industry. Into the 1980s, government intervention largely reinforced the traditional organization of industry in the region. But in the 1980s, regional industries began to emphasize decentralization in the organization of production. This required government, banks, and industry to construct or transform regional institutions needed to support this new model of industrial organization.

Chapter 5 examines Baden-Württemberg, one of the most industrialized and successful regional economies in Germany. In contrast to North Rhine–Westphalia, the institutional preconditions for organized capitalism are weak in this region: economic concentration is lower because of the large number of SMEs, and industrial finance is controlled to a comparatively high degree by relatively small, local banks. This region's industry is governed to a greater degree by markets and networks of direct and indirect cooperation among firms in the region. The decentralized organization of production and smaller-firm structure of the region are supported by a dense network of public and private institutions. In Baden-Württemberg, government policy has interacted successfully with the financial sector to expand the capacity of SMEs to adapt to economic change and sustain the decentralized organization of production in the region.

Chapter 6 examines the process of restructuring the East German economy after reunification in 1990. It shows how participation of the banks in the restructuring process fell considerably short of what the organized capitalism model would predict. The banks' actions in the East demonstrate with great clarity the limited capacity of the banks to guide firm and sectoral adjustment processes. This has meant that the state and other economic institutions have had to bear the greatest burden of guiding the restructuring of the eastern German economy. In many respects, the task of reconstructing the East presents the greatest challenge to the adaptive capacity of the German model.

Part 1

Organization of the Banking Sector and Its Relations to Industry

Origins and Evolution of the Federalist
Banking System

This chapter analyzes the organizational development of the German banking system. It shows how the three major bank groups emerged and evolved based on two distinct organizational models: a hierarchical branch bank model that dominates in the commercial banking sector, especially in the three major national banks (commonly referred to as the Big Banks); and an association model that governs the savings and cooperative banking sectors. The origins of each model go back to the late nineteenth century, but their consolidation occurred primarily in the 1920s. Since that time, and especially since the late 1960s, these two models have converged to a significant, albeit limited, degree toward a federal model of bank organization. A federal model is characterized by legally or functionally autonomous operating units in local, regional, national, and international markets. In such a model, the success of any given individual unit depends importantly on regular cooperation with units operating at other levels within the bank or bank association. Relations among units are better characterized as consensual and interdependent than as hierarchical.

The savings bank sector is based on a three-tier associational model. On the primary level are nearly 700 savings banks. These banks are legally independent banking organizations but are owned and supervised by communal governments. They operate in a wide variety of commercial markets and seek to make profits, but as public institutions they also support communal policy initiatives in numerous ways. These banks are subject to federal banking laws and regulation but are chartered and primarily regulated under Länder savings bank laws. The secondary level of the savings bank sector, or group, consists of regional savings bank associations and regional banks known as *Landesbanken* (or *Girozentrale*). With some exceptions (notably among the five new federal states), there is one Landesbank for each federal state, and traditionally, in most cases, ownership of the Landesbank is divided between the Land government and the regional savings bank association(s) in that Land. This division of ownership reflects the fact that most Landesbanks have multiple functions: a Landesbank serves its Land government in financial matters; it competes directly with banks outside the savings bank group; and it assists local savings banks by providing numerous banking services that these local banks alone cannot do, either because Land regulation prohibits them from doing so or because they lack sufficient scale economies. The tertiary level of the savings bank sector consists of a national association and a national central bank (Deutsche Girozentrale–Deutsche Kommunalbank, or DGZ Bank). For historical reasons, the DGZ Bank plays a relatively limited role in the savings bank sector. The national association, in contrast, plays a major coordinating and policy leadership role in the group and represents the sector's interests in federal politics.

The cooperative banks also have a three-tier associational structure. On the primary level are more than 2,700 member-owned credit cooperatives. They are subject to the Federal Cooperative Law, which, among other things, places special requirements and privileges on them. On the secondary level are regional cooperative banks and regional cooperative associations, though in contrast to the savings bank sector the regional banks of the cooperative sector are relatively few and play a less significant role in the group. On the tertiary level are the national cooperative banking association and a national bank (Deutsche Genossenschaftsbank, or DG Bank). The DG Bank is one of the 10 largest banks in Germany and, along with the national association, exercises a powerful leadership role within the cooperative banking sector.

The three big banks (as well as several large regional banks) also have a federalist character, since each encompasses a large network of local branches overseen by a dozen or so main regional branches. In the last two decades, the big banks have greatly increased the autonomy of their local and regional branches, allowing them to act much like independent banks. The functional division of labor, relations of authority, and distribution of resources between local, regional, and national units (branches) in the big banks have converged to a significant extent toward those that characterize the association banking groups: the headquarters and specialized subsidiaries now provide an internal capital market and more expensive and sophisticated financial and informational services to autonomously operating regional and local branches.

Understanding the federalist character of the German banking system is essential to understanding both the historical preconditions for German industrial success and the current role of the banking system in the process of economic adjustment. First, recent scholarship shows that there have been at least two distinct and successful regional models or patterns of industrialization and industrial organization in Germany. The first pattern is characterized by the predominance of production in large, vertically integrated firms. These firms became large in part because of the technical nature of production, but also because "the lack of surrounding infrastructure forced them to incorporate most of the stages of manufacture under their control" (Herrigel 1989, 193; also Herrigel 1996; Tipton 1976; Fischer 1972; Megerle 1982). The high capital requirements of these industries also meant that they developed close relationships to the big banks. The prime example of this autarkic industrial order is the Ruhr area of the Land of North Rhine–Westphalia—the traditional stronghold of the German coal, steel, and other heavy industries. The second pattern of industrial organization is characterized by decentralized production in small firms clustered within a geographically specific region. Spatial proximity facilitates direct cooperation among these firms, as well as indirect cooperation via local organizations that provide them with private and collective goods essential to their success. Because firms in such regions typically produce specialized but complementary goods, the region as a whole may be analyzed as a loosely connected unit of production.[1] Baden-Württemberg is a leading example of a region with a decentralized industrial order.

Reflecting such regional variations in industrial organization, substantial variation among Germany's regions in the relative strength of the different banking groups emerged in the nineteenth century and continues to the present. The major commercial banks concentrated in and around the Ruhr, and in most major cities in Germany. Conversely, where the major commercial banks were weaker, the cooperative and public banking sectors tended to be stronger.[2] Indeed, some of the most prosperous sectors (e.g., machine tools) and regions in Germany (e.g., the Bergische, Siegen, and Württemberg regions) are those where the market presence and influence of the major commercial banks are more circumscribed. This suggests, contrary to the widely held view, that the industrial leadership of the major banks is not necessarily a prerequisite to industrial success.

Second, the federalist character of the banking system is the foundation of group competition among banks in Germany. The logic of this competition dictates that nationally operating commercial banks and the two association banking groups compete head-to-head in all financial market segments, in all geographic markets, and with all categories of firms. Thus each major commercial bank and the two association banking groups are continuously seeking the capacities to serve the needs of virtually any firm—whether a small craft firm or an international conglomerate. Success in this endeavor requires not only having the operating units for each type of market and firm, but also achieving group- or concern-internal coordination and synergies. For example, through the provision of collective goods to member banks, the associations enable their banks to expand their range of financial market services and thus remain competitive with the other major banking groups. To prevent competition between member banks, both groups also have a self-imposed regional principle that largely prohibits any single member bank from operating outside of its assigned area. One primary outcome of group competition is that both large and small German firms are benefiting from intense competition among the banks for their business. Understanding the logic of group competition is therefore fundamental to understanding the institutional evolution of the German financial system and its relations to industry and the state.

Third, it is widely recognized that small and medium-sized firms—the Mittelstand—are an integral element of the nation's industrial success. The Mittelstand has traditionally been financed primarily by the savings and cooperative banking sectors. In the postwar era, these two association banking groups successfully adjusted to the changing needs of the Mittelstand and growing bank competition. In doing so, they have played a crucial role in sustaining the provision of long-term finance to Mittelstand firms, even in a world of rapidly growing international capital mobility. In other words, the association system helps preserve a strongly Mittelstand-oriented banking system by providing smaller banks the advantages of scale economies through the association. Through internal decentralization—that is, federalization—the major commercial banks have sought since the mid-1970s to capture these same advantages of local autonomy and flexibility.

The emergence and maintenance of a banking system based on three major bank groups was, and is, a highly political process. From the nineteenth century through to the present, the state promoted the savings and cooperative banking groups in order to counter economic concentration and support particular social groups. State actors, at both the national and Länder level, were motivated in part by their own policy goals but also very importantly by political pressure from these social groups—notably small firms, the self-employed, and farmers—who sought to protect their economic interests through a decentralized banking system attuned to their needs. Länder governments also saw the maintenance of this banking system—above all the savings banks—as crucial to maintaining their policy autonomy and thus the essence of federalism.

From the early twentieth century onward, growing market competition among the three banking groups frequently spilled over into political conflict over financial regulation. Preserving three bank groups therefore meant that the state also played a crucial role in maintaining fairness in market competition among these three groups, especially as the state itself promoted greater bank competition in the postwar period. The challenge of maintaining this three-sector, federalist banking system grew as the international integration of financial markets accelerated during the 1980s and 1990s. But even in this era of liberalization and European integration, the historical coalitions supporting this model of banking remain firmly committed to it, for its undoing would shock the very institutional core of the German political economy.

This chapter will briefly summarize the emergence and consolidation of the three major bank groups up to World War II. It is in this period that the three groups developed their mature organizational forms and rooted them in broader market, social, and political institutions. The remainder of the chapter will trace the development of the industry in the postwar period. It highlights the state's role in promoting bank competition and the response of each banking group to the changed conditions of competitiveness.

The Federalist Banking System in the Nineteenth Century

In the first half of the nineteenth century, political fragmentation in Germany hindered the integration of the loosely connected local capital markets. Industrial finance came largely through personal and familial relations (Tilly 1967, 151–57). During the second half of the century, industrialization began to accelerate, and the capital requirements of industry grew tremendously. To meet these needs, private bankers began to form consortia in the form of joint-stock credit banks. From here the traditional story of German banking is a very familiar one: The joint-stock, or great, banks of Berlin promoted rapid industrialization through their tutelage of industry.

The story of the cooperative and public savings banks, however, is not well known or understood outside of Germany. From the nineteenth century to the present, the savings and cooperative banks not only survived, they were able to gradually expand their market share vis-à-vis commercial banks because of three factors: the supportive actions of the state, the development of cooperation in associations, and their tight links to local economic institutions and firms. The close, symbiotic relationship between smaller banks and smaller firms helped both succeed in competition with larger banks and firms during Germany's period of rapid industrialization and later. Maintaining competitiveness also required the savings and cooperative banks to "universalize"; that is, over time these banks expanded their range of activities until they became, with some exceptions, universal banks like the major commercial institutions.

The history of the savings banks goes back to the late eighteenth century, when the first banks were established for the purpose of poor relief. They were simple, usually private institutions that collected savings deposits and invested them, primarily in state bonds and, to a lesser extent, in loans to local governments and individuals (Pohl 1976, 30–31). After the post-Napoleonic political reconstruction of the German states, local governments began to use their recently expanded authority to bring existing private savings banks under their administration, or to create new ones.[3] The savings banks quickly became an important resource to local governments, especially for financing urban infrastructure (Weinberger 1984). In the mid-nineteenth century, several German states began actively promoting savings banks, partly to prevent the growth of an urban, industrial proletariat through support for production in agriculture and small craft firms (Trende 1957, 82, 131; also Wysocki 1983, 169–70).[4] Encouraged by new legal regulations and support from the states, the number of savings banks grew rapidly, and they began to increase their local lending to merchants, craftworkers, and farmers.[5] Though they continued to expand steadily, restrictive regulations led savings banks to invest primarily in low-risk mortgage loans or state securities rather than small-business loans (Henze 1972, 35–46). Thus, for most of the nineteenth century, the savings banks played a relatively limited direct role in German industrialization.[6] This vacuum in the small-firm lending market was filled by the cooperative banking sector.

The growth of centralized industrial production in the second half of the nineteenth century threatened urban craftsmen and rural cottage industry. The general lack of credit available to these groups was translated by the emerging cooperative movement into the creation of small cooperative banks throughout the German states. The founding father of the commercial cooperative banking movement was Hermann Schulze-Delitzsch. While Schulze-Delitzsch established the first credit cooperative in 1852, it was through his writings that he made the greatest impact. Seeking a third way between socialism and large-scale capitalism without resorting to state protection, he promoted the formation of associations of production workers based on the principles of self-help and mutual liability among members (Conze 1973). His work had powerful appeal among the increasingly threatened craft sector, and by 1859 there were 80 commercial credit cooperatives with more than 18,000 members spread over Germany.[7]

Early cooperative banks were little more than a simple form of interfirm cooperation network: members pooled their money and borrowed from the bank as needed (Pohl 1976, 36–38, 68–71). The banks were also typically operated on a part-time, honorary basis. Since the liability of these banks was generally unlimited, the members needed to know and trust each other a great deal. To refinance their loans and circulate funds among themselves, cooperative banks joined in regional associations and created regional clearing banks (*Verbandskassen*).[8] Despite these early organizational successes, in the 1860s competing groups of cooperative banks emerged, separated by varying philosophical principles. Establishing organizational unity within the cooperative banking sector—including a single national association and national clearing bank for all cooperatives—evolved gradually over the following decades. Nonetheless, the credit cooperatives played a crucial role in the economic survival and development of Mittelstand firms through the late nineteenth and early twentieth centuries.

The unification of the German states in 1871 generated a wave of economic growth and entrepreneurial activity. In order to finance the projects of the growing industrial concerns, private bankers all over Germany led a second major wave of joint-stock bank foundings.[9] By the late 1870s, the mostly Berlin-based big banks began to build continuous financial relations with large firms, providing short- and long-term capital to industry, primarily through current account credits. Thus was born the German tradition of the "house bank."[10] From the 1880s onward, the Berlin banks continued to expand their dominant position in industrial finance, firmly establishing the very close ties to industry that ostensibly empowered them to organize German capitalism.

In contrast, during the last two decades of the century the savings banks faced a panoply of changing circumstances that threatened their long-term survival. First, the inability of the savings banks to create additional lending capital through float mechanisms (e.g., cashless transfer payments) severely limited their expansion. Second, the cooperative banks, and to some extent even the Berlin banks, were expanding their share of the deposit-taking and small-business loan markets. Meanwhile, the rapid growth of large-scale industry intensified pressure on the Mittelstand to modernize production, in turn causing the capital demands of the Mittelstand to outrun the capacity of both the savings and cooperative banks to satisfy them. Together, these threats spawned a reform drive within the savings bank sector to make these banks more universal banking institutions. While these reform efforts would not reach fruition until the early twentieth century, in the closing decades of the nineteenth century the savings banks made important moves toward organizing themselves. Motivated by the desire to stifle a proposed Imperial postal savings bank and to provide some form of liquidity equalization among themselves, savings banks began to form regional associations. In 1884 several regional associations joined together to create a national peak association, the Deutscher Sparkassenverband

(Wysocki 1983, 186). Through the association and its publications, the representatives of the banks pressed their demands on government and carried out the debate over the future of the savings bank sector.

As in the savings bank sector, the cooperative banking sector found it increasingly difficult to meet the growing needs of its members toward the end of the nineteenth century. To remedy this situation, they sought and obtained a new and improved Imperial Cooperative Law in 1889. The law opened the door to an expansionary phase for the cooperative banks, since it enabled the cooperative banks to offer short-term current account and acceptance credits to their members, just as the big commercial banks offered to large firms. With these new forms of credit, the cooperative banks made a qualitative jump in their functional and organizational character, from simple loan associations toward more formally organized universal banks.[11] The cooperatives got a further boost in 1895 when the Prussian government, eager to protect farmers and craftsmen from proletarianization, created the Preussenkasse—an independent organization under public law and capitalized by the Prussian government—to act as a central bank for cooperatives.[12] However, a large segment of the cooperative sector refused to work with the state on the grounds that to do so would compromise the principle of self-reliance and instead used other banks for their central banking needs (Faust 1977, 539–40; Pohl 1976, 68–71). This division within the cooperative sector would only be resolved after World War I. In the meantime, the combined institutional stimuli of the 1889 Cooperative Law and the Preussenkasse unleashed a wave of new cooperative foundings.

In summary, the German banking sector underwent dramatic growth and change in the nineteenth century. By 1895 the commercial banking sector was represented primarily by the eight big Berlin banks and 86 provincial joint-stock banks. The commercial cooperative banks grew from 80 banks with 18,000 members in 1859 to 1,068 banks with over 500,000 members in 1895. The savings banks expanded from some 300 banks around 1840 to well over 2,000 in the 1890s (Deutsche Bundesbank 1976, 122; Pohl 1976, 65). The savings and cooperative banks were not yet universal banks in the same sense as the commercial banks, though the growing demands of the Mittelstand were pushing them in this direction. More importantly, both made significant gains in organizing their respective sectors into associations. In the early part of the twentieth century, the organizational cohesion of these associations would solidify and lend them an indispensable tool to sustain their market position, as well as to wage the political battles necessary to maintain the legal protection of their distinct organizational principles and thus their ability to finance adequately the Mittelstand.

1895–1931: Consolidating the Foundations of the Federalist Banking System

This period begins with the economic boom starting in 1895 and ends with the Depression and the banking crisis of 1931. During this time there was tremendous concentration in German industry and in the commercial banking sector. The Berlin banks dramatically expanded their presence in the provinces. The savings and cooperative banks responded to this by universalizing and strengthening cooperation within their respective associations. In this way they were able to marshal a collective strength against the big Berlin banks. Thus, in this period, the cooperative banks gradually moved toward a resolution of their internal divisions. The savings banks also made great strides toward organizational unity and closer cooperation, due in large part to their eventual adoption of a *giro* (checking) system. With the endorsement of the Länder governments in the Weimar period, the savings banks moved more and more into commercial banking business. The commercial and cooperative banks joined together in a political campaign to push the savings banks back out. But the savings banks, with state support, successfully defended their new role. Thus by the 1920s the hierarchical branch model of the commercial banks and the association banking model of the savings and cooperative banks reached their mature form, and the basis for group competition was in place. The growing dominance of these three banking groups can also be seen in their combined control of bank sector assets (table 1).

The single most important and divisive issue in the savings banks' long-running reform debate was over the ability to conduct cashless transfer, or checking (giro) accounts, an activity that at that time only the commercial banks were allowed to conduct.[13] Within the savings bank sector, there were many who believed the savings banks should not engage in such "commercial" activities, as this would take them away from their public mission of promoting savings and serving communal needs.[14] Reformists, in rebuttal, saw the savings banks as having a public mission to help preserve the threatened Mittelstand, as well as to provide a market counterweight to the growing power of the commercial banks (Mura 1987b, 51; Wysocki 1983, 169–72; Wysocki 1985, 34–43). This argument was particularly persuasive as the big Berlin banks were steadily increasing their efforts to gather funds from local markets, which they typically channeled to large industry elsewhere, not back into the local Mittelstand.[15]

While the reform debate had raged for nearly three decades, it was a severe capital shortage in 1907 that provided the needed catalyst for change. To help

TABLE 1. Number of Banks and Total Assets in 1913 and 1928

Bank Groups	1913			1928		
	Number of Institutions	Total Assets (mio. of M)	% of Total	Number of Institutions	Total Assets	% of Total
Berlin big banks	9	8,391	13.9	8	12,673	23.3
Provincial banks	151	7,839	13.0	70	2,471	4.5
Mortgage banks	40	11,514	19.1	39	5,508	10.1
Savings banks	3,133	19,689	32.7	2,651	10,038	18.5
Girozentralen				34	7,926	14.5
Commercial cooperatives	963	1,680	2.7	1,418	1,843	3.3
Cooperative central banks	47	684	1.1	44	1,676	3.0
Other banks		10,412	17.3		12,243	22.5
Total		60,209	100		54,378	100

Source: "Deutsches Geld- und Bankwesen in Zahlen, 1876–1975." Frankfurt: Deutsche Bundesbank, 1976, pp. 67, 92–94, 114, 121.

Note: Not all bank groups are separately listed.

ease the shortage and secure their own future, the national savings bank association lobbied for, and secured, Imperial legislation in 1908 that opened the door for savings banks to implement transfer and checking accounts, to operate current accounts, and to hold securities on deposit (Pohl 1976, 64–68; Henze 1972, 58–61; Wysocki 1987, 25–27). This empowerment of the savings banks was a huge step in the transformation of the savings banks into universal banking institutions. More importantly, the giro system cemented unity among more than 3,000 savings banks existing in the 1910s, because giro accounts required central clearinghouses to carry out interbank transfers.[16] Thus the savings banks joined together in regional "giro associations" (*Giroverband*) and established regional giro clearing banks known as *Girozentrale*. In 1916 the Prussian regional associations united into a central giro association (Deutscher Zentralgiroverband) and two years later established a central clearing bank, the Deutsche Girozentrale, in Berlin.[17] Thus, with the introduction of the giro system and the Girozentrale, the savings banks' federal associational structure was solidified and extended. Moreover, with the introduction of the giro system and other "banklike" activities, individual banks began to rely on cooperation with other banks in the association for their own competitiveness.

It was probably the inflation of the early interwar years, however, that made the transformation of savings banks truly irreversible. To survive inflation, the savings banks needed to do more short-term and cashless business, and the recently adopted giro system quickly became indispensable. As inflation worsened, the Länder found themselves forced to liberalize further restrictions on the permitted activities of savings banks (Wysocki 1986, 40). The Länder, however, were not simply reacting to an emergency situation. Länder governments widely believed that the private banking sector was not providing sufficient capital to the Mittelstand and saw liberalization as essential to rectifying this serious problem (Born 1983, 52). Indeed, in regions where the big Berlin banks had taken over provincial banks—which, in fact, they had been doing in great numbers—they generally provided less credit to the Mittelstand than the provincial bank had done. In the 1920s the Berlin banks were frequently reproached by regional and national political authorities for this (Gehr 1959, 103–8). Thus, by the end of the inflationary period in 1923, most German Länder had greatly expanded the range of financial activities open to their savings banks, in the process making them universal banking institutions (albeit with some important restrictions remaining).

The hyperinflation of the early 1920s was a mixed blessing for the cooperative banking sector. On the one hand, inflation wiped out much of their equity, and many cooperatives dissolved. The state, acting through the Preussenkasse, put a large number of the remaining cooperatives—and the firms that depended on them—back on their feet with an infusion of much-needed capital.[18] On the other hand, inflation-induced recapitalization of the Preussenkasse in 1924 enabled the cooperative banks to take a capital position in the bank. Permitting the cooperative sector to have direct influence over the bank represented a compromise solution over the "state versus no state aid" debate that had long divided the cooperative movement. With this achievement, the vast majority of cooperative banks committed themselves to working with the Preussenkasse.[19]

Thus by 1925 the cooperative sector had developed a strong three-tier associational system: on the primary level were 1,349 commercial and 20,855 agricultural credit cooperatives;[20] on the secondary level were 43 regional banks (now known as *Zentralkassen*) and associations; on the tertiary level were the Preussenkasse and national association (Deutsche Bundesbank 1976, 122).[21] Aided by further amendments to the Cooperative Law, during the 1920s the cooperative banks also began to expand into new financial services such as insurance (provided through association-owned subsidiaries).[22] In short order the cooperative banks, especially the commercial cooperatives and the Zentralkassen, made a breakthrough into the traditional markets of the commercial banks and provided strong competition to savings banks. They were increasingly oriented toward short-term credit markets and developed significant securities business (Pohl 1986, 76–83). But more than anything else, the intensifying competition among the cooperative, savings, and commercial banks in the 1920s was occurring through the incursion of the Berlin banks into local markets.

A rapidly expanding economy after 1895 led to dramatic changes in the commercial banking sector. The voracious appetite of large industry for capital induced the big Berlin banks to reach out into the provinces with deposit banks and branches to gather more funds. But, eager to expand their market share in corporate banking, the eight big banks soon began taking over provincial banks, especially in the primary industrial regions of the Ruhr, Silesia, and Württemberg. Between 1914 and 1921, the eight big banks together absorbed 83 provincial banks, in the process becoming truly national banks.[23] While expansion brought the big banks many Mittelstand customers, they nonetheless continued to focus on business with large corporations and now had few competitors other than themselves in large-scale industrial finance. Through consortia, the banks also expanded their underwriting of state and industrial bonds—in the process taking a strongly dominant position over the domestic German securities market.

1924–31: A Brief Era of Bank Group Competition

The post-inflation 1920s were the first years of relatively intense bank group competition in Germany and a key period in German banking history. Invigorated competition came primarily from the cooperatives and the savings banks and their Girozentrale, which were utilizing the opportunities gained during and after the war to expand their commercial banking activities, especially short-term lending via current accounts—the traditional sphere of the private banks.[24] Indeed, between 1913 and 1928 all public banks together raised their share of short-term credit markets from 9.2 percent to 32.2 percent (Born 1983, 87–90)! Intensifying market competition spawned a major political conflict between the savings banks on the one hand, and the cooperative and especially the commercial banks on the other (Dieckmann 1981, 66–78; also Kluthe 1985, 105). Sensing growing competition from the savings banks at a time when they themselves were financially weakened, the commercial and cooperative banks launched a campaign to push the savings banks back into their comparatively limited prewar role.[25] They wanted the savings banks to get out of the short-term lending business and argued that this sort of business (particularly current account lending) was a taxable commercial activity and therefore did not belong in the tax-free savings bank sector. Even the major interest association of the business sector—the Reichsverband der Industrie (RDI)—backed the demands of the commercial banks.[26]

This battle went beyond the pursuit of narrow self-interest by the different banking groups. Conservative social forces, including the right wing of industry (associated strongly with the heavy industry of the Ruhr), warned repeatedly that the socialists were slowly extending their power over society via the state (Abrahams 1980, 88–128). And, in fact, during this time state-owned companies were dramatically expanding their market presence (Wurm 1969, 211–13).[27] In their attempt to beat back the savings banks, the private banks therefore repeatedly invoked the specter of creeping socialization. Against this background struggle between socialism and capitalism, the battle between the public savings banks and the private banks drew a great deal of public attention.

Forced to defend their growing engagement in commercial banking activities, the savings banks developed a new self-definition of their social and economic role as serving a subsidiary function. Namely, they sought to fill the gaps left between the large commercial banks and the small cooperative banks—such as in the area of public infrastructure and Mittelstand finance—or to undertake activities where the common good required a public presence. The savings banks also characterized their role as providing an essential counterweight to the growing centralization and concentration in the economy, behind which lurked the monopoly ambitions of the private sector.[28]

After several years of intense political fighting, the conflict was largely defused in early 1928 when the Prussian government issued its new savings bank ordinances and the Imperial Finance Ministry issued new tax regulations. Both rulings made clear that the current account and Mittelstand lending (with some exceptions) of the savings banks would continue to be tax-free. Having failed to win an outright victory, the commercial and cooperative banks decided to cut a deal with the savings banks that would limit bank competition. In 1928 the three banking groups concluded a private (albeit state-sanctioned) Competition Accord in which the private banks agreed to drop their opposition to the savings bank sector's commercial activities, if the latter agreed to stay away from large industrial loans.[29]

Though the savings banks agreed to self-limit their role in commercial banking activities, they made tremendous gains in other respects through their battle with the private banks. First, the attack of the private banks helped to create a stronger sense of collective identity in the savings bank sector and thus to solidify internal unity among the banks. Second, through their public campaign, the savings banks gained a much greater and more positive profile among the public, as well as greater influence with the authorities, parliaments, the press, and business associations. Finally, the protracted transformation of the savings banks' public mission was completed: from poor relief and protection of the lower classes to supporting the middle classes, including Mittelstand firms.

While the Competition Accord brought some much-needed relief to the big banks, their balance sheets were still weak. Moreover, concentration in German industry and growing access to foreign capital meant the Berlin banks had even less influence over increasingly independent industrial concerns.[30] This combination led to a consolidation within the ranks of the big Berlin banks in 1929. While these mergers returned some financial health and power to these banks, the commercial banking industry as a whole remained weak. This structural weakness, as well as poor management decisions by many of the banks in the 1920s, was laid bare by the economic depression, growing political uncertainty, and the banking crisis of 1931. The crisis and the responses to it would definitively end the brief period of vigorous competition among the three major banking groups in the interwar period—competition that would not reemerge until the 1960s.

The 1931 Banking Crisis: Codifying the Three-Sector
Bank System

In May 1931 a massive run on German banks began (Born 1967, 28–30). Unable to collect on many of their loans, the banking system soon faced imminent collapse. International efforts to maintain Germany's liquidity through a capital infusion and rescheduling of war reparations payments floundered until it was too late. Confidence in the German economy was destroyed, and capital flight surged. On July 13, the fourth-largest commercial bank—the Danatbank—went under. Hundreds of banks, including many savings banks and Girozentrale, were likewise tottering on the brink. Despite concerted efforts to prop up the banks through loans, the state was soon forced to bail out and merge numerous banks. When the dust settled, only the three big banks of today were remaining from among the eight big Berlin banks, and all but the Deutsche were majority-owned by the state.[31]

Even more than the commercial banks, the savings bank sector suffered severely in the banking crisis. More than 70 percent of the credits disbursed to shore up the banking system by the state-sponsored guarantee bank went to the savings banks (Pohl 1986, 93). With growing social expenditures and declining revenues after 1929, communal governments had borrowed heavily from their savings banks. When the banking crisis hit, many communal governments were unable to pay back their loans, thus rendering their banks insolvent. In an emergency regulatory decree, the national government sought to protect the savings banks from further abuse by local public authorities by transforming them into legally independent banks (though with local public ownership and liability for deposits maintained).[32] The legal and organizational separation of the savings banks from local governments led to a significant change in the character of the banks. Whereas until then they were more or less instruments of communal governments and thus local politics, the partial independence gained in 1931 gave them more influence over their own business practices, decisions, and goals. In the postwar era, this new autonomy would prove crucial to an expanded role for the banks in the area of industrial finance.

The commercial banks used the banking crisis as an excuse to once again attack the commercial activities of the savings banks, but the head of the Reichsbank, Hjalmer Schacht, defended the savings banks. The Imperial Bank Sector Law (Reichskreditwesengesetz, or KWG) passed in 1934 reconfirmed the right of the savings banks to exercise commercial banking activities (Dieckmann 1981, 82). In fact, the banking commission that prepared the KWG cited the overextension of credit on easy terms to large firms by commercial banks—to the detriment of small- and medium-sized firms—as one of the causes of the 1931 crisis (Born 1967, 156–57; Wandel 1983, 153). The KWG therefore focused on preserving liquidity in the banking system in good part through redirecting capital away from large firms toward the Mittelstand.[33]

The cooperative banks survived the 1931 banking crisis relatively well, though in the following year it became necessary once again to reorganize the Preussenkasse. Predominant government influence in the bank passed from the hands of the Prussian to the national government, which now owned 42.5 percent of the bank. It was renamed the Deutschlandkasse and placed under the jurisdiction of the Imperial Finance Ministry. Nonetheless, the state gave the cooperatives substantial influence over the bank's policies while continuing to use the Deutschlandkasse as a channel to provide subsidies to agriculture and the Mittelstand.[34]

In addition to new banking legislation and regulation, after 1931 the government finally permitted the different banking groups to hammer out loan and deposit interest rate agreements, which it then sanctioned. In December 1936 the banking industry was formally cartelized through another Competition Accord (Wettbewerbsabkommen).[35] But neither cartelization, reprivatization, nor Nazi benevolence could restore the big banks to their pre-1931 position.[36] The combined volume of business of the big three commercial banks was substantially lower in the 1930s than in the previous decade, especially in securities business and international lending.[37] The major commercial banks would not reach the same equity capital levels of 1913 until well after World War II. The savings and cooperative banks, on the other hand, reattained their 1913 equity levels by the late 1930s (Pohl 1986, 85). As the vast majority of savings deposits were held by the cooperatives and savings banks, they became the primary intermediaries of war finance. Consequently, during the 1930s the total assets of the savings and cooperative sectors outgrew those of the Berlin banks many times (Häuser 1988, 11–38). This asset growth helped the savings and cooperative banks begin the postwar era in a relatively favorable position vis-à-vis the big commercial banks.

The Political Construction of Bank Competition in the Postwar Era

As a result of their drive to move into the traditional markets of the others, over time the internal organization of the three banking groups began to appear more similar, though this convergence was just beginning to become apparent in the Weimar period. Interrupted by the Depression, the banking crisis of 1931, and the era of National Socialism, the twin processes of universalization and organizational convergence (federalization) between the three banking groups continued in the postwar era. In this period, bank competition became predominantly group competition. In turn, group competition fostered changes in the internal organization of the three banking groups that, in turn, reinforced bank competition.

Beginning in the 1970s, the major commercial banks extensively decentralized internal decision-making authority in order to compete more effectively for the business of consumers and Mittelstand firms. In so doing, the major commercial banks became more like a federation of regional and local banks. The association banking groups, especially the cooperative banks, significantly centralized decision-making authority and concentrated resources within their respective associations. All three bank groups now attempt to combine the advantages of decentralization and centralization within one organizational structure. They do so because continued success in one market segment increasingly requires each bank or group to be competitive in all. With the aid of their associations, small banks competed successfully with local branches of the major commercial banks: from 1952 to 1981, the combined assets of the three major commercial banks declined from 16.9 percent to 8.8 percent of total bank industry assets, while the combined asset share of the savings banks and Girozentrale (Landesbanks) rose from 32.7 percent to 38.6 percent, and the cooperative sector's share increased from 8.5 percent to 15.2 percent (Büschgen 1983, 149).[38]

In the postwar period, the state actively promoted the expansion of market mechanisms in the banking sector, sometimes even against the opposition of the industry. The liberal tenets of the social market economy laid down in the 1950s by Erhard set the market liberalization process in motion. After 1969 the Social Democrats pushed the banking industry toward even greater competition in order to promote their social and economic objectives. Länder and local governments used regulation and direct control to further reshape the savings bank sector, partly in order to pursue industrial policies and partly to maintain the competitiveness of savings banks. However, constructing stronger markets required the state to ensure that all three banking groups remained competitive. This was not an easy task, all the more so because intra-industry conflicts over bank regulation and the like were typically further complicated by intergovernmental conflicts that arose out of the public nature of the savings banks and their control by subnational governments. More recently, European integration and the growth of European financial regulation has forced the German banking groups and state to adapt to growing intra-European competition while sustaining group competition in Germany.

Reconsolidating the Three Bank Groups (1949–57)

In the first decade after the war, the banks were preoccupied with reconstructing their previous organizational systems. Disrupted most by the war were the
major commercial banks. The victorious Allies—fearful of any concentration
of power—broke the three big banks into a total of 30 independent regional
banks. But as the Cold War intensified, Allied policy toward the new Federal
Republic was increasingly concerned with reconstructing a successful economy. Thus the banks were allowed to gradually reconsolidate, a process completed by 1957 (Pohl 1976, 122).

Immediately following the war, the occupation administrations viewed the
Girozentrale (Landesbanks) as an unnecessary form of concentration and
sought to eliminate them. But the savings banks managed to convince the
authorities that they were essential. In most Länder, the Land government also
became a major shareholder in the regional Girozentrale.[39] The Länder were
generally seeking a bank that could help them administer the vast number of
reconstruction programs, as well as serve their general financial needs. The
savings banks were largely willing to accommodate their respective Land governments because they needed scarce capital, and it would reduce the probability that the Land government would establish a competing bank for these
functions. In 1953 the regional associations reestablished the central association (Deutscher Sparkassen- und Giroverband, or DSGV), and in 1954 the central savings bank was permitted to resume its activities, thus completing the re-
assembly of the savings banks' three-tier associational structure.

With reconstruction moving ahead quickly, the DSGV set out to modernize the savings banks, making them more market-oriented and competitive enterprises without losing their status as communal institutions. Despite resistance from some corners of the savings bank sector, after 1953 the Länder began
to promulgate new savings bank laws that firmly entrenched this direction of
change.[40] The cornerstone of this new orientation was the extension of the
"self-administration" principle of the savings banks: each bank would now be
able to hire and fire its own personnel without interference (at least direct) from
the communal government.

After the war, the cooperatives also found themselves in the position of
having to rebuild their sector, and once again they needed the state. In 1949 the
Deutsche Genossenschaftskasse (DG Kasse)—successor to the Deutschlandkasse—was established in Frankfurt. The federal and Länder governments contributed capital to the new bank, but their share was not allowed to reach 50 percent of total equity.[41] The public-private nature of the DG Kasse and its

treatment by the state reflected the still enigmatic institutional nature of the co-operative sector as a whole.[42] In certain respects the state (and many coopera-tive banks as well) viewed the cooperative system as serving an important public interest function, since promoting economic prosperity and individual self-sufficiency among the membership was the chief goal of the cooperatives, not profit maximization. Accordingly, the DG Kasse was granted a tax-free sta-tus. As in times past, in the reconstruction era the DG Kasse was an important channel through which state funds (including Marshall Plan funds) flowed to rebuild the Mittelstand (Kluthe 1985, 149). But over the postwar period, the DG Kasse would move away from this more limited role to become a true univer-sal bank.[43]

A conjuncture of several events made 1957–58 an important watershed in the evolution of the German banking system. First, in 1957 the new central bank—the Bundesbank—was established. Second, the deutschmark was made freely convertible and capital controls were eliminated, thereby opening the door for the gradual integration of domestic and international capital markets. Third, in 1958 branching restrictions instituted in the early 1930s were elimi-nated by a decision of the Federal Constitutional Court (Bundesverfassungs-gericht).[44] With the new branching freedom in their hands, the banking sector sought to capture the rapidly growing pool of national savings through an ex-plosion of branches (see table 2). Thus, owing in part to key state actions, by the late 1950s the German banking sector had been reconstructed largely in its prewar form and deregulated enough so that an upswing in competition would ensue.

The Social Market Economy and Bank Competition

During the reconstruction era, Federal Economics Minister Ludwig Erhard laid the foundations of a neoliberal economic order known as the social market economy. Two constituent elements of the social market economy were of par-ticular relevance for the banking sector. First, in contrast to prewar Germany, the Cartel Law of 1957 sought to prevent the kind of economic concentration that had traditionally prevailed throughout much of German industry (Stolper, Häuser, and Borchardt 1967, 233–36, 258–61, 277–95). This would later fa-cilitate the state's revocation of the banking industry's interest rate cartel. Sec-ond, with the completion of the reconstruction era, attention turned to revising the Banking Law of 1934 to make it more consistent with the liberal principles of the social market economy.

After the war, the state had assumed the task of setting interest rates in the

TABLE 2. Number of Banks and Branches by Group

	1957 Domestic		1987 Domestic		1987 Foreign		1995 Domestic		1995 Foreign	
	Banks	Branches	Banks	Branches	Branches	Subsidiaries	Banks	Branches	Branches	Subsidiaries
Major banks[a]	8	787	6	3,120	54	47	3	3,624	123	148
Landesbanks (including DGZ Bank)	14	191	12	231	18	20	13	433	31	59
Savings banks	871	8,192	586	17,307	—	—	624	19,071	3	1
Regional cooperative institutions (including DG Bank)	19	89	6	36	7	10	4	43	8	11
Credit cooperatives	11,795	2,305	3,476	15,910	—	—	2,591	17,205	10	2

Source: Monatsbericht der Deutschen Bundesbank 40, no. 11 (November 1988); Statistical Supplement to the Monthly Report of the German Bundesbank, series 1 (January 1997): table 4.

[a]For 1957 and 1987, three of these are the Berlin subsidiaries of the three major banks.

banking sector. The banks wanted to return to a private cartel in which they would set interest rates with state approval. But in the new Banking Law (KWG) of 1961, the state retained its control over interest rate regulation, while indicating that interest rates would be entirely deregulated in the near future (Bähre 1981, 23–33). In spite of concerted opposition by the Länder, which sought greater influence over banking legislation, the KWG also centralized banking supervision in the Bundesbank and a new Federal Banking Supervisory Office (Bundesaufsichtsamt für das Kreditwesen, or BAKred).[45]

In the debates leading up to the KWG revision, each of the banking groups sought regulations that would improve its competitive position. The private banks—especially the cooperatives—once again leveled charges of unfair competition against the savings banks, arguing that the public guarantee of the savings banks' liabilities allowed them to operate with less equity than other banks. In addition, the fact that the savings banks were under much less pressure to maximize profits enabled them to emphasize market share over profit, thereby placing even more pressure on private credit institutions. So if they were going to become more "banklike" in their activities, the private banks reasoned, then the savings banks must also be subject to the same tax and regulatory rules (Meyer-Könster 1979). As in the interwar period, in the final KWG the savings bank sector was successful in defending its commercial banking activities while retaining many privileges associated with its public status. In accord with the savings banks' demand, federal lawmakers agreed to maintain different equity and liquidity requirements for the various banking groups. Since the KWG did not resolve the "fair competition" question to the satisfaction of the commercial and cooperative banks, the federal government established a Competition Commission to make further recommendations for promoting fair competition among the banks.

The year 1967 was another watershed for the banking industry, as it was for the Federal Republic as a whole. The Social Democratic Party (SPD) had recently come to power in the federal government through a Grand Coalition with the Christian Democratic Union (CDU). With Ludwig Erhard—the "father" of the social market economy—as chancellor and Karl Schiller of the SPD as federal economics minister, the Stability and Growth Promotion Law (Stabilitätsgesetz) was passed in 1967. The law marked a shift in national economic policy toward Keynesianism. The Social Democrats intended to place more emphasis on growth and employment than their predecessors, who stressed price stability and balanced trade. In support of this new policy direction, Schiller, with the concurrence of the Bundesbank, overrode industry opposition and fully deregulated interest rates in 1967.[46] Schiller and the SPD believed that the resulting price competition among the banks would lead to a reduction in interest rates and thereby assist their new growth-oriented economic policies in ending the ongoing recession.[47]

Two further important competition measures were taken in 1967. First, the Competition Accord from 1936—which among other things prohibited banks from advertising—was eliminated. Second, the tax burden of the savings banks was raised. After the KWG of 1961, the issue of tax privileges had become hotly contested. The rapid growth of savings deposits during the 1960s translated into ever larger profits for the savings banks, since they dominated these markets.[48] The commercial and cooperative banks strongly lobbied the federal government to create fairer competition by, among other things, taxing the savings banks more. Rhetorical arguments with supporting empirical examinations flourished on both sides of the political debate.[49] Even though the final report of the Competition Commission established in 1961 to examine these issues had not yet been submitted, the federal government decided to proceed with eliminating some of the tax advantages of the savings banks. The federal government wanted to raise its revenues and, moreover, believed that the savings banks no longer deserved such a high rate of subsidization. But this did not occur without a final battle, and, with political backing from the Länder, the savings banks forced a compromise (Dieckmann 1981, 185).[50] But if there had been any hopes to the contrary, the following year would show that this was only a temporary reprieve.

In 1968 the federal government published the final report of the Competition Commission. The commission sought the middle ground in resolving the struggle among the banking groups over fair competition. On the one hand, the commission recommended the removal of several regulatory advantages that the savings banks enjoyed and the gradual elimination of their tax-free status (Meyer-Könster 1979, 178–79). On the other hand, the commission refused to entertain the suggestion of the private banks that public banking per se automatically had unfair advantages and, moreover, was superfluous. The report cited the importance of the corrective (counterweight) function of the savings banks—in other words, ensuring that all social groups and the Mittelstand everywhere had access to banking services at competitive prices (Henze 1972, 120).[51] While the subsequent decision to gradually eliminate much of the tax privileges of the savings (and cooperative) banks reduced the intensity of the competition debate, growing competition among three banking groups operating under varying rules meant that the fairness question would continually be examined, debated, and fought over in the future (e.g., Grunwald 1978).

The conjuncture of various policy changes in 1967 and 1968 accelerated the pace of change in the banking industry. The state's actions brought down the industry's interest rate cartel and other competition-limiting practices that had helped maintain stability in the German banking system since the banking crisis of 1931. For the association banking groups, this new era of competition led to growing identity problems and difficulties in defending their regulatory privileges. As the cooperative banks grew and their membership expanded across social groups, they found it increasingly difficult to distinguish themselves from other commercial banks. The savings banks groped to find a new definition of their public mission. Ultimately, these banking groups responded to the introduction of stronger markets in banking through a stronger orientation to commercial banking activities. This was not, however, a foregone conclusion. Rather, it involved considerable struggles within these banking groups and critical actions by the state to maintain competitive markets.

The Savings Banks after 1967: "Departure for New Shores"

The events of 1967 and 1968 had a catalytic effect on the savings bank sector. In several Länder, discussions began over the construction of larger Girozentrale or Landesbanks through the fusion of public sector banks. Since Länder such as Baden-Württemberg, North Rhine–Westphalia, and Lower Saxony were themselves created through the postwar merger of previously separate political territories, there were typically several Girozentrale and public special purpose banks in each Land. The economic and political circumstances of the late 1960s suggested that the time was ripe for a consolidation of these banks. First, the savings banks and Girozentrale needed to have larger banks operating within the group that could keep pace with the growing credit demands of large firms. Competition from domestic and foreign banks was also beginning to put pressure on the profitability of the Girozentrale. In general, greater commercial lending was very appealing because it was a market where the savings bank sector could utilize the excess liquidity it built up over the two postwar decades. Second, for the savings bank associations the fusion of banks, especially where there were two Girozentrale in one Land, would cut costs, strengthen the central bank function of the Girozentrale, and help restore an appropriate size differential between the ever larger savings banks and their Girozentrale (Stein 1971, 8–50; Biehal 1984; Völling 1969). Third, for the Länder governments, fusing Girozentrale and other public banks would build large Landesbanks with greater capacity to implement Länder economic policy.[52]

At the beginning of 1969, the first Girozentrale fusion occurred in North Rhine–Westphalia, between the Rhenisch Girozentrale (RGZ) and the Westphalian Girozentrale (WGZ). With the top leadership of both banks and the Land government promoting the fusion, the Land legislature readily approved it.[53] The new bank was named the Westdeutsche Landesbank, or WestLB. On the basis of total assets alone, the WestLB was then the largest bank in West Germany and the ninth-largest in Europe (Stein 1971, 15).[54] The creation of the powerful WestLB hastened fusion discussions in other Länder. Without similar fusions, the other regional savings bank associations ran the risk of ceding more market and policy influence within the savings bank sector to the WestLB. Moreover, many Länder governments considered it desirable to have an equally powerful bank at their disposal.

Thus in 1970 the Norddeutsche Landesbank (NordLB) was created through the fusion of four public sector banks in Lower Saxony. In Bavaria, several bank fusions involving major regional private and public banks occurred with support from the Land government. The first merger was completed in 1971 between the private Bayerische Vereinsbank and the public Staatsbank (Bössenecker 1972, 68–79; Girke and Kopplin 1977, 19–21). In 1972 a second fusion created the Bayerische Landesbank out of the Girozentrale of Bavaria, the Bayerische Gemeindebank, and another public special purpose bank. After these two bank fusions, the Bavarian government had significant ownership in three major regional banks: 20 percent of the private Vereinsbank (10 percent of voting shares); 50 percent of the Bavarian Landesbank; and 100 percent of the Bayerische Landesanstalt für Aufbaufinanzierung (LfA), an economic development bank created in 1950 (Huber 1980).[55] The Land government of Baden-Württemberg and the two regional savings bank associations in the Land also attempted to fuse their two Girozentrale. After numerous rounds of negotiations, an agreement could not be reached, though the Land government did manage to create a state industrial development bank—the Landeskreditbank—through the merger of two state mortgage banks in 1972. Like the LfA in Bavaria, this bank became the primary industrial development bank of the Land government.

Change in the savings bank sector, however, was not limited to the fusion of Girozentrale.[56] Ludwig Poullain, head of the WestLB, had much more in mind. At the annual national congress of the savings banks in 1969, Poullain, who had also become president of the national association in 1967, outlined a nine-point reform plan. Poullain was convinced that the savings bank sector needed to be shaken of its public bureaucratic mentality. If the savings banks did not adopt an offensive, market-oriented strategy, he argued, they would be overtaken by the other banks. Moreover, the future public mission of the savings banks must be different than in the past: rather than supporting weaker social groups, the public mission of the savings banks must place greater emphasis on the corrective function, that is, assuring effective competition in the banking industry.[57]

In emphasizing this corrective function, Poullain drew avid support from Federal Economics Minister Schiller. At the 1969 congress, Schiller expressed his support for Poullain's plans and underscored his own belief that, because the savings banks were regionally anchored institutions, they must counter economic concentration and animate competition in the banking industry. By continuing their focus on local communal and Mittelstand business, but also by expanding into new market segments, especially international and large-firm business, the savings bank sector was to be the guarantor of bank competition in the Federal Republic.[58] Since the reduction in the savings banks' tax privileges in 1967 was part of the federal government's attempt to introduce more competition into the banking industry, Schiller was deploying both a carrot and a stick to prod the savings banks into more aggressively challenging the other banking groups.

The 1969 congress of the savings banks was hailed in the press as a "new era for the savings banks" (Poullain 1979, 49–50; also Korbach 1986, 52–54). The sector was invigorated with a new sense of purpose and self-understanding, though the realization of the goals set out by Poullain was a long, difficult, and, in the view of many today, still incomplete process. For the Landesbanks, the new era consisted primarily of two new directions. First, they began to develop international connections. The WestLB, for example, joined with three foreign banks to establish a consortial bank in London and by 1976 achieved its goal of having 25 percent of total assets in international transactions (Poullain 1979, 276). Second, the Landesbanks began to pursue more aggressively the business of large firms. In Germany's system of universal banking, this also meant that they would begin to acquire equity holdings in large firms. Because nearly all Landesbanks were co-owned by Land governments, several Land governments therefore became more directly involved in the affairs of regional industry. By the early 1970s, the Landesbanks were forcing their way into the elite club of the big banks, and the savings banks were firmly on their new market-oriented path.[59]

The Cooperatives: Adjusting to the Pains of Success

In terms of overall market share expansion, the liberalization measures of 1967 benefited the cooperative banking sector the most. With their vast network of banks and branches, the cooperatives were well positioned to capture the fast-growing consumer banking business. But growth had a large downside for the cooperative banks. After 1967 the rate of cooperative bank fusions grew quickly, reaching several hundred per year in the early 1970s. By and large, it was simply growing competition with the other banking groups that forced the cooperatives to improve cost-efficiency through greater size. But fusions also reflected success. As cooperative banks expanded, they encroached on each other's markets, and many mergers were undertaken in order to eliminate group-internal competition.

The rapidly expanding membership ultimately transformed the demographics of credit cooperative membership and thus the banks themselves. Until the mid-twentieth century, the membership of commercial credit cooperatives was generally dominated (if not always in numbers, then at least in terms of control) by business owners. But by the early 1970s, two-thirds of cooperative members were not self-employed, but blue- and white-collar employees. The consequent growth of retail consumer business represented a crucial change for cooperatives, since their original major purpose was commercial credit provision. The growth of membership also changed the way the cooperatives conducted business. Through World War II, the cooperatives typically had a few hundred members. On this scale, the members were frequently well acquainted with each other, if not personally then with each other's business qualifications. But with the growth of membership, this personal knowledge became rarer, and the cooperative banks needed to become more formal in their lending practices. The cooperative identity as a closely knit group providing mutual aid was severely strained (Hahn 1986, 24).

Like Poullain for the savings banks, Georg Draheim, president of the DG Kasse from 1964 to 1972, sought to redefine and clarify the nature of cooperative banks. Draheim argued that cooperatives have a double, sui generis nature: they are at the same time both business enterprises and "member communities" in which the goal of the members is mutual aid. Market-oriented management was essential, but profit maximization as a primary goal did not fit the cooperative ideal (Faust 1977, 599–615). Their survival as a unique species, however, required greater cooperation and unity within the group. To this end, a new joint association of agricultural and commercial credit associations—the Bundesverband der deutschen Volksbanken und Raiffeisenbanken (BVR)—was created in 1971–72.[60]

The cooperatives also demanded and got further amendments to the Cooperative Law in 1974. The amendments lifted several restrictions on the business activities of cooperative banks and thereby provided the legal basis for their further universalization. The most important change was the new possibility to conduct business with nonmembers *if* it served the interests of the cooperative's members. In recognition of the diminished capacity of cooperative members to directly operate their bank, the governing board of each bank was made legally responsible for bank actions (though the board of each bank is still ultimately controlled by the membership through elections). Despite these changes, the cooperative banks are not full-fledged universal banks in the sense of the commercial banks, as certain restrictions on them remain intact.[61] A critical distinction between cooperative and other banks remains the personal liability of members for the organization. Since their beginning, this liability has been institutionalized in a "liability surcharge" (*Haftsummenzuschlag*). This principle obligates each member to pay in additional capital in proportion to the number of shares each holds in the bank should the bank's equity prove insufficient to cover losses (Schramm 1984). The liability surcharge has been critical to the success of the cooperatives, because it is legally recognized in the KWG as bank equity. The 1974 amendments permitted cooperative banks to set lower limits on this surcharge. This preserved the equity-enhancing advantages of the surcharge while reducing the risk of membership and therefore enhancing its attractiveness.

Fulfilling its 1968 commitment to reduce tax privileges and create fairer competition in banking, the federal government gradually eliminated the tax-exempt status of the DG Kasse. As compensation, in 1976 the DG Kasse was given a new law and renamed the Deutsche Genossenschaftsbank (DG Bank). In accordance with the growing market orientation of the cooperative sector, the new law lifted most restrictions on the bank's activities. The state now accepted large-scale commercial credits and domestic and international consortial lending by the DG Bank insofar as they promoted the welfare of cooperative members. For the first time in its history, the cooperative banking sector had a central bank with negligible direct government control.[62] In the process, the DG Bank also became another major competitor to the big banks.

In sum, by the mid-1970s the cooperative and savings banks responded to market pressure and state policy changes through a transition to a stronger market orientation. The change required the association bank groups to recast their distinctive identities in order to successfully defend their special privileges. This transition was neither easy nor smooth. The preservation of market competition and the market orientation of these bank groups would need to be fought for and reaffirmed by them and the state many more times in subsequent years.

The Big Banks Fight Back

Recession, major losses at several of the Landesbanks, and the collapse of West Germany's second-largest private banking house (I.D. Herstatt) in 1974 dealt a severe blow to the public's trust in the banking system. The events raised questions about the security of deposits in the banking system and, more importantly, about the so-called power of the banks (*Macht der Banken*)—a highly charged issue in German public debate. The first question was addressed through a series of emergency regulations and the strengthening of the banking sector's private deposit insurance programs.[63] The second question was turned over to a new commission known as the Gessler Commission. The commission was charged by the federal government with a thorough examination of the industry's social and economic role and, in particular, the merits of a universal banking system with the associated accumulation of power in the banks. Over the next few years, the banking industry—especially the big banks—was subjected to close scrutiny and numerous ad hominem attacks from the public and the press (Studienkommission "Grundsatzfragen der Kreditwirtschaft" 1979, 3).

Ironically, the growing market orientation of the Landesbanks, which rightfully could have been viewed as a positive contribution to controlling the power of the big banks, was also seriously questioned by large segments of the public and political establishment. This started in 1973 with a series of large loan defaults that brought scandals to three of the largest Landesbanks—the WestLB, the NordLB, and the Landesbank of Hessen (HELABA). In Hessen alone, the losses amounted to more than DM 2 billion between 1974 and 1976, forcing the Land government to cover the bank's losses out of its own treasury. In several cases, though, Länder governments were partly responsible for these scandals: unable to resist the power of the banks in their hands, several Länder had begun using Landesbanks to aid troubled regional firms, often with little consideration for sound banking practices.[64]

The mid-1970s crisis of the Landesbanks reached its peak in 1977 when Ludwig Poullain, the man who symbolized the new role of the savings banks in West Germany, was ousted from his post over allegations of corruption.[65] Under pressure from the public, the savings banks, and Länder opposition parties to end their high-flying expansion, the Landesbanks liquidated many of their foreign offices and refocused on their regional markets (Pohl 1986, 128–30).[66] Land governments were forced to considerable lengths to defeat political campaigns that threatened to reverse the growing market orientation of the savings banks. The Land and federal governments remained committed to the market role of the Landesbanks, in part because local and regional efforts to overcome growing structural economic crises needed the help of strong public banks.[67] Nor could the savings banks and Landesbanks afford to retreat too far or allow their internal problems to sap their collective strength. In the 1970s the major commercial banks were stepping up their efforts to capture more of the consumer and Mittelstand banking markets.

For the major commercial banks, the Herstatt crisis and bank power debate coincided with an important juncture in their internal development. Since their reconsolidation in the late 1950s, the major commercial banks had been steadily increasing their branches, buying up mortgage banks and other financial service organizations and expanding their international presence (Pohl 1986, 116–23). By the 1970s the major banks realized they needed to rethink their market strategies and undertake a major reorganization in order to effectively accommodate their ever broader range of activities and growing number of customers. Reorganization at this time was further motivated by declining profitability and growing competition from domestic and foreign banks (Wielens 1977, xiv, 6, 101). Finally, the rise of international capital markets provided large firms with an alternative source of industrial finance. For the commercial banks, this meant that lending to the Mittelstand was an increasingly important source of growth, and they would need to reorganize internally to meet the needs of this customer group.

The Dresdner Bank was the first to initiate a major reorganization. In 1972 the bank created one head office (out of three); concentrated its middle level from 40 to 14 main regional bank offices; and increased the competencies of the 14 regional offices and the branches below them. In 1975 the Deutsche Bank followed, likewise forsaking the three-head-office structure and consolidating the number of regional offices from 23 to 14 (Hahn 1977, 83–84; Büschgen 1983, 214–20). But the Deutsche Bank took this decentralization one step further by making its 14 regional offices and major branches into individual profit centers. The reduction of hierarchical control within the two banks made them much more like the two association banking groups. Despite this evident convergence, critical differences between the three major bank groups remained, which each sought to protect. In the early 1980s, this attempt to protect institutional (chiefly regulatory) advantages flared again in a new round of intense political fighting among the groups. This was one of the most pitched battles ever among the three groups to gain competitive advantage. It was all the more intense because during the 1970s the savings and cooperative banks made large market share gains vis-à-vis commercial banks, and especially the big banks, in commercial lending. And once again, the state was in a position to shape the competitiveness of each banking group.

The 1984 KWG Revision: The Struggle
for Regulatory Advantage

In 1979 the Gessler Commission, called by the federal government in 1974 to examine the fundamental principles and operation of the banking system, finally published its report. The commission found no major faults in the universal banking system. Nor did it find there was an undue concentration of power—let alone its abuse—in the banking industry. Nonetheless, in the interest of fairer competition the commission recommended that the KWG's definition of equity capital for the different banking groups be amended and that the liability surcharge of the cooperative banks be eliminated. The report also recommended that banks be limited to holding no more than 25 percent plus one share of a company's voting stock, exceptions being made for cases of firm rescues. This last recommendation fell far short of the limitations on bank shareholdings demanded by the Federal Monopoly Commission, the unions, and many Social Democrats—all of whom supported a 5 percent limit (Mario Müller, "Reform des Bankwesens—Die Machtfrage wird nicht mehr gestellt," *Frankfurter Rundschau,* 8 August 1981).

Within two years of the Gessler report's publication, however, the main issue of political debate switched from the power of the banks to the "equity" question. The "power" question faded under the weight of two financially bad years for the major banks in which they not only parted with many of their largest shareholdings, but had a difficult time finding buyers for others. Renewed concern about increasing foreign control of German firms made the power of the banks seem more benign, if not desirable, to the federal government. But if political support to curtail bank ownership in industry through legislation was fading, there was still ample support to force more competition into the banking industry.

In 1981 the federal government proposed the elimination of all remaining tax privileges for the savings and cooperative banks. The government maintained that the business restrictions placed on the savings banks by Länder regulations were no longer significant (what the savings banks were not allowed to do, their Landesbanks could), and thus the justification for tax privileges was no longer present.[68] This proposal unleashed a great outcry among both of the association banking groups, but especially the savings banks. The issue of eliminating tax privileges was intimately linked to the debate over the impending reform of the banking law (KWG) and the equity capital question. The savings banks argued that the previous increases in their tax rate had already severely inhibited their ability to maintain an adequate capital base and, moreover, the other banking groups could access outside sources of equity capital while they could not. If taxes were raised further, the growth potential of the savings banks would be severely and unjustly limited.

The national savings bank association also argued that its own decentralized structure and focus on the Mittelstand helped preserve a decentralized economic structure. If the lawmakers wished to force the savings banks to be just like other banks—so argued Helmut Geiger, president of the national association—then they must be prepared to accept the broader social, political, and economic consequences (Geiger 1981). Communal and Länder politicians and representatives of the savings bank sector also suggested that failure by the state to maintain an adequate basis for the savings banks to continue as communal organizations could be considered unconstitutional, because the Basic Law (Grundgesetz) guarantees communal self-administration and the savings banks are an indispensable cornerstone of this guarantee.[69] The Länder, acting through the Bundesrat, opposed the federal government's attempt to raise the taxes on the savings banks, since it would raise the budget expenditures of Länder and local governments to maintain adequate capitalization of their banks.[70] But the Länder also supported the savings banks for many of the same reasons that the banks themselves put forth—namely, their focus on providing local banking needs to consumers and the Mittelstand (Koschnik 1982, 181–82).

Despite these efforts, the savings and cooperative banks could not prevent the passage of the Subsidy Reduction Law in 1981, which eliminated their remaining tax privileges. As compensation, the savings banks demanded the KWG be amended so as to allow them a liability surcharge (*Haftungszuschlag*) similar to that of the cooperative banks. For the savings bank sector, such a surcharge would do justice to the unlimited liability of communal and Länder governments for their banks by acknowledging this liability in the form of un-paid-in capital. During the ensuing KWG hearings and debate, the savings banks found broad support in the federal, Länder, and local parliaments and governments for their demand.[71] Among the major political parties, only the liberal Free Democratic Party (FDP) seemed clearly opposed to the measure (Hahn 1986, 436).[72]

Naturally, the cooperative and commercial banks vehemently opposed a liability surcharge for the savings banks.[73] Instead, they argued that the lawmakers must expand the possibility for all banks to build their equity. The definition of what counts as liable capital was critical because German banks are permitted by the KWG to lend up to a sum equaling 18 times their capital. And in a banking industry with three major banking groups operating on different definitions of "liable capital," these definitions have been the subject of recurrent and often sharp conflict.[74] Despite these objections, in June of 1982 the federal government proposed KWG amendments that included a liability surcharge for the savings banks.

Unfortunately for the savings banks, the government of Chancellor Schmidt fell on a rare vote of no confidence before the KWG law could be amended. The new conservative-liberal coalition led by Helmut Kohl subsequently presented a new KWG proposal that did not include a savings bank liability surcharge.[75] In 1984 the KWG was finally amended. An uneasy peace settlement among the warring banking groups, and between the federal government and the Länder, was accomplished through the introduction of a new form of equity that all the banks could use—the *Genussschein,* or special participation right.[76] The compromise also included a gradual reduction (to half its previous value) of the liability surcharge of the cooperatives.[77] Thus the 1984 KWG revision pushed the association banking groups further along the path to greater market orientation and universalization, since they would have to rely more than ever on profits to maintain an adequate capital base.

Accelerated Convergence and Internationalization

After the 1984 KWG, both association bank groups initiated new reform drives to meet the challenge of intensifying domestic and international competition. Since the savings and cooperative banks already had an overwhelming local presence, organizational reform efforts focused heavily on rationalizing their secondary and tertiary levels. The national associations of the cooperative and savings banks believe that only by further raising their efficiency on this level and maintaining a group-internal division of labor can the vast majority of the local banks they serve provide the growing range of essential financial services at competitive prices. But reform is a long, difficult process in the association groups, where decision making is highly complex. The creation of the Single Market and the advance of European financial regulation and integration have not altered the central debates in each group about organizational issues, though they have intensified reform pressures.

A Future for Public Banking?

Since the 1984 KWG amendments, the German savings bank association (DSGV) has faced corrosive internal division over the future direction of the group. Indeed, in the late 1980s the group sometimes appeared to verge on civil war. In spite of an enormous financial potential, the savings bank association perceives itself as lacking long-term competitiveness. The group's dominant market share—close to one-half of the German banking market—rests in large part on traditional savings instruments that are steadily declining in popularity. In international/export and investment banking, which are dominated by the major banks and expected by all banks to be the key markets of the future, the savings banks are relatively weak.[78] Competitive pressures are driving many savings banks and Landesbanks into competition with each other. Four key issues divide association members: the further liberalization of business restrictions on the savings banks; public ownership versus privatization; the association-internal division of labor; and fusion of the Landesbanks.

By law, savings banks are permitted to engage only in the activities that are expressly authorized by the lawmakers or supervisory authorities of the Land government. Many savings banks, especially the larger ones, find this increasingly cumbersome.[79] Hence in recent years several Länder governments have worked with their savings banks to liberalize further savings bank regulations. One of the chief problems with such liberalization is that it enables the large savings banks—several of which are really superregional banks—to compete in markets previously reserved for Landesbanks. While this might benefit larger savings banks, the competition engendered tends to undermine cooperation and thus the ability of the association to support effectively the smaller savings banks.

All savings banks are especially concerned about their limited capacity to raise sufficient equity capital to remain competitive. The EU's Solvency Ratio Directive, which took effect in 1993, also forced most savings banks to substantially raise their capital. In response to these pressures, since the mid-1980s a small but vocal group of rebels within the association has pushed the DSGV and Länder governments for the privilege of privatization.[80] But the opposition to privatization by most local and Land politicians, and the majority of savings banks, is overwhelming. Opponents argue first that privatization of even just a few large savings banks would destroy the regional principle, and thus organizational unity, by enabling these banks to compete with other savings banks. If the association is thus weakened, the smaller savings banks would suffer a great disadvantage vis-à-vis their chief local competitor, the cooperative banks, since the cooperatives would still have the advantages of a strong association (Günther Olthof, "Stille Gesellschaft vor den Kassen," *Die Welt,* 21 March 1989). From a national perspective, many fear that privatized savings banks would eventually fall into the hands of domestic or foreign commercial banks. Greater concentration in the banking sector, rather than more competition, would be the likely outcome (Fahning 1987; Nierhaus 1985). German reunification added more fuel to the ongoing privatization debate, as several prominent national political figures called for privatizing public banks. While privatization advocates remain vocal, resistance is very strong, and there has been little success in pushing bank privatization onto the domestic legislative agenda.[81]

The third major problem for the savings bank group centers around the group-internal division of labor and the Landesbanks. Once relatively confined to their respective regions, as Landesbanks became more and more directly engaged in commercial banking activity they inevitably expanded their activities to the national and international markets. While this was essential for competing successfully with the major commercial banks, it also led to competition among Landesbanks and created redundant organizational capacities that could be more effectively and cheaply utilized by the group as a whole if combined. Moreover, the Landesbanks' profitability is low, and long-term business lending, their chief source of income, is in decline. The bigger savings banks are not only using them less and less, they are also competing with them. This makes the cost of serving the smaller savings banks that much higher to the Landesbanks ("Rebellen und Funktionäre," *Wirtschaftswoche,* 9 June 1989). Lastly, the group-internal division of labor, which assured the Landesbanks a large portion of their income, is coming apart. For example, a cornerstone of cooperation in the savings bank group is the "liquidity association." Under this arrangement, the local banks are required to deposit their excess funds with their Landesbank, which lends these funds to other savings banks in the region or invests them. The Landesbanks, in turn, refinance the loans of the savings banks and act as lender of last resort. The Landesbanks are also assigned all the investment banking functions of the group, issuing bank bonds when more cash is needed and buying securities for savings bank customers. Though this system served the savings banks well, it is being undermined through attempts by individual banks and/or Länder to gain competitive advantages for themselves, rather than for the group.

As its major strategy for preserving the savings bank group, the leadership of the DSGV began in the mid-1980s to promote the fusion of western Landesbanks. The DSGV believed that fusing the Landesbanks would directly or indirectly solve the majority of the group's problems and would be critical to becoming more competitive in the international and export finance activities including, most importantly, the export finance business of Mittelstand customers.[82] While some advocated the fusion of the then 11 Landesbanks into one bank, the more immediate goal promoted by the DSGV was the creation of three or four Landesbanks. Numerous fusion discussions among Landesbanks were subsequently initiated, but all of them failed. The chief obstacle, among many, was the resistance of the Länder governments, which did not want to surrender control over one of their chief economic policy instruments.[83] The only fusion that did occur was between the two Girozentrale of Baden and Württemberg. After nearly two decades of trying, these banks finally merged in the new Südwestdeutsche Landesbank (SüdwestLB) in 1990.[84]

The reform struggles took a new turn with reunification of the two Germanys in 1990. Reunification had the potential to be either a golden opportunity or a disaster for the savings banks. Initially, the DSGV managed to form a united front regarding a singular, comprehensive strategy for integrating nearly 200 eastern German savings banks into the western savings bank group. Among other things, this required the difficult task of getting western Landesbank managers to throttle their urges to grab market share in the East. The plan was to place all eastern savings banks into one regional association with one Girozentrale to serve their central banking needs. This was initially accomplished through the creation of an eastern savings bank association (Ostdeutscher Sparkassen- und Giroverband, or OSGV) and by a revitalized DGZ Bank assuming central banking functions for eastern savings banks at the time of monetary and economic union in July 1990.[85] At first the unified front strategy seemed to work, but in 1991 the savings banks of Thuringia announced that they intended to leave the OSGV and join the Hessen savings bank association, making the Landesbank of Hessen (HELABA) the Landesbank and Girozentrale for Thuringia as well. The government argued that its savings banks would be better served by the HELABA and, moreover, a joint venture with the state of Hessen would give the Land government of Thuringia more influence over the bank, since it meant joint decision making with one, rather than four, other Land governments (Bohn 1991).

With this move, savings bank unity was dealt a severe blow. Each of the other major western Landesbanks felt an ever powerful pull to grab as much as it could in the East before its competitors did. Within a short time, the next blows fell. The NordLB—the Landesbank of Lower Saxony—became the house bank of the Land governments of Mecklenburg–West Pomerania and Saxony-Anhalt, as well as Girozentrale for their respective savings banks (Schildt 1993). The Saxon government and its regional savings bank association decided to establish their own Landesbank, though with a 25.1 percent equity participation by the SüdwestLB. Later in 1993, a major bank merger involving four banking institutions, including the Landesbank of Berlin, was sealed. Thus, rather than serving as a force of unity and the restoration of order in the savings bank sector, the eastern savings banks were mostly drawn into different fiefdoms of western Landesbanks.

Immediately on the heels of this turmoil in the East, however, in 1992 the long-sought breakthrough in Landesbank mergers in the West finally came. It was not in the form of mergers between Landesbanks, but rather in the form of strategic alliances based on equity participations by the bigger, financially stronger Landesbanks in smaller, weaker Landesbanks. As the dust began to settle in early 1993, all but one of the smaller Landesbanks had either merged with or sold a large equity stake to at least one of the larger Landesbanks. Together with the realignments in the East, the 13 Landesbanks in unified Germany were essentially reduced to five major banks or bank alliances. By far the largest and most powerful bank alliance is that centered around the WestLB, the Landesbank of North Rhine–Westphalia. The other Landesbanks in this alliance are those of Baden-Württemberg, Rhineland-Palatinate, Schleswig-Holstein, and Saxony. The alliance is cemented by a cooperative agreement between the WestLB and SüdwestLB (Baden-Württemberg), as well as large equity stakes by one or both of these two Landesbanks in the other three.[86] This alliance controls roughly half of the assets of the savings bank sector. The other two strategic alliances center around the Bavarian Landesbank and the NordLB respectively. The newly enlarged Landesbanks of Hessen-Thüringen and Berlin round out the list. In early 1997, partly prompted by expectations of European monetary union and heightened competition in Europe, further consolidation among Landesbank alliances occurred. The Landesbank of Schleswig-Holstein acquired a 49.5 percent stake in the Hamburg Landesbank, thereby strengthening the WestLB alliance. Partly in fear of the WestLB's growing power, the NordLB and Bank Society of Berlin (Bankgesellschaft Berlin), the recently formed holding company that contains the Berlin Landesbank and Berliner Bank (a private bank), announced their intention to merge. Such a merger would create the third-largest bank in Germany in terms of asset size.

Restructuring the savings bank sector in the East cannot be considered the primary cause of the eruptive Landesbank movements in the West, but this process, and the unification process as a whole, were important (if not necessary) facilitative conditions. First, the open struggle in the East accelerated alliance formation in the West by creating an atmosphere of change and the need for bold and risky measures. Second, the massive public financial transfers from West to East, combined with recession in 1992 and 1993, also strapped the resources of western Land governments. This occurred exactly at a time when all the Landesbanks urgently required increased equity to remain competitive in an integrated European financial market and to meet the new EU solvency ratio requirements. Without the money to contribute to their Landesbanks, several western Land governments came to view strategic alliances as the best solution to their problems. Allowing equity participations by large Landesbanks generated revenue for cash-strapped governments while solving their Landesbanks' equity problems. Yet forming an alliance rather than an outright sellout allowed a certain amount of autonomy and government influence to remain in the smaller Landesbanks. Finally, cooperation within the alliance could potentially achieve cost savings and product improvements to benefit the smaller savings banks for which Land governments bear a certain amount of responsibility (Heidenreich 1993).[87]

In terms of competition among the three major banking groups, the formation of these Landesbank alliances seems likely to produce fewer but stronger Landesbank rivals to the major commercial banks. For individual savings banks, the extent to which the Landesbank restructuring produces cost savings and more competitive products—particularly in the areas of securities and international business—could enhance their competitiveness in local markets, especially with the export-oriented Mittelstand. Combined with a new DSGV president in 1993 and a strengthened commitment to cooperate by the heads of the Landesbanks, the savings bank sector moved closer to resolving some of its long-term organizational problems (Balzer 1993).

Cooperative Banking in an Internationalized Era

Until the mid-1980s, the cooperative banks were the success story of the post-1967 era. In less than two decades, they doubled their market share of total bank business, while their membership grew almost exponentially. Explanations for their success are many, and none is convincing by itself. One factor was surely the repeal of the prohibition on nonmember business in the early 1970s; another their ability to capture a large share of the rapidly growing retail market. Many would cite their efficiency in cross-selling the specialized banking and other financial services (e.g., insurance) of association organizations. The cooperatives themselves see their decentralized structure and the individual's identity as a member as responsible for their success (Gundlach 1985, 255–67).

In the mid-1980s, however, the cooperative banks ran into problems. Group-internal competition—mostly among the regional banks and DG Bank—began to plague the cooperative banks, albeit to a lesser extent than the savings banks.[88] More importantly, the cooperatives' steady expansion curve in market share flattened after 1985, thereby raising concerns about their future. Like the savings banks, the cooperative banking sector is weak in the key growth markets—securities trading, investment and international banking—that are increasingly important for their traditional Mittelstand customers

(Rudolf Kahlen, "Die Basis Streitet um den Überbau," *Die Zeit,* 30 September 1989). To do these kinds of activities, the cooperative leadership has worked to strengthen the market capacities of its upper-tier banks.

The more pressing problem for the cooperative sector, however, is that the vast majority of cooperative banks are still very small—too small to afford the products, services, and specialized staff with the know-how necessary to compete effectively in an integrated European financial marketplace. The association therefore continues to promote mergers among the smallest banks, and dozens of independent cooperative banks merge every year (compare table 2). Yet these local banks are the very reason for the success of the group. Hence the association is seeking ways to reduce costs and enhance the efficiency with which services are delivered from the upper levels to the primary banking institutions. In the late 1980s, the DG Bank and national association sought to achieve this end through the merger of the regional banks with the DG Bank, in effect moving from a three-tier to a two-tier organizational structure. But three of the four regional banks refused to merge, and a major securities trading scandal involving the DG Bank in 1990 forced association leaders to suspend further fusion negotiations. Finally, in 1995 the DG Bank gave up the goal of merging the remaining regional banks, instead seeking to strengthen cooperation between itself and the regional banks ("Kreditgenossenschaften wollen ihren Streit in einer Klausur bereinigen," *Handelsblatt,* 2 November 1995).[89]

Even without the completion of a two-tier associational structure, the process of rebuilding and integrating the former East German cooperative banking sector into the western group strengthened further the already powerful leadership role of the DG Bank and the national association within the group. The first measure by the DG Bank was to assume the central banking functions for the 362 eastern cooperatives, thus preempting any need for regional cooperative banks.[90] With this measure, the cooperative banks quickly established a two-tier associational structure in the East in which the cooperative banks would serve local markets and cooperate directly with the DG Bank in consortial lending, international transactions, and securities business (Pleister and Hennigsen 1991).[91] The reinvigorated role of the DG Bank is perhaps the most significant consequence of reunification for the internal structure of the cooperative banking sector. Already in the 1980s, many outside observers described the cooperative association as being concernlike, because the DG Bank had achieved considerable direct influence over the small cooperatives, much like the head office of a commercial bank exercises over its branches (Hahn 1986). Developments since then have generally strengthened the DG Bank's position, though it is very unlikely that cooperative banks would ever surrender their formal independence. Thus, under the pressures of growing domestic and European competition, organizational convergence among the banking groups continues.

The Major Commercial Banks: Anywhere and Everywhere?

The first major organizational development of the big banks since the mid-1980s is further internationalization through the purchase of foreign banks and joint ventures with foreign banks. As elsewhere, this was driven in large part by the rapid internationalization of financial markets. The Deutsche Bank has gone the furthest toward establishing a comprehensive presence throughout Europe. The Dresdner Bank and Commerzbank have instead relied more on cooperation agreements with major European banks. After a heavy push in the early 1990s, the banks slowed their European branch expansion while stepping up their efforts to build international investment banking capacities in Frankfurt and other major financial centers.

The second major organizational development of the big banks is a continuation of the decentralization or federalization process that they initiated in the 1970s.[92] One prominent measure of decentralization within banks is the lending authority of each level of the bank. Since the 1970s, all the major banks have delegated much greater authority to lower levels (Zapp 1975, 57–66; Heye 1985).[93] The credit needs of nearly all small- and medium-sized firms can now be decided upon in the local, or at most the regional, branch in all major commercial banks.[94] In early 1987 the major banks made another bold step when, for the first time in their history, they gave their regional offices (and in some cases key branches) the freedom to set their own interest rates on savings deposits (Otto Schwarzer, "Schlagkraft von der Basis: Wie die Grossbanken sich für den Wettbewerb Rüsten," *Süddeutsche Zeitung*, 21 March 1987).

With this devolution of authority, the role of the central office vis-à-vis the regional and local branches changed. The relationship between center and periphery within the bank became less authoritative and more consensual. Both strategic (long-term) and especially operative (short-term) planning are done in all three major commercial banks through a dialectical process between the central, regional, and local offices.[95] In many respects, the central office acts more like a service provider to regional and local branches. The major banks outwardly portray their regional offices as similar in their autonomy to independent regional banks.[96] These "banks within a bank" typically have their own network of institutional relations with larger Mittelstand firms. For example, in 1988 representatives from 643 firms sat on the 14 regional advisory councils of the Deutsche Bank. Many of these same firms in turn offer a seat on their advisory board to a bank member (Eglau 1989, 248–51). While these boards have minimal decision-making roles, they help cement bank-firm relations and firmly root regional offices in their immediate corporate environment. In the mid-1990s, the Deutsche Bank announced another major reorganization that would put even further competencies in the hands of local and regional branches.[97]

Finally, the big three commercial banks benefited considerably from German reunification. They were the quickest among all the West German banks to expand into the new Länder (table 3). In anticipation of unification, on April 1, 1990, the Staatsbank, the former East German central bank, was transformed by the East German government into the Deutsche Kreditbank AG. After a subsequent period of competitive negotiations involving the big three western banks, the Deutsche Kreditbank AG formed two joint ventures in July 1990—one each with the Deutsche Bank and the Dresdner Bank. These joint ventures brought 122 branches of the former Staatsbank under the control of the Deutsche Bank and 72 under the control of the Dresdner Bank. Because the Staatsbank was the bank for virtually all company accounts, with this move the two largest West German commercial banks immediately established a dominant market position in corporate business in the East. Simultaneously, the Deutsche and Dresdner banks were establishing wholly owned branches in the East.[98] Thus, at the start of German monetary union on July 1, 1990, the

TABLE 3.   Banks and Branches in the Five New States by Type

	July 1, 1990	December 1991	December 1992
Commercial banks	4 banks	73 banks	68 banks
	268 banks[a]	599 branches	864 branches
Savings banks	196 banks	191 banks	181 banks[b]
		2,641 branches	
Credit cooperatives	362 banks	301 banks	261 banks[b]
		2,528 branches	
Other banks	4 banks	14 banks	16 banks[b]
		165 branches	

Source: Deutsche Bundesbank, "Regionalergebnisse der Monatlichen Bilanzstatistik für Kreditinstitute in Ostdeutschland," *Beilage zur statistischen Beihefte zu den Monatsberichten der Deutschen Bundesbank,* series 1, no. 11 (1992); and Klaus Krummrich, "Strukturwandel in der ostdeutschen Kreditwirtschaft." *Sparkasse* 108, no. 10 (1991): 468–76; "Banken und Aufbau Ost—das Konzept," *Die Bank,* no. 4 (1993): 244–47.

Note: The Girozentralen (Landesbanks) and eastern cooperative central bank (DG Bank) are included in the "Other banks" category.

[a]Includes only branches from the Deutsche Bank (140); Dresdner Bank (107); and Commerzbank (21).
[b]September 1992

Deutsche Bank had 140 branches in the East and the Dresdner Bank had 107 branches.

The other western commercial banks moved quickly to gain market share in the East, but building a new branch network was hindered considerably by shortages of suitable office space, appropriately skilled personnel, and a client base. While the number of commercial banks engaged in the East grew rapidly, the big three (Deutsche, Dresdner, and Commerzbank) dominated among them: at the end of 1990, commercial banks operated 451 branches in the East, 322 of which belonged to the big three (compare table 3). Thus, in the short term, the biggest impact of reunification on the commercial banking sector was to strengthen the market share in corporate business of the big three vis-à-vis other commercial banks and the other two major banking groups (though, as discussed in chapter 6, this later reversed itself). None of the major commercial banks' organizational strategies was noticeably altered in response to reunification. Rather, the East was taken as an opportunity to extend their branch networks and increase market share.

German Banks and EU Regulation

Given the long history of growing bank competition within Germany, the real and anticipated growth of intra-European bank competition does not present German banks with a radically different market reality, even though it adds further competitive pressure. Thus the real question for German banks in regard to European integration is whether EU regulation will accommodate the legal and regulatory differences that sustain three distinct banking groups and thus the basis for group competition. One of the most important tests of this was the Solvency Ratio Directive, which was translated into German law through the fourth KWG revision taking effect in 1993. The key question was what forms of equity the EU would recognize. If, for example, the EU failed to recognize the liability surcharge of the cooperatives, these banks would be dealt a devastating blow. In the end, the EU directive and the KWG revision actually expanded the kinds of equity instruments that all banks could use. Thus there was no repeat of the early 1980s battle over the KWG revision, as each banking group gained expanded opportunities to raise equity capital (Gröschel 1993).

This does not mean, however, that all conflicts among the three German banking groups will be suppressed in favor of fighting jointly on the European front. For example, the German commercial banks continue to fan the fire of the savings bank privatization debate in Germany ("Brüssel und Bonn sollen nicht 'überregulieren'," *Handelsblatt,* 11 March 1994). While privatization opponents were always more powerful in the past, future intervention by the EU may shift the balance of power in the domestic German debate. In 1995 the European Commission, at the request of the German private banks, announced that it was reviewing the status of German public banks—that is, the savings bank group and especially the Landesbanks—to determine if they gain an unfair competitive advantage from the public guarantee of their liabilities ("Banken sollen Wettbewerbsregeln der EU einhalten," *Frankfurter Allgemeine Zeitung,* 20 October 1995). The revocation of this guarantee would raise the cost of equity for savings banks and Landesbanks, thus adding (more) market pressure to the political pressure for privatization. As discussed above, significant privatizations in the savings bank group would severely strain, if not destroy, the association. In short, one of the greatest threats to the German three-sector banking system and group competition may soon be the EU. The Kohl government and the Länder strongly opposed any EU action that would undermine public banks and are hoping that a domestic resolution can be achieved and thereby preempt such action (Neubauer 1997).

The second challenge presented by European integration and regulation is to the German model of universal banking. In the effort to expand securities markets and accommodate other financial systems, the EU challenged some of the practices that were long part of German universal banking. In the view of German banks, the original commission proposals for its Investment Services and Capital Adequacy Directives (both took effect in 1996) would have given the investment banks coming from the Anglo-Saxon segmented banking systems unfair advantages in securities markets. The German financial community and federal government mobilized and lobbied Brussels aggressively, forcing a compromise solution (Gröschel 1993; Coleman and Underhill 1995). The future viability of the German universal banking model will be increasingly tested through direct competition with other European banking systems. In sum, EU regulation has added another cleavage dimension to organizational competition among banks, only this time it is German universal banking against Anglo-Saxon banking—a theme we turn to in the next chapter.

Summary

The process of institutional change in the German banking system is complex, incremental, and driven by both exogenous and endogenous sources. First, exogenous events altered the strategies market actors pursued within the banking system. For example, the state eliminated many institutions or rules that restricted competition, such as branching restrictions, interest rate cartels, and tax privileges. The extension of large-firm financial autonomy in the postwar period, combined with the expanding size and demands of the Mittelstand during the late 1970s and 1980s, shifted the demand for bank loans and services. Another important source of exogenous pressure for change was the desire by subnational governments, particularly Länder governments, to use the savings banks and Landesbanks to promote the competitiveness of regional firms. There were also endogenous sources of change. The natural drive among bank managers for expanding market share was one key source, as was the emergence of key industry leaders such as Ludwig Poullain, who sought to transform the savings bank sector in the pursuit of both old and new goals.

All these factors together produced specific strategic and organizational responses in the banking sector. These responses were characterized as universalization and convergence toward a federal bank model. The logic of group competition ensures that each group seeks to have strong decentralized and centralized financial capacities, since any group would suffer as a whole if it could not achieve substantial success in any major market segment. Once group competition coalesced during the 1920s, it ensured that the universalization and federalization processes were self-reinforcing.

The state played a crucial role in the creation and maintenance of a banking system based on three distinct banking groups. A historically recurrent motive for state actors—particularly Länder and local governments—to promote such a banking system was the desire to preserve the lower classes, farmers, and small business as important groups in Germany's economic and social order. A second motive was to minimize economic concentration and contain the influence of the major commercial banks by promoting competition among banks. Thus the state—alternately through legislation, regulation, and direct intervention—expended considerable efforts to establish and maintain locally oriented rival banking systems to the commercial banking sector. The state was also important as an arena in which the different banking groups—and the different social groups they served and represented—fought over the rules that would help them develop and preserve their distinct organizational and group identities. In resolving these intra-industry conflicts, the state—at both the federal and Land level—sought to preserve market governance in the banking industry by ensuring that fair competition and group competition were maintained. In fact, while competition and other factors furthered centralization and concentration in the association banking groups, a surprising amount of deconcentration has been preserved through the combined impact of state actions, the logic of group competition, and structural economic changes that favored production in smaller firms and regions where the major commercial banks have been traditionally weak.[99] Maintaining three distinct banking groups and group competition is likely to be a major economic and political challenge in an increasingly integrated European financial marketplace.

The expansion of market mechanisms and group competition, the federalization of the three banking groups, and broader structural economic changes (not least of which was international financial market integration) produced significant changes in bank-industry relations in postwar Germany. Intense competition for the financial business of both large and small firms has generally raised the negotiating power of nonfinancial firms vis-à-vis the banks. Moreover, it has forced the banks to seek out a new role for themselves in industry that enhances their importance to firms without (or with less) reliance on the traditional institutional sources of bank influence. These changes in bank-industry relations are the subject of the following chapter.

CHAPTER 3

Anglo-Saxonization of the German
Financial System?

How has intensified competition among the three major banking groups affected bank-firm relations in Germany? How have the internationalization of
financial markets and European regulatory harmonization affected the German
financial system and its role in nonfinancial sectors? How are the processes of
firm and sectoral restructuring altered by changes in the financial system? This
chapter provides answers to these questions through an examination of changes
in the banking sector's relations to industry. In the still dominant standard organized capitalism perspective, it is primarily the "tutelary" role of the banks
vis-à-vis industry that distinguishes the German system of industrial finance (or
economic governance, if more broadly formulated) from those of other industrial nations. A central tenet of the organized or finance capitalism model is that
the close relations among large nonfinancial firms and the major commercial
banks enable these banks to extensively influence firm management and therefore coordinate, to a significant degree, economic activity throughout the nation. Thus the pattern of firm and sectoral adjustment is a negotiated or coordinated process. Most scholarly accounts further accept, implicitly or explicitly,
the logical conclusion that this economic governance role of the banks allevi-
ates, if not obviates, the need for state economic intervention.

However, a growing number of recent studies provide evidence that suggests that this model has always been seriously flawed. Moreover, like so many
national financial systems, the German system has come under assault from
powerful domestic and international forces. These forces have led to significant
changes in the structure of the financial sector and its relations to industry. Signs
of convergence toward the Anglo-Saxon model of market-based finance are
strongly evident. Several traditional functions of the German banks in corporate governance and industrial adjustment have eroded considerably. In general,

73

the institutional sources of bank influence in large German firms—loans and equity stakes in firms, supervisory board seats, and proxy votes—have been altered in a way that reduces bank influence. Consequently, banks have lost significant capacity to coordinate market adjustment by individual firms, but especially across several firms in a given sector. Two general processes are producing these changes. First, intensified domestic bank competition significantly shifted the balance of market power from the sellers of finance to the buyers. This is true for both large and small firms in Germany. Firms are now much less dependent on one or a few banks for finance. Second, the internationalization of financial markets (especially European market integration) provided firms, especially large firms, with new sources of finance not under the control of the German banks. Increased financial autonomy generally weakens bank influence. Financial market integration also generates pressures toward regulatory and structural convergence in financial markets. In the case of Germany, this is reflected in the intense effort to develop domestic equity markets as sources of corporate finance. This effort stems from a widely shared desire in Germany to achieve a globally competitive financial services sector. Deeper and more open equity markets, in turn, mean greater possibilities for firm financial autonomy and therefore weakened bank influence. In this respect we can speak of an Anglo-Saxonization process of the German system of corporate finance.

The chief implication of these changes is that the capacity for collective action by business is weakening. Moreover, if German firms come to rely more heavily on equity and short-term market finance, as the movement to a market-based financial system implies, management strategy is more likely to focus on short-run rather than long-run optimization. There has already been sufficient institutional change in the German financial system that it might well have switched to a different institutional developmental trajectory, that is, becoming a market-based system of finance. Such a change would have potentially far-reaching consequences for the German economy or national framework more broadly, including its capacity to pursue diversified quality production.

Nonetheless, in spite of these critical changes, several core institutional features of the German organized capitalism model remain largely in place. The dense web of corporate interlocks—both in terms of boards of directors and financial interlocks—that has long characterized the German system remains intact. In fact, in several respects these interlocks appear to be deepening in response to the opening of German financial markets and European market integration. First, many such interlocks serve the purpose of providing firms with a small set of long-term shareholders who collectively control enough shares to prevent undesirable external interference with management. The more German equity markets are expanded and opened to foreign investors, the more important this function actually becomes to management. Second, many such interlocks serve as a basis for interfirm cooperation to compete jointly against intensified domestic and foreign competition. As long as such interlocks remain tightly in German hands, the Anglo-Saxonization process will be limited— among other things, in the sense that managers' autonomy can remain relatively high, thus allowing them to continue long-term strategizing.

Paradoxically, the bank-based system of finance for Mittelstand firms has been expanding and deepening in response to increased domestic bank competition and globalization. Mittelstand firms continue to rely heavily on traditional bank finance. As discussed in the previous chapter, the growing emphasis of all the banks on Mittelstand finance, combined with greatly increased state financing of Mittelstand firms, has strengthened the provision of long-term financing to Mittelstand firms. Moreover, banks are providing Mittelstand firms with an ever wider array of financial and nonfinancial services. As will be discussed in the following chapters, in this role local banks and branches are increasingly embedded in local and regional institutional networks engaged in Mittelstand firm promotion. Thus, rather than loosening connections in the real economy for the lure of profits in capital markets, a large segment of the German banking industry is becoming even more firmly rooted in its relations to nonfinancial firms. This development is explained by the logic of group competition and key state actions.

The next section of this chapter reviews briefly the organized capitalism model. The third section reviews evidence regarding the financial dependence of large firms on the banks. The fourth section examines trends away from a bank-based to a market-based system of corporate finance. The fifth section analyzes more closely the question of how much power the banks derive from their shareholdings, board seats, and proxy votes in large firms. The sixth section uses the evidence of the preceding sections to reexamine the supposed competitive advantages of intimate bank involvement in industrial affairs. This section also examines the bank's role in corporate management or governance. The final section analyzes the changing relationship between banks and Mittelstand firms.

Revisiting the Organized Capitalism Thesis

From unification in 1870 to the eve of World War I in 1914, the exploding economic might of Germany propelled it into a new, powerful position among European states. In contrast to other European nations, Britain in particular, the hallmark of German industrialization was the degree of economic concentration in large industrial concerns and large banks. The apparent dominance of large firms was increased by their deepening ties to each other within cartels, which in turn were linked to the banks. For the Austro-Marxist theorist Rudolf Hilferding ([1910] 1981, 224–26), this concentration of capital in large firms and the growing interlock between bank capital and industrial capital were an essential stage in the process of capitalist development.[1] For Hilferding, Germany and Austria represented the supreme examples of the high degree of bank capital invested in industry—what he called finance capital. His functionalist argument begins with the emergence of joint-stock corporations in the late nineteenth century: the resulting possibility to profit from stock trading stimulated the centralization of capital and the growth of large corporations. The banks invested capital in industrial corporations, and a mutually reinforcing process of industrial and financial concentration set in, resulting in the formation of cartels closely associated with the banks. Because of their heavy investment in industry, the banks themselves became de facto industrial capitalists. Even more importantly, the dependence of firms on the banks for capital enabled the banks to assume a hierarchically dominant position vis-à-vis firms. The pervasive market presence and power of the cartels and banks introduced planning and overall control into an otherwise anarchic market, eventually yielding a system of "organized capitalism."[2]

Probably the most widely accepted non-Marxist theory of German industrialization and bank dominance is that of Alexander Gerschenkron (1962, 1966). Briefly and simply stated, Gerschenkron argued that Germany, like other late-industrializing countries, had to industrialize on a large scale in order to overcome its "backwardness." Industrialization had to be large both in terms of the average size of an investment and in terms of the number of sectors that must simultaneously begin to industrialize. The German solution to this need to mobilize large sums of capital for investment at a time when there was a general shortage was the universal bank: a bank able to both extend credits to firms and own shares in them. Like Hilferding, Gerschenkron attributed a tutelary role to the German banks vis-à-vis industrial firms; the heavy credit dependence of firms on the banks enabled banks to influence or even dictate the most important management decisions of the firms. The banks used this control to organize industry into cartels in order to limit competition among firms in the industry and thereby raise bank profits. Gerschenkron acknowledged the eventual emancipation of the large firms from the tutelage of the banks, though in his view the banks retained considerable, though not clearly specified, power in industry. Complementarily to Hilferding and Gerschenkron, the Imperial German state is generally viewed as an important facilitator—but not the leader—of industrialization through its benevolent attitude and policies toward industrial concentration, as well as through provision of the necessary economic and social infrastructure.[3]

Both Hilferding and Gerschenkron were challenged in their assertion of bank dominance over industry during Germany's initial industrialization. Riesser (1911) and Jeidels (1905), contemporaries of Hilferding, acknowledged the economic strength of the big Berlin banks and their close relations to firms but argued against any treatise of bank dominance over industry. Jeidels and Whale ([1930] 1968) also argued against Hilferding's contention that competition among the banks was largely eliminated. They maintained that strong competition among the banks in the pre–World War I era limited bank influence. More recently, Jürgen Kocka (1978, 1981) and others (Feldenkirchen 1979; Tilly 1966; Wellhöner 1989; Born 1977; Wixforth 1995; Edwards and Ogilvie 1996) argued against the notion of bank dominance over industry during the Second Empire and Weimar period. In general, these historians argue that the power balance between banks and large firms varied considerably, even in heavy industry, where bank power was supposedly strongest. In numerous cases large, financially strong industrial firms could dictate the terms of financial investment to the banks. Gerschenkron's thesis that the banks came to such preeminence because they represented an efficient solution to the problem of development has also been criticized. Critics charge that the preference of the banks for investment in heavy industry disadvantaged other sectors, thereby preventing an optimal allocation of resources in the economy and keeping the German economy from reaching its fullest growth potential (Eistert 1970; Neuburger and Stokes 1974; Tilly 1986, 136). Finally, it has recently been argued that large joint-stock companies were not as crucial to German industrial development as generally viewed and, moreover, that these companies self-financed the vast majority of their investment—that is, banks were not a critical source of finance. This implies, in turn, that it was the nonuniversal banks— savings banks, cooperatives, and mortgage banks—that provided the great bulk of external finance to the Mittelstand firms, which collectively accounted for the bulk of German industrial output.[4]

Regardless of the serious questions regarding the bank dominance thesis, nearly all scholars writing on the postwar German political economy continued to argue in support of, or simply assume, substantial bank influence over industry. In the post–World War II period, one of the standard interpretations of the West German economic model, and the one on which so many subsequent studies in the Anglo-American social science literature have been based, is that of Andrew Shonfield ([1965] 1980, 239–97). Writing in the mid-1960s, Shonfield adopted the central tenets of the organized capitalism model in arguing that key industrial adjustments in West Germany occurred most importantly via negotiated or bargained agreements among private economic actors, not via market mechanisms. Thus cartel-like arrangements in industry were often an integral part of sectoral rationalization programs. The political counterparts of the cartels were centralized, hierarchically ordered trade associations with semipublic status. The associations acted as intermediaries in negotiations and bargaining between firms, as well as between government and industry. The final and critical linchpin of this institutional framework for "private collective economic management" was the banking system. While the major commercial banks no longer had quite the power over industry that they once did, their large holdings in industry still placed them in a unique position to participate in, if not direct, the negotiated changes of industry. For Shonfield, it was the combination of four elements—the high degree of economic concentration, cartel-like arrangements, the trade associations, and a tutelary banking system—that continued to make the West German political economy distinct from others and accounted for its postwar economic miracle.

In the course of the postwar years, the trade unions were gradually included in industry negotiations, primarily via codetermination rights in firms. But this did not alter the basic tenets of organized capitalism. German labor unions generally pursued goals beyond individual worker benefits to include macroeconomic stability and continued industrial competitiveness through firm and sectoral rationalization programs. Thus, rather than continually challenge the authority of business leaders to organize the economy, the unions participated as junior partners in the endeavor (e.g., Markovits 1982; Paterson and Smith 1981; Parnell 1994). According to the organized capitalism thesis, the German state generally avoids direct government intervention in favor of providing investment incentives to industry. Even in times of sectoral crisis, the state presumably plays a subsidiary role to the private sector, supporting the sectoral rationalization plans worked out by private industry and the major commercial banks (e.g., Dyson 1983; Esser and Fach with Dyson 1983). Government's role is therefore generally considered "arm's length" or market-conforming. As Dyson (1983, 54) argues, "compared with Britain, [the West German] government is better insulated by a de-politicized system of self-organization of capital from the difficult process of managing industrial crises."

In sum, the essential principles of the German system of organized capitalism as outlined first by Hilferding and later by Shonfield are still widely seen as intact (e.g., Zysman 1983; Hall 1986; Cox 1986; Smyser 1993). The banks ostensibly use their influence over firms to help coordinate decisions within individual firms and relations between them. The process of firm and sectoral adjustment in Germany is thus characterized by a relatively high degree of nonmarket coordination among firms. But in a piecemeal fashion, the organized capitalism model has been increasingly undermined in the last few years. Various studies of sectoral restructuring in West Germany over the 1980s suggest a far more decentralized process of adjustment has occurred (Katzenstein 1989). In most cases the banks appear to have played a supportive, but hardly leading, role. The role of the banks in rebuilding the East German economy after reunification has also been surprisingly modest. In concurrence, several recent studies have tended toward greater skepticism regarding the influence of the banks in industry (Edwards and Fischer 1994; Oberbeck and Baethge 1989; Esser 1990).

The Undoing of Finance Capitalism

This chapter develops an alternative analytical framework with which to characterize the present role of the banks in industry. To date, no truly comprehensive study of bank intervention in German industry has appeared. But by focusing on changes in key structural and institutional factors that tend to reduce bank influence, a broader argument can be made that qualitative dimensions of the relationships between banks and large firms in Germany have significantly changed since the late 1960s. While incidents of direct bank intervention in firm management are still clearly evident, direct bank intervention and coordination of a broad range of firms is increasingly difficult. The definitive relationship between large banks and large firms is not one of bank tutelage, but one of cooperation based on bank provision of multiple services. Increasingly, banks are sellers of services to large firms. More arm's-length market relationships between banks and firms are increasingly replacing traditional cooperative or nonmarket relationships. Where such nonmarket relationships do exist between bank and firm, it will be argued that these relationships can be better understood by their function within various types of firm networks. Small and medium-sized firms continue to rely heavily on bank financing, but this does not translate into unusual bank influence over them.

The loosening of ties between banks and industry is not without direct implications for the role of the state in the economy. Quietly and surely the German state itself, particularly at subnational levels, has become increasingly involved in the affairs of industry. The growth of state intervention, discussed in part 2, is evident first in the steady expansion of subsidies and long-term loans to industry. But this is not the benign state support for private restructuring plans as expounded in the Shonfield model. State subsidies have concrete, if not always obvious, investment-steering consequences for the private economy. Moreover, state funds have played a growing role in the most critical processes of industrial restructuring, such as technology development and transfer and labor force skill development. Banks play a central role in these broader economic adjustment processes, but that role is increasingly dependent on coordination with state action.

The Financial Autonomy of Large Firms

Central to the organized capitalism thesis is the assumption that a high degree of capital concentration in a relatively small number of financial institutions (among which competition is limited), combined with a high level of financial dependence by firms on the banks, translates into considerable bank leverage over nonfinancial firms. Some of the most commonly examined statistics continue to suggest that bank loans are the major source of industrial finance in Germany. In spite of a relatively large number of new stock issues since the early 1980s, capital markets continue to play a comparatively minor role as a source of industrial finance in Germany. Underdeveloped capital markets and apparently heavy reliance on bank borrowing suggest that the institutional prerequisites favoring the tutelary role of the banks are still intact. But other data clearly indicate that the majority of large firms are no longer—if, indeed, they ever were—financially dependent on the banks.[5] Edwards and Fischer (1994, 61) conclude, "Over the period 1950–1989, internally-generated funds (the sum of retained profits and depreciation) were by far the largest net source of finance for investment in physical assets by the producing enterprises sector." Jenkinson and Corbett (1997) find concurring evidence and argue in addition that "the share of bank finance in financing physical investment is not higher in Germany than in the US or UK."[6] Finally, a wide range of evidence indicates that the largest West German firms substantially increased their financial autonomy even more from the big banks over the past two decades. They have been able to do so first because greatly intensified bank competition and new sources of funds have increased the *supply* of capital available to large firms while their *demand* for bank loans has declined. Increased competition among banks also hinders their ability to act jointly vis-à-vis any given firm, thus giving firms greater bargaining leverage with banks.

Since the late 1960s, a growing number of banks have become "big banks," not only in terms of size but also insofar as they compete vigorously and successfully for the business of large firms. Of the 20 largest banks, only seven are private commercial banks (table 4). The growth of competition increased the available supply of capital and put downward pressure on the cost of capital for large firms. The Landesbanks in particular drew on the large pool of cheap savings account funds available in the group in order to gain market share through price competition. Reflecting this change, in this period the big three commercial banks lost a substantial portion of their share of industrial lending markets to the other two banking groups, especially to the savings banks and the Landesbanks. Table 5 (figs. 1 and 2) shows a decline in the big three commercial banks' market share of loans to firms from 15.4 percent in 1972 to 11.9 percent at the end of 1982. In this same period, the market shares of the savings and cooperative banking groups increased from 33.2 percent to 36.7 percent and from 12.9 percent to 17.4 percent respectively. In the mid-1970s the savings bank group surpassed the entire private commercial banking sector as the largest source of business loans. When only loans to manufacturing industry are considered, this shift between the three banking groups is even stronger. The savings and cooperative groups together provided roughly one-half of all loans to manufacturers in the early 1980s—the big three commercial banks provided less than one-fifth. Thus, when many firms and industries were amidst deep restructuring processes in the 1970s and early 1980s and were increasing their demand for credit (Deutsche Bundesbank 1996a), the savings and cooperative banks made tremendous gains over the big commercial banks in business lending.

Between 1982 and 1990 this trend was reversed, as the big commercial banks were able to make up some—though less than half—of the ground they had lost to the other banking groups in the 1970s. Given the growing emphasis by the big commercial banks on business with small and medium-sized firms, as well as the fact that domestic lending to large firms is declining, the ability of the big banks to gain back some lost market share in firm lending in the 1980s was due primarily to increased loans to Mittelstand firms. In the 1990s the commercial banks again lost market share in business lending, despite their initial dominance in eastern credit markets.

On the demand side, the largest German corporations have used various tax laws and accounting rules to literally stash away billions of deutschmarks annually, thereby reducing their overall demand for external financing. Table 6 shows a more than 100 percent increase in the reserves held by firms from 1971 to 1995 (from 10 percent of liabilities to 22 percent). What this table does not reveal is that a disproportionate share of this growth in reserves has accumu-

TABLE 4. Twenty Largest Banks, End of 1995

Ranking of Bank	Total Assets in Billion DM	Sector
1. Deutsche Bank AG, Frankfurt/M.	721,655	Private
2. Dresdner Bank AG, Frankfurt/M.	484,482	Private
3. Westdeutsche Landesbank Girozentrale, Düsseldorf	428,622	Public
4. Commerzbank AG, Frankfurt/M.	404,167	Private
5. Bayerische Vereinsbank AG, Munich	359,543	Private
6. Bayerische Landesbank Girozentrale, Munich	318,447	Public
7. Bayerische Hypotheken- und Wechselbank AG, Munich	298,563	Private
8. DG Bank Deutsche Genossenschaftsbank	291,221	Cooperative
9. Bankgesellschaft Berlin AG, Berlin	281,553	Private[a]
10. Kreditanstalt für Wiederaufbau, Frankfurt/M.	249,798	Public
11. Norddeutsche Landesbank Girozentrale, Hannover	208,941	Public
12. Südwestdeutsche Landesbank Girozentrale, Stuttgart-Mannheim	180,365	Public
13. Landesbank Hessen-Thüringen Girozentrale, Frankfurt/M.	157,191	Public
14. Deutsche Pfandbrief und Hypothekenbank AG, Weisbaden	151,216	Private
15. Landesbank Berlin Girozentrale, Berlin	143,296	Public
16. Landeskreditbank Baden-Württemberg, Karlsruhe	115,974	Public
17. Postbank AG, Bonn	99,221	Public
18. Landesbank Schleswig-Holstein Girozentrale, Kiel	93,228	Public
19. Deutsche Girozentrale–Deutsche Kommunalbank, Frankfurt/M.	87,188	Public
20. Hamburgische Landesbank Girozentrale, Hamburg	83,555	Public

Source: "Die 100 grössten deutschen Kredinstitute," Die Bank, no. 8 (1996): 506.
[a]The Bankgesellschaft Berlin combines private and public banks under the umbrella of a private sector holding company.

TABLE 5. Share of Bank Loans by Major Bank Groups, 1972–96

Bank Group	Year	Loans to all Firms[a]	Loans to Industry[b]
Commercial	1972	36.7	54.2
	1977	31.8	48.5
	1982	30.1	38.8
	1986	27.0	39.3
	1990	31.3	42.1
	1992	34.5	46.1
	1994	29.2	40.2
	1996	30.7	38.8
Of which:			
Big banks	1972	15.4	28.2
	1977	13.2	25.1
	1982	11.9	18.2
	1986	10.7	18.8
	1990	13.8	22.4
	1992	13.2	22.8
	1994	12.5	22.7
	1996	12.9	21.1
Savings banks[c]	1972	33.2	26.1
	1977	34.6	27.9
	1982	36.7	33.2
	1986	35.9	31.8
	1990	33.6	30.6
	1992	32.0	28.2
	1994	33.7	29.5
	1996	36.5	32.8
Cooperatives[c]	1972	12.9	11.3
	1977	15.1	14.9
	1982	17.4	17.5
	1986	16.1	18.4
	1990	15.3	17.3
	1992	13.8	16.0
	1994	13.2	16.8
	1996	15.0	18.3
Special banks[d]	1986	4.0	7.6
	1990	4.2	7.6
	1992	8.4	7.5
	1994	14.2	11.3
	1996	5.1	7.3

Source: Figures for 1972 and 1982 from K. J. Lubitz, *Bankmarketing gegenüber mittelständischen Betrieben* (Frankfurt: Fritz Knapp, 1984), 11. Figures for other years are from Deutsche Bundesbank, *Statistische Beihefte zu Monatsberichten der Bundesbank,* series 1, *Bankenstatistik nach Bankengruppen.* Author's own calculations. Percentages do not total 100 because not all bank categories are included.

Note: Figures for 1992, 1994, and 1996 include eastern Germany. 1977 figures are for September and do not include mortgage loans on commercial property.

[a]Includes mortgage loans on commercial property and loans to self-employed.

[b]This category includes manufacturing industries only.

[c]Including Girozentrale and cooperative central banks, respectively.

[d]Special banks are public economic development banks.

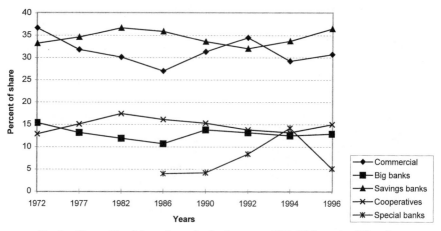

Fig. 1. Share of bank loans by major bank groups, 1972–96 (loans to all firms)

lated in the largest firms. In effect, much of these reserves represent hidden equity, since they are provisions for future costs that firms can actually use in the
present to invest in plant and equipment, securities, and the like. For example,
the investment boom of the West German automobile industry between 1979
and 1983 was financed entirely by the auto firms themselves with their reserves
(Welzk 1986, 93). The share of bank credits in the total working capital of all
AGs (public limited companies) declined from 16.9 percent in 1974 to 6.6 percent in 1984. In the automobile, electronics, and chemicals industries—three
of Germany's leading economic sectors—this share was even lower (Welzk
1986, 67).[7]

Edwards and Fischer (1991; 1994, 54–55) come to similar conclusions.[8]
After examining the sources and uses of funds by German industrial firms from
1970 to 1989, they concluded that retained earnings financed 62 percent of firm
investments; bank loans accounted for only 18 percent. If one focused only on
purchases of physical assets, German banks financed only 11 percent of such
investments. British firms, by comparison, used bank loans to finance 24 percent of their investments. In its own study, the Bundesbank arrived at similar
results: from 1978 to 1989, the bank debts of large firms declined from 13.7
percent to 7.6 percent of balance sheet liabilities—mostly due to a decline in
long-term borrowing. In the same period, the balance sheet provisions of large
firms rose more than 50 percent. The Deutsche Bundesbank (1992b, 30) wrote,
"trends in long-term bank debts show . . . a consistent tendency towards de-
coupling large enterprises from lending by the banking system. This tendency

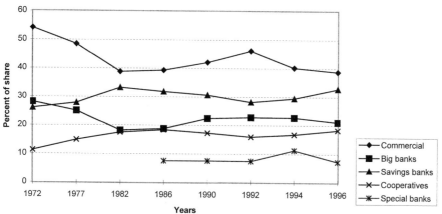

Fig. 2.   **Share of bank loans by major bank groups, 1972–96 (loans to industry)**

is probably ascribable to the increasing assumption of banking functions by large enterprises and groups in the context of systematic financial management and to the growing significance of inter-company lending ('industrial clearing')."

As suggested by the Bundesbank, the finance departments of the largest, typically multinational German firms have become increasingly sophisticated in the financial activities they conduct directly with capital markets. Firms such as Volkswagen and Siemens have turned their treasury departments into so-

TABLE 6.   Structure of Liabilities of West German Firms, 1971–95 (in percentage of total)

	1971	1981	1989	1995
Equity Capital	26	19	19	18
Debt	74	81	81	82
Of which:				
Short-term	42	48	44	45
Long-term	20	19	16	15
Provisions[a]	10	14	21	22

Source: Figures for 1971 and 1981 are from "Business Finance in the UK and Germany," *Monthly Report of the Deutsche Bundesbank* 36, no. 11 (1984): 3. Figures for 1989 are from "West German Enterprise's Profitability in 1989," *Monthly Report of the Deutsche Bundesbank* 42, no. 11 (1990): 21; and "West German Enterprise's Profitability and Financing in 1995," *Monthly Report of the German Bundesbank* (November 1996): 43. Author's own calculations. Figures rounded to nearest full percentage point.

[a]Reserves against future claims, including pension provisions.

called corporate banks, conducting financial services for their own departments and subsidiaries, but also increasingly for outsiders. Large firms are finding that they can manage many of their financial needs better than their banks.[9] Many corporate banks are also deeply engaged in managing the myriad shareholdings of their parent corporation, including corporate restructuring through mergers and acquisitions. The challenge presented by corporate banks to the major commercial banks is considerable. Neither the firms nor the banks believe that the latter have become superfluous, but it does mean that banks must focus on highly specialized services that they can provide more efficiently and cost-effectively.[10]

In sum, on the supply side, the growing number of domestic (and foreign) banks competing in the commercial lending market for large firms, and the increased access to international capital markets, have greatly enhanced the general availability and sources of capital for firms.[11] On the demand side, there has occurred a long-term shift in the structure of demand by firms for external finance. Since the early 1970s, the degree of self-finance among large nonfinancial firms has significantly increased. Like the provision of loan capital, the rate of self-finance by firms is subject to cyclical changes in the economy. But the self-finance trend is largely the result of stable regulations and practices that enable firms to retain more of their earnings.[12] The recent translation of the Fourth EC Banking Directive into German law further expanded the scope for forming provisions (Deutsche Bundesbank 1992b). As a result of competition and thus very thin margins, even the major banks themselves are less interested in lending to large firms (Eglau 1989, 173–75). Increasingly, banks are earning their income through service provision and trading activities. Unlike the traditional German house bank relationship, the provision of such services by banks to large firms typically embodies a market relationship—the bank secures a contract through a competitive process to perform a specific service at a predetermined price. When large firms do use external finance, they are increasingly utilizing domestic and foreign securities markets rather than bank loans (Deutsche Bundesbank 1997, 32). Thus financial dependence does not constitute a systematic basis for bank influence in large firms. Stock ownership by banks remains an important potential source of influence, but for reasons explored below, this too appears to be weakening. In response to the growing autonomy of large firms, to growing competition in Germany from foreign financial firms, and to the rapid integration of national financial markets, the German banking industry and public authorities are pushing dramatic changes in German financial markets. The push to make Frankfurt a globally competitive financial center—referred to as *Finanzplatz Deutschland*—is both a reflection of these changing conditions and a response to promote them further.

Finanzplatz Deutschland

As traditional business with large German firms declined, the major German banks were forced to devise new market strategies. One strategy was to extend business with the Mittelstand, where traditional bank lending is still strong. But retaining the business of large corporate customers required a more radical change in strategy. During the 1980s it became clear to the major German banks that future success would hinge on their ability to provide sophisticated financial and investment banking services to these firms. Many of these services are trading-based services, such as currency and interest rate swaps, futures contracts, and options. There is also growing demand for traditional investment banking services such as bond and equity issues underwriting, and consulting in mergers and acquisitions. Investment banks in the United Kingdom and the United States had considerably more experience and expertise in many of these areas than German banks. As long as national capital markets were relatively insulated, this difference had little consequence for German banks. But as financial markets became increasingly integrated, large German firms either went abroad with their business or sought out foreign investment banks operating in Germany to provide them with these services.[13]

Thus the major German banks began to push for the development of German securities markets through an assortment of institutional changes and market liberalization measures. Large firms also welcomed this development, as did the German federal government. The push for Finanzplatz Deutschland is, in effect, an effort to move to a considerable degree from a bank- to a market-dominated financial system, or at least an attempt to capture the benefits of both. It is a reaction by the German financial sector and the state to both the growing autonomy of large firms and to the competitive pressures arising from the integration of national financial markets, especially within the European Union. If the German financial sector was to be globally competitive, it needed a home market that was attractive to large domestic and international investors. This requires that the German financial system—especially its securities markets—increasingly approximate the structures, products, and especially the regulatory rules of the U.S. and U.K. financial systems.

The formal campaign for Finanzplatz Deutschland began in the early 1990s, but its real beginnings reach back well into the 1980s. Since the mid-

1980s, a wide variety of measures intended to facilitate this institutional transformation have been adopted by the financial sector and the state. Starting in 1985, several liberalization measures were enacted to permit the adoption of new financial products: zero-coupon and floating-rate notes, and interest and currency swaps in deutschmark. To facilitate the introduction of more firms to the stock market, the Free Market was opened in 1987 for trading in unlisted shares. In 1989 the Stock Exchange Law was amended to permit trading in options and futures contracts. In 1990 the German Options and Futures Exchange was opened (Deutscher Terminbörse, or DTB).

In 1990 the First Financial Market Promotion Law was promulgated. Among other measures, the law eliminated many of the taxes that hindered securities trading and enabled German investment funds to trade in derivatives. This law, coupled with the Bundesbank's suspension of its approval requirements for debt issuance, enabled the creation of a deutschmark commercial paper (CP) market at the beginning of 1991. Long a part of Anglo-Saxon capital markets, a CP market was absent in Germany due to a combination of regulatory and tax barriers. Most importantly, the Bundesbank long opposed CP for fear that it would lose some of its capacity to control the money supply and that a CP market would encourage excessive short-term borrowing. But competition across international financial centers led large banks and firms in Germany to pressure state authorities for liberalization.[14] German firms were increasingly issuing CP in foreign currencies and markets—especially in London's Euro-CP market. Thus both German firms and especially banks wanted to bring this business back home. Large German firms reacted strongly to this new market: by early 1993, over 50 issuers had established CP programs valued at over DM 35 billion (Michels 1993; Rohleder and Schäfer 1991). This same bank-industry coalition, with support from the federal government, finally convinced the Bundesbank to permit money market funds in mid-1994.[15] The introduction of money market funds was expected to spur short-term capital markets in Germany by creating more demand for the short-term debt instruments (e.g., CP) of large firms and other institutional borrowers—another crucial step toward an Anglo-Saxon style of corporate finance (Kudiss 1991). The CP market represents the further development of short-term financial markets as an alternative to short-term bank finance. The consolation for the banks is the fee income gained through the placement of CP issued by nonfinancial firms. Since financial regulators also dropped their approval process for the issuance of debt instruments, securities-rating companies rather than banks will be evaluating the credit risk of an increasing proportion of corporate debt—a measure that should further reduce the influence of the major banks over debt financing. In early 1997 the Federal Banking Supervisory Office liberalized its regulations regarding asset-backed securities. If the banks begin securitizing a significant amount of their assets, as is expected, this will give a further boost to both short- and long-term securities markets.

Several measures have also been adopted to stimulate equity market expansion. To facilitate cheaper and faster trading of Germany's leading stocks, an electronic exchange system (IBIS) was created in early 1991. While Frankfurt dominates German securities trading, market trading was long hindered by a fragmented exchange system built upon eight regional exchanges. The major German banks and the federal government sought to unify regional exchanges for many years but faced stiff resistance from Länder authorities who feared a loss of jobs and financial clout. In 1992 the German Exchange Company (Deutsche Börse AG) was finally established to control the Frankfurt exchange and link the regional exchanges. While each exchange will continue its independent existence, they are now linked via an electronic trading system. The major financial institutions are counting on electronic trading and growing specialization of the leading exchanges to overcome the deficiencies of a fragmented exchange system. In its continuing effort to develop securities trading, in early 1997 the Deutsche Börse AG introduced its New Market (Neuer Markt) for listing and trading in smaller, innovative companies.

All of these changes facilitated the further opening and deepening of German capital markets. From 1982 to 1996, equity market capitalization grew from DM 170 billion to DM 1,034 billion, and trading volume grew from DM 40 billion to DM 1,940 billion ("The 1992 Guide to European Equity Markets," *Euromoney,* January 1992 (supplement); Balzer and Wilhelm 1997b). Competition among banks to underwrite new stock issues also helped stimulate equity markets. Traditionally, when a firm wished to go public or issue new shares, it gave this business to its house bank(s), and the terms of sale were strongly influenced by the banks. Until 1986 the Deutsche Bank was the dominant market leader in new issues, bringing 15 of 26 new issues to the stock market in that year. But now all the banks compete vigorously for the lead in underwriting consortia, thus shifting the balance of power from underwriters to issuers of debt. Accordingly, in 1988 the Deutsche Bank led only two of the 14 new issues ("Die Banken konkurrieren zunehmend um Neuemissionen," *Frankfurter Allgemeine Zeitung,* 13 April 1991). The 1980s also marked a rapidly growing readiness on the part of medium-sized firms to go public. From 1977 to 1986, there were 85 initial public offerings (IPOs); from 1987 to 1995 there were 152.[16] It is widely expected that the going-public trend will continue, since thousands of midsize companies suffer from a deteriorating equity position and face a succession crisis from company founder to nonfamilial management.

Bank Strategy

Despite their long history as universal banks engaged in a full range of financial services, the major German banks have realized that to be internationally competitive they must have much better developed international investment banking capacities. Some banks are seeking to be global players. To this end, the Deutsche Bank bought a leading British investment bank—Morgan Grenfell—in 1989 and has since invested huge sums in building up its global investment banking operations. The bank is pursing a highly ambitious aim of raising its revenue from investment banking from between 10 and 20 percent of global revenues to one-third to one-half (Peter Truell and Edmund L. Andrews, "Accelerating a Risky Strategy," *New York Times,* 31 October 1996). In a similar pursuit, the WestLB took over the European operations of another British bank—Standard Charter—in 1990. The Dresdner Bank bought the British investment bank Kleinwort Benson in 1995. Other German banks are seeking to be niche players in the domestic or European markets. The association banking groups, especially the savings banks, continue to believe that their strategic advantage lies in their local orientation and are seeking to combine closeness to the customer with a European reach by pursuing collaboration with their counterpart associations in other European states.[17] But whether global or niche player, investment banking has become a strategic focus for all three major banking groups, and they are modernizing their technological capacities, reorganizing departments internally, and retraining their personnel, who are more accustomed to the traditional domestic credit business. The strategic push to develop investment banking is a response to five major market developments: first, the global and increasingly German pattern of securitizing debt demands stronger underwriting, trading, and investment management capacities; second, global economic integration requires more and more interest and currency risk management; third, firms are demanding more financial consulting; fourth, new forms of equity finance are emerging, and corporate restructuring through mergers and acquisitions, spin-offs, and management buyouts and buy-ins is growing; and fifth, more sophisticated project-specific investments, especially for large-scale undertakings, are being sought by large firms (Reimpell 1990).

Foreign banks, especially investment banks, have become increasingly aggressive in marketing these services to German firms. These banks are expecting—and helping to create—a dramatic growth in investment banking markets in Germany (Kaven 1991). Foreign and German investment banks are especially looking for growth in mergers and acquisitions through the sell-off of subsidiaries by large German multinationals, the privatization of state firms, strategic mergers among Mittelstand firms, and continued reorganization in eastern Germany ("Goldman Sachs erwartet Zunahme des 'M&A'-Geschäftes in Deutschland," *Frankfurter Allgemeine Zeitung,* 9 August 1993). In line with the German and European market liberalization efforts, the access of foreign banks to German financial markets has been growing. For example, in mid-1992 the Bundesbank permitted the subsidiaries of foreign banks operating in Germany to become consortium leader for new securities issues. Foreign bank representatives now sit in the governing bodies of the major equity and futures exchanges. The Bundesbank also opened the DM commercial paper market to foreign firms, a move criticized by German banks who feared greatly intensified competition for underwriting CP ("Bundesbank verteidigt Liberalisierung," *Frankfurter Allgemeine Zeitung,* 13 August 1992; Gaddum 1993). But neither is the Bundesbank neglecting the interests of German banks. In early 1993, for example, the Bundesbank dramatically lowered the minimum reserve deposit requirements on banks (Meyer-Horn 1993). This measure was intended to enhance the competitiveness of German banks, especially the savings and cooperative banks because of their market prominence in savings deposits.

Changes on the demand side are also pushing for stronger equity markets in Germany. By one estimate, approximately DM 200 billion (7 percent of total domestic savings) are inherited each year by a younger generation ("A Survey of World Banking," *The Economist,* 2 May 1992). Younger investors are showing that they want higher returns for their savings and are increasingly willing to invest them in securities. Foreign investment funds generally outperform their German counterparts and are increasingly marketing their services in Germany. The major banks have therefore targeted investment and asset management for private and institutional investors—not only in Germany, but throughout Europe—as a primary growth field for them.[18] In order to provide their clients with adequate investment opportunities (and the bank with profit opportunities), the banks are seeking to stimulate both the demand and the supply of securities.[19] Foreign investors—who held about one-quarter of quoted German equities in 1991—can be expected to increase further their buying as the depth and breadth of securities markets expand.

The Campaign

All of these efforts to stimulate securities markets have become embodied in the Finanzplatz Deutschland concept. Facing the imminent completion of the Single Market and possible currency union, the Federal Finance Ministry first presented its concept of Finanzplatz Deutschland in early 1992. The plan focused on negotiations between the German government and banking community over extensive regulatory changes intended to increase the attractiveness of German equity markets to domestic and foreign investors. The forces driving these changes are numerous and are both domestic and international. First, the German financial sector has long realized that its own future hinges critically on its ability to make Frankfurt an international financial center. From the mid-1980s on, it became increasingly clear to the banks that they were also losing the more sophisticated financial business of large German firms (and other European multinationals) and German investors to other markets. For example, it has been estimated that between 5 and 25 percent of German stock turnover actually occurs in London.[20] Second, foreign banks and investors operating in Germany are also pressuring the German government to liberalize and modernize financial markets (Engel 1991). Third, EU directives regarding financial markets are pushing the German financial system in this direction. The German federal government also pushed for extensive reregulation of its securities markets in part because it discovered that it needed a central state regulatory agency to be accepted as a participant in international regulatory regimes.[21] A final push came from the collapse of communism and the expected demand for equity by public authorities and private firms in eastern Germany, and East Europe more generally—the German financial community did not want to see this business go to other financial centers.[22] Thus Finanzplatz Deutschland is the cumulative product of efforts to liberalize German equity markets, to harmonize financial regulations with the EU, and to institutionalize new financial market regulation by codifying and elaborating rules, establishing legal controls, and extending formal state regulation (compare Moran 1992).

The first major result of the formal Finanzplatz Deutschland campaign was the omnibus Second Financial Market Promotion Law, promulgated in mid-1994 after being introduced in parliament a year earlier. Negotiations involved a wide range of public and private actors. There was disagreement over certain details, but widespread consensus existed over the general goals and objectives.[23] The law focused heavily on the future development of securities markets by significantly harmonizing the content and form of German regulation with international norms. To oversee the transformation of German securities markets, a new, independent securities supervisory office was established (Bundesaufsichtsamt für den Wertpapierhandel, or BAWe). The new watchdog agency will assume much of the self-regulation traditionally exercised by the financial community. The institutionalization of such authority in an independent public body is essential to establish the international credibility of capital markets regulation in Germany. One of the key functions of the agency will be to enforce a new legal ban on insider trading, a measure widely seen as necessary to win the confidence of international investors and to comply with EU banking directives.[24] Strengthened information-reporting rules were also put in place, including the requirement that all stakes of 5 percent or more, and shareholdings moving over or under the 10 percent, 25 percent, 50 percent, and 75 percent thresholds, must be publicly announced and registered with the new agency. Financial institutions will be required to inform the BAWe of all securities and derivative trading for their own and other accounts.[25] All firms that have issued publicly traded securities must immediately and publicly disclose all information relevant to the value of their securities.[26] Such stringent information requirements represent a dramatic break with the past. German firms and banks are hardly accustomed to extensive public knowledge of their dealings—a secrecy that facilitates the insider system of corporate control. Even so, more stringent information-reporting requirements, as well as further amendments made to the stock exchange law, are seen as necessary to promote the objective of greater market transparency and hence to protect individual investors. In line with the campaign to stimulate market-based finance, financial regulation in Germany is shifting from the oversight of traditional bank liabilities and assets to oversight of market trading activities. The omnibus law also embodied measures to stimulate demand in capital markets.[27] In early 1997 a Third Financial Market Promotion Law was proposed by the Kohl government. Among its more than 100 measures, the proposal calls for stimulating securities markets through the expansion of investment funds and reducing transaction costs associated with equity issues.

The majority of these regulatory and institutional changes are necessary to conform with international standards and with EU directives. EU regulation is largely intended to strengthen the trend toward market-based financial systems in Germany and throughout the union. The EU's Second Banking Directive and the Investment Services Directive created a "passport" system for banks and traders to move more easily across borders, thus further stimulating competition among banks for the underwriting and trading business of large firms. The commission also seems intent on creating significantly more liberal equity markets including rules that would foster U.S./U.K. style takeovers on the Continent. More stringent information disclosure rules, limits on proxy voting, limits on bank shareholdings, and other rules are all under consideration. Such regulation would tend to further weaken close links between banks and firms in Germany—links that constituted the core of German finance capitalism.

Barriers to Change

In spite of all these efforts, there remain many barriers on the long road to making Frankfurt an international financial center and transforming Germany from a bank- to a market-based financial system. In Germany there are still only about 650 publicly listed companies (and of these, fewer than 10 percent are actively traded) versus nearly 2,000 in the United Kingdom and nearly 7,000 in the United States (Stefanie Burgmaier and Michael Friedrich, "Strammer Marsch," *Wirtschaftswoche,* 2 April 1993). "Near the end of 1996 the ratio of domestic enterprises market capitalisation to nominal gross domestic product came to 27 percent in Germany, compared to figures often way above 100 percent in the United States, the United Kingdom, Switzerland and Sweden" (Deutsche Bundesbank 1997, 28). In comparative terms, the rate of IPOs in Germany also remains paltry: between 1991 and 1996, there were 77 IPOs in Germany but well over 3,000 in the United States (Deutsche Bundesbank 1997, 28). Despite growing interest, individual investors still own relatively little stock. The share of private German households in total shareholdings declined from 27 percent in 1960 to less than 15 percent in 1995 (compare table 7). Only 6 percent of private wealth is held in stocks (Karsch 1992). The brokerage business is still dominated by the German banks, which tend to encourage their customers to buy shares in (mostly bank-controlled) investment funds, rather than directly in stocks. Insurance companies have increased their holdings, but there

TABLE 7.   International Comparison of Share Ownership Profiles (percentage of total shares in circulation held by different sectors in the respective country, end of 1995)

	United States	Japan	Germany	France	United Kingdom
Households	36.4	22.2	14.6	19.4	29.6
Enterprises	15.0	31.2	42.1	58.0	4.1
Public sector	0.0	0.5	4.3	3.4	0.2
Nonfinancial sector	51.4	53.9	61.0	80.8	33.9
Banks	0.2	13.3	10.3	4.0	2.3
Insurance enterprises and pension funds	31.3	10.8	12.4	1.9	39.7
Investment funds and other financial institutions	13.0	11.7	7.6	2.0	10.4
Financial sectors	44.5	35.8	30.3	8.0	52.4
Rest of the world	4.2	10.3	8.7	11.2	13.7
Total	100	100	100	100	100

Source: Table reproduced from "Shares as financing and investment instruments," *Monthly Report of the Deutsche Bundesbank* 43, no. 1 (1997): 29.

are few other independent institutional investors, such as pension funds, that might stimulate equity issues. Deregulation of the insurance industry by the EU will likely promote more direct buying by these firms, but this will take time.

German tax laws still favor debt over equity finance by firms. Concentration in shareholdings is encouraged, inter alia, by a tax break for holdings greater than 10 percent (whether individually held or in pools) and by a stiff capital gains tax on sales of shares by long-term shareholders. New equity issues and trading are also discouraged by limits on voting rights and other preemptive rights for existing shareholders. Moreover, domestic and international institutional investors in Germany tend to favor stocks in the largest and most actively traded firms: in 1993, 85 percent of stock market turnover consisted of trading in just thirty listings (Wolfgang Köhler, "Die Banken spielen falsch," *Die Zeit,* 26 August 1994). The vast majority of listed shares are hardly traded because there is little demand.

Reflecting the slow process of transforming the German financial sector, the Deutsche Bank announced in late 1994 that London, not Frankfurt, would headquarter its global investment banking activities. The next two leading German investment banks, the Dresdner and WestLB, are making similar moves. Perhaps the greatest obstacle to change is the desire among banks and firms to preserve elements of the old system that lent it stability and therefore predictability. Chief among these elements are the close financial and personal interlocks among leading corporations. At the end of 1995, nonfinancial firms held over 40 percent of total shareholdings in Germany (see table 7): "It is estimated that three-quarters of the equity interests of domestic producing enterprises consist of cross-holdings—a fact which is especially prevalent among manufacturing and utilities" (Deutsche Bundesbank 1997, 39). In short, the significance of equity finance and investment remains comparatively circumscribed in Germany and, while expanding, is only slowly changing. But even if the Finanzplatz campaign fails to make Frankfurt Europe's chief financial center, the relationship between banks and firms in Germany has already undergone significant transformation.

The Decline of Bank Influence

The push to develop Finanzplatz Deutschland is importantly driven by the banks' changing relationship to large German firms. This section examines changes in the traditional institutional basis of bank influence or power in nonfinancial firms that are transforming the bank-firm relationship and the broader economic functions of banks.[28] In the mid-1970s a trend among the major private commercial banks to reduce the number of industry holdings they control emerged. An initial explanation of this decline in the quantitative dimension of the banks' investor role focuses on two factors. First, regulations in the revised Banking Act (KWG) of 1984 made it less rewarding for banks to carry large holdings of nonbank shares on their balance sheets.[29] In effect, the banks faced stronger incentives to either sell some of their holdings or find ways to get them off their books. Available evidence suggests both strategies have been pursued. The Dresdner Bank and the Commerzbank significantly reduced their industrial holdings by the late 1980s. While some have speculated that this was done to bolster their income, the solid profitability of the banks in this same period suggests—as their leaders contend—that the reduction of holdings was part of their long-term strategic plan to reduce risk exposure (Gerald Braunberger, "Die deutschen Grossbanken blicken gestärkt auf eine Zukunft mit wachsenden Risiken," *Frankfurter Allgemeine Zeitung,* 16 April 1991; "Dresdner Bank: Starker Volumenzuwachs bei stabiler Ertragslage," *Frankfurter Allgemeine Zeitung,* 13 April 1991). And this leads to the second, and perhaps more powerful, explanation for the reduction of bank shareholdings. Increasingly competitive and integrated financial markets, as well as the new emphasis by the banks on market trading activities, have put pressure on the banks to reduce their traditionally undifferentiated risk structure (Sabel, Griffin, and Deeg 1993). Large holdings in a relatively small number of large nonfinancial firms expose the banks to the market risks of those firms. And those firms themselves face increasingly competitive markets and complex management issues that go beyond the capacities of the banks to monitor the associated risks. Thus the banks are seeking to reduce risk through greater diversification while continuing to engage in profitable equity investment opportunities.

Bank Shareholdings

Several studies affirm this trend to smaller equity stakes. Examining the 10 largest private banks in West Germany, Cammann and Arnold (1987) found that the number of firms in which banks held at least 10 percent of the shares (directly or indirectly) declined from 129 in 1976 to 86 in 1986.[30] Perhaps more importantly, the number of firms in which banks controlled more than 25 percent of the shares—a blocking minority—fell from 86 to 45 in this period.[31] By 1986 the private banks held more than 25 percent in only two of the 50 largest firms in the Federal Republic.[32] More than three times as many holdings were sold (63) as were purchased (20) in this period. Of the 20 purchases in this period, five were undertaken as a means to support a weak firm through

an infusion of needed capital, six were made primarily for the bank's investment purposes, five were made as a step toward placement of the firm's shares
in private hands, and of the remaining four, one was to prevent a takeover and
one was to secure the bank's loans to the firm (Cammann and Arnold 1987,
122). Roggenbuck (1992, 173–74) estimates that from 1976 to 1991, all banks
together (public and private) acquired or accumulated 25 percent or greater
holdings in 13 nonfinancial firms. Of these 13, most were later reduced such
that only seven remained significant long-term holdings. In this same period,
banks reduced 78 holdings below the 25 percent mark; of these, roughly two-
thirds were completely sold by the bank in question.[33] Thus, while in a few
cases the banks may purchase or hold shares in industry in order to guide the
development of particular firms, in most cases they seem to acquire holdings
for far less ambitious reasons, such as preventing loan defaults or simply
to make a substantial profit through speculation in securities trading.[34] This
hardly supports the common view that the banks act strategically in the acquisition of firm holdings to guide industry through periods of rapid economic
change. In short, most holdings by banks were not acquired to exert control or
influence in industry. And only about 3–3.5 percent of total shares outstanding
are held by banks as part of their participating interests (significant, long-term
holdings) in nonfinancial firms (Deutsche Bundesbank 1997, 39).

Even the Deutsche Bank, by far the bank with the most extensive industrial holdings, reduced at least the number of its large industrial holdings (25
percent or more), if not its total holdings. In the postwar era of Hermann Abs—
who as head of the Deutsche Bank sat on dozens of corporate boards—the bank
purchased several large holdings as part of its competition strategy with the
other big banks (Eglau 1989, 66–67). But in the face of growing public concern over the power of the banks in the mid-1970s, the Deutsche announced its
intention to gradually sell off shareholdings and especially to acquire no large
packets on a permanent basis. Though there were some exceptions to this, the
Deutsche Bank did sell many large holdings.[35] Under the leadership of Alfred
Herrhausen, the Deutsche Bank's proclivity for industrial intervention revived
somewhat in the mid-1980s. But following his death in 1989, the bank returned
to an equity investment strategy of reducing many of its long-established and
largest domestic shareholdings, including a reduction in its Daimler-Benz stake
below the 25 percent threshold. With growing concern for its own profitability,
the Deutsche Bank would like to sell off or substantially reduce the many
underperforming shares in its portfolio and is pressing the federal government
to reduce the hefty 40 percent tax it would have to pay on most such sales
(Balzer and Wilhelm 1997a). The bank's strategy also calls for more equity in-

vestment abroad to further reduce risk while enhancing the profit opportunities associated with buying and selling equity stakes. Observers also suggest that the Deutsche's reduction of large holdings is intended to be a signal to foreign investors that the German corporate community will be increasingly open to them (Hans Otto Eglau, "Abschied von alten Schachteln," *Die Zeit,* 1 April 1994; "Deutsche Bank wird Horten-Aktien abgeben: Die Beteiligungspolitik soll internationaler werden," *Frankfurter Allgemeine Zeitung,* 1 June 1994). It has long been argued that the tight interlocks among financial and industrial companies in Germany prevented outsiders from achieving a greater role in German corporate governance and thus reduced foreign investment interest.

On the other hand, the Deutsche and other large German banks continue to see equity investments as a profitable and therefore important line of business that they will continue to engage in. The bankers also continue to argue in public that their equity investments in nonfinancial firms are an important contribution to German corporate development because banks tend to be long-term investors, thus allowing management to focus on long-term development, rather than short-term profits.[36] Accordingly, the number of bank holdings of 10 percent or more in publicly traded corporations continued to decline into the early 1990s, while the number of bank holdings in nontraded and generally much smaller firms increased from the mid-1980s to the early 1990s.[37] Most of these investments were made as capital investments, as preparation for public listing, or to support Mittelstand firms with external equity.[38] There is also substantial evidence that the banks have simply reduced many of their holdings in large firms to less than 10 percent or placed them in separate holding companies. Many of these holding companies are investment pools in which several banks or industrial firms combine their common shareholdings in a third firm. Such pools achieve tax advantages and spread risk while obscuring who really owns the shares: holdings of less than 10 percent—whether individual or pooled—do not have to be identified individually in bank balance sheets.[39] In short, many bank holdings have become smaller and therefore hidden.

Thus several scholars continue to argue that a relatively small number of insiders (i.e., banks and other large firms) continue to control collectively a substantial number of the largest firms in Germany through direct, indirect, and combined shareholdings (e.g., Böhm 1992).[40] And public debate over the power of the banks continues to be popular, especially whenever there is a spectacular corporate fiasco involving banks, such as the insolvency of Metallgesellschaft in 1994 or the bungled attempt at a hostile takeover of Thyssen steel by Hoesch-Krupp in early 1997. Thus politicians continue to propose and debate stricter limits on bank shareholdings but never muster the political will to realize them.

On the other hand, smaller holdings do reduce the potential influence of the banks since one of the advantages of 25 percent or greater holdings was the veto power it gave the holder in major corporate decisions (*Sperrminorität,* or blocking minority). Ten percent alone will not grant the bank such a right. Through coordination with other "friendly" shareholders, the banks can still affect major decisions even where their own holdings may be small. The ability of the Deutsche Bank to build a voting bloc of more than 25 percent among large German firms to frustrate Pirelli's attempted takeover of Continental in 1991 is a good example of such a capacity. But the bank's inability to later convince these same coalition partners to buy back Continental shares from Pirelli also shows that a bank-led coalition is not the equivalent of a large bank holding.

Proxy Votes

Aside from their own holdings in industry, it has traditionally been argued that extensive bank control of proxy votes greatly enhances the banks' power in a significant number of Germany's largest firms because it allows them to vote more shares in annual meetings than they actually own, as well as help them gain seats on firm supervisory boards. There is little dispute that the banks collectively control the majority, or a blocking minority, of votes in dozens of the country's largest firms (Gottschalk 1988). But closer analysis reveals the fact that only in a few cases does proxy voting really create potential bank power. A recent study examined the 24 of the largest 100 German firms in which the majority of shares were widely dispersed—it is in such firms where proxy voting has the greatest potential to leverage bank influence. If one excludes the banks themselves, in 16 of these firms the majority of shares were voted *by all banks together;* in only six cases did a single bank control more than 25 percent, and three of these resulted largely from bank ownership in that firm. In other words, there were only three firms in which a single bank attained a blocking minority through proxy voting. In the remaining 10 cases, it was all banks together—all big banks, savings banks, Landesbanks, cooperatives, etc.—that controlled the majority votes. It is very unlikely that so many competing banks coordinate their votes in an effort to control management. The fact that the vast majority of annual meeting votes are close to unanimous indicates as well that banks follow the suggested vote of firm management (Baums and Fraune 1995).

Thus, more than anything else, bank control of proxy votes is used to protect the autonomy of—not influence—incumbent management and to help the bank secure access to business with the firm.[41] This protection of management extends to the big banks themselves, since bank managers are the single largest vote holders in their own shareholder meetings![42]

Supervisory Boards

The extent to which board seats are controlled by the banks has probably also been overestimated. According to Edwards and Fischer (1991, 20), in 1984 banks occupied only 8.4 percent of supervisory board seats and represented 16.8 percent of shareholders' equity in the top 100 AGs—a substantial decrease from 10 years earlier. Thus bankers rarely muster the majority of votes on a supervisory board. Even more importantly, the actual role of supervisory boards in firm decision making is overrated. Most boards meet only twice a year, at most four times per year for a half day. They rarely discuss strategic planning; roughly one-half discuss the sale or purchase of equity in other firms; and only one-third deal with questions regarding bond issues or loans (Edwards and Fischer 1991). Based on his study of the Deutsche Bank, Eglau (1989, 135) argues that power has shifted from the supervisory to the management board. Supervisory board members tend to follow the lead of the management board, partly in order to show solidarity vis-à-vis worker representatives on the supervisory board.[43] Moreover, representatives from competing banks often sit on the same boards, and even then the firms do not limit their bank connections to these banks. As discussed above, most large corporations have extensive in-house finance operations, and the remaining business increasingly goes to the cheapest bidder, not necessarily to the banker(s) sitting on the firm's board.

Thus supervisory board seats do not in themselves give banks influence in the firm. Since supervisory boards do hire and fire the firm's management board, there is the potential to influence firm decision making indirectly, through personnel changes. And case evidence indicates that banks do sometimes initiate changes in management. But the principal role of bankers on the boards is to act as advisor in financial matters such as financing large investments and foreign exchange hedging. Therefore, under conditions of low firm financial dependence, formal mechanisms of bank control, such as bank representation on corporate boards, are more likely to serve an information rather than control function (see also Stearns 1990, 197). Bank representation on supervisory boards often does make a difference when the bank representative controls the chair of the board, because the chair has the greatest potential to exercise external control over management. When it comes to supervisory board chairs, equity holdings, and proxy votes, the Deutsche Bank stands above all other German banks. In 1988 the Deutsche Bank occupied 38 supervisory board chairs; the Dresdner, 11; and the Commerzbank, five (Eglau 1989, 136). By mid-1994, however, the Deutsche Bank held only 13 chairs and intended to give up more (Eglau 1994).[44] The leadership of the bank and a growing number of corporate managers believe that the interests of corporate clients would be better served if this board position is held by professionals with experience in the firm's industry—generally by the most recently retired CEO. In the early 1990s, a series of major strategic blunders by several large German corporations in which the Deutsche or other banks held strong equity positions and controlled the supervisory board's chair underscored this growing conviction among both bankers and industrialists (Antrecht, Luber, and Stiller 1993; "Deutsche Bank: Total überlastet," *Wirtschaftswoche,* 22 April 1994). The Deutsche Bank is apparently also increasingly sensitive to the possibility that its business could suffer from conflicts of interest stemming from its control of supervisory board seats ("New Dreams at Deutsche Bank," *The Economist,* 22 June 1991). For example, capturing a part of the growing and lucrative mergers and acquisitions business requires a bank to be able to present itself as a neutral advisor, a position that is compromised if the bank is too close to one of the parties involved.

In sum, there are still several reasons for the banks to continue buying equity stakes in firms. Investment-oriented shareholdings are purchased as a financial investment or as reserve assets to be liquidated in financial need, as well as to help firms in their restructuring, prevent takeovers, or facilitate ownership change in Mittelstand firms and prepare them for public listing. Both the banks and outside observers argue that one of the primary reasons for bank holdings is to secure some advantage in gaining the banking business of that firm.[45] Banks that want to manage the global financial needs of German multinationals, for example, generally must get on the list of those firms' house or main banks. Yet even though equity holdings will get a bank on that list, they no longer guarantee business. For example, in 1995 Daimler-Benz passed over the Deutsche Bank—its largest single shareholder—and chose American investment banks to help reorganize its AEG subsidiary and underwrite a major new issue (Peter Truell and Edmund L. Andrews, "Accelerating a Risky Strategy," *New York Times,* 31 October 1996). Big German firms have on average seven to nine house/main bank connections (which get roughly 75 percent of the firm's financial business) and a total of 20 to 30 bank connections (Juncker 1992). Many of the largest firms, such as Veba and Daimler-Benz, are deliberately diversifying and internationalizing their investor base (Antonia Sharpe, "Daimler Shows Its Friendly Side," *Financial Times,* 17 June 1996). Given this situation, industry holdings are increasingly viewed with an eye to the bank's bottom line, not to the long-term strategy of that firm, let alone an entire sector. In general, the banks seem more intent on attempting to realize profits through the later resale of shareholdings. In fact, the Commerzbank says it will only acquire investment-oriented holdings—risky firm bailouts or reorganizations are to be shunned ("Haus Banques," *The Economist,* 16 November 1991).[46] The reduction of large holdings is consistent with this strategy, but it also suggests a reduction of bank influence and the role of the banks in corporate governance generally—a conclusion supported by a survey of 350 finance directors of the 500 largest German firms, which indicated that the traditional bond between a firm and its house bank had noticeably loosened, largely as a result of bank competition.[47]

Banks, Corporate Governance, and Corporate Restructuring

Bank shareholdings in industry, bank control of board seats, and proxy votes have traditionally empowered the banks with a major role in German corporate governance—that is, the system that provides for investor control over firm management. The German system of corporate governance can be characterized as an "insider" system because the majority of publicly traded firms are majority-controlled (or at least 25 percent) by a handful of long-term investors. Ownership is thus highly concentrated. While most of these owners are families or other nonfinancial companies, the banks are still said to play an especially prominent role because of their connections to a wide range of firms. The insider system of corporate governance is argued to have several competitive advantages over the system of corporate governance in market-based financial systems. As large, long-term investors, banks, families, and other companies allow management to focus on long-term growth through long-term investment strategies. In market-based systems, most large firms are owned by a large number of small investors who are more concerned with short-term profits, and thus management must also focus short-term. Banks in Germany also presumably actively monitor firm management (even in widely held firms), ensuring that it takes proper account of investor (and possibly even employee) interests in all its decisions. Thus the banks overcome the commonly lamented situation in market-based economies where most equity in firms is so widely distributed that investors find little incentive to actively monitor and influence management, instead preferring to sell their shares if they disapprove of management decisions. These are "outsider" systems of corporate governance, in which firm management is disciplined by changes in stock price or (even the threat of) outside takeover (Franks and Mayer 1994).

Dyson (1982, 39–59) probably best states some of the other widely hypothesized benefits that derive from this bank role in corporate governance. First, the banks provide an "early warning" system to identify weaknesses in industry and mount firm rescue operations. Second, close relations between banks and firms enhance the availability of capital to German firms because the banks can better monitor how management uses funds. Third, the banks exert financial discipline in industry. Fourth, the banks as initiators or organizers of industrial activity help screen industrial policy from the general arena of politics. Fifth, banks assume a long-term perspective regarding the firms in which they invest, helping firms secure market share and improve their long-term cost structure through the mobilization of financial, technical, and managerial resources.

Contrary to what is widely asserted or assumed in the literature, the question remains open whether the major banks are capable of managing their industrial holdings in a manner that is beneficial for the individual bank and its client firms, and whether close bank-firm relations promote the long-term economic development of individual firms, sectors, and the whole economy. This section briefly reviews the presumed consequences or "benefits" of intimate bank involvement in industry. The question of to what extent banks actually monitor and influence corporate management, and with what consequences, is an empirical one and the subject of this section.

Benefits of Bank Power?

One of the supposed advantages of the German bank-based system and insider control is that banks act as initiators and organizers of industrial activity, thus keeping industrial policy a largely private affair. The banks have been presumed to develop new growth sectors and assist the restructuring of those in trouble. Shonfield ([1965] 1980), and later Zysman (1983), cited the steel industry as a prime example of this bank function. But (as will be discussed in chapter 4) despite a large volume of loans, equity holdings, and supervisory board seats in the major steel firms, the banks' effort to generate a sectoral rationalization plan in the early 1980s was defeated by hostilities among the steel firms and political opposition. The state, through subsidies and other forms of intervention, has arguably had as much or more to do with the steel industry's adjustment path as the banks. The case of steel and evidence from other sectors suggest that it is increasingly difficult for banks to achieve the coordination among themselves and control over firms needed to mastermind and implement sectoral development plans.

The German banks are also said to use their inside knowledge and influence to aid or financially restructure weak firms before they reach insolvency. And if this does happen, then the banks take a long-term perspective and rescue the firm. But Edward and Fischer (1991, 1994) argue that rescue operations are becoming more difficult for the banks to carry out. In the 1980s a series of court battles indicated that banks could be held liable if their attempt to rescue a firm by delaying insolvency hurt other creditors. Now outside management consultants must approve all rescue plans. Surprisingly, even before these changes, German banks let firms go under more often than they rescued them.[48] Moreover, several cases suggest the banks failed to foresee trouble in the firm before it was too late. Or, worse, that bank intervention led to subsequent problems for the firms. The financial collapse of the energy and metals group Metallgesellschaft in 1994 was the most spectacular recent indictment of banks as monitors: the company's massive losses in oil futures speculation suggested that either the banks were poor monitors or their ill-conceived intervention in fact precipitated the losses. In other cases, especially where a firm is still largely family-held, the banks prefer to avoid conflict and defer to family leadership. In some cases this deference probably contributed to the subsequent demise of the firm (Eglau 1989, 138–43). While banks continue to assist individual firms in their restructuring, it is much more accurate to see this as the exception rather than the rule. There appear to be three situations in which a bank rescue is likely: (1) the bank already has a large equity holding in the firm; (2) there is a long-standing and close relationship to a large or family-owned firm; or (3) the bank sees a strong threat to its reputation or image with the public (e.g., where a firm's collapse would cause obvious economic hardship) or other business partners (who wish to view the bank as a reliable partner).[49]

Standard accounts suggest that another important role of the banks is to assure firms ready access to long-term funds. But bank finance is not especially important for large German firms. While Mittelstand firms receive a high level of long-term funds, this is attributable in large part to state efforts to ensure long-term financing and the lending patterns of savings and cooperative banks. It has also been claimed that the extensive involvement of the banks in industry exerts financial discipline among firms. But it is rather difficult to ascertain whether disciplined firms are so because of their own diligence or because of bank monitoring. In the case of the largest firms, however, their financial dealings are extensive and largely conducted by in-house staff. There is probably far too much activity for banks to oversee firms, especially on a daily basis.

Another presumed consequence of close bank-industry relations is that the major banks take a long-term perspective in their dealings with firms. The banks use long-term sectoral analyses and mobilize financial, technical, and managerial resources to help firms reduce their long-term cost structure and thus improve potential profitability.[50] A widely cited study by Cable (1985), for example, analyzed the correlation between banks' control of firms—defined by the number of supervisory board seats and voting shares they controlled—and the profitability of 48 of the 100 largest German firms. He concluded that bank control was positively correlated to firm profitability, primarily because a better flow of internal information between bank and firm made the bank willing to extend more credit on more favorable terms. But this study rests on several questionable assumptions. First, as noted above, the largest German firms are less and less dependent on the banks for funds, and the price of capital for large firms is now more determined by international market conditions than by the banks. Second, it is not certain that supervisory boards have access to all the important information about a firm. Third, it is not clear whether bank control produces superior profitability or whether banks try to gain influence in the firms that were already very profitable and thus lucrative clients. Finally, what German firms report as profits is problematic, given the relatively loose accounting distinctions between profits and reserves for future claims. Several other recent studies have attempted to assess the impact of bank influence on the cost of firm financing and profitability and have found that close bank ties have no, or even negative, effects on these variables.[51]

A Network Approach to Bank-Industry Relations

It has been suggested that the role of the major banks in the economy be analyzed in terms of financial groups (Pfeiffer 1989). Such groups are understood as involving strong linkages that hold over time between one or more house banks and one or more nonfinancial firms. The capacity for collective planning in the economy—the essence of organized capitalism—presumably resides within such groups. The questions of who dominates whom within the relationship—extremely difficult to ascertain—and how these groups came into being can be considered secondary (Esser 1990, 30). But this notion of groups implies a clear and purposive demarcation between sets of firms with close relationships—something more akin to the Japanese *keiretsu*. The available evidence for the German case suggests that the multitude of close bank-firm relationships cannot be so clearly ascribed to distinct groupings. I think it more fruitful to analyze the nonmarket relationships between banks and nonfinancial firms according to their function within distinct varieties of firm networks. Each type of network entails a particular form of interfirm relations and serves particular goals, though the exclusiveness of each kind of network is compromised by the fact that they often overlap and one type can sometimes be transformed into another type. These three types of firm networks are monitoring, obligational, and promotional.[52] The relationships between banks and firms vary between types of networks.

Monitoring networks are the most encompassing of these networks. They cut across many sectors and involve more informal multilateral exchanges among firms—usually characterized by webs of interlocking directorates. Monitoring networks generally serve the primary purpose of facilitating the flow of information among the financial-industrial elite. They help "corporate leaders identify problems concerning large numbers of companies, and facilitate the search for general solutions to those problems" (Lindberg, Campbell, and Hollingsworth 1991, 23).[53] For example, in 1988, of the 170 shareholder representatives on the supervisory boards of the 12 largest industrial concerns, the big three commercial banks, Germany's largest retailer (Karstadt), and its largest insurer (Allianz), about one-half (86) came from one of these very same 17 firms.[54] Through such a network, Germany's economic elites can follow each other's activities. But monitoring networks rely more on peer pressure and consent to obtain compliance among members. Coercive mechanisms are generally lacking. Monitoring networks in Germany appear to be largely unaffected by the changes in the financial system and bank-firm relations discussed above. While banks are clearly involved in such networks, especially as conveyors of information from one firm to another, it is through networks of the obligational variety that one firm is more likely to influence another.[55]

Obligational networks involve primarily bilateral relations between firms or among a small clique of firms and serve the purpose of stabilizing resource flows among them—particularly capital and information. Obligational networks entail relationships between firms that are less precisely specified and therefore more flexible and open-ended than market or "classical" contracts. Interlocking corporate directorates, mutual cross-shareholdings, and some types of joint ventures are examples of such networks. Many relations between banks and large firms in Germany fall into this category.[56] As suggested above, the exact purpose of these bank-firm network relations, and the degree and (a)symmetry of dependence between firms, varies from case to case. In some cases these networks serve to coordinate the buying and selling of products, such as the Dresdner-Allianz cooperative pact designed to promote the sale of banking and insurance services.

In fact, within the financial services sector itself there are growing financial interlocks among banks and insurance firms in Germany. As part of the trend to Allfinanz, several partnerships and mutual equity positions have been agreed to among insurance firms and banks. These developments—evident in other European countries—have been given a further boost by the anticipated opening of European banking and insurance markets. Perhaps unique to Germany, many of these obligational networks also serve the purpose of exploiting tax regulations: increasingly common are financial holding companies in which various firms pool their shares in a particular firm in order to reach the tax-exempt 10 percent threshold (Hans Otto Eglau, "Abschied von alten Schachteln," *Die Zeit,* 1 April 1994).

Many managers of the large German firms are also content to have a large portion of their shares held by friendly firms, including banks. In fact, it is not unknown for a firm's managers to deliberately seek out a particular individual or group of potential shareholders. First, managers want to avoid hostile takeovers. German industry's defense of Daimler in the mid-1970s and Continental in 1991 shows how a small group of large German firms can protect one of its own. In an interview, the head of the Federal Cartel Office, Wolfgang Kartte, suggested that large German firms typically do not acquire minority holdings in other firms in order to control them, but in order to prevent a competitor from gaining control of that firm ("Wir sind doch nicht blind," *Der Spiegel,* 6 April 1992). While many see the prevention of unwanted takeovers as a positive feature of the German system, some analysts have suggested that German banks may in fact hinder unwanted takeovers of their corporate clients because they imply to other investors that the bank was not effectively monitoring the firm's (presumably less-than-effective) management (Franks and Mayer 1990, 213). Networks of mutual cross-shareholdings as a means to prevent hostile takeovers have probably been growing in Germany over the last decade (Wilhelm 1991). But in this respect Germany is not unique, as such networks are evident in other European countries such as France (compare table 7 and Schmidt 1996).

The second major incentive for managers to have stable, long-term shareholders is that such close control, combined with commonplace restrictions on shareholder voting rights, minimizes small shareholders' control over management. Managers' autonomy is consequently quite high, allowing them to pursue their own agenda, even if it means lower dividends and/or share prices in the short term. On the other hand, many domestic and large foreign institutional investors are demanding more active shareholder control of management and greater emphasis on shareholder value (i.e., maximizing the value of share price and dividends and judging investment opportunities primarily on the basis of their return on capital). Many German large-firm managers are beginning to adopt this approach to investment decisions. Indeed, the Deutsche Bank and Daimler appear to be orchestrating a major campaign for shareholder value. In mid-1996 both firms broke new ground in Germany by creating stock option plans as part of executive compensation. Following the Anglo-Saxon model, the firms are hoping this will focus managers more on enhancing share performance. Under the urging of several leading banks and firms, in mid-1997 the Kohl government proposed a revision to company law that would permit German firms to buy back their own shares—something hitherto illegal—as a means to boost share prices. But this newfound fascination among German managers with shareholder value does not mean abandoning all the aspects of the traditional approach to corporate governance that emphasized the interests of all stakeholders, notably those of employees alongside owners. Nor does it mean firms will necessarily have a more dispersed shareholdership (Christian Deutsch, "Stochern im Nebel," *Wirtschaftswoche,* 20 June 1996; see also Deutsche Bundesbank 1996b, 36).

While banks therefore play an important role in influencing ownership of large German firms, the evidence indicates that the German banks are not usually at the center of such obligational networks. Franks and Mayer (1994) analyzed 171 publicly traded German companies in which there was at least one shareholder owning more than 25 percent. In 27.5 percent of cases, that major shareholder was another German company; in 20.5 percent it was a family group; and banks were major shareholders in only 5.8 percent. Bank ownership and supervisory board presence are declining while those of nonfinancial firms are rising. Large German nonfinancial firms are net purchasers of equity and thus have extensive shareholdings in other firms (see also table 7). The huge energy utility VEBA, for example, purchased some 300 shareholdings in the 1970s and 1980s ("Mehr Filz, weniger Wettbewerb," *Der Spiegel,* 30 December 1991)! A large number of the cross-shareholding networks involving large German firms do not involve a bank at all. Where banks are involved, such networks can also be used by firms to influence the banks. Some 45 percent of the Dresdner Bank's stock, for example, is controlled by a group of insurance and industrial firms led by the insurance giant Allianz.[57] Thus the major commercial banks are also dependent on the goodwill of other firms in their respective cross-shareholding networks. In sum, despite the decline in large shareholdings by the banks, the dense and obscure web of financial and directorate interlocks among many large German banks and firms appears to be intact. Recent regulatory changes have increased, and will further increase, the transparency of such interlocks, but only an outright ban on interlocking holdings in industry is likely to undo them—and such a ban is nowhere on the horizon. Thus this form of obligational network in Germany has been altered somewhat in response to broader market and regulatory changes, but such networks so far remain firmly entrenched.

Achieving cooperation among a number of firms in an industry for the purpose of sectoral rationalization is a form of promotional network. This kind of network is based on explicitly negotiated and defined rules of resource exchange among a large number of organizations, generally for the purpose of promoting their collective interests. In Shonfield's model, it is the banks that are the linchpin of such coordination, but the experience with sectoral rationalization in the last decade indicates the growing difficulty of creating such networks involving large firms. Extensive as the German system of corporate interlocks may be, the flow of information and resources in them is not subject to the control of any single actor, nor are conflicts between firms eliminated— even those that may own shares in each other. At the end of 1991, for example, the German steelmaker Krupp completed a successful hostile takeover of its rival Hoesch by quietly buying up large packets of stock from other firms and securing the backing of other major Hoesch shareholders. Hoesch's lead bank, the Deutsche Bank, apparently knew nothing until it was too late ("Europe's Corporate Castles Begin to Crack," *The Economist,* 30 November 1991). This episode echoes the inability of the major commercial banks to pressure the steel firms into a bank-designed sectoral rationalization plan in the early 1980s. Sectoral rationalization in steel now appears to be occurring through a much less cooperative process than in the past. It suggests further that it may be increasingly difficult for the banks to turn obligational or monitoring networks into promotional networks for the purpose of restructuring ailing industries. Effective sectoral cooperation in the form of industry associations still exists in Germany, but a growing amount of evidence suggests the banks often cannot function, or are not needed, as the linchpin of this coordination.

In sum, the potential influence of the banks over large firms has probably never been as strong as the organized capitalism model suggests and has declined significantly since the 1970s, due in large part to more intense bank competition and declining large-firm financial dependence on banks. Under certain conditions the banks can still play a tutelary role for firms, but these conditions seem to obtain less and less frequently. Promotional networks are increasingly difficult to construct. Monitoring networks flourish but do not provide the banks with substantial influence. Within obligational networks, most large firms have achieved financial autonomy and, to a significant degree, maintain close non-market relations (e.g., mutual cross-shareholdings) with banks as a matter of their own (strategic) choice. As banks become less involved in corporate decision making (governance), as banks rely more on selling services instead of capital to firms under conditions of strong competition, the relations between banks and large firms become increasingly of a market nature.

Reflecting the declining capacity for bank monitoring, in the 1990s a debate emerged in German financial and business circles over reforming the system of corporate governance. This debate was inspired to a certain extent by outside pressures (the EU, international investors, etc.) to make the German system more open and accessible. But for the most part, the debate is driven by the widespread perception in industry and government that the system is no longer working. Many critics argue that supervisory boards are ineffective at controlling management.[58] Some add that bank representatives should be replaced on corporate supervisory boards by independent shareholder representatives. Whatever the outcome of this debate, it clearly indicates the reduced role of banks in the corporate governance system and the consequent struggle to find new institutional alternatives to fulfill these functions.

Banks and Corporate Restructuring

The changing relations between banks and firms and the development of capital markets are also contributing to a changing pattern of corporate adjustment. In the past, large firms commonly adjusted through internal restructuring of organization and operations. Banks typically supported this pattern through loans and equity provision. More and more, however, a pattern of corporate adjustment through the buying and selling of firms or subsidiaries is emerging. In Anglo-Saxon capital markets, one frequently speaks of a market for firms. German managers generally reject the creation of such a market in Germany and particularly the experience of hostile takeovers and leveraged buyouts associated with this.[59] But the number of mergers, acquisitions, buyouts, spin-offs, and management buyouts and buy-ins has grown dramatically in Germany. In 1984 there were approximately 1,000 such transactions; by 1990, before the massive M&A (mergers and acquisitions) rush in eastern Germany, there were nearly 3,000 ("Die Dealmaker auf der Pirsich," *Industriemagazin,* August 1991). German banks and foreign investment banks operating in Germany expect this dramatic growth to continue, if not accelerate. To encourage (friendly) takeovers, protect the interests of smaller shareholders, and meet the expectations of international investors, in late 1995 a committee organized by the major banks agreed to a takeover code. While the code is voluntary, dozens of the largest German firms have since pledged to honor it.

There are three primary motors behind the shift to adjustment through a market for firms (Lennertz 1993). The first is the actual and anticipated intensification of competition associated with the completion of the European internal market. Mittelstand firms are looking for partners to strengthen their ability to compete. Large firms are more commonly shedding subsidiaries or making them independent and publicly traded, and they are buying new firms as part of their strategy to focus on core business segments and to enhance shareholder value.[60] Second, the German Mittelstand is also on the beginning edge of a wave of company-founder retirements. Thousands of such firms have no suitable family successor and will end up being sold to external investors. Third, restructuring the East German economy involved a tremendous amount of buying and selling of firms. This helped stimulate firm deals in West Germany as well and gave German bankers greater experience in managing them. It could be added that the efforts at Finanzplatz Deutschland, to the extent that it succeeds in stimulating equity-based finance, will make changes in ownership and control of firms easier and therefore probably more frequent.

As universal banks, the big German banks are in the best position to offer services in all the aspects associated with mergers and acquisitions—from brokering deals to financing them with loans or equity. This ability lends them definitive advantages vis-à-vis their competitors, especially in regard to Mittelstand firms. A handful of German banks, especially the Deutsche Bank and the WestLB, offer firms M&A consulting services as part of a complete corporate restructuring strategy in which the bank plays an important role in preparation and implementation. Most other banks, however, including the Dresdner Bank and Commerzbank, focus more on the brokering function of M&A (Bross, Caytas, and Mahori 1991, 39). But the German M&A market is no longer controlled by the big German banks. There are now well over 100 firms engaged in the M&A advising market, including the big German banks, foreign investment banks, German and foreign management consulting companies, and international accounting firms. For larger firms, especially deals involving cross-border transactions, the German banks still fare poorly in competition with foreign investment banks. German banks are hampered by their comparatively limited international presence and experience, as well as the reality and perception by firms that the banks have too many conflicting interests (Bross, Caytas, and Mahori 1991, 52–65). A bank that has extended loans or equity to a firm does not make an ideal advisor on an M&A deal involving that firm. Despite moving their M&A business into independent subsidiaries or autonomously operating corporate finance units separated by "Chinese walls" from the rest of the bank, the big German banks are having difficulty in this market segment in good measure because of the perception of conflicting interests.[61] Thus the ambitions of the German banks to develop investment banking conflict to an important degree with an extensive role in corporate governance. This new pattern of corporate adjustment, less subject to coordinated control by the big three banks, adds further evidence to the argument that banks are less able to steer firm and sectoral adjustment.

Banks and the Mittelstand

It is widely recognized that Mittelstand firms play a central role in industrial production in Germany.[62] Despite widespread expectations of economic concentration, this role has not diminished in the face of increasing product and financial market integration. If anything, Mittelstand firms have become more important as a result of restructuring trends, including a significant shift in employment from large to smaller firms.[63] Beginning in the 1980s, the new concepts of production spreading quickly in Germany were: to produce a diversity of products of high quality; to flexibly automatize the manufacturing process; to integrate production, maintenance, and quality control functions; and to recruit and train highly skilled labor (Kern and Schumann 1989). Alternatively labeled post-Fordism or diversified quality production (DQP), production according to these principles means a shift away from mass-produced, standardized goods to more customized goods produced in comparatively small batches. Many of these new concepts—in particular higher-quality goods achieved through intensified R&D and production with higher-skill labor—are widely seen as essential prerequisites for all advanced industrial nations to remain internationally competitive (Piore and Sabel 1984; Hage 1988). And there is growing recognition that continued competitiveness increasingly requires collective goods—such as education and research—that the market as a governance institution frequently fails to produce in sufficient quantities.

Streeck argues that DQP requires a rich set of institutions that create enforceable social constraints on rational market participants and encourage them to restructure toward higher diversity and quality. Free markets and private hierarchies are insufficient for generating and supporting DQP, "because DQP is dependent on an industrial order or social structure that can only provisionally or precariously exist on a voluntaristic-contractual basis, rather where it is fully developed it is the result of long-term developments and collective 'cultural' choice mediated by and crystallized in a set of social institutions" (1992, 31). In this view there are three broad institutional requirements for DQP. First, there is the requirement of congenial organizational ecology, because markets and hierarchies are not well equipped to govern the complex mixture of cooperation and competition required for DQP. Other organizational mechanisms, such as trade associations, are necessary to help firms to act on their self-interest in their competitors' and suppliers' competitiveness and well-being. For example, DQP for large firms depends on their successful interaction with economically and technically independent smaller firms. And for smaller firms to achieve and maintain this position, there must be mechanisms that support the interfirm transfer of know-how and technology. Second, DQP requires redundant capacities, both within the firm and collectively, in order to respond to rapid market changes. This requires investment in general capabilities for as yet undefined purposes. For example, a broadly and highly skilled workforce will possess skills not in use at any given time but that will probably be needed at some point in order for the firm to successfully adapt. But without institutionally imposed pressures to train workers at a high level, the skill level of the workforce is likely to decline. Such redundant capacities are more likely to be provided through collective institutional obligations. Third, DQP requires collective production inputs from the state, not necessarily through the direct provision of nonappropriable inputs, but through behavioral regulation of the market participants that creates obligations for cooperative behavior.

The banking system is an additional central institutional element to the German system of DQP.[64] Under DQP, firms require high levels of long-term investment in research and product development, in labor force training, and the like. By providing long-term loans and stable, long-term relations, banks enable Mittelstand firms to pursue long-term objectives. In this manner, firms in Germany avoid or minimize pressures to maximize short-run returns. The strong preference for short-term investment horizons inherent in equity-market-based finance systems is unlikely to support all the kinds of investments needed for DQP. The rapidly changing relationship between banks and large firms raises questions about the future ability of such firms to follow a DQP strategy. But even in a more equity-based system, large German firms may be able to focus long-term if they continue to self-finance at a high rate and if control over their equity remains primarily in the hands of large, long-term shareholders. For Mittelstand firms, rapid changes in product markets, technology, and intensified competition from domestic and international sources intensify short-term adjustment pressures. For example, firms with adjustment difficulties because of inadequate financing are more likely to disengage from R&D

and other activities that make DQP possible. Successful adjustment by Mittelstand firms operating within a DQP strategy (or even for firms not engaged in DQP) is conditioned much more heavily by factors exogenous to the firm, since smaller firms typically lack many resources that large firms have (Tichy 1990). Intensified product market competition and technological changes drive Mittelstand firms to seek greater assistance from outside—especially from banks (Juncker 1988). In the 1990s, many German firms were forced to adapt further their DQP strategy in response to the competitive pressures emanating from the lean production model developed most successfully in Japan. While many of the basic concepts of DQP and lean production are similar, lean production achieves similar quality to DQP but at lower costs, through methods such as cellular manufacturing, multifunctional team-based production, and worker control for quality and continuous improvement.

Allfinanz

Responding to these adjustment needs, since the early 1980s each of the three major banking groups has been working toward the goal of providing Mittelstand firms comprehensive financial and business services.[65] This Allfinanz strategy embodies an explicit attempt to become the external management arm of the small firm. The adoption of Allfinanz was strongly conditioned by the growth of group competition, particularly in the Mittelstand market. The successful implementation of the Allfinanz strategy is heavily contingent upon the federal character of the banking system. To compete, all banking groups must offer comparable services, and for each group these services can only be offered through successful coordination of local, national, and international units. For commercial banks, this means cooperation between increasingly autonomous local branches and other bank divisions or subsidiaries. For savings and cooperative banks, this means cooperation between local and regional or national banks in the group and with their respective associations. The Allfinanz strategy of the banks signifies that they are not only providing long-term financing, they are also facilitating the flow of nonfinancial resources to firms useful for DQP that can be understood broadly as information: information about technology, business management, business partners, and markets.

Thus a central element of the Allfinanz strategy is to provide Mittelstand firms with comprehensive consulting services. All the banks provide consulting services on a wide range of topics: foreign and domestic market analyses, technological development and innovation, joint ventures and partnerships, organizational administration, and extensive short- and long-term financial and investment planning—the kind of planning that many Mittelstand firms do not have the resources to undertake.[66] Banks seek to provide such consulting primarily with in-house staff. All banks are demanding and training their loan officers to be knowledgeable advisors to client firms on all business matters. For Allfinanz to succeed, loan officers are expected to pull together the right resources within, or even outside, the bank to satisfy the customers' demands. But more than that, the officer is expected to actively help the firm identify internal and external threats to its present and future health and to develop a long-term business strategy.[67] Taking this strategy one step further, in the mid-1990s the Deutsche Bank established some 260 special centers of competence in various branches to act as in-house firm consulting units (Bauer, Sybille, Stefanie Burgmaier, and Bernhard Jünemann, "Schätze nützen," *Wirtschaftswoche,* 9 November 1995).

In addition, all three major banking groups acquired or established management consulting companies. The banks have done so for several reasons: first, it is a growing market segment from which they seek to profit; second, they hope consulting companies will increase their ability to understand the market risks that their firm customers face and thus enable banks to manage better their risk diversification; third, bank consulting companies are sometimes used to assist a bank customer with severe difficulties, thus preventing loan defaults; fourth, consulting companies can help bank customers in their strategic, nonfinancial planning and thus solidify a long-term relationship between bank and firm (Schäfer 1993; Marner and Jaeger 1991).

In-house consulting and external consulting companies are part of a broader effort by banks to become information and education centers for Mittelstand clients (Bredemeier 1992). It is now commonplace for a local bank, whether a cooperative or savings bank or the local branch of a major bank, to organize seminars, workshops, and discussion groups for local business people.[68] Banks use databases to advise firms on patents and technologies. Banks are also establishing direct electronic information linkages between themselves and SMEs (small and medium-sized enterprises) in order to provide continuous services such as cash management, liquidity planning, and payments transfers (Musil and Nippa 1993). More and more local banks and branches are using the international resources of their group or concern to help local firms identify new export markets or find potential business partners abroad.[69] For example, as part of this effort several commercial and public sector banks have initiated and funded (often in conjunction with German state governments) several commerce centers, mostly in Asia, from which German Mittelstand firms can build up export markets or local production relations. Finally, as part of this strategy

banks are using their firm contacts, consulting companies, and databases to me-
diate interfirm cooperation in production, innovation, or distribution.[70] Interfirm cooperation is a central institutional feature of DQP, since product development and manufacturing in this production model involves extensive
cooperation among small and large firms. Where cooperation is insufficient to
maintain firm competitiveness, banks seek to tap into their investment banking
services by facilitating mergers and acquisitions and management buyouts and
buy-ins among SMEs.

The Framework for Long-Term Financing

While these nonfinancial aspects of the Allfinanz strategy are beneficial to Mittelstand firms, adequate long-term finance is even more critical to their competitiveness and ability to engage in DQP. Mittelstand firms have not been able
to build the kind of financial reserves that many large firms have, and thus they
remain much more dependent on bank loans to finance investment (Deutsche
Bundesbank 1997, 32). German SMEs receive substantial amounts of long-
term finance from banks, both in the form of loans and increasingly in the form
of limited equity.[71] Adequate long-term finance is assured by three factors—
strong bank competition, the comprehensiveness and competitiveness of savings and cooperative banks, and state regulation and long-term lending. The
savings bank group, which has the largest market share in commercial lending
among the three major groups, specializes in low-cost, long-term financing and
uses this to compete with the other banking groups. This places pressure on the
other groups to provide long-term funds. Savings and cooperative banks also
have unique institutional incentives to provide SMEs with adequate long-term
funds. First, these banks are limited by their group or association to a local market, and thus they are dependent for their own success on the long-term vital-
ity of their local client base. They also have a strong incentive to protect their
reputation for being a reliable long-term bank partner to SMEs. Second, savings and cooperative banks' charters and governing laws obligate them to pursue profit as a means to other goals, not as an end in itself: savings banks are
obligated to promote the local economy; cooperative banks are required to
serve the interests of their members.

For these reasons, these banks can be characterized as rent-seeking institutions, rather than profit maximizers (Allen and Gale 1995). For these banks,
rent-seeking behavior is likely to produce excess service provision to firms (as
compared to a profit maximizer) because it creates jobs and managerial rewards
(rents). In the case of savings banks, rents are also likely to include the satis-

faction of communal political leaders who have a formal governing role over these banks and expect them to fund all reasonable investment projects by local firms. Rent seeking may also help explain the pursuit of Allfinanz, since it facilitates investment in service provision capacities. But rent seeking has not made these banks uncompetitive. The ability of savings and cooperative banks in West Germany first to increase and then largely maintain their market share of commercial lending over the postwar period verifies this. Rather, because so many banks in Germany are rent-seeking, it is likely that this forces *all* banks toward similar behavior.

Increased financing by federal and state development banks over the past two decades also increased the availability of long-term funds to SMEs and lowered the cost of borrowing by lending at subsidized or low-margin interest rates.[72] The majority of state loans to firms are on a long-term basis (typically 7–10 years) for new fixed capital investment (but also for business start-ups, firm rationalization and expansion, technology projects, and liquidity assistance). Most important among these development banks are two federal-Länder development banks—the Deutsche Ausgleichsbank (DtA) and the Kreditanstalt für Wiederaufbau (KfW).[73] While both banks have been operating several programs for the Mittelstand since the early postwar years, the growth in lending under these programs has been especially strong since the 1970s.[74] The KfW, the largest special credit bank, estimates its market penetration in Mittelstand finance to be quite high: for manufacturing firms with annual revenues less than DM 5 million in 1985, the KfW financed 45 percent of their total investment; for firms with revenues between DM 5 million and DM 100 million, the share of the KfW in total investment ranged between 20 and 25 percent (Götte 1988).[75] Between 1982 and 1987, over 10 percent of all firms in the Federal Republic with annual sales between DM 5 million and DM 10 million received one or more KfW loans; this percentage climbs steadily with the size of the firm, reaching nearly 30 percent of all firms with sales between DM 50 million and DM 100 million.[76] Vitols (1994, 13) estimates that the 17 special credit institutes in Germany currently account for just over one-quarter of all long-term loans to manufacturing. After German reunification, new Länder development banks were established in the East to administer loan programs, while several of the old Länder reorganized and expanded their own development banks to do more economic promotion. Federal subsidies and loans for Mittelstand investment in eastern Germany have been massive, as discussed in chapter 6.[77]

Extensive government lending has demonstrated leveraging effects on at-risk lending by the banks. It also decreases the difference between smaller and larger firms in their average cost of capital.[78] By minimizing this structural disadvantage for smaller firms, the state increases their potential growth. Moreover, the presence of state loans for the Mittelstand reduces to some extent price competition among the banks on Mittelstand loans.[79] This helps push the banks to also compete on the basis of their ability to provide other resources and services—that is, to expand their Allfinanz role for firms. Since long-term government loans flow to firms largely via the banks, the growth of such loans strengthens long-term relations between banks and SMEs. Banks screen loan applicants and carry the credit risk (but not interest rate risk) of state loans and therefore must maintain a relationship with the firm in order to monitor government (and most likely their own) loans. Government loan programs are so widespread that SMEs expect their banks to incorporate such loans whenever possible into investment financing packages. Thus the preservation of long-term financing mechanisms essential for Mittelstand firms to engage in DQP is importantly attributable to the state.

Since most SMEs in Germany are still reluctant to go public, efforts by the banks and the federal government to encourage this have met with limited success. Instead, banks and public authorities have sought to produce a functional equivalent through an alternative form of limited equity finance. This form of finance has grown dramatically since the early 1980s, as the banking industry was encouraged through regulatory and legal measures by the federal and state governments to expand funding for new and existing capital, or equity, participation corporations—*Kapitalbeteiligungsgesellschaften,* or KBGs (Breuer 1997). All of the three major banking groups operate KBGs.[80] In each German state there also exists a state-supported, nonprofit KBG (also supported by the major banking groups and local business associations). KBG equity investments are made for a fixed period of typically 10 to 15 years, receive an annual (in some cases profit-dependent) dividend, and generally do not involve a management role for the KBG. Firms use KBGs for a variety of purposes such as seed money, expansion finance, facilitating management buyouts, or leveraging additional bank loans (Fromman 1991; Stedler 1993). KBGs are generally not a vehicle for bank control over SMEs. Some KBGs, however, function more like venture capital funds, investing in technology-oriented projects and realizing much of their profit only after ending their participation. These KBGs are more frequently involved in assisting firm management where they have invested. The KfW and DtA have also become important providers of equity capital. In 1989 the DtA established an equity participation company to provide equity to young high-tech firms. By 1996 it had mobilized nearly half a billion marks of public and private venture capital for hundreds of firms (Deutsche

Ausgleichsbank 1996). And in 1996 the KfW initiated a massive equity participation program for eastern Germany. Altogether, from 1980 to 1989 the total number of equity participations in SMEs grew from 910 to 1,701, and total invested capital rose from DM 620 million to DM 2,500 million (Gröshel 1989, 53–55). At the end of 1993, KBGs held DM 5,400 million of equity in over 2,700 SMEs (DM 511 million of this was invested in 343 firms in eastern Germany; Hummel 1995). Despite this rapid growth, this still represents less than 1 percent of all SMEs. Moreover, German KBGs show a clear bias to invest in established industries such as machine tools, rather than new industries such as computers or biotech. This is partly attributable to the fact that it is easier for KBGs to sell their holdings in more traditional firms to other firms than it is to sell their holdings by taking the firm public (Deeg 1997; Breuer 1997). Thus, as discussed earlier in the chapter, German policymakers and the banking community continue to debate further measures to stimulate public offerings by Mittelstand firms.

Banks and Regional Embeddedness

While each of the three major banking groups is pursuing an Allfinanz strategy, there are comparative differences in their capacity to provide different services. For example, the major banks still dominate export finance markets.[81] This strength is a key factor in acquiring new Mittelstand firm clients and a major reason why the savings and cooperative banking associations invested so much effort in building their international capabilities.[82] The savings and cooperative banks' strength in deposit markets, on the other hand, enables them to undersell the major banks with greater frequency. The savings and cooperative banks also have strong, and in certain ways almost exclusive, connections to local government, trade associations, education, research, and other institutions. For example, some banks have developed special lending programs for high-technology start-ups and other innovation investments. Usually lacking in-house technical expertise, local banks readily refer their customers to local outside technical advisors for assistance and use these experts to aid in the assessment of technology loans. In 1996 the national savings bank association initiated a national system to help savings banks provide loans for technology-oriented investments. Working through the publicly funded Frauenhofer research institute in Karlsruhe, savings banks will be connected with appropriate experts who can provide them with a technical assessment of investment projects planned by their firm clients. The purpose of the program is to facilitate more lending by savings banks to innovative firms by overcoming the banks' information deficit regarding innovative investments (Landrock 1997). Success in Allfinanz and Mittelstand business therefore means that banks must be integrated into the institutional networks that sustain DQP by Mittelstand firms. Local branches of the major banks have been learning to utilize such local institutions yet still prefer to rely more on their own resources. I discuss this embeddedness in greater detail in chapters 4, 5, and 6.

The pursuit of Allfinanz and the strengthening of long-term bank-Mittelstand relations cannot, however, be associated with a growth of bank influence over such firms. Bank ownership or representation on governing boards is uncommon in Mittelstand firms.[83] Intensified competition among banks has encouraged even Mittelstand firms to develop several banking connections, thus minimizing dependence on a single bank. The more ambitious goals of the Allfinanz strategy have generally not met with success. The Deutsche Bank, for example, intended to achieve synergies between its consulting firms, investment banking subsidiary, and bank branches that would enhance the bank's ability to oversee and influence individual firm and sectoral adjustment. But this ambition foundered on the resistance of firms that wanted to minimize the Deutsche Bank's influence. Thus Allfinanz has not turned out to be an effective strategy for banks to monitor and shape sectoral adjustment in Germany according to their plans (Sabel, Griffin, and Deeg 1993). On the other hand, Allfinanz has turned out to be a strategy that helps preserve and extend the traditional German system for financing SMEs, as well as one that enhances firm capacity to adjust and pursue DQP.

In this respect, the implementation of many Allfinanz services is coordinated with the growing efforts by state actors to promote Mittelstand firms. For example, SMEs in financial distress draw on several assistance mechanisms that involve close cooperation and risk sharing between banks and government or government-supported institutions. First, in each German state there is a publicly supported loan guarantee bank and KBG. Firms turn regularly to these organizations for equity injections or loan guarantees when their house bank(s) alone can no longer sustain them. In many cases, state governments also provide loan guarantees directly to firms. Many state development banks provide liquidity assistance through long-term loans to financially distressed SMEs. Such loans are usually provided when the firm's banks cannot provide sufficient liquidity to keep an otherwise competitive firm afloat. In the state of Baden-Württemberg, for example, several hundred SMEs received such liquidity loans during 1993, when the regional economy was in a severe recession. Finally, several states occasionally use their Landesbank to aid troubled firms through the purchase of equity in the firm. In the vast majority of cases, though, state aid (regardless of form) is contingent upon continued bank participation in the firm's credit risk, thus reducing the likelihood that noncompetitive firms will be sustained through state subsidies. Through these public-private finance mechanisms, banks and government increasingly share the risk of the riskiest SME investments, such as start-ups and product innovation. They help viable SMEs survive through short-term downturns in demand or financial bottlenecks and sustain diversified quality production: since DQP typically involves extensive long-term contracting relations among a large number of firms, if too many firms in a production network succumb to a recession, the whole production system could be seriously disrupted.

Summary

This chapter argued that the standard organized capitalism model of the German economy must be revised. While banks continue to have influence in a very limited number of large firms, when examined in the broader context of economic structural change and other roles that the banking industry plays in the economy, its relative importance for the functioning of the economy appears exaggerated by most accounts. Relations between large banks and large nonfinancial firms in Germany have become more arm's-length, or market, relationships. Nonmarket relationships, here characterized as various forms of network relationships, continue to survive and in many cases have expanded. But much evidence suggests that within such networks banks do not exercise nearly as much influence over other firms as standard accounts suggest.

These changes in the relationships between banks and large firms result in large part from the growing financial autonomy of large corporations, as well as intensified competition among a growing number of large banks for corporate business. Concurrently, the banks themselves have become less willing to assume the substantial risks involved with turning around individual firms and, even more so, entire industrial sectors. Given the decline in traditional business with large German firms, the banks have actively promoted the transition to a more market-based system of industrial finance in which the banks can profit from a wide range of trading and investment banking activities. However, there is much evidence that the impact of financial market integration is not unequivocally that of convergence or harmonization in economic structures, corporate governance, and patterns of adjustment. In many cases the German system has accommodated such pressures while finding ways to preserve old patterns. For example, the banks have reduced their industrial holdings and their role in corporate monitoring, but the system of insider control or governance continues because other large German firms are buying stakes in each other. The banks' Allfinanz strategy for Mittelstand firms is a further example of adaptation that preserves much of the traditional system of Mittelstand finance.

Because of the unique institutional character of the German banking system itself and the broader institutional context in which banks operate, German banks do therefore perform economic functions to a degree not found in market-based systems. Most important is that banks provide (1) high levels of long-term financing and (2) market and managerial information, primarily to Mittelstand firms. These first two bank functions contribute importantly to a third function, namely, shaping firm choices in their organization of production (DQP). The institutional structure of the banking industry is therefore significantly correlated to the organizational structure of nonfinancial sectors. These bank functions, though, are only sustainable because of a particular mix of institutional incentives—secured primarily by state economic and regulatory policy—that shape bank behavior. These state and bank functions are explored in more detail in the three regional case studies in part 2.

Part 2

Banks and the Process
of Economic Adjustment

CHAPTER 4

North Rhine–Westphalia: The Decline
of Organized Capitalism

If there is a single region that captures the spirit of organized capitalism, it is surely the Ruhr in North Rhine–Westphalia. In the mid-nineteenth century, the rich, hard coal under the green pastures surrounding the Ruhr, Ems, and Lippe Rivers fueled the emerging industrial revolution in the German states. By the end of the century, the Ruhr was the most heavily industrialized and densely populated region in Germany. Large, vertically integrated firms employed most of the region's labor force to produce most of Germany's coal, steel, and iron and much of its heavy machinery. The leading industrialists of the Ruhr and the nearby Rhine region were among the nation's most politically powerful. Producer cartels and finance capital—bank funds invested in industry—were copious. Thus all the elements of classic organized capitalism were present and operating. On the strength of these industries, the region enjoyed a century of prosperity.

But in the postwar period, the Ruhr suffered the same fate as similarly structured regions across Europe. Beginning in the late 1950s, successive and protracted sectoral crises in coal and steel slowly transformed Germany's premier growth pole into a vortex of decay. The shrinkage of these industries dragged along many of the smaller firms in the region that supplied them. The comparatively low number and weakness of firms in other sectors in the region prevented them from absorbing the vast amounts of labor released by the large firms. By the late 1970s, the onetime symbol of German industrial might was widely scorned in the Federal Republic as the filthy relic of a bygone era.

If we accept the standard organized capitalism argument, then we would expect this adjustment process to have been managed according to the negotiated agreement of the large firms and big commercial banks. And in numerous respects it was. Production capacity was reduced, productivity greatly improved, and the labor force drastically reduced while the big firms diversified and moved toward higher-quality production, all while maintaining a comparatively high degree of industrial and social peace. But to describe the process of adjustment in the Ruhr as "*private* industrial policy" or "organized *private* enterprise" would be an injustice to the role of governments and other regional actors in producing the underlying consensus and funds that made this adjustment possible. Major changes in the organization of production in these sectors were shaped by a corporatist bargaining process involving the unions, the federal and Land governments, firms, and the banks. In the cases of coal and steel, state intervention has been frequent and extensive, at times imposing solutions on industrial sectors unable to develop a consensus plan on their own. Banks were an important part of this process, but they were unable or unwilling to lead it.

Even in the classic case of German organized capitalism—the steel industry—the big three banks so intricately involved in its affairs were eventually incapable of managing its adjustment. Contrary to the widely held view, it is state intervention that saved the large firms and the bank capital invested in them, rather than the banks' saving the state from being bothered with the problems of industry.[1] This points to the limits of private industrial policy and, second, to the critical and often underestimated role of governments in the economy. The cases of coal, steel, and other sectors suggest that the capacity of the major banks to organize industry is effective only on the individual firm level. When whole industries require drastic adjustment measures, the system of private industrial policy is overwhelmed and governments must step in.

Because economic adjustment in Germany is increasingly shaped by the interaction of a wide range of national and regional organizations, including governments, we must examine the banks' activities within the broader institutional context that shapes the adjustment process. For this reason, the case studies presented in this and the next two chapters focus on both the role of banks in the adjustment process and the growing role of Land governments and other organizations linked in what I call regional economic policy networks. A regional policy network consists of the set of relations and interaction among public and private organizations involved in the formulation and implementation of regional economic policy. Such interorganizational coordination or cooperation is based on an exchange of mutually valued resources such as information, legitimacy, authority, and money.[2] Organizations that might typically form a regional policy network include Land governments, business and trade associations, public and private banks, Chambers of Industry and Commerce, Crafts Chambers, credit guarantee cooperatives, cooperative equity participation corporations, and unions. Through cooperation in the network, these organizations channel resources such as capital, technology, and information to firms. For this reason, these networks can be thought of as the kind of promotional network discussed in the preceding chapter, except they are organized on a regional rather than sectoral level. It will be argued in this and the following chapters that, concurrent with the declining capacity of banks to organize *sectoral* promotional networks, banks have become increasingly important within *regional* policy or promotional networks.

Through the 1970s, government intervention and the process of industrial adjustment in North Rhine–Westphalia were consistent with the tenets of the organized capitalism model to the extent that large, centralized actors frequently managed (or at least attempted to) the process of industrial change. The comparative dominance of large firms and banks in North Rhine–Westphalia encouraged a form of Land government intervention that relied heavily on sectoral policy and direct influence over large firms. To this end, the most important institutional development in the regional economic policy network was the utilization, beginning in the early 1970s, of the Landesbank of North Rhine–Westphalia (the Westdeutsche Landesbank, or WestLB) as a major instrument of state industrial policy. By developing and using the capacities of the WestLB, including its ability to purchase large holdings of industrial firms, the Land government has been able to influence directly adjustment in particular firms and sectors. Like the major commercial banks, however, the Land government and WestLB learned that bank influence could only go so far in shaping firm and sectoral adjustment.

As the structure and organization of the regional economy shifted away from large, autarkic firms toward a more Mittelstand economy pursuing diversified quality production, the primary role of banks and government in the adjustment process also shifted. Thus, in the 1980s and 1990s, the Land government moved toward decentralizing the economic policy–making process to local actors, toward greater use of nongovernment organizations to formulate and implement policies, and away from sectoral policy (in traditional sectors) toward more support for Mittelstand firms. In a dramatic turnaround from decades of traditional roles and processes, local governments, chambers, firms, banks, and other actors in the Ruhr launched countless local cooperative initiatives aimed at promoting structural change. The dominant strategy has become that of fostering growth, jobs, and innovation by supporting the growth of the Mittelstand through the provision of collective goods. Large banks continue to exercise influence in selected large firms, but over the last decade the banks have sought increasingly to facilitate, rather than direct, the process of structural economic adjustment through the provision of expanded Allfinanz services and participation in the regional policy network.

The Reconstruction Period

Badly discredited by their owners' support of the Nazi government, the coal and steel firms of the Ruhr were politically weak and faced serious challenges to their autonomy in the early postwar years.[3] Workers demanded they be socialized. In an attempt to deflate this pressure, several steel firms gave their workers codetermination rights in 1947.[4] Still, in 1948 the parliament of the new Land of North Rhine–Westphalia passed legislation—initiated by the SPD but with substantial support from the CDU—that provided for the socialization of the coal industry. But the Allies did not warm to this idea and gradually returned ownership of the firms to the previous shareholders, a policy supported by Federal Chancellor Adenauer (Schaaf 1978, 20–50). By transferring limited sovereignty to an international body, the accession of the Federal Republic to the European Coal and Steel Community (ECSC) further solidified private ownership (Rombeck-Jaschinski 1989, 52–57). With the blessing of the ECSC and the federal government, the industrialists of the Ruhr were also allowed to reestablish to a large degree their vertical and horizontal concentration and control over production.

Economic reconstruction and the outbreak of the Korean War placed great demands on the industries of the Ruhr and kept the federal government intimately involved in the economic management of the region. Under pressure from the Allies, the federal government passed the 1950 Investment Assistance Act and a special industry tax to divert private capital from other sectors to coal and steel. As before the war, the major commercial banks invested equity and lent funds to all the major coal and steel firms. Still, between 1950 and 1954, 77 percent of long-term funds invested in these sectors came from the state (Schaaf 1978, 45–47). All this suggests the state was more crucial to the reconstruction of Germany's key industrial sectors—both as a provider of resources and through the preservation of private control—than the commercial banks. At a critical historical juncture, heavy state intervention stabilized the traditional economic structure and institutions of organized capitalism in the Ruhr.

Extensive investment in Ruhr industries and the broader economic miracle of West Germany in the 1950s brought growth and prosperity back to North Rhine–Westphalia. Social partnership embodied in the institution of codetermination became the symbol of West Germany's successful postwar compromise between capital and labor. In economic policy, the Land government of North Rhine–Westphalia adhered to the liberal principles of Erhard's social market economy. To the extent that the state still intervened in North Rhine–Westphalia's economy, it was done primarily by the federal government (Petzina 1988, 502–5).

Yet in the midst of this prosperity, a coal crisis emerged that would test the Land's commitment to economic liberalism and the capacity of organized capitalism to manage industrial change. In the late 1950s, the growing competitiveness of heating oil presented coal producers with tremendous pressures to reduce costs and capacity. Erhard based the federal government's coal policy on his belief that private market actors, with some government-provided financial incentives to reduce overcapacity, could adequately deal with the industry's problems. The Land government introduced some coal assistance measures of its own, but largely deferred to Bonn. The CDU-led Land government had neither the political will nor the capacity to intervene in the industry.[5] This reliance on the federal government, however, may well have cost the CDU control of the Land government.[6] In the 1966 elections, the SPD overtook the CDU for the first time as the largest party in the Land.[7] After a few months of negotiation, the FDP switched its allegiance and formed a coalition government with the Social Democrats. Once in power, the SPD sought to reward its supporters by publicly committing the Land government to responsibility for the more than five million inhabitants of the Ruhr. The deepening crisis of coal in 1966–67 tested the strength of this commitment and the ability of the new ruling coalition to generate policies that could affect long-term economic developments. More importantly, the coal (and later steel) crisis bared the weakness of organized capitalism and the commercial banks to manage sectoral transformation.

Coal and Steel in the Social Democratic Era

With the emergence of the Grand Coalition (CDU-SPD) in Bonn, and a Social-Liberal (SPD-FDP) coalition in North Rhine–Westphalia in 1966, the political basis for the SPD's Keynesian-inspired approach to economic management was set. In March of 1967, Federal Economics Minister Karl Schiller brought together leaders of the unions and mining companies, officials from the Land governments of North Rhine–Westphalia and the Saarland, and economic experts for a series of negotiations known as the Concerted Action Coal. In the talks, Schiller pushed the union proposal for a consolidated coal mining company as a solution to the crisis. The Land government and unions of North Rhine–Westphalia supported this but wanted a stronger social plan and codetermination measures, as well as greater efforts by the federal government to maintain higher levels of coal demand. The coal firms were also divided, with firms more dependent on coal opposing those that were controlled by the steel industry (the latter group included leaders of the Deutsche Bank and key national business associations, the Bundesverband der deutschen Industrie and the Deutscher Industrie- und Handelstag; Schaaf 1978, 280–90).

After extensive bargaining, the federal government passed the Coal Adjustment Act in 1968 based on the negotiated settlement of the Concerted Action Coal. The act provided for the consolidation of the Ruhr mining companies on a voluntary and private basis into one conglomerate—the Ruhrkohle AG (RAG). The federal and Land governments guaranteed the corporation's assets (up to DM 3.3 billion).[8] This benefited the coal and steel firms (and indirectly the major commercial banks) by saving them from having to close mines and write off large losses. In order to remain economically viable, it was agreed that coal production should be reduced according to a negotiated timetable.[9] In the 1970s RAG continued to lose money, and the owners, unions, and Land and federal governments had to negotiate several capital infusions to maintain RAG. Though Ruhrkohle nominally remained largely in private hands, it became so dependent on the state that it became de facto a nationalized concern.[10]

The steel firms and the major commercial banks that were so heavily involved in them were thereby unburdened of a very troublesome problem by the state. This was not trivial state assistance, since at the time several steel firms were facing considerable difficulties in steel markets and could ill afford to lose money through their coal operations. Continued generous financial support of the federal and Land governments in subsequent decades enabled RAG to rationalize coal production but also to diversify and substantially reduce its dependence on domestic coal production.[11] The Concerted Action Coal came to be the model for numerous subsequent sectoral rationalization plans in the Federal Republic. In this new, corporatist model, production remained in private hands while the state, firms, and banks would negotiate and finance firm restructuring and social plans for laid-off workers. But the sector that most reveals the limits of bank power, as well as the growing role of governments in firm and sectoral adjustment, is steel.

Restructuring Steel

In his seminal work, Shonfield ([1965] 1980) depicted the rationalization measures of the steel industry in the early 1960s as a prime example of what he called organized private enterprise. Underscoring this portrait, in 1967 the big commercial banks rescued the giant steel firm Krupp from bankruptcy and aided its reorganization (Esser and Fach 1989). In the first few years following the onset of the world steel crisis in the mid-1970s, the West German steel industry managed to modernize, reduce capacity, and shed tens of thousands of jobs. Thanks to successful social partnership with the unions, this process also occurred without substantial industrial strife. The German steel industry was one of the healthiest in Europe. Inspired by Shonfield and these successes, in 1983 Zysman also cited the West German steel industry's ability to manage crisis without state subsidies as a tribute to the tutelary role of the big banks and the possibilities of "private collective management of industrial change" (258–60). Indeed, the comparative success of German steel producers through the 1970s can be attributed to a significant degree to the cooperative strategy they pursued: in the 1966–67 recession the German steel firms, with state approval, formed four regional cartels that helped avoid ruinous price competition through market-sharing agreements and price coordination (Howell et al. 1988, 175–76).

However, by the late 1970s conditions in the German steel industry began to deteriorate rapidly. Cooperation among the steelmakers eroded as each firm sought to ride out the downturn in demand without reducing its capacity. Each firm hoped that competition would weed out the weaker steelmakers in West Germany and Europe. Though the German state had not played a leadership role in its steel industry since the early 1950s, by the early 1980s it became clear that none of the major firms and banks involved in the industry could provide the leadership—either alone or in consort—needed to orchestrate its orderly rationalization. As in the case of the coal industry, state involvement and subsidies became crucial to the restructuring of steel.

Beginning in 1980, a series of concerted negotiations involving the firms, unions, and federal and Land governments, including North Rhine–Westphalia, took place. Out of these talks came agreements from the federal and Land governments to provide subsidies to steel firms for R&D and pollution control investments, social assistance for laid-off workers, and job-creation programs. A special program for steel regions was also added to the federal-Land joint-task regional policy program (*Gemeinschaftsaufgabe "Verbesserung der regionalen Wirtschaftsstruktur,"* or GA) that provides tax incentives to steelmakers for investment in economically depressed areas. In the Saarland, state involvement went even further. After pouring hundreds of millions of deutschmarks into Saarstahl, the firm was taken over in 1986 by the federal and Saar governments.[12]

However, these ad hoc measures were insufficient to deal with the long-term needs of the industry. As the crisis deepened in 1981–82, the major steel-makers came under strong pressure from the banks to negotiate a sectorwide rationalization plan. With billions lent to the steel firms, significant equity stakes, and numerous bank representatives on the supervisory boards of the five largest steel firms, the three big banks were in the strongest possible position to exercise influence. Moreover, the banks, fearing default on already outstanding debts, began withholding new credits from firms, thereby adding more pressure (Vitols 1995, 34). Nonetheless, the banks' pressure on the steel firms to produce a plan for capacity reduction (through mergers, if necessary) failed. Instead, each firm sought to enhance its own position in the market while lobbying for massive state aid. In the summer of 1982, the federal government faced demands from several large steelmakers for aid totaling DM 14 billion.

Seeking a solution to the crisis without taxing its budget, the new conservative-liberal coalition in Bonn formed a strategic alliance with the big banks, asking them to generate a private sectoral plan that the state could back with DM 3 billion in subsidies. The bankers came up with a plan to form two steel groups—one in the Rhine region and one in the Ruhr (both are in North Rhine–Westphalia). But this, too, failed. Several steel firms, the unions, municipalities in the Ruhr, and the Land government of North Rhine–Westphalia opposed the plan on the grounds that the Ruhr steel group would be the inherently weaker of the two. Subsequent merger or sectoral rationalization proposals also fell apart—sometimes due to intense conflict among steelmakers, sometimes due to conflict among the federal and Land governments (Howell et al. 1988, 186–89).

Thus the steel industry responded to the early 1980s crisis without significant sectoral coordination. Individual firms continued to modernize, closing old plants, reducing capacity, and shifting from mass-produced, standardized steel products to high-quality specialty products made according to DQP principles. Negotiation and bargaining between the firms and workers were central to the success of this restructuring. The Land and federal governments significantly raised their subsidies to steel, largely for R&D subsidies and social plans.[13] The federal Loan Corporation for Reconstruction (KfW) also established a modernization program that provided substantial loans on favorable terms to the steel firms, but only in conjunction with capacity reduction plans. Private banks continued to provide financing, but at a reduced level. Social partnership and state intervention enabled the steel firms to return quickly to profitability and increase levels of investment.[14] Despite another minor crisis in 1987, throughout the 1980s and into the early 1990s the steel firms were profitable in most years and managed to steadily reduce external debts from about 20 percent of net assets in 1980 to less than 10 percent in 1992 (Vitols 1995, 21, 25).

The story of the steel industry demonstrates that Germany's system of organized capitalism—particularly the presumed industrial leadership of the big banks—has greater limits than is widely assumed. Bank influence in the industry could not produce a sectoral plan nor protect the state from demands for subsidies. In fact, sectors dominated by large firms and the banks may actually be more successful at gaining subsidies in times of dire need, as the coal and steel cases suggest. In contrast, the extensive rationalization of the clothing and textile industries in North Rhine–Westphalia, which are characterized by a large number of smaller firms, proceeded without large amounts of direct government aid nor any attempt by the banks to lead the process (Esser and Fach 1989, 246–47). In short, in two major industrial sectors where the big banks were best positioned to exercise influence, they failed to provide the sort of industrial leadership that the organized capitalism model suggests they would. The coal and steel cases also highlight the emergence of the Land government of North Rhine–Westphalia as a significant economic actor and how the banks and the state became increasingly complementary—rather than alternative—institutions for influencing sectoral adjustment.

The WestLB and the Regional Policy Network

In the late 1960s, the Land government of North Rhine–Westphalia adopted long-term structural adjustment policies with particular emphasis on regional and sectoral policies. The Land government attempted to steer and shape market processes by altering incentives for firms and occasionally through direct intervention into markets. The Land government did not seek to replace the market but did believe that it could smooth the process of change and slow it where necessary for social reasons (Landtag of North Rhine–Westphalia, publication, 16 July 1974). This new activism was undergirded with solid union support, even if the government's planning efforts did not go as far as they preferred (Adam 1988, 283–86). The pursuit of structural policies also meant that Land ministries became the central coordinating authorities for a wide range of state policies and funds.[15]

The first major regional policy initiative of the Land government was a special five-year Ruhr Development Program, introduced in 1968. The program entailed a variety of new Land government initiatives but focused primarily on infrastructure development—transportation, schools, and universities. By improving the infrastructure of the region, the Land government hoped to improve the conditions for structural change and diversification away from large-scale heavy industry through the development of new firms and industries.[16] But diversification was slow, and thus considerable funds and effort were expended by the Land government to prop up the coal and energy sectors through extensive direct subsidies to RAG and other coal producers.[17]

In the 1970s the Land government changed tactics, increasingly pursuing its industrial policy goals through direct market intervention. The primary instrument for intervention became its Landesbank—the WestLB. The Land government and the WestLB attempted to influence firms and the adjustment process in the region's most important industries—notably coal, energy, construction, and steel. The case of the WestLB is the most prominent example of how several Land governments tapped the possibility for direct intervention in industry presented by the German system of universal banking. The relationship between the WestLB and the Land government also shows how the state has influenced the institutional evolution of the banking sector according to its own economic policy goals.

This relationship, as well as the WestLB's relations to firms in the region, evolved gradually through a dynamic and at times rocky process. First, while the interest of the bank and its managers in pursuing a more activist industrial role was shared by key political leaders in the Land, their interests did not always coincide. Sustaining the industrial policy role of the bank required frequent reconciliation of conflicting interests. It also required keeping interests opposed to the bank's industrial role at bay. Second, as a commercial bank, the WestLB had the potential to influence firm decisions directly through the traditional mechanisms of bank influence, but the exercise of such influence according to industrial policy objectives was not inevitable and had to be constructed through the political will of the Land government. As an instrument for economic intervention, the WestLB offered several political advantages. It was further removed from direct bureaucratic and parliamentary control, thus allowing for greater executive autonomy in industrial policy. Since the bank operated as a commercial bank, it could also pursue state policy objectives from within the market process itself, thus avoiding the appearance (and some of the financial costs) of direct state intervention.

Remaking the WestLB

In the early 1950s, the Land government negotiated an agreement with its two regional savings bank associations that permitted the government to buy into their respective Girozentrale. Like other Länder, the government wanted to have a public bank at its disposal to handle financial matters on its behalf. Through the 1950s and 1960s, the Girozentrale administered some government business lending programs but were otherwise not involved in the government's economic policies. When the two Girozentrale fused in 1969, the initiative came from the savings bank sector itself. After negotiating a settlement within the savings bank sector, Ludwig Poullain, head of the Girozentrale in Westphalia, teamed up with the Land's finance minister, Wertz, to persuade the Land government that a larger and more industrially active Landesbank would offer advantages to it and the regional savings bank sector (Poullain 1979, 66–107). Once convinced, the Land government quickly moved enabling legislation through the parliament, and the Westdeutsche Landesbank took form.[18]

The ambitious new head of the bank, Ludwig Poullain, wasted no time in launching the WestLB into new market activities. Poullain, like many of his predecessors in the savings bank sector, believed that an important function of all the Landesbanks was to provide a competitive counterweight to the big commercial banks. This imperative was all that much greater given the deregulatory measures of the late 1960s that opened up banking markets for greater competition. In Poullain's view, the Landesbanks were sleepy, provincial banks that faced a bleak future unless they became much stronger in commercial banking markets. Poullain also wanted to make the WestLB itself—*his* bank—a more profitable, competitive, and influential bank. The WestLB's new objectives were therefore to increase long-term industrial credits to large firms, to enter into international banking, and to begin acquiring shares in industry. The last two activities were controversial and required significant public relations campaigns waged by the bank and the Land government to assuage skeptical politicians and the fears of the public. Critics of the bank's internationalization were concerned about the Land government becoming financially responsible for transactions conducted abroad, well beyond its purview. In rebuttal, the WestLB argued that international banking was absolutely necessary for it to compete as a universal bank with the big banks. The Land government supported the international expansion of the bank because it believed that its export-oriented economy would benefit.

However, the most prominent and controversial new activity of the WestLB was its involvement in industry through the purchase of shareholdings in several large firms between 1969 and 1971. The bank itself claimed this new industrial policy was necessary to expand its market share and attain a better risk distribution in its asset portfolio (Korbach 1986, 63; Girke and Kopplin 1977, 70–71). Moreover, Poullain argued that for a Landesbank to win the business of large firms, it must offer the full range of universal banking services—

including equity investments—anywhere in the nation, not just in a regional market.[19] Poullain was also intent on breaking the cartel-like practices of the big banks in underwriting, loan consortia, and international business: by holding shares in a firm, the WestLB could demand a significant quota, if not the lead, in any underwriting consortium for that firm. And in fact, after a year or so of resistance, the WestLB was accepted by the big three into their elite banking club (Poullain 1979, 80).

Pursuing such an industrial policy also served the more immediate interests of the Land government. Buying shareholdings in firms would enable the WestLB to promote structural adaptation in North Rhine–Westphalia by providing capital to promising firms and supporting troubled firms through capital infusions or preparing their merger with a stronger firm. Thus the transformation of the WestLB was made possible by the emergence of new actors in government and the bank whose response to their respective challenges yielded a mutual interest in an activist industrial bank.

The first, largest, and most widely publicized WestLB purchase was 26 percent of Preussag—a conglomerate active in construction, energy, and metals (Girke and Kopplin 1977, 66–68). The Preussag holding, one the WestLB still holds today, became the cornerstone of its industrial portfolio. The Preussag purchase also became the first instance in which the Land government used the WestLB to support its own economic intervention. In 1970 and 1971, Preussag's diversification strategy led to a growing number of loss-making operations, and its share price plummeted. In mid-1972 Poullain's patience ran out, and he forced Preussag's CEO to resign. Poullain took over the chair of the firm's supervisory board in order to oversee the sale of loss-making operations. But one operation presented the WestLB with a dilemma: Preussag's coal mines in Westphalia were unprofitable, but it would be politically disastrous for the Land's industrial bank to destroy coal mining jobs. With the global energy crisis breaking out, the Land government thought it prudent to save the mines and arranged for assistance to Preussag in order to keep the mines open (Girke and Kopplin 1977, 75–77). As part of its "preference to coal" sectoral policy, the Land government also made sure that the WestLB supported Ruhrkohle AG, even though the bank could have made a much better profit with its funds elsewhere (Poullain 1979, 84–85). Thus, while the bank pursued its own market interests, it also had to fulfill its political obligation to support industry in North Rhine–Westphalia.

By the mid-1970s, the WestLB had radically transformed itself. The bank had opened several foreign branches, and one-quarter of its balance sheet consisted of international activities (Poullain 1979, 276). From 1969 to the end of

1974, the WestLB increased the value of its equity holdings in other firms from DM 15 million to DM 791 million (Girke and Kopplin 1977, 69). Many of these early purchases were in large industrial firms, and most were initiated by the bank itself for a variety of business reasons. Several of the bank's purchases were also clearly made partly or primarily for reasons of structural policy.[20] Preussag, for example, was seen as particularly important for the government's coal policy.[21] In all cases, however, the decision to purchase major long-term shareholdings in a firm necessarily involved the Land government through its representatives—most importantly the finance minister—on the bank's administrative board. Thus, if the government was not always using the bank as an instrument of industrial policy, it was always aware of, and in a position to veto, major bank decisions.

Fighting Political Challenges to the "New" WestLB

The commitment of the Land government to the new activities of the WestLB was strongly tested on several occasions during the 1970s. In 1973, several industrial holdings of Landesbanks went sour, forcing these banks, and indirectly their governments and taxpayers, to cover large financial losses. The WestLB also had some smaller engagements that failed, but it was rocked mostly by the loss of DM 250 million in 1974 through currency trading. These spectacular losses drew national attention to the Landesbanks and stirred much debate about the merits of their new activities. The Landesbanks, including the WestLB, were criticized for their risky ventures in international finance and industrial engagements. Many argued that the banks had bought into high-risk, low-margin business in order to expand into markets where they had few skills and still fewer reasons to be.

In the face of heavy criticism from the public, the political opposition, and the major commercial banks, several Landesbanks scaled back their ambitions. But the WestLB saw no reason to alter its basic strategy and maintained that its industrial holdings were beneficial for the regional economy (Girke and Kopplin 1977, 92–95). The Land government agreed, and to underscore its commitment and involvement in the bank it put more of its ministers on the bank's administrative board after 1975 (Landtag of North Rhine–Westphalia, publication, 25 July 1974; protocol, 14 November 1974). The readiness of North Rhine–Westphalia's government to back the WestLB also had implications well beyond its borders. The WestLB was the premier Landesbank leading all the savings banks toward a greater market orientation. If the Land government had backed down, the transformation of the savings bank sector would have been slowed, as well as the intensification of group competition among the major banking groups.

Though the government was resolute in defending the new role of the WestLB, the late 1970s became a period of struggle in North Rhine–Westphalia and other Länder to find an agreeable and effective balance between the commercial interests of Landesbanks and the policy interests of their Land governments.[22] Growing structural economic adjustment problems put increasing political pressure on Länder governments, and Landesbanks were too attractive as industrial intervention tools for the Länder to ignore. But this often ran against the interest of Landesbanks as commercial organizations. Resolving the tensions between these interests would prove to be essential to the successful institutional transformation of the Landesbanks in particular, and the savings bank sector more generally. In North Rhine–Westphalia, the achievement of a stable and mutually agreeable relationship between the Land government and bank managers took several more years and was realized only after a series of conflicts and subsequently negotiated agreements.

Given his ambitious agenda for the WestLB, Ludwig Poullain began to find political control of the bank increasingly bothersome and sought to circumvent it (Poullain 1979, 85–95). For example, in 1977 Poullain bought land in London to be used for the WestLB's new branch without consulting the Land government. He had discovered that with the agreement of the government's representatives on the bank's board, the support of representatives from the regional savings bank and provincial associations was sufficient to make major decisions without informing the government itself. When the bank's action later came to light, the agitated Minister-President Kühn immediately sought to gain stronger oversight and control over the bank by forcing the provincial associations to sell their stakes in the bank to the Land government.[23] The Land parliament also decided at this point that it too should be more involved in supervising the bank ("Westdeutsche Landesbank im Parteienstreit," *Frankfurter Allgemeine Zeitung*, 19 December 1977). But this political struggle over the bank ended without any major shift in control among these political institutions. Even before the dust had settled on this matter, it was quickly overshadowed by a new scandal.

In January of 1978, Poullain was forced to resign after being accused of accepting bribes. Poullain contended they were legitimate consulting fees. An investigation by the Land parliament concluded that, legal or illegal, Poullain acted improperly and his removal was warranted.[24] But the scandal would not subside without costing the Land government a major political sacrifice. Minister-President Kühn and his finance minister, Halstenberg, were charged with hindering the investigation into Poullain's activities. Consequently, Halstenberg was forced to resign shortly after Poullain did so.

Yet one more serious scandal befell the WestLB and the Land government in 1979. This scandal traces its roots back to the early 1970s when the WestLB undertook an extremely ambitious industrial policy for the regional construction industry. Through its position as a Land, communal, and mortgage bank, the WestLB already had long-standing and extensive lending engagements in the construction sector. Now the bank wanted to use its new industrial activism to offer a more complete range of financial services in commercial, communal, and housing construction. To this end, the bank bought into numerous public and private development corporations. It also purchased holdings in construction firms in order to promote the development of construction technology and stabilize construction prices through rationalization measures. Through market analyses, the WestLB also sought to inject more systematic long-term planning into the regional construction market. The potential power of the WestLB to remake the Land's construction sector was further enhanced by its role in the distribution of public construction contracts. In effect, the WestLB aspired to achieve a position where it could lead a sectoral promotional network in the regional construction industry. In this ambitious plan, the Land government saw beneficial consequences for its growing urban renewal and development programs. In addition, as construction was a highly cyclical sector dominated by small firms and providing hundreds of thousands of jobs, the government had much to gain if the WestLB succeeded in stabilizing employment (Girke and Kopplin 1977, 72–73).

But the WestLB and the Land government eventually discovered that their powerful position did not necessarily enable them to successfully guide the development of the sector. The failure of this effort was symbolized in 1979 by a scandal involving a large construction firm—Beton und Monierbau AG (BuM). In the previous year the Land government, with approval of the parliament, had given a DM 80 million guarantee for a loan by the WestLB to BuM. The following year the firm went bankrupt, and the WestLB was charged with having deceived the Land in order to save the bank's previous loans and equity in BuM. The bank was also sued by other investors who believed the bank delayed BuM's bankruptcy to their detriment. The CDU charged the Land's finance minister, and by implication the government, with complicity in this deception, incompetence, and misfeasance (Landtag of North Rhine–Westphalia, protocols, 8 February 1980, 16 April 1980). While this scandal did not lead to a reversal of the WestLB's industrial intervention, it nonetheless underscored the point to political leaders that a more activist WestLB could cause serious polit-

ical problems. It also taught the government and bank managers that controlling the development of an entire sector is extremely difficult and risky. The
episode forced both to become more cautious in their approach to industrial intervention.

In the aftermath of the Poullain and BuM scandals, there was wide agreement in North Rhine–Westphalia that more effective supervision of the
WestLB was needed. Accordingly, the Land government and parliament
charged a new commission with developing a supervisory process that would
allow the bank sufficient freedom to operate in commercial markets while hon-
oring the government's political obligations in the bank. But most important for
the government and all the parties in the parliament was that, regardless of who
was responsible for the problems of the bank, the WestLB should get out of the
national and international headlines as quickly as possible in order to minimize
damage to the bank's image (Landtag of North Rhine–Westphalia, protocol,
25 October 1979).

In summary, by the late 1970s the industrial role of the bank had withstood
several attacks, and acceptance of this new role—in the political arena and the
marketplace—was firmly entrenched.[25] Even the opposition CDU in North
Rhine–Westphalia no longer questioned the bank's industrial activities or state
ownership per se, only the manner in which the government operated the bank.
But it was clear that not only did the supervisory process need improvement,
the bank itself needed to rethink its market strategy. In the 1970s the WestLB
grew strongly, but not as fast as the big banks. In 1980 the bank was unable to
pay a dividend, and in 1981 the bank's profits dropped 30 percent, forcing its
owners to kick in more capital (otherwise the bank would have been forced to
sell off assets). While the big commercial banks had a difficult year as well, the
WestLB's poor results were attributed by many, especially its managers, to the
low-profitability or even loss-making business that the bank did on behalf of
the Land and local governments. Many politicians blamed the managers and
called for more state control over the bank. Others floated the idea of privatizing it (Hugo Müller-Vogg, "Die Landesbanken und die Politiker," *Frankfurter
Allgemeine Zeitung,* 30 June 1981). Toward the end of 1981, a new and lasting
compact between the WestLB and the Land government finally began to emerge
with the appointment of Friedel Neuber to head the bank.

WestLB: From National to Global Player

One of the most visible components of the new compact was the agreement to
expand the commercial operations of the bank. As the 1980s unfolded, this

expansion accelerated as the WestLB increasingly sought to become a global player in international finance. The Land government actively promoted this expansion, in part because it believed that having one of Europe's, if not the world's, leading banks in its backyard could not help but have a powerfully positive impact on the regional economy. First, to sustain the bank's expansion, the Land government needed to assure steady increases in the bank's equity. Because the financially strapped local governments had not been willing to keep up with necessary capital increases, over time the Land government was able to raise its share of the WestLB's equity from 33 percent to just over 43 percent ("Nordrhein-Westfalen prüft Kapitalerhöhung bei der WestLB," *Frankfurter Allgemeine Zeitung,* 18 March 1991). With the provincial associations now holding less than 25 percent of the bank's equity, effective control is shared between the Land government—the largest shareholder—and the two regional savings bank associations.

Second, in 1988 the Land government transferred several economic grant and lending programs from its ministries into a new Investment Bank (IB) division of the WestLB. For the Land government it promised a more efficient administration of its programs. For the WestLB it provided more business. For the other banks in the Land it constituted an unfair advantage for the savings banks, since one of their banks—the WestLB—would be in charge of administering government grants and loans to firms for which all banks compete. Despite continuing political challenges by the Land's other banking groups, the government did not rescind this measure (Mussler 1989).

Finally, with the approval of the Land government, in 1989 the WestLB made a major push to expand its international capabilities with the purchase of the European branches of the British Standard Charter Bank. The Land government expected that a more internationalized WestLB would promote exports by regional firms, including the Mittelstand. The WestLB itself knew that to remain competitive in business with large firms and capture new market opportunities, it would need to have a stronger international presence. This purchase was very expensive and politically controversial within North Rhine–Westphalia. Moreover, to help finance the WestLB's international expansion, the Land government agreed to merge its housing finance agency with the WestLB in 1991. This added DM 4 billion to the equity of the WestLB, creating a tremendous potential for expansion. The other banking groups howled in protest, but to no avail. The Land government was convinced that the capital and political cost was justified by the potential benefits for regional firms.[26] The WestLB has since been using its strengthened equity base to build up its domestic and international investment banking capacities.

The new compact between the WestLB and the Land government did not mean the withdrawal of the WestLB from active industrial intervention. Indeed, in an era in which the big banks have tendentiously reduced their shareholdings, the WestLB has systematically expanded its industrial portfolio. Shortly after assuming control of the WestLB in 1981, Friedel Neuber reorganized the bank and announced that decisions to purchase holdings in firms would henceforth be made with greater consideration of profitability and less consideration of the Land government's structural policy requirements. The bank was still burdened with vestiges of its pre-1969 civil service bureaucracy, and Neuber eventually went outside to hire the industrial management experience that the bank still lacked.[27] The Land government, for its part, was willing to let the bank orient its operations more toward market requirements. Yet by no means did this mean the end of the WestLB as an instrument of economic policy. This role of the WestLB, in fact, expanded further in subsequent years. This was possible in part because the Land government showed greater self-restraint in not forcing the bank into engagements with little or no hope of eventual profitability. The new working relationship between the bank and the Land government kept both intimately involved in the affairs of regional industry.

In 1986 the WestLB announced a long-term strategy to build up its equity holdings in industry in order to compensate for declining loan business with large firms. And the WestLB held to its plan: in 1990 alone the WestLB bought 30 (and sold 18) holdings in firms, raising the total value of its holdings to DM 3.2 billion—a level comparable to the Dresdner Bank and Commerzbank ("WestLB: Europastrategie kommt gut voran," *Frankfurter Allgemeine Zeitung,* 17 May 1990). Despite this expansion, the WestLB's industrial holdings portfolio is still firmly rooted in the region. Nearly all of the WestLB's major holdings are in firms that have headquarters or extensive operations in North Rhine–Westphalia (Neuber 1993). The Land government thus continues to support—and largely makes possible—this industrial strategy because it facilitates the adjustment of regional firms to changes in the European and global markets.

For example, in 1990 Germany's largest charter airline, LTU, was on the verge of moving from Düsseldorf (the North Rhine–Westphalia capital city) to Munich, no doubt with encouragement from the Bavarian government. The jobs of LTU were important to the Land government, but LTU was also a critical part of the government's long-term plan to build up the Land as a center for air traffic in Europe. To preempt this move, the WestLB, acting with the support of the Land government, purchased a controlling interest in the firm.[28] Since the initial purchase of LTU, the WestLB has supported LTU's plan to become a major tourism and travel conglomerate through further acquisitions.[29]

The WestLB views these as long-term holdings and expects to profit from the rapidly growing tourism industry ("Neuber kritisiert Sachverständige," *Handelsblatt,* 27 June 1994).

Even more driven by the Land government's regional economic concerns are the WestLB's holdings in the machinery industry. The most important of the bank's many holdings in this sector is Gildemeister, one of Europe's largest machine tool companies and located in North Rhine–Westphalia. Since the WestLB first purchased a holding in 1969 (it had a 20 percent stake by 1995), the bank has gone to great lengths—including several debt cancellations—to support the expansion of the firm. During the early 1990s national crisis of the machine tool sector, the Land government gave the firm DM 40 million in loan guarantees ("Gute Zeiten, schlechte Zeiten in Ostwestfalen," *Handelsblatt,* 10 October 1995). Despite its weak financial position, in mid-1994 Gildemeister acquired another major and bankrupt machine tool firm (Deckel Maho) with the help of the WestLB.[30] In 1994 the WestLB sought to raise from 25 percent to 50 percent its stake in Autania, a holding company that owns shares in close to 30 machine tool companies. These moves prompted observers to speculate that the WestLB sought sufficient influence to shape and force the pace of sectoral change. In other words, the WestLB may be attempting to construct a promotional network in the sector. Indeed, the WestLB itself indicated that it would like to use its holdings to promote sectoral rationalization through consolidation among smaller firms ("Die WestLB zielt verstärkt auf den Werkzeugmaschinenbau," *Frankfurter Allgemeine Zeitung,* 18 May 1994). To the extent the WestLB succeeds in this, it is surely only possible because the bank and the Land government are willing to accept losses or low returns in these investments. Even so, the bank's plans created considerable unrest within the industry and were challenged by other machine tool makers in North Rhine–Westphalia.[31] This resistance probably contributed to the bank's later decision to not raise its holding in Autania (Lothar Schnitzler, "Wieder aufatmen," *Wirtschaftswoche,* 31 August 1995). As was the case with the regional construction industry during the 1970s, this suggests it will not be easy for the WestLB to transform its obligational network with machine tool makers into a sectoral promotional network.

More generally, as part of a strategy to stabilize Ruhr industry, since the early 1970s the Land government and especially the WestLB came to be intricately involved as major actors in the various networks of interlocking shareholdings and directorates involving banks and the major firms in the coal, steel, and energy sectors.[32] This insider position within the regional corporate monitoring network enables them to gain extensive information about the plans of key large firms. Both parties have used this information to pursue various objectives. The Land government, for example, has used it to prepare for impending plant closings or layoffs; the WestLB has used it to track sectoral developments that affect its business and occasionally to influence firm and sectoral developments. This insider position also enabled the Land government and the WestLB to compete with the big banks for influence in regional industry.

For example, at the end of 1991 the steelmaker Krupp successfully completed a hostile takeover—a rare event in West Germany—of Hoesch, a fellow Ruhr steelmaker. The takeover was masterminded by Krupp boss Gerhard Cromme and Friedel Neuber, head of the WestLB and chair of Krupp's supervisory board. In the year leading up to the takeover, Krupp secretly acquired 24.9 percent of Hoesch's voting stock. With another 30 percent of Hoesch's stock controlled between the WestLB and a collaborating Swiss bank, Hoesch's managers had little chance to mount a defense (Ferdinand Protzman, "Krupp Takes Control of Hoesch's Stock," *New York Times,* 11 November 1991).[33] But the WestLB did far more to make the takeover possible than simply throwing its vote behind Krupp. Over several years preceding the deal, Neuber managed to displace the Deutsche and Dresdner Banks as two of Krupp's major house banks. Since the Deutsche Bank was Hoesch's chief house bank and controlled the chair of Hoesch's supervisory board, the takeover proved to be an embarrassment for the Deutsche Bank.[34] On the one hand, this example illustrates again how banks still influence certain firms. On the other hand, it demonstrates the incapacity for collective negotiation of a sectoral rationalization plan: earlier merger talks in the industry—including between Krupp and Hoesch—intended to reduce capacity and financially strengthen the steel firms had failed. Thus the Hoesch takeover was orchestrated through market mechanisms more characteristic of Anglo-Saxon capitalism. When Krupp attempted a hostile takeover of Thyssen, another major steel firm, in early 1997, it turned to Goldman Sachs and the Deutsche and Dresdner Banks, rather than the WestLB. But it was Johannes Rau who brought the CEOs of the two firms together and mediated their ultimate agreement to merge their steel operations (Balzer and Wilhelm 1997c).

In summary, the Land government's policies for the coal, energy, and steel sectors—all vital to its economy—constitute more than the absorption of the costs of economic adjustment by the state, as the widely held view of the German model would have us believe. The Land government and the WestLB came to be important market actors in the regional economic adjustment process. Moreover, the expansion of markets as economic governance institutions in the EU makes it that much more valuable for the Land government to be itself a powerful market actor via the WestLB.[35] The bank and the Land government have shown they can compete with the major commercial banks for such influence in industry. But like the big banks, they discovered that controlling sectoral developments is extremely difficult and that bank influence is likely to be consistently effective only on the individual firm level.

Diversified Quality Production and New Policy Directions

Despite the decline of regional industry, in 1987 North Rhine–Westphalia still accounted for 27.7 percent of total national revenue in the mining and manufacturing sector. In all major branches within this sector, North Rhine–Westphalia's national share was greater than 27.7 percent, except in electronics and motor vehicles.[36] In this respect North Rhine–Westphalia is the mirror image of its two fast-growing southern rivals—Baden-Württemberg and Bavaria—where electronics and motor vehicle production constitute a disproportionately large share of total output. More importantly, through the 1970s the Land's growth rate had only slowly fallen behind the national average. But in the 1980s North Rhine–Westphalia fell far behind, seemingly uncoupled from the rest of the nation (table 8). Consequently, North Rhine–Westphalia's share of national gross domestic product dropped from 31.9 percent in 1950 to 26.1 percent in 1988 (Burdack 1990, 62). Much of this relative decline is attributable to the continuing problems of the Ruhr region.

TABLE 8.   Selected Länder and Federal Economic Data

	NRW w/o Ruhr	NRW	Ruhr	FRG	BAV	B-W
Population (1988; millions)	12.1	16.8	4.7	61.3	11.0	9.4
Workforce in manufacturing (%, 1987)		42.7		40.4	41.8	48.1
Workforce in services (%, 1987)		55.2		54.5	49.2	47.0
Unemployment rate (1989)	8.3	9.4	12.1	7.3	4.9	4.3
Workforce in large firms[a] (%)	34.5	40.5	58.1	39.2	37.4	36.9
Real GDP growth (%)						
1960–70		53.6		60.3[b]	66.2	70.8
1970–80		25.4		32.6[b]	39.3	32.1
1980–88		7.7		16.9[b]	22.3	17.7
Total R&D personnel in FRG[c] (%)		22.3			23.1	24.3

Source: Burdack 1990; Schatz and Maas 1988, 248.

Note: NRW = North Rhine–Westphalia; FRG = Federal Republic of Germany; BAV = Bavaria; B-W = Baden-Württemberg.

[a]Firms with more than 1,000 employees (1988)

[b]FRG without NRW

[c]R&D personnel employed in firms (1983)

In addition to sectoral decline, there have been significant changes in the organization of production in the regional economy. Key indicators of these changes are the size distribution of firms and the production strategy of firms, including the nature of relations between large and small firms. While large firms remain very prominent in North Rhine–Westphalia (in the Ruhr they still accounted for nearly 60 percent of employment in the late 1980s; table 8), they no longer dominate production and employment as they did in earlier decades. For example, of the more than 600,000 coal miners in 1957, fewer than 150,000 remained in 1989; in the steel sector, employment declined from 375,000 workers in 1970 to 181,000 by 1988 (Hamm and Wienert 1990, 154). Conversely, the number of manufacturing firms with *more* than 20 employees in North Rhine–Westphalia rose from 26,023 in 1978 to 27,352 in 1984. Since total industrial employment declined in this same period, the average manufacturing firm dropped from 83.3 employees to 69.3.[37] In addition, the Land government's figures show that the number of industrial firms with *fewer* than 20 employees increased between 1977 and 1986 (by 1,471 firms, to 16,594; Landtag of North Rhine–Westphalia, protocol, 15 December 1988, 8885). Many of these firms were established by former employees of large firms in the region (which also encouraged this) in order to provide their former employer with specialized production or production-oriented services. This type of decentralization of production and supplier-contractor relations is consistent with the general requisites of DQP.

The case of the turnkey plant construction industry is a prime example of this decentralization process in the Ruhr. Several of the huge industrial concerns in the Ruhr, especially the big steel firms such as Krupp, diversified into the construction of ready-made production complexes such as power plants, steel mills, and chemical factories.[38] But unlike in the past, when large firms centralized production internally, in this industry the large concerns of the Ruhr offer integrated system solutions to their customers—from manufacturing to maintenance to finance—but rely on a host of other, smaller firms to provide the individual components (Grabher 1990).[39] This case exemplifies what appear to be broader changes in the organization of production in North Rhine–Westphalia's economy. Traditionally, the small firms of the Ruhr were heavily dependent on the large firms. Rigid, hierarchical relations in which the large dominated the small were typical. Now many small firms are thriving, and interfirm networks based on nonauthoritative cooperation are beginning to form. Many of the smaller supplier firms of the Ruhr are finding new markets, thereby decreasing their dependence on a few large firms (Hamm and Wienert 1990, 158–68).

Yet the revival of the Ruhr remains elusive. Many of the Mittelstand firms still remain dependent on the large firms, and the overall level of R&D activity in Ruhr Mittelstand firms—a key element of DQP—was slow to increase (Schatz and Maas 1988, 247). The provision of production-oriented services and critical business information for Mittelstand firms is also comparatively weak (Lehner, Geile, and Nordhaus-Janz 1987). Thus there is an important deficit in the institutional environment that enables smaller firms and interfirm networks—hallmarks of DQP—to thrive. It is exactly this deficit that the Land government sought to close with new Mittelstand policies adopted during the 1980s and 1990s. It is also a deficit that the banks increasingly sought to close through their participation in creating or sustaining organizations that support the Mittelstand and DQP, as well as through the pursuit of Allfinanz.

A Social Democratic Mittelstand Model

When the provision of government support to the Mittelstand became popular in regional and national politics in the mid-1970s, the Land government of North Rhine–Westphalia had followed suit. Between 1975 and 1978, a series of Mittelstand promotion measures were adopted, including the introduction of a liquidity assistance program for troubled firms, export promotion, technology promotion, and the extension of soft loan programs beyond craft and retail firms to manufacturing Mittelstand firms. The regional policy network was also expanded through the creation of new institutions, such as a quasi-public capital participation corporation.[40] Despite these measures, throughout the 1970s the Land government decidedly emphasized centrally developed and administered regional and sectoral policies focused on the Ruhr and its key industries.[41] In the 1980s, however, the Land government began shifting its policy emphasis from centralized structural policies toward the Mittelstand promotion policies typical of the southern German states. This Mittelstand model of firm promotion relies primarily on indirect government support for firms through aid to private and quasi-public organizations that provide production-oriented services and goods. In turning to this model, the Land government expanded the scope and intensity of resource exchange among organizations within its regional economic policy network. More organizations, especially ones with a local focus, were incorporated into this network. As part of its new compact with the Land government, the WestLB took a primary position in this Mittelstand-oriented network by supporting organizations that assist the Mittelstand. This new direction in economic policy was symbolically reflected in a change of government rhetoric from planning and steering to decentralization and endogenous development.

The adoption of this new direction can be attributed to several factors. First, the change was driven in part by the Land government's rapidly growing debt burden, due in good measure to its Ruhr subsidies. It was clear that after pumping billions of deutschmarks into the Ruhr, the loss of coal and steel jobs had only been slowed, while too few new ones had arisen to take their place. Moreover, throughout the 1970s the government had been repeatedly criticized for focusing too heavily on the Ruhr and its large firms. Even the head of the German Federation of Labor in North Rhine–Westphalia criticized the Land government's structural policies as being crisis-driven and neglectful of Mittelstand firms and their workers (Landtag of North Rhine–Westphalia, publication, 5 August 1981). Second, the lesson was not lost on the government, unions, and other key producer groups that jobs were being created to a large extent in smaller firms in other sectors and other regions of the Land. Thus Mittelstand-oriented policies were developed to reinforce these structural changes and the movement to DQP in both large and small firms. And finally, the runaway economic success of the southern Länder fueled the belief in North Rhine–Westphalia that the government must do more to stimulate the growth and creation of innovative Mittelstand firms.

The conversion of the Land government to a more Mittelstand-focused economic strategy began in earnest in 1982 when the CDU introduced a measure in the Land parliament that opened lengthy discussion and debate about technology policy. There was growing belief among all the political parties and social groups in the region that new technological challenges necessitated a new political and social approach to economic policy. On the more tangible side, the microelectronics industry was seen in West Germany, as throughout the industrial world, as the key sector of the future. In Bavaria and Baden-Württemberg, this sector was strong and growing fast at the same time as these Land governments were heavily subsidizing R&D and technology transfer in Mittelstand firms.[42] The fact that federal technology funds flowed disproportionately to the southern Länder reinforced the belief that North Rhine–Westphalia was falling behind and that its firms were unfairly disadvantaged (Jens 1989).[43] Competition from the south, the weakness of North Rhine–Westphalia's high-tech sectors—especially electronics—and the low research intensity of its firms caused alarm among North Rhine–Westphalia's policymakers.

Finally, in 1984 the Land government called for a concerted action approach to economic modernization and held a conference with representatives from the unions, industry, and academia to develop and legitimize new policy initiatives, especially in technology policy. While the content and implementation process of North Rhine–Westphalia's technology policies came to resemble those of the southern Länder, in North Rhine–Westphalia the Land government sought to secure greater union involvement in the technology decisions of the government and individual firms.[44] While this was heavily criticized by business as giving workers de facto veto rights, the Land government needed to show workers that it would safeguard them from a one-sided adjustment burden due to technological change and the reorganization of work. Moreover, the willingness of the unions and the SPD party faithful to deemphasize sectoral policy and the Ruhr in order to back a more Mittelstand-oriented policy (with a heavy technology focus) provided indispensable political support that needed to be rewarded.[45]

As in Bavaria and Baden-Württemberg, the cornerstone of the Land government's Mittelstand promotion model came to be technology policy implemented through greater cooperation with organizations in the regional policy network. Technology policy in particular was intended to stimulate the creation of networks of firm cooperation and networks of cooperation among local governments and other organizations that could provide firms with essential resources needed for DQP. In 1984 the government initiated this strategy by providing funds for a new technology transfer center called ZENIT (Zentrum für Innovation und Technik). The initiative for this project came from a group of Mittelstand firms in North Rhine–Westphalia. These firms wanted to create an organization run by the private sector that would provide technical information to firms, supply information about capital sources such as venture capital, and find cooperation partners for firms. ZENIT was also intended to act as a central consulting office for the local technology centers or parks rapidly proliferating throughout North Rhine–Westphalia.[46] A few years later, the Land government encouraged the WestLB to join ZENIT and contribute both capital and know-how to the consortium.[47]

The shifting content of policy (from structural to technology), as well as changes in its formulation and implementation (more decentralized), was aptly stated by the economics minister, Reimut Jochimsen, when he wrote regarding ZENIT and the growing number of local technology initiatives.

These enormous and admirable local efforts are not to be replaced through a centralized planning and steering "from above." The Model North Rhine–Westphalia in technology promotion therefore means decentralization, local consensus, cooperation, and financial support as an impulse to self-help. In this sense the Land government will promote new forms of cooperation, setting in motion self-steering processes with financial support for a limited time and degressively structured. . . . The Land government is resolved to answer the new technical challenges with new forms of state action. (Economics Ministry of North Rhine–Westphalia 1988, 6; my translation)

In line with this technology emphasis, the Land government expanded its Mittelstand-oriented technology program from 1978 (Technologieprogramm Wirtschaft, or TPW) with an additional program in 1985.[48] The new TPZ (Technologieprogramm Zukunft) program provided financial support for research projects in eight technology fields.[49] In contrast to the TPW, the TPZ program emphasized indirect support to Mittelstand firms through an expansion of the research capacity of the Land's universities (Lehner et al. 1989). These technology efforts were substantial, as attested by the fact that in the mid-1980s the proportion of all R&D spending in North Rhine–Westphalia provided by the Land government was relatively higher than that in other Länder.[50]

However, the Land government did not limit its Mittelstand support to technology policy. In the mid-1980s, the government also established a working group to overhaul its export promotion policies, an increasingly important policy area given the traditionally strong export orientation of North Rhine–Westphalia and the new Single Market initiative of the EC. Made up of government, bank, and industry representatives, the group worked out a variety of new measures by which the Land government could promote the activities of and further coordination among the chambers, industry organizations, and other associations that provide export-related services to Mittelstand firms.[51] As a complementary measure, the Land government supported the international branch expansion and other measures of the WestLB intended to promote the exports of regional Mittelstand firms. In the mid-1980s, for example, the WestLB established a trade promotion department to develop export markets and identify foreign production partners for regional Mittelstand firms. This service to the individual savings banks and their Mittelstand clients enables these banks to compete more effectively with local branches of the big banks that have strong foreign trade experience.[52] The WestLB also played a formative role—along with the city of Cologne, the Cologne Chamber of Industry and Commerce, and the Trade Fair Corporation of Cologne—in the establishment of several specialized export consulting firms intended to promote Mittelstand exports from North Rhine–Westphalia to China, Japan, and Korea.[53]

In the late 1980s, regional policy was also reoriented to provide more support for the institutional support network of Mittelstand firms. Since the early 1970s, the joint federal-Land regional promotion program (GA) had been a central instrument of the Land government's economic intervention. In the 1980s the GA came under heavy criticism from many directions. The Council of Experts (Sachverständigenrat), a group that advises the federal government on its economic policies, criticized the GA and used the example of the Ruhr to argue how numerous factors, including overly centralized control of the GA in Land government hands, hindered structural change in the region (German Bundestag 1988). The Land government of North Rhine–Westphalia responded by petitioning the federal government to alter the GA rules so that GA funds could be used to support Mittelstand consulting offices, innovation in manufacturing and service firms, and the creation of local economic development plans (Landtag of North Rhine–Westphalia, protocol, 26 January 1989, 9063).[54]

Decentralizing the Regional Policy Network

In the midst of another major Ruhr crisis in 1987, the Land government launched a new regional development program, (Zukunftsinitiative Montanregion, or ZIM). On the surface, ZIM appeared a throwback to earlier centralized Ruhr development programs, but the real innovation of ZIM was not its content but the process by which funds were to be dispensed. Under ZIM, the infrastructure projects to be funded were to be selected at the local level by consensus among local unions, government, chambers, business associations, and other relevant organizations. ZIM was thus intended to increase further cooperation among local actors and allow them to better use local knowledge in promoting structural adjustment.[55] In designing ZIM, the Land government consciously sought to follow what it perceived to be the national and international trend toward decentralization and public-private partnership (Landtag of North Rhine–Westphalia, publication 10/3552, 21–22). In the 1990s, the Land government continued this process of decentralizing its own regional policy network through the ZIN (Zukunftsinitiative Nordrhein-Westfalen) program of 1989. Under ZIN, the Land government began sharing responsibility for the development and implementation of structural policy with 15 subregions covering the entire state. Each region developed a regional structural plan tailored to local needs that would be coordinated and supported by the Land government. The chief effect of this change has been a further strengthening of interorganizational cooperation in the subregions and North Rhine–Westphalia as a whole (Economics Ministry of North Rhine–Westphalia 1992; Jochimsen 1992).

With the advent of the Single Market and other steps to greater market integration in Europe, the Land government stepped up its emphasis on support

for the Mittelstand and technology in the 1990s. The government has stated explicitly and repeatedly its belief that the best strategy for promoting regional
competitiveness in the broader European market is through support for leading
technologies and the production of quality products, and that the motor of regional development is the Mittelstand ("Schnittstellen zwischen Forschung und
Produktion," *Handelsblatt,* 7 April 1993; "Landesregierung strafft Förderung
kleiner and mittelständischer Unternehmen," *Handelsblatt,* 26 July 1993).
More generally, it is widely recognized, including in North Rhine–Westphalia,
that market integration enhances the mobility of capital. Thus state promotion
of less mobile resources—education, technology, firm networks, etc.—is gaining further significance. From the perspective of the Land government, the
WestLB and savings banks are essential to these efforts through the expansion
of their Allfinanz capacities and their support for other regional policy network
organizations that promote the Mittelstand and DQP.

The Savings Bank Sector in the Regional Policy Network
In chapter 2 it was argued that the savings and cooperative banks have been successful in commercial banking, in large part because of their focus on the Mittelstand. But in North Rhine—Westphalia, the historic dominance of the big
banks and large firms limited for a long time the expansion of these other bank
groups. The savings banks profited from the payroll and savings deposits of factory workers, but the dearth of entrepreneurs meant relatively few cooperative
banks were formed in North Rhine–Westphalia (Siepmann 1968). Savings and
cooperative banks were more successful in regions of North Rhine–Westphalia
where production was traditionally done in smaller firms, such as the Bergische and Siegen regions. Despite these historical disadvantages, since the
1970s savings and cooperative banks in North Rhine–Westphalia have done
very well in commercial banking, partly as a result of the shift in employment
and production from large to smaller firms. The current success of all three
banking groups in North Rhine–Westphalia is attested by the fact that all now
have regional market shares above their respective national averages: in loans
to businesses, the big banks have a 21.1 percent market share in North
Rhine–Westphalia, while their national market share is 13.2 percent; savings
banks have a 28.9 percent market share in North Rhine–Westphalia but only
20.3 percent nationally; and cooperative banks have 13.3 percent and 11.9 percent respectively.[56]

The relative success of the savings banks can also be attributed to government policy. Just as the Land government supported the growth of the WestLB
to promote regional adjustment, in the 1980s the Land government undertook

numerous measures to increase the competitiveness of its savings banks in Mittelstand finance. In this sense the government's savings bank policies are designed to flank its Mittelstand promotion strategy. An example of this is provided by equity participation corporations (KBGs). Since savings banks are generally prohibited from holding equity in nonfinancial firms, establishing a KBG requires approval of a Land government. In the late 1980s, the North Rhine–Westphalia Economics Ministry approved several savings bank KBGs in order to improve the availability of equity capital for Mittelstand firms.[57] To minimize risk, the ministry required these savings banks to demonstrate sufficient technical knowledge, either in the form of in-house personnel or through cooperation with another local organization such as a university, Chamber of Industry, or Landesbank (Brockhaus 1984).

The government's savings bank policies also strengthened the federalist structure of the savings bank sector, that is, intensified vertical cooperation between the savings banks and the WestLB. For example, cooperation between the WestLB and savings banks enables many savings banks to help selected Mittelstand firms go public. The ability to provide such services is crucial for savings banks to remain competitive with the major commercial banks in North Rhine–Westphalia (Prautzsch 1990). The impact of such bank services on Mittelstand firms is multiplied through their frequent combination with the services and resources provided to Mittelstand firms through other local organizations.

The city of Aachen demonstrates quite well how many local savings banks have become involved in building local interorganizational networks that promote Mittelstand firms. While not located in the Ruhr, Aachen is an old coal mining town and has therefore suffered similar decline. In the early 1980s, the city government, the local Chamber of Industry and Commerce, local savings banks, and other organizations formed a nonprofit organization for technology promotion. In 1983 this group established a technology center to house new, innovative firms, many of which were started by students from the city's technical university. The Chamber of Industry and the university also established a program to promote technology transfer out of the university into local firms. At the same time, the savings bank of Aachen created a special lending program for innovative firms and built contacts to local research institutes and universities to help it assess technology loans. In 1987 this local group was joined by the Land government and the WestLB in the creation of another center to promote the transfer of computer integrated manufacturing technology into local firms. And in 1988 six local savings banks, with permission of the Land government, established an equity participation corporation to provide investment capital for promising local Mittelstand firms (Rosen 1990).[58] By early 1997, there were 12 technology centers/small business parks in the region housing 370 firms (90 have already outgrown them and resettled in the region), and the regional savings banks were planning a new venture capital fund to promote high-risk, high-tech ventures (Bräutigam and Bartz-Adrian 1997). Building on this kind of successful cooperation, in 1995 the government launched a new campaign, in conjunction with organizations from the regional policy network and especially the savings banks, to stimulate new firm formation. In 1997 the government proposed the creation of a regional risk capital fund (with major contributions from the banks) to provide DM 100 million in equity to small, innovative firms (Clement 1997).

Given the demonstrated commitment and capacity of the WestLB and savings banks to support local and Land economic policy, the Land government remains strongly committed to preserving the competitiveness of its public banking sector and realizes that these banks must have greater flexibility to compete successfully in a more integrated European marketplace. To this end, in 1994 the government amended its savings bank law. The amendments liberalized restrictions on savings bank activities, thus enhancing their ability to adopt or develop new financial products, especially in securities markets. In light of growing pressures to privatize public banks, the amendments also raised the legal barriers to privatization of savings banks while making it easier for savings banks to raise equity and thus minimize the temptation for the banks themselves to seek privatization (Heinz Schleusser, "Mehr Bewegungsfreiheit für die Sparkassen," *Börsen-Zeitung,* 19 February 1994). In sum, North Rhine–Westphalia continues the long tradition of actively promoting a public banking sector in order to maintain group bank competition, to support Mittelstand firms, and to support local and Land governments in their economic development policies.

Summary

The pattern of sectoral adjustment in North Rhine–Westphalia's coal and steel industries demonstrates the limited capacity of the big banks to manage the process of industrial change. In the face of severe contraction and long-term sectoral decline, the burden of adjustment was increasingly assumed by the federal and Land governments. But the state did more than simply subsidize the decisions and production strategies of private producers. Through various mechanisms, including the WestLB, the state frequently shaped the decisions of firms and thus sectoral adjustment. Through the 1970s, the process of industrial adjustment in North Rhine–Westphalia appeared consistent with the organized capitalism model to the extent that a relatively small group of actors exercising extensive control or influence over their respective social, economic, or political spheres negotiated agreements on major industrial changes. The predominance of large firms and banks in the region also favored the pursuit of centralized and more direct government intervention into the regional economy. The Ruhr policies of the Land government and support for traditional producers favored the preservation of the traditional hierarchical organization of production in these sectors. Thus centralized public crisis management replaced to a significant extent private collective management. However, in the course of the 1980s, both types of centralized management became less and less viable (see also Katzenstein 1989, 341).

The organization of production and the process of industrial adjustment in particular sectors and North Rhine–Westphalia as a whole began to change perceptibly starting in the late 1970s. Large firms began to decentralize, while the number of smaller firms began to grow. Diversified quality production became an increasingly common strategy for producers, linking large and small firms in new ways and giving the latter an increasingly important role in production. Through its investments in organizations of the regional policy network that provide collective goods such as technical training and R&D, as well as through aid to firm networks and associations, the Land government began to promote Mittelstand firms and DQP strategies. Sounding more like CDU-dominated Länder, by the late 1980s the SPD and Land government in North Rhine–Westphalia were praising the Mittelstand as the motor of the region's economy.[59]

Clearly, however, the extent to which smaller firms and DQP principles expand their presence in various sectors in North Rhine–Westphalia will be determined by and large by private actors, not the state. Sectors dominated by large hierarchies are far more amenable to direct state control and direction than are sectors dominated by a large number of smaller producers. But the evidence suggests that the state can play an important role in promoting these latter sectors by producing and allocating essential resources and information to them. The expansion of the banks' Allfinanz capacities must also be viewed as an important component of a supportive institutional environment for Mittelstand firms. The Land government's support for its Landesbank and savings banks through resources and regulatory changes was to a significant degree designed to expand their role as a critical element of such an institutional environment. Hence these bank and state strategies are highly complementary in promoting the Mittelstand and DQP.

CHAPTER 5

Baden-Württemberg: Economic Adjustment
in a Decentralized Regional Economy

In Baden-Württemberg, the institutional preconditions for organized capitalism are, and have always been, weaker than elsewhere in Germany. Economic concentration is low because of the large number of small- and medium-sized firms. Well-developed patterns of direct and indirect cooperation among firms are institutionalized in collaborative contracting relations, associations, and numerous other forms. Large firms are comparatively decentralized, relying on long-term subcontracting arrangements with local Mittelstand suppliers. Industrial finance is provided to a high degree by relatively small savings and cooperative banks that own no shares in regional industry. Indeed, the maintenance and strength of a decentralized (federalist) regional financial system was a critical institutional precondition for Baden-Württemberg to maintain its system of decentralized production. In Baden-Württemberg, government intervention is largely subsidiary or market-conforming. The Land government relies on close cooperation with chambers, associations, banks, and the like to promote individual firms, sectors, and subregions. In all these and other respects, production in Baden-Württemberg was always closer to the diversified quality production than the Fordist model of production. Thus, in the 1970s and 1980s, as other sectors and regions in Germany moved toward DQP, Baden-Württemberg and its Mittelstand firms and banks found themselves in a favorable position to profit from changed domestic and international economic conditions.

This does not mean, however, that producers in Baden-Württemberg did not face structural economic adjustment pressures. When faced with such pressures, the Baden-Württemberg economy adjusted quite successfully by deepening its traditionally decentralized pattern of industrial organization with its emphasis on DQP. The Land government and regional producer groups responded collectively to adjustment pressures through the dramatic expansion of the regional policy network. Adjustment in individual firms and sectors was thus facilitated through the provision of essential resources via the public and private organizations of this network. The regional banking sector facilitated adjustment through the continued provision of long-term financing and deeper cooperation with other organizations in the regional policy network. Direct bank intervention in firms plays a comparatively minor role in facilitating regional economic adjustment. Given this interdependence among producers and the institutions of the regional policy network, industrial adjustment in Baden-Württemberg is best analyzed at the regional level, not simply at the firm or sectoral level.

This chapter proceeds first with a brief overview of the historical development of Baden-Württemberg's regional economic policy network and decentralized production system. The chapter then examines three periods of crisis and adjustment in Baden-Württemberg: the first period follows the recession of 1974–75, the second follows the 1982–83 recession, and the third follows the 1992–93 recession.

Decentralized Industrialization and the Regional Policy Network

Until World War I, the state of Württemberg was considered an impoverished industrial laggard. By the end of the 1920s, the region had become Germany's second most industrialized and prosperous region (Megerle 1982).[1] In the Depression era, Württemberg's unemployment rate was approximately half that of the Reich. The prevalence of small, widely distributed firms producing goods with skilled and flexible labor helped them to change quickly their output to other goods in higher demand.[2] Stability was also aided by a broad industrial base. The early consumer goods sectors (notably textiles/clothing and food products) were augmented by rapidly growing investment goods industries— machinery, electronics, and motor vehicles—in the early 1900s.

This pattern of small-scale, decentralized industrialization arose out of particular social and economic traditions of the region. The scarcity of natural resources and high cost of energy and transportation favored industrial production that emphasized skilled processing and finishing.[3] In turn, the emphasis on skill and quality in production also restrained the centralization of production, as work had to follow the widely dispersed and generally immobile labor force. Reflecting the organization of production, the banking sector in Baden and Württemberg was heavily dominated until the 1920s by a large number of widely dispersed savings and cooperative banks and a few regional commercial banks.[4] The Württembergische Vereinsbank and the Rheinische Creditbank had a virtual duopoly over banking business with larger firms in the region until taken over by the Deutsche Bank in the 1920s.[5] However, the spread of the big banks into the region did not affect the predominance of the savings and cooperative banks in Mittelstand business.

The pattern of state-society relations and the early regional policy network—formed in the second half of the nineteenth century—also reinforced production in small firms. In 1848 the government of Württemberg created the Centralstelle für Gewerbe und Handel (Central Office for Trades and Commerce) (Wauschkuhn 1977).[6] Under the direction of Ferdinand Steinbeis, the Centralstelle worked closely with the new chambers of commerce and industry (in the key industrial cities of Stuttgart, Heilbronn, Ulm, and Reutlingen) to promote the technical modernization of local industry.[7] Probably most important of all, Steinbeis and the Centralstelle were leaders in creating a new system of higher-level vocational schools under the control of local business and community leaders. Starting from the first school in 1854 in Heilbronn, by the early 1870s Württemberg was covered with 155 vocational schools educating over 100,000 students. Many of these *Fachschulen* were the direct precursors of today's engineering polytechnics known as *Fachhochschulen* (FHS) (Klagholz 1986).[8] The creation of a skilled labor force and technical innovation through these schools were central to the region's production system.

Through such combinations of public and private resources focused on vocational education, technology development and transfer, and capital provision, the Centralstelle and chambers became the core of a regional policy network that still today provides essential collective and selective (e.g., firm consulting) goods to Mittelstand firms needed for the success of decentralized production. Through this network, Mittelstand firms share, with each other and the state, the costs and risks associated with production. Relations between the state and the economy came to be guided by the principle of state "help for self-help." These patterns of decentralized industrial organization and state-society relations developed in the nineteenth century continued through the twentieth century.

By the 1970s the postwar state of Baden-Württemberg was heralded as West Germany's *Musterländle*—the "little model state." Through this turbulent decade, the state's unemployment rate consistently hovered around one-half that of the Federal Republic, and its per capita GDP was a dependable 5 percent over the national average. With only 15 percent of the nation's population, Baden-Württemberg provided over 20 percent of its manufacturing workforce in the mid-1980s; in the regionally dominant sectors of machinery, electrical products, and automobiles, this percentage climbed to over 25 percent.[9] In the mid-1980s, the region exported roughly one-third (32.2 percent) of its industrial output.[10] Mittelstand firms accounted for 48.2 percent of commercial revenues in the state, compared to the nationwide average of 41.8 percent (Economics Ministry of Baden-Württemberg 1986). In the manufacturing sector, 80 percent of the state's firms have fewer than 500 employees and account for more than half of industrial employment.[11] Industrial production in Baden-Württemberg continues to display a relatively high degree of geographic decentralization, in spite of the large industrial agglomerations around Stuttgart and Mannheim. The extensive presence of flexible and innovative small firms undoubtedly contributes to more informal and multilateral production strategies, even in sectors normally seen as dominated by large, hierarchically organized firms and mass production. In a study of the German auto industry, for example, Streeck notes that auto producers in southern Germany—Daimler-Benz in Baden-Württemberg and BMW in Bavaria—rely considerably more on external local supplier firms (especially craft firms) for parts than do northern firms (VW, Opel, and Ford). The southern auto firms developed a greater number of long-term contracting relations with suppliers that frequently involve shared responsibility for research and development (Streeck 1989, 121–49). Thus many of the state's big and small firms are linked through intricate and efficient networks of long-term contracting, each accounting in good part for the success and expansion of the other (Sabel et al. 1989; Herrigel 1996).

The region also developed a tradition of cooperative research and technology transfer through dozens of industry-oriented research organizations. Most of these are funded jointly by firms, trade associations, and the Land and federal governments.[12] In accordance with the precepts of DQP, skilled labor is employed to a comparatively high degree in Baden-Württemberg.[13] The importance of skilled workers to the state's industries is also reflected in their demonstrated propensity to put their workers on shorter workweeks rather than fire them when times get tough.[14] The labor force reciprocates in part through a comparatively greater willingness to participate in continuing education.[15]

In short, Baden-Württemberg epitomizes the diversified quality production model. Its success has been generated by innovative large and small firms that seem particularly adept at integrating new technologies into traditional industries—machine tools, autos, electrical products, textiles, office machinery, clocks, and other fine mechanical instruments. The key factors of production—capital, knowledge, and skilled labor—are generated and distributed to a high degree through extensive networks of cooperating institutions. Production occurs extensively through vertical and horizontal subcontracting networks.

These interfirm networks, in turn, draw importantly on resources provided through the regional policy network. The internal dynamic and resilience of this model can be seen over several periods of economic crisis and adjustment.

Crisis in the 1970s: Decentralized Adjustment

Until the early 1970s, Land government aid to industry expanded slowly, and top priority was accorded by both the government and regional economic actors to enlarging the capacity of the regional vocational training system and the publicly supported business consulting system.[16] In the vein of the traditional "help for self-help" principle, the government relied heavily on the chambers, trade associations, and other economic organizations to provide resources to the Mittelstand.[17] However, the Land government and regional economic organizations were not passive in the face of growing government intervention elsewhere in the Federal Republic. Less enthused about the philosophy of state economic planning being propagated by the SPD, the Baden-Württembergers focused instead on expanding the regional policy network through three new organizations (all established in 1971).[18]

The first was an equity participation corporation called the Mittelständische Beteiligungsgesellschaft Baden-Württemberg (MBG), which provides equity capital to Mittelstand firms.[19] The second organization—the Surety Bank (Bürgschaftsbank)—provides guarantees to local banks on a broad range of loans to Mittelstand firms. Both the MBG and the Surety Bank were established through the financial support of, and cooperation among, the Land and federal governments, the regional associations of the cooperative and savings banks, the private banking sector, the chambers, and dozens of regional business associations. Accordingly, the credit and investment committees of these two organizations are composed of representatives from their founding partners.[20] The third organization created was the Steinbeis Foundation. Named after the legendary "father" of Württemberg's industrialization, the private foundation's purpose was to support the region's Mittelstand through expanding the provision of technical consulting services.

The early 1970s were also the beginning of a new era in the relationship between the government of Baden-Württemberg and the region's banks (discussed in greater detail later in this chapter). In other Länder, Landesbanks (many newly enlarged through recent fusions) provided governments convenient access to capital markets and assisted in government policy implementation. Since Baden-Württemberg as a political territory was created in 1952 through the union of Baden and Württemberg, there were two regional Girozentrale and two regional savings bank associations. Thus the Land government sought to create a Landesbank with government ownership through a merger of the two Girozentrale with two smaller Land-owned special purpose banks.[21] However, the fusion efforts failed because the Baden Girozentrale and regional savings bank association feared their interests would be subordinated to those of the Württembergers. Despite this defeat, the Land government succeeded in merging the two smaller banks in 1972 to create the Landeskreditbank Baden-Württemberg (LKB). Responsibility for most of the state's Mittelstand financial support programs was transferred out of the bureaucracy into this relatively autonomous institution.

The Steinbeis Foundation, the Surety Bank/MBG, and the LKB were critical additions to the regional policy network, since they provided additional arenas in which public and private actors coordinate their activities and share the risks of achieving collectively defined economic goals. The definition of goals is done, in part, through the supervisory boards and committees of these organizations, where leaders of the Land government and representatives of industry and the craft and banking sectors regularly discuss the needs of the regional economy. Though other Länder have similar organizations to these, the amount of resources that came to be provided to firms through Baden-Württemberg's regional policy network is significantly higher in relative terms. This results from a combination of the strongly Mittelstand structure of the regional economy and the willingness of regional firms and institutions to share risks.

Bringing the Network to Life

The first global oil crisis and subsequent recession in 1974 were critical tests for the regional economy and regional policy network. Though Baden-Württemberg suffered far less than other regions of the country, the number of bankruptcies and the regional unemployment rate rose dramatically. Gross capital formation and industrial employment had already been sliding since 1970. Most alarming, however, were emerging sectoral crises in the Mittelstand-dominated, and regionally important, sectors of textiles and clothing, leather goods (including shoes), and clock making (Economics Ministry of Baden-Württemberg 1977). These threats to the small firm raised concern not only among the Mittelstand itself, but also among Land politicians in all parties. The Land government and regional economic actors responded through a dramatic expansion of resources flowing to Mittelstand firms through the regional policy network. The region's industries drew on these resources to aid their restructuring through strengthening diversified quality production.

As an emergency response measure, at the beginning of 1974 the government created a special program for the textile and clothing, leather goods, and shoe industries. Firms in these sectors were eligible for interest-subsidized loans from the LKB for rationalization measures or to hire workers laid off in other firms in their industry. These loans were channeled to firms through their local house bank, which also carried a portion of the risk of the loan. Demand for these loans was tremendous, and in mid-1974 this special program was turned into a general liquidity assistance program for Mittelstand firms in all sectors.[22] Originally scheduled for a limited time period, the program is still in existence today.

After lengthy consultations with the chambers, business associations, regional labor federation, and other organizations, the Land government passed a Mittelstand Promotion Law (Mittelstandsförderungsgesetz) in 1975. The new law made Mittelstand promotion a permanent, legal obligation of the Land government and paved the way for an expanded set of promotion measures and expansion of funds for all existing promotion programs.[23] From approximately DM 28.5 million in 1970, these expenditures had already risen to DM 93.5 million in 1975. In 1976, they rose to DM 147.4 million, and in 1977, to DM 179.5 million. Funds were expanded the most for construction of new vocational training centers, applied R&D, and loans and investment grants to firms.[24]

Sharing the belief that greater government action was necessary, the Land government and actors in the regional network launched several new cooperative initiatives to promote structural adjustment in firms. Perhaps the most visible new direction in government activism was export promotion. While the economy of the region had long had a strong export orientation, the government now claimed it had a duty to help the Mittelstand achieve greater stability and growth through expansion in foreign markets. The first measure (taken in 1977) was an export loan guarantee program at the LKB.[25] The government also began encouraging firms to join in export "communities" or cooperatives that would help firms establish and administer export and foreign operations, particularly in areas outside the Western industrialized countries.[26] Funding was expanded for export consultancies to be provided through the existing Mittelstand consulting network.[27]

Finally, at the end of 1976 the government introduced a new Innovation Promotion Program—the first technology program among the Länder that awarded R&D grants directly to firms.[28] In justifying this new policy direction, the Land government argued that global structural changes were forcing the economy to concentrate on technically demanding products and processes; thus economic policy would increasingly have to be technology policy. The Land government characterized its new innovation program as a long-term "risk community" (*Risikogemeinschaft*) in which the decision to innovate would be left to industry, but the risk of innovation shared (Landtag of Baden-Württemberg, 10 February 1977). This new policy direction was also justified on the grounds that federal technology policy focused intentionally on large firms and was therefore promoting economic concentration and centralization at the expense of the Mittelstand. Through cooperation with the Chambers of Industry and Commerce, the Steinbeis Foundation, and several cooperative industrial research institutes, the number of technology transfer offices in the Land was dramatically increased within a few years.[29]

In nearly all of these initiatives, the Land government shared the functions of policy-making and implementation with a range of quasi-public and private organizations. This practice not only helped legitimate government policies, it also spread the costs and risks associated with them. Indirect government promotion of industry, that is, aid to organizations that support the Mittelstand, was consistent with long-standing relations between state and society in Baden-Württemberg. These indirect measures expanded tremendously in the second half of the 1970s. What grew even faster in the late 1970s, however, was direct government financial support to firms.[30] This shift is accounted for in part by a changed political perception of the region's economic problems. In contrast to the 1966–67 recession, which was generally perceived as a cyclical phenomenon, the 1974–75 downturn was seen to be a consequence of structural economic changes that the market alone could not master in a socially acceptable manner.

However, the growing emphasis by the Land government on direct firm support met somewhat greater resistance and skepticism from private sector organizations. In the late 1970s, the Chambers of Industry and Commerce warned that the Land government was becoming increasingly *dirigiste* through the LKB and thus violating the tradition of help for self-help. But no concerted opposition to the expansion of direct government lending emerged. Once in place, subsidized loans and grants became too popular among firms in the region for any business association to strongly oppose them. Moreover, because local business representatives participated in the decision-making process for a large percentage of government grants and loans, they could influence the flow of capital and thus became partly accountable for them.[31] The strong showing of the CDU in the 1976 Land elections—which kept it as the sole governing party—also suggested that the broader electorate approved of the government's response to the economic crisis.

The last half of the 1970s was a period of relative prosperity in the Federal Republic, and especially in Baden-Württemberg. The Land government felt confirmed in its expanded economic role in the region. Demand by firms for the state-supported consulting network, continuing education, and technology programs was rising strongly. As a result, direct and indirect government subsidies to the Mittelstand increased roughly tenfold within the decade.[32] Notably, the failure to achieve a large, government-owned Landesbank in the early 1970s inhibited the Land government from engaging in the sort of large-scale firm bailouts that other Land governments were attempting in the 1970s. While the LKB had become a major instrument of industrial policy, it was not suited for direct firm intervention. More importantly, there was little political support for the Land government to get so directly involved in the affairs of large firms in the region.

Thus, unlike the cases of coal and steel in North Rhine-Westphalia, in Baden-Württemberg sectoral crises in the 1970s were not addressed through a centralized crisis management effort involving concerted efforts among governments, banks, firms, and unions. Rather, sectoral governance and the process of industrial adjustment remained comparatively decentralized. Firms called upon the organizations of the regional policy network, their trade associations, their own production partners, and state subsidies to aid them in their adjustment. Though a few sectors in Baden-Württemberg began an irreversible decline, such as (noncuckoo) clock making, several other traditional sectors, such as textiles, adjusted very successfully.

Successful adjustment and the expansion of the regional policy network were also predicated on the strong participation of the many small banks in the region. The cooperative and savings banks of Baden-Württemberg had regional market shares well above their respective national averages—together they controlled nearly 70 percent of regional bank business in the early 1970s. All banks headquartered outside the state had just over 10 percent of Baden-Württemberg's banking business.[33] The success of organizations such as the LKB, Surety Bank, and MBG depends importantly on the willingness of the banks to use them. The savings and cooperative banks, which provide the majority of Mittelstand finance, readily draw on these organizations. Mittelstand firms in trouble were frequently stabilized, or even rescued, through the coordinated efforts of their house bank, the LKB, and other organizations in the regional policy network. Thus the combined predominance of small firms and small banks created both the demand and the support for strong institutions organized in a regional policy network.

**Crisis in the 1980s: Strengthening DQP
through Technology Promotion**

The early 1980s presented a new set of economic adjustment pressures for
Baden-Württemberg and Germany as a whole. The recession of 1981–82 was
compounded by the explosive technical revolution in microelectronics and the
emergence of Japan as an economic superpower. This time, the region's key industries—autos, electronics, and machine tools—were the ones most challenged to reorganize their production and technology efforts in order to remain
globally competitive. Firms in the region pushed their traditional strategy of diversified quality production even further, utilizing the new microelectronics
technology to modernize and move further up-market. Collaborative contracting—in which firms share the risks and costs of innovation—spread further,
both horizontally across Mittelstand firms and vertically between large and
small firms. In this sense, production became even more regionalized. The key
response of the regional policy network was to expand dramatically its technology promotion efforts. The Land government, under the leadership of Minister-President Lothar Späth, also attempted to achieve greater influence over
the structural adjustment process through more direct forms of intervention in
the banking sector and elsewhere. By the end of the decade, it was clear that the
regional economy had adjusted quite successfully to the changed conditions of
competition.[34]

A New Round of Network Expansion

Confronted with recession and fast-rising unemployment, the government began hearings on a reordering of its economic policy. To achieve a high media
profile and mobilize political support for a new economic strategy, the Land
government established three expert commissions in 1982 (one each for research, export promotion, and new communications technologies) to generate
medium- and long-term policy proposals. In December of that year, the government brought the commissions together to present their proposals to the key
political and economic elite of Baden-Württemberg. While these commissions
were dominated by representatives from regional firms and business organizations, the economic policies that emerged out of them were strongly influenced
by Lothar Späth. Späth, a powerful political figure, advocated a more activist
state that had to force modernization by promoting technological change, because the market alone would not sufficiently develop the information infrastructure and know-how needed in the coming information society (Späth

1984). In practice, his policy program would entail supply-side measures—which the regional policy network of Baden-Württemberg had long emphasized—and innovation promotion policies that targeted Mittelstand firms and particular sectors. However, Mittelstand firms and many organizations in the regional policy network resisted Späth's most interventionist efforts, especially when they were intended to aid large firms. Thus many of Späth's practices did not become institutionalized but remained ad hoc.

In 1983 the Land government set about finalizing its reorganized economic development model based on the commission reports. Meanwhile, the government wasted no time in acting upon some of its most important technology policy objectives. Immediately following the conference, the Land government named a Government Commissioner for Technology Transfer to support and accelerate the adjustment of the Mittelstand to rapid technical change. Heeding warnings of further bureaucratization by key private sector leaders, the government proposed that the main instrument of the commissioner be not a state agency, but the Steinbeis Foundation. By April of 1983, an agreement was reached through which the commissioner—Johann Löhn—became head of the Steinbeis Foundation. In exchange, the government financed a major expansion of the foundation's capital and ongoing operations. Within this expanded (quasi-public) apparatus, the Land government began implementing several new technology initiatives to promote R&D and technical modernization in Mittelstand firms.

The now 16 technical advising offices of the Steinbeis Foundation were so successful that they were approaching the limits of their capacity.[35] The solution to this problem was to create technology transfer centers that would conduct product- or production-oriented R&D in very specifically defined technologies. The centers were to be largely self-financing through contracts with industry and staffed primarily by recent graduates of the engineering polytechnics. The centers also provided a forum for educating the workers in the firms for which the new technologies were destined. Since they were built on traditional cooperation between the polytechnics and industry, new centers were rapidly established: by 1985, 22 new centers had been established, and more were planned.[36] While research in these centers does not typically involve direct interfirm collaborative research, they nonetheless promote the diffusion of technology by using knowledge gained in one project to solve the technical problems of another firm client.

The year 1984 began with the introduction of the government's long-awaited new Economic Promotion Program (Wirtschaftsförderungsprogramm, or WIP). Under the WIP, and with broad political support, the government devoted substantial resources to a much-expanded technology policy (Schmid 1989, 103–13). Like many other subnational governments around the industrial world, the first technology initiatives of Baden-Württemberg were motivated in good part by an attempt to re-create the Silicon Valley phenomenon. Through the technical assistance of the Steinbeis Foundation and financial support from the Economics Ministry, the Land government eagerly supported the creation of technology parks intended to be "incubators" for new technology-oriented firms and to stimulate collaborative research among firms and research organizations. By the late 1980s, over a dozen parks had been established, and more were planned.[37]

Baden-Württemberg, however, lacked the venture capital firms that played such a crucial role in the Silicon Valley phenomenon. The German financial system did not make it easy for such firms to emerge (compare Deeg 1997). Instead, Baden-Württemberg attempted to achieve a functional equivalent through the concerted efforts of the regional policy network. From the State Commerce Office (LGA) came project-specific innovation grants; from the LKB came innovation loans; from the Surety Bank came loan guarantees; and from the Mittelstand Equity Participation Corporation (MBG) came equity finance.[38] All of these efforts required coordination with commercial, savings, and cooperative banks in the region, which vetted applicants for technology loans and typically carried most of the credit risk.

One of the most prominent new programs under the WIP supported the introduction of modern, unproven technologies into firms, either through a low-interest loan from the LKB or a grant from the LGA (all projects required technical approval from the Steinbeis Foundation). In practice, this form of direct firm support typically financed the introduction of CAD/CAM, numerically controlled machine tools, and other related microelectronics technology into the production systems of Mittelstand firms. During the mid-1980s, a substantial portion of regional Mittelstand firms, particularly in the machine tool and electronics sectors, received support under this program (see appendix to this chapter). The government complemented these measures by promoting the expansion of continuing education courses related to these technologies. Though much fanfare and media attention centered around these new initiatives, funding for research at the universities, Fachhochschulen, and the numerous applied industrial research organizations in the region was also greatly expanded.

The mid-1980s were also years of high-profile export promotion by the Land government and Lothar Späth in particular. In between jumping from one international trade fair to the next—with a full entourage of business representatives from home in tow—Späth sought partner regions in Europe, North

America, and Asia. While many of these vaguely defined cooperation agreements brought few immediate results, the minister-president held them out as promising long-term opportunities to promote industry in Baden-Württemberg ("Plusterländle ohne Potenz," *Der Spiegel,* 29 January 1990).[39] On a more modest level, and in keeping with the traditional pattern of state-society relations, the Land government, the Chambers of Industry and Commerce, and the Land Association of Baden-Württemberg Industry (Landesverband der Baden-Württembergischen Industrie) established a new Export Promotion Foundation in 1984 to support and coordinate the numerous sources of export information, consulting, and education in the region.

By the late 1980s, the number of organizations in the regional policy network and the extent of resource exchange among them had once again dramatically expanded. From 1972 to 1987, the total assets of the LKB rose from DM 9 billion to DM 40 billion, making the LKB one of the nation's top 20 banks. Under the government's economic promotion programs, the bank granted over 5,000 new loans, grants, and guarantees valued at DM 1.142 billion in 1987— a tenfold increase over lending in 1972.[40] In 1986 the Surety Bank made over 1,100 loan guarantees worth DM 200 million; this represented one-third (by volume) of all guarantees granted by credit guarantee cooperatives nationwide (Surety Bank of Baden-Württemberg 1986). Baden-Württemberg's cooperative equity participation corporation (MBG) made nearly 900 equity participations in Mittelstand firms between 1972 and the end of 1986, investing a total of DM 126 million. As of 1986, the MBG held investments worth DM 75.7 million in 541 firms. The significance of this is all the more apparent when compared to the fact that all of West Germany's private venture capital firms together had investments totaling roughly DM 150 million in 1986 (Mittelstand Equity Participation Corporation of Baden-Württemberg 1986).

The Land government also attempted to use the regional policy network and especially the LKB to influence the price and allocation of capital in accordance with its policy priorities. For example, under the technology programs of the mid-1980s, a considerable amount of low-cost capital was directed to Mittelstand firms in the vital machine tool sector. In 1983 only 2 percent (by volume) of the LKB's subsidized loans to firms were for innovation and technology promotion, while 56 percent went to business start-ups; in 1986, 38 percent of the LKB's loans were for technology promotion and 34 percent for start-ups (Landeskreditbank Baden-Württemberg, 1987). In 1986 almost half of the MBG's new participations went to technology-oriented investments, including firm start-ups (Mittelstand Equity Participation Corporation of Baden-Württemberg 1986). The evidence suggests these efforts did have some impact on

firm investment decisions (see appendix). Moreover, the technical modernization of the Mittelstand benefited larger firms in the state via the modernization
of their suppliers. One of the key adjustment patterns during the 1980s was the
increased reliance of large firms on collaboration with supplier firms in product innovation and development.[41] More generally, as the pace of technological change accelerated, Mittelstand and even large firms came to rely more
heavily on access to the many sources of technical information and know-how
provided by the various organizations linked in the regional policy network.

Probably the most dramatic institutional development within the regional
policy network during the 1980s was the expansion of the Steinbeis Foundation. Within a few short years, the Steinbeis Foundation had become the primary coordinator for technology promotion and cooperation in Baden-Württemberg.[42] Internally, it is a highly decentralized organization in which the
central administration minimally coordinates the activities of the numerous
technology centers and advising offices. When the foundation is asked to provide a technical evaluation for the LKB, Surety Bank, or other project, it calls
upon appropriate experts from the state's universities and polytechnics. In keeping with the decentralized organization of production, the decisions over which
research projects should be conducted rest with local firms and the researchers
in the technology centers.

Through early 1986, the regional and national press, unions, the SPD, and
business associations all seemed to find something positive in the Baden-Württemberg model. Lothar Späth seemed like an increasingly rare political leader
with a vision that could draw wide social support for his policy agenda (Schmid
1989, 44–48). But the rapid expansion of the Land's economic intervention
was not without its critics. The federal economics minister, Graf Lambsdorff,
was most vociferous in his condemnation of growing subsidy competition
among the Länder as federal mercantilism (Michael Jungblut, "Manchmal
helfen Ideen mehr als Geld . . . ," interview with Lothar Späth, *Die Zeit,* 20 December 1985).[43] At home, the eagerness of the Land government to promote
local industry was beginning to make it appear as little more than a promotion
agent of the economy—the minister-president's State Ministry was dubbed by
some critics as the Stuttgart MITI (Horst Bieber, "Per Ritterschlag vom Lan-
desfürsten," *Die Zeit,* 18 March 1988). The Chambers in Baden-Württemberg
voiced again their long-standing disapproval of growing direct government financial assistance to firms, arguing that the best Mittelstand policy would be a
reduction of the overall tax and social wage burden and the cessation of unjustified subsidies to large firms (Winkel 1981, 599; Chamber of Commerce and
Industry, Middle Neckar 1984). Such warnings represented an attempt to limit

the growing influence of the Land government over the regional policy network. In response to such criticism, the government asserted its intention to dismantle subsidies, but they continued to rise (Bettina Wieselmann, "Land zahlt mehr an die Wirtschaft: Entgegen Späths Ankündigung sind Subventionen in diesem Jahr erhöht worden," *Südwestpresse,* 21 October 1987). This tension within the regional policy network has been present since the mid-1970s, when government subsidies first rose dramatically. However, with each subsequent economic downturn, these organizations and firms in the region found government assistance programs quite useful. In the 1990s this would once again be reaffirmed.

Confronting the Weaknesses of DQP in the 1990s

During the second half of the 1980s, and into the post-reunification economic boom, Baden-Württemberg's economy was an economic juggernaut. Its firms pulled in strong profits, hampered in their expansion mostly by a shortage of skilled labor. But in late 1992, as the German economy began to fall in line with the sluggish global economy, Baden-Württemberg's economy started to nosedive. During 1993, manufacturing production dropped 9 percent, and exports dropped 5.6 percent. Production in the auto sector, which accounts for one-third of manufacturing revenue in the region, dropped 15 percent (Iwer 1994, 6, 15). Regional electronics and machine tool producers, many of which are heavily dependent on the auto sector, suffered in turn.[44] In all these sectors, many small and large firms began rapidly shedding workers, even skilled workers.

The crisis in Baden-Württemberg was both cyclical and structural. Domestic and international demand for its products, especially autos, sloughed off quickly in the early 1990s. But producers in Baden-Württemberg were also clearly suffering from structural competitiveness problems. The strategy of diversified quality production, which they honed and exploited so well during the 1980s, ran up against its inherent weaknesses. DQP allowed firms to absorb their higher production costs by emphasizing quality and technical/engineering content in their products. In the 1990s, however, Japanese, American and other competitors were finding ways to achieve similar diversification and quality at significantly lower costs. German producers quickly realized that DQP also had to become "lean production." To achieve cost levels comparable to those of their competitors, German producers began experimenting with their competitors' organizational principles: flatter management hierarchies, more decentralized responsibility for quality and decision making, teamwork, shorter product development cycles through simultaneous engineering (e.g., using teams of engineers and production and marketing people), and tighter collaboration with key suppliers in product innovation. Big firms in Baden-Württemberg, as elsewhere in Germany, stepped up their efforts to cut costs by buying more parts, and producing in lower-cost locations, abroad. The intensified globalization of large firms in the region creates strong cost pressures on thousands of supplier firms, and many are not likely to survive.[45]

The all-important auto sector moved rapidly to adjust its organization of production. Mercedes-Benz, the largest firm in the region and the dominant firm in the regional auto sector, is critically shaping this adjustment process. In 1992 Mercedes purchased some 40 percent of its parts (worth about DM 30 billion) from Baden-Württemberg suppliers ("Zweifel, ob die Struktur noch stimmt," *Frankfurter Allgemeine Zeitung,* 21 October 1993). But the 1993 crisis forced Mercedes to speed up its globalization targets, and in 1994 Mercedes announced plans to reduce its vertical integration from 45 percent to 38 percent of value added and to purchase 25 percent of its parts from abroad by 1997 (up from 10 percent in 1990).[46] The company also planned to reduce substantially the number of its supplier firms (some 2,000) and rely more heavily on first-tier system suppliers (Dieter Schweer, "Nummer kleiner," *Wirtschaftswoche,* 18 May 1995). The other major auto producers in the region, Porsche and Audi, are following similar strategies (as are key auto suppliers like Bosch) (Cooke and Morgan 1994). In the course of this restructuring, tens of thousands of jobs were shed by these and other firms in the auto sector.[47]

The machinery industry, the classic Mittelstand sector of Baden-Württemberg, suffered considerably from the troubles of the auto sector and the general recession.[48] But this sector, too, was not without its own structural problems. Japanese and other Asian competitors are making inroads into traditional German machinery and especially machine tool markets. Many machinery firms responded to the early 1990s crisis and rising competition by slashing costs, in good part through layoffs. Many of them, however, also pursued long-term strategies to enhance their competitiveness and cost-effectiveness by adopting several principles and methods of lean production, notably the introduction of group work and increased collaboration with other machinery firms (both at home and abroad) in distribution, R&D, and purchasing (Institut der deutschen Wirtschaft 1993b).[49]

Collectively Reorganizing Regional Production

The process of sectoral adjustment in the 1990s, however, cannot be fully analyzed without incorporating the regional dimension. For, even more than in the past, firms that adjust successfully in Baden-Württemberg rely on the information, skills, and capital provided through the organizations of the regional policy network. Even large firms, despite their increasingly global orientation, are, paradoxically, drawing more heavily on this network to facilitate their own adjustment. As these large firms intensify their collaborative relations with regional suppliers, the big firms draw indirectly (and to some extent directly) on the resources provided by the network to their (mostly) Mittelstand suppliers (Herrigel 1993b). This helps explain why it is the largest firms in the region that intensively engaged in a dialogue with the Land government and other regional actors over the current and future initiatives of the regional policy network.

The Land government, ruled by a CDU-SPD coalition since early 1992, reacted to the breaking economic crisis with a series of joint initiatives (*Gemeinschaftsinitiativen*). These initiatives, organized along sectoral lines, brought together key sectoral representatives (including unions) under the auspices of the Economics Ministry to discuss the conditions and prospects of their industry (an industry analysis was prepared in advance by the Economics Ministry) and agree upon a range of short- and long-term measures to deal with sectoral problems. The first initiative, in October 1992, brought together representatives from auto producers and suppliers in the region. Other joint initiatives soon followed in machinery, textiles and clothing, and telecommunications (Hirn 1993; "Gemeinschaftsinitiative im Maschinenbau," *Frankfurter Allgemeine Zeitung,* 8 February 1993). The measures adopted called extensively upon the regional policy network to assist sectoral adjustment.

In the auto sector joint initiative, for example, the first measure was to improve the flow of information about sectoral structural adjustment problems to supplier firms through a variety of initiatives carried out by the large auto manufacturers, the metal industry association, the Chambers of Industry and Commerce, the metalworkers' union, and the Economics Ministry. The second measure charged the Steinbeis Foundation and chambers with initiating programs to address the problems of auto suppliers in production and organization. The third measure entailed Economics Ministry financial support for joint technology development projects of Mittelstand auto suppliers. The fourth measure again called upon the Economics Ministry to finance a project that would promote the adoption of simultaneous engineering in horizontal and vertical collaborative contracting relations. The fifth measure was to promote the adoption of lean production and lean management practices. The sixth measure called for the promotion of interfirm cooperation and strategic alliances in production. The final measures targeted improved educational training in metalworking, and export promotion.[50] While the specific impact of these measures is difficult to measure, these talks clearly facilitated discussion among regional firms about how to adjust, both individually and collectively. The mediating role of the Land government was essential, since it helped create more even-handed bargaining between the generally weaker (in market power terms) suppliers and the manufacturers.[51]

As in past crises, during the early 1990s the Land government and regional policy network were also called upon to act as a "fire department," that is, to save the rapidly growing number of firms tottering on the brink of bankruptcy. In 1993 alone, several hundred Mittelstand firms in Baden-Württemberg received a total of DM 324 million in liquidity loans from the L-Bank (formerly the LKB)—up from DM 56.6 million in the prior year ("Autoindustrie setzt jetzt auf Partnerschaft," *Frankfurter Allgemeine Zeitung,* 9 July 1993). More than a third of these loans went to the greater Stuttgart region where the auto, electronics, and machinery industries are concentrated.[52] Loan guarantees granted by the Economics Ministry, L-Bank, and Surety Bank also rose substantially.[53] From 1992 to 1995 (inclusive), the Land government reputedly handed out DM 2.5 billion in liquidity loans and loan guarantees (Michael Heller, "Die Lasten einer Industrieregion," *Frankfurter Allgemeine Zeitung,* 20 March 1996). Ironically, just before the crisis, there was widespread talk among government and business leaders about the need for subsidy reductions and even the elimination of direct financial promotion to firms. The sudden, deep economic slump in 1992–93, however, reminded these regional actors that the financial support network they themselves had constructed was still essential for the successful adjustment of firms and the regional economy as a whole. The capacity of the regional network to save many supplier firms also prevented a more serious disruption of the interfirm production networks needed for DQP.

Long-Term Responses of the Regional Policy Network

As a decade earlier, one of the first responses of the Land government to the emerging economic crisis was to call together a regional commission (Zukunftskommission Wirtschaft 2000, or ZK) with 40 representatives from regional industry (mostly large firms), academia, unions, and government. After nearly a year of meetings, the group's mid-1993 report called for increased federal and Land support to research consortia and promotion of key technologies of the future—technologies in which Germany is generally behind the United States and Japan.[54] The Land government immediately followed the report with several new technology measures. The most visible was a new project in multimedia technology involving collaboration among a host of large firms in the region and financial support from the Land government. The regional alliance behind the project believes it will promote German competitiveness in this new technology, as well as benefit the traditional sectors in Baden-Württemberg that could utilize the technology ("Stuttgart will mit Multimedia das High-Tech-Image aufpolieren," *Frankfurter Allgemeine Zeitung,* 15 February 1995). The Land government planned other model technology projects (e.g., in laser technology), planned for the construction of industrial parks to "incubate" biotech firms and for the expansion of the regional research infrastructure, and created a permanent innovation council to advise it on technology policy.[55] At the behest of regional industry, the Land government also announced its support for the construction of a series of industry and commerce centers abroad that will support the efforts of regional Mittelstand firms to expand their exports and foreign production.[56]

Bank Behavior during Crisis

The case of liquidity assistance loans and loan guarantees provided through the regional policy network reveals a good deal about the role of banks in the regional adjustment process. Virtually all of these loans and guarantees require cooperation between the firm's house bank and loan/guarantee-granting organization. In the case of liquidity assistance loans granted by the L-Bank, the house bank or banks must carry half the credit risk of the loan. Because liquidity assistance loans are also long-term loans, they reinforce the house banks' long-term commitment to the firm while sharing the risks of this commitment with the government. In Baden-Württemberg, it is the savings banks followed by the credit cooperatives that most readily use the liquidity assistance program (interview with director of L-Bank liquidity assistance program, 28 July 1993).[57] Private commercial banks are much less likely to draw on the regional policy network for such loans or loan guarantees. The reasons for this difference are several. First, savings and cooperative banks account for the majority of loans to Mittelstand firms; thus they are more likely to need such programs. Second, these are smaller banks that cannot balance the assumption of greater credit risk in one geographic market through less risk in another, as the big commercial banks can. Third, and not the least significant, there also appear to be systematic differences across the major banking groups in their long-term commitment to Mittelstand firms.

In late 1992 and early 1993, as red ink spread from firm to firm like wildfire, the regional banking system was thrown into crisis. After a decade of hefty profits for firms and banks alike, no one was prepared for the sudden reversal of fortune. Firms once considered golden customers were posting losses that kept growing from week to week. Loan losses mounted rapidly for many banks in the region. For example, the Stuttgart branch of the Deutsche Bank, which oversees 80 branches in Baden and Württemberg, was forced to write off DM 1 billion in nonperforming loans between mid-1991 and the end of 1993. Long the star among the bank's 14 main regional offices, the Stuttgart office was heavily engaged in lending to the larger regional Mittelstand firms, especially in autos and machinery ("Ungewohnte Sorgen bei der Vorzeige-Filiale der Deutschen Bank," *Frankfurter Allgemeine Zeitung,* 19 August 1994).

In response to the crisis, many banks began to call in their loans, especially if they were a minority lender to the firm.[58] The banks, especially the big banks, were criticized by the L-Bank and Land political leaders for a lack of commitment to financially troubled Mittelstand firms ("Landeskreditbank kritisiert die Grossbanken," *Frankfurter Allgemeine Zeitung,* 5 February 1993; "Rekordarbeitslosigkeit im Musterländle," *Frankfurter Allgemeine Zeitung,* 11 February 1993). The savings and cooperative banks, meanwhile, turned to the L-Bank for help in rescuing their most troubled firms.[59] As 1993 wore on, however, the big banks showed a greater willingness to write off more of their credit claims on struggling firms and to work with the L-Bank and Economics Ministry in aiding troubled firms ("Kreditausfälle bereiten noch keine Sorgen," *Frankfurter Allgemeine Zeitung,* 5 July 1993). Even so, the severity of the 1993 crisis dampened the willingness of the big banks to engage in business lending. During 1994, when the economy was recovering and loan demand rising, total business loans by the big banks in the region dropped 5.3 percent. Meanwhile, business loans by the savings banks rose 5.5 percent, and loans by the cooperative banks rose 7.3 percent (Landeszentralbank in Baden-Württemberg 1994, 72). The savings and cooperative banks together account for approximately 56.2 percent of all credits to firms in Baden-Württemberg; the big banks for 11.3 percent (Landeszentralbank in Baden-Württemberg 1994, 72; "Sparkassen halten Unternehmen die Treue," *Frankfurter Allgemeine Zeitung,* 4 February 1994; Baden Savings Bank Association 1994, 53; Württemberg Savings Bank Association 1994, 44). Thus it is the two association banking groups that carried the greatest burden in financing the Mittelstand through the crisis.

The crisis in Baden-Württemberg (and elsewhere in Germany) was also a test of the banks' Allfinanz capacities. It is partly for just such crises that the big banks established management consulting and equity participation corporations.[60] While the banks surely used these capacities to aid adjustment by a select number of individual firms, the evidence suggests that their Allfinanz capacities were insufficient to influence broader sectoral adjustment patterns. In 1991 the Deutsche Bank, for example, supported an auto industry conference organized by its management consulting subsidiary Roland Berger. At the conference, firms were informed about global trends in management and production changes and advised to follow suit. Apparently, few firms listened, as the Deutsche Bank's massive losses in the auto supplier sector in Baden-Württemberg (and elsewhere) indicate. These losses prompted the Deutsche Bank to carefully review its lending and equity engagements in the auto industry to see if it should reduce its overall exposure (interview with senior vice president of Deutsche Bank, 4 April 1993). Thus, rather than pursuing a grand restructuring strategy for the auto industry, the bank appears more concerned with avoiding excessive dependence on the industry.

Banks and Large Firms

An analysis of the role of the banks in regional restructuring would hardly be complete without examining the relationship between banks and large firms headquartered or with major operations in the region. With the exception of AEG, a subsidiary of Daimler-Benz, the largest firms in Baden-Württemberg's electronics sector are foreign-owned (Alcatel-SEL, Hewlett-Packard, IBM Deutschland, and Sony). All of these firms (with the exception of Sony) underwent significant restructuring in the early 1990s, but these restructuring efforts were made under the direction of the foreign headquarters and had little direct involvement by German banks.[61]

In the auto sector, the most prominent role of the banks is obviously in Daimler-Benz, in which the Deutsche Bank holds a 24.4 percent stake and controls the supervisory board chair. There is little question that Deutsche Bank has influence in Daimler-Benz, but this is an unusual, if not unique, case of bank-firm relations in Germany. Yet, even in the case of Daimler, it appears that the Deutsche Bank's influence over firm strategy was surprisingly minimal in the 1990s. Despite several years of growing dissatisfaction with the company's results and Edzard Reuter's leadership, the Deutsche Bank would not (or could not) alter the firm's strategy. Only with Reuter's retirement in 1995 has Daimler begun to move away from its 10-year high-tech diversification strategy (Dieter Schweer, "Nummer kleiner," *Wirtschaftswoche,* 18 May 1995).[62] To finance its current restructuring, Daimler-Benz has drawn primarily on its deep reserves and gone directly to the national and international capital markets.[63]

The second-largest auto firm in Baden-Württemberg is actually one of the world's largest auto parts suppliers—Robert Bosch GmbH. No differently than for Mittelstand parts suppliers, in 1993 Bosch began to lose money as demand and prices for auto parts began to fall. Bosch's response was to accelerate an already ongoing restructuring program that required no special assistance from banks: Bosch is owned 90 percent by the Robert Bosch Foundation, and no bankers sit on its supervisory board. Of the other major auto firms in the region, Audi belongs to the VW concern (headquartered in, and substantially controlled by the Land government of, Lower Saxony) and Porsche is privately held by the founders' families. Porsche in particular underwent radical restructuring after demand in its elite market collapsed in the late 1980s, in the process becoming a model of lean production (Iwer 1994, 73–74). Only one banker, Walther Zügel, head of the Landesgirokasse Stuttgart (a savings bank), sits on the firm's supervisory board.[64] While the banks do not own shares in the company, they have obviously been patient financiers, given the very slow turnaround of the firm.

In the machinery sector, the largest firms in the region are considerably smaller than the multinational concerns of the electronics and auto sectors, but they are no less international in their market orientation. They all face strong adjustment pressures and draw importantly on their bank partners for support, but very few of them have any bank ownership. Probably the largest machinery firm in Baden-Württemberg is Heidelberger Druckmaschinen AG. While the firm has bank representatives on its supervisory board, the firm is majority-controlled by the energy-based conglomerate Rheinisch-Westfälische Elektrizitätswerke, or RWE (which itself is controlled by communal governments in North Rhine–Westphalia). Trumpf GmbH, a major machine tool maker in the region, has close connections to the Deutsche Bank and the Landesgirokasse Stuttgart but is a privately held firm.[65] Traub AG, another large and family-owned machinery firm, had serious financial difficulty in the early 1990s and was saved through a financial restructuring supported by its banks. The key decision was that of the banks to cancel DM 80 million in debt.[66]

These prominent examples further support the depiction of Baden-Württemberg as a regional economy in which the banks, especially the savings and cooperative banks, play a central role in financing firms, but there is little evidence of big bank tutelage of firms. By 1996 the regional economy appeared on the road to recovery as sales and exports began to rebound. More importantly, it appears that firms were successfully adopting many lean production concepts (on adjustment in the automobile industry, see Schumann 1997). But the price of this success, and one that weighs heavily on the region (and the nation as a whole), is lost employment. Thus Baden-Württemberg and Germany are still confronted with major and perplexing structural adjustment challenges that will continue to test the capacity of the regional policy network(s) and national institutions to meet them.

Evolution of the Regional Public Banking Sector

Despite the continuing dominance and success of savings and cooperative banks in Baden-Württemberg, since 1970 there have been numerous attempts by political and public banking sector leaders to construct a very large regional public bank.[67] Though few firms in the region felt inadequately served by the banking system, the Land government, particularly under Späth, wanted control of a bank large enough to carry out large-scale industrial finance, boost the export business of regional Mittelstand firms, and support the economic promotion efforts of the regional policy network. The Land government also played a crucial and probably more important role in strengthening Mittelstand financial services in the region by liberalizing its savings bank regulations and thus enabling these banks to expand their commercial banking activities.

The stories of regulatory liberalization and bank mergers show how the savings bank sector and Land government are each dependent on cooperation with the other to maintain their respective capacities to adapt to economic change. Furthermore, the bank merger and regulation stories teach us that change in Germany's banking system is not simply an economic process driven by market competition, but a process strongly influenced by political actors and their interests. They also show that the institutionalized patterns of cooperation, trust, and the mutual exchange of resources among the savings banks and local and regional governments built up over a long period of time delimit the pace and possibilities for change. Finally, these stories illuminate the region's reaction to the internationalization of product and financial markets as an attempt to maintain local control over capital resources and preserve a regional financial structure that is attuned to the needs of its decentralized organization of production.

The Long Road to Fusions

In September of 1973, the two largest savings banks in Baden-Württemberg announced their intention to merge.[68] Both savings banks were eager to expand their business in the lucrative, heavily industrialized Middle Neckar region around Stuttgart. Greatest resistance came from the savings banks in Württemberg and their Girozentrale, which would face increased competition from a very large savings bank.[69] The Land government argued that invigorated bank competition would benefit the Mittelstand and make an important contribution to the widely agreed upon need to strengthen the competitiveness of the public banking sector. After lengthy negotiations, Baden-Württemberg's savings bank law was amended in 1975 to allow the merger and creation of the Landes-girokasse Stuttgart (LGK), with ownership divided equally between the city of Stuttgart and the Land government. The LGK became the dominant savings bank in the region and achieved considerable success in the regional industrial finance market.

When the Land parliament approved the LGK merger, it also voted over-whelmingly that the government should continue to promote (and, if necessary, force) the fusion of the two Girozentrale in the Land.[70] Given its failure to achieve the fusion of the Girozentrale in 1970–71 (out of which came the LKB, later L-Bank), this time the Land government pursued two potential routes to a large Land-owned bank. While negotiations over the Girozentrale proceeded, the government initiated a parallel merger involving the government-controlled Badische Bank and Württembergische Bank with the only significant private regional commercial bank in Baden-Württemberg—the Handelsbank Heil-bronn.[71] After long and difficult negotiations with the principal shareholders of the Handelsbank—among them the Deutsche Bank and Bosch—a merger agreement was finally reached in late 1977. The new Baden-Württembergische Bank, or BW-Bank, was expected to function primarily as a private commer-cial bank, though the Land government was the majority shareholder. With the BW-Bank, the Land government believed it had not only created a bigger in-digenous commercial bank, but also an enticement to coax the Girozentrale merger by offering to include the commercially strong BW-Bank in a new Girozentrale/Landesbank (this would have also given the Land government an ownership stake in a Landesbank).

However, after two years of direct merger negotiations, the attempt to merge the Girozentrale foundered once again on the resistance of the Baden savings bank association. The government chose not to use its legal authority to force a merger, since this would risk alienating the savings bank sector. In addition, a series of bad loans at the Württemberg Girozentrale and the serious financial problems of government-owned Landesbanks in other Länder soured the readiness of legislators to attempt a momentous political battle for a some-what discredited cause (Biehal 1984). Various discussions continued between the Land's two savings bank associations in subsequent years, but no agreement was reached.

With his highly touted technology policy up and running, in 1984 Lothar Späth decided it was time to see if his string of political successes could be extended into a government-controlled Landesbank. Envious of Bavaria and North Rhine–Westphalia, where big public regional banks cooperated closely with government, Späth also wanted a powerful regional bank that would complement the government's industrial policy through a strong focus on technology finance. Through a strong Landesbank, Späth and many leaders in the savings bank sector also hoped to break the monopoly of the commercial banks in the export finance market.[72] According to the Land government, a big Landesbank was needed above all for the Mittelstand, since only a strong bank oriented to Baden-Württemberg could ensure that regional capital would benefit regional firms—in good times and bad (Dieter Ferber, "Ein Neuer Anlauf für die Landesbank-Fusion," *Stuttgarter Zeitung,* 4 February 1985).

Späth favored a four-way fusion model that, in addition to the two Girozentrale, would include the LKB and the Landesgirokasse.[73] The LKB was an attractive fusion partner because of its strong equity base; the Landesgirokasse, because it had 240 branches and was the only bank of the four with any tangible export finance experience. If the four-way fusion were to succeed, the new bank would become the nation's second largest. But in this latest attempt at a Landesbank merger, Späth would encounter much of the same opposition as his predecessors. The commercial banking association was conclusively opposed, arguing that Baden-Württemberg's export business was already well served by the private banking sector ("Bankenfusion in Baden-Württemberg," *Wirtschaftswoche,* 4 April 1986). The cooperative banks opposed the fusion on the grounds that a competitive disadvantage would arise because the government economic programs operated by the LKB would be administered by the rival savings bank organization via the new Landesbank (Württemberg Cooperative Association 1985). Finally, some politicians were still concerned that a big Landesbank might embroil the government in monstrous financial fiascos, as they had continued to do in other Länder.

Through 1985, negotiations dragged on, and the endless shift of proposals, strategies, and tactics made it seem that an agreement would be impossible to reach. But by April of 1986, after relentless pressure and persuasion from Späth, informal agreement had been given by all parties except the Baden savings banks, and even they were now expected to follow suit ("Ruhig schlafen," *Der Spiegel,* 21 April 1986).[74] However, as negotiations entered the finalizing stage in June, the Landesgirokasse, citing the recently mounting losses of the Baden Girozentrale, backed out of the deal. Späth felt personally betrayed by Walther Zügel, the ambitious head of the LGK, and Manfred Rommel, mayor of Stuttgart, because both men had been avid supporters of the fusion plan from the beginning. Späth was convinced that Zügel backed out only so that he could pursue privatization of the Landesgirokasse and free himself of the "yoke" of the savings bank law.[75] A few days later, Späth gave up his eighteen-month-long battle for a Landesbank in announcing that he would not pursue the legal channel to force a merger, claiming that with all the trust destroyed among the parties, a fusion could no longer have a positive outcome ("Späth beerdigt seine Fusions-Vorstellungen," *Handelsblatt,* 25 June 1986).

The two Girozentrale and the Baden and Württemberg savings bank associations, however, actually continued talking to each other after the collapse of the four-way Landesbank fusion plan. The persistent structural problems of the Girozentrale—primarily declining business with their own savings banks—kept them at the negotiating table.[76] By late 1987 a merger agreement was reached, and in 1989 the new bank took up operations as the Südwestdeutsche Landesbank Girozentrale, or SüdwestLB. As the central bank of Baden-Württemberg's savings banks, the SüdwestLB could now strengthen its service role through expanded economies of scale. As a large commercial bank, the Süd-westLB would focus on expanding its international and investment banking operations. In justifying the fusion, the savings bank associations pointed in particular to the need to better serve Mittelstand firms and effectively compete for their business (Faisst and Rühle 1988).

Still not satisfied with the competitive status of the regional public banking sector, at the annual Württemberg savings bank congress in 1988 Lothar Späth, to the dismay of many of those present, announced that his government would continue to liberalize savings bank regulations and consider allowing a partial privatization of selected large savings banks. This would build upon the liberalizations of the Baden-Württemberg savings bank law in 1986 and 1987 that enabled the savings banks to substantially expand their commercial banking activities.[77] In his speech, Späth made clear his belief that the coming integrated European market presented an even greater challenge to the regional public and private banks than it did to regional industry. In his view, the government had to take an offensive strategy to prevent Stuttgart from falling further behind Frankfurt and Munich as an attractive location for the European financial community ("Späth ist mit Bankstrukturen immer noch unzufrieden," *Schwäbische Zeitung,* 8 November 1988). True to his words, in 1990 and 1991 Späth actively promoted several merger attempts involving various combinations of major regional public banks (within and outside the savings bank sector), but for many of the same reasons as earlier, all these fusion attempts failed. In early 1995, yet another failed merger attempt involving the Landesgirokasse and the BW-Bank occurred.[78] Merger among public banks in the region continues to be a hot and controversial economic and political topic, in no small part because both regional savings bank associations would like to see a stronger Landesbank.

Even without additional bank fusions, the Land government has found ways to increase further its influence over regional industrial finance. In 1990, the law governing the Landeskreditbank was successfully amended to permit the LKB to expand its commercial banking operations in which it competes directly with other banks. This change also raised the chances that the L-Bank might be used for direct government intervention into firms.[79] And in late 1994, the L-Bank and BW-Bank negotiated a cooperation pact that will assist the L-Bank in commercial business with larger firms and the BW-Bank in business with the Mittelstand.[80] This alliance should strengthen both banks in the regional industrial finance market.

Neither has the lack of direct control by the Land government precluded the SüdwestLB from playing a supportive role in the regional policy network. For example, one of the SüdwestLB's first actions was to sign a cooperation agreement with a Tokyo trading house to advise and assist Baden-Württemberg firms entering the Japanese market ("SüdwestLB wird in Japan Aktiv," *Frankfurter Allgemeine Zeitung*, 5 December 1989). To quickly establish a presence in foreign markets and investment banking, the SüdwestLB took a 25 percent stake in WestLB Europa AG—a subsidiary created by the Westdeutsche Landesbank to operate its vastly expanded European branch network—and a 25 percent stake in West Merchant Bank, also a WestLB subsidiary ("SüdwestLB beteiligt sich an WestLB Europa AG," *Frankfurter Allgemeine Zeitung*, 23 February 1990). The SüdwestLB later sold both of these holdings back to the WestLB because of differences in international strategies: the WestLB wants to focus on large firm customers abroad while the SüdwestLB wants to focus on helping regional Mittelstand firms in their export markets. For the SüdwestLB, this means building up foreign offices and a network of cooperation with banks in other countries, as well as providing financial support for such measures as the German House in Singapore, which houses Mittelstand firms from Germany ("SüdwestLB hat Kooperationspläne in Frankreich und Italien," *Frankfurter Allgemeine Zeitung*, 1 February 1996). In contrast to other Landesbanks, however, the SüdwestLB has not purchased any significant shareholdings in nonfinancial firms. The savings banks in Baden-Württemberg are resisting such activities, and the Land government has too little direct influence in the bank to initiate such an industrial policy.

In summary, though the Land government failed to realize its most ambitious bank sector goals, along the way it managed to significantly change the structure and development of the region's banking sector. In its alternating roles of owner and regulator, the Land government successfully stimulated or guided four major bank mergers yielding the Landesgirokasse Stuttgart, the Landeskreditbank, the BW-Bank, and the SüdwestLB. Each of these banks represents one of the region's major banks today, and in all but the SüdwestLB the Land government has a major ownership stake.

The fusion (and liberalization) stories are also a microcosm of the issues, interests, and institutions shaping the ongoing national debate over the future of the public savings banks (as discussed in chap. 2). The suggestion of altering the regional principle, public ownership, or three-tier structure—all of which were threatened by one or more of the attempted mergers in the region— is enough to incite passionate warfare between factions.[81] As in the national arena, within Baden-Württemberg competing alliances emerged between government and savings bank officials who seek to preserve all of the fundamental association principles and structure, and those who are willing to greatly modify or even abandon some of these principles. Such debates and struggles will undoubtedly continue as the market pressures associated with financial internationalization and European integration mount.

Summary

In the traditional model of business-government relations in Baden-Württemberg, government plays a largely subsidiary role in the economy, providing aid to firms directly and indirectly via subsidies to organizations in the regional policy network. Government policy also promotes diversified quality production and interfirm cooperation primarily through its extensive support for collective goods such as education and technical training, as well as research and development. This model was built on the particular needs and preferences of the strongly Mittelstand-dominated regional economy.

In the 1970s and 1980s, the Land's regional policy network was greatly expanded in terms of new organizations and resources flowing through it to firms. Through the rapid growth of direct subsidies to firms, the Land government was able to influence the price and flow of capital to particular firms, sectors, and market activities (such as innovation). This expansion was at times initiated unilaterally by the Land government, at other times by business organizations in cooperation with the government. The expansion of the network was facilitated by several factors: the ascendance of the CDU to stable political dominance allowed a durable business-government policy coalition to emerge; economic crisis and structural changes also raised the demand by Mittelstand firms for the resources provided through the network; and the existence of the LKB, Surety Bank, and MBG and very effective cooperation with banks in the region enabled the flow of resources through the network to firms to expand quickly without requiring organizational or procedural changes.

The success and expansion of the organizations of the regional policy network were not solely conditioned by the expansion of government subsidies. Many of these organizations provide collective and noncollective goods and services directly to firms that are not state-subsidized. In fact, some critics in the region suggested that state industrial policy is redundant, that is, that technical and business information is already provided by the self-help organizations of the Mittelstand and that banks provide adequate capital. However, such redundancy appears to be a contributory, if not necessary, institutional feature of the decentralized networks of production (and by extension DQP) that are so pervasive in Baden-Württemberg. Redundancy enables smaller firms to access multiple providers of resources, thus reducing the negative impact if one provider is no longer available (Grabher 1993). Arguably, regional firms and their organizations also learned to accept such intervention as beneficial to their long-term ability to survive problem periods and facilitate firm adjustment. Moreover, much of the state subsidies were used to expand the capacity of private industrial research organizations, chambers, the RKW, and other organizations that support the Mittelstand in the region. There was also a marked trend toward transferring the implementation of government economic policies out of government agencies to the quasi-public or private organizations of the regional policy network. This helped maintain the political support of the dominant business groups, because the programs would be implemented by organizations that were completely, or at least partially, under their control.

Finally, the predominance and resilience of small firms and small banks circumscribed the kind of bank dominance over industry associated with organized capitalism—Baden-Württemberg is hardly a system of economic coordination by bankers. Rather, it is a system of multiple loci of direct and indirect cooperation—as well as competition—among firms. Cooperation is frequently mediated and supported, but not controlled, by the Land government. The government's actions in the banking sector were largely intended to promote the Mittelstand and its supportive institutions. Unlike North Rhine–Westphalia, the Land government of Baden-Württemberg failed to build the kind of institutional capacity in the form of a Landesbank that would have enabled it to intervene and shape the strategies of large firms. Thus, in Baden-Württemberg, industrial governance and change remain comparatively decentralized.

APPENDIX: IMPACT OF INDUSTRIAL POLICY ON
FIRM MODERNIZATION

In this appendix I examine briefly the growth of subsidies for business start-ups and technology promotion and attempt to assess the extent to which these influenced the process of firm and sectoral adjustment. After a relatively slow start in the mid-1970s, the support of business start-ups by the government of Baden-Württemberg exploded: from 441 loans worth about DM 20 million in 1974 to 3,800 new loans worth DM 223.1 million in 1979—a level roughly maintained since then (Landeskreditbank Baden-Württemberg 1982). An independent study of the Middle Neckar region in Baden-Württemberg showed that in 1974, 3.4 percent of all business start-ups received state loans; by 1979 this percentage had reached 17.9 (Economics Ministry of Baden Württemberg 1982, 60). Because the start-up loans of the government of Baden-Württemberg, granted by the L-Bank, can be combined with federal loans, a firm receiving assistance could potentially finance 50–80 percent of its initial investment with state funds.[82]

Results of studies by the LKB and outside institutes indicate that firms that received state loans at their founding, in comparison to those that did not, demonstrate higher rates of growth and profitability, employ and educate more people, and have a substantially lower insolvency rate.[83] In a 1985 study, roughly half the firms surveyed said they would not have started their business without state support and that state aid was an important factor in the firm's success.[84] Consulting subsidized through the regional policy network was used by about half of all start-up firms.[85] Firms that received state funds and participated in state-supported educational seminars, or received state-subsidized consulting, demonstrated significantly higher growth and employment rates than those that did not (Zahn et al. 1985). The expanded supply of business consultancies offered by the regional policy network was met with equal demand: between 1975 and 1985, the overall number of state-subsidized consultancies rose 64 percent (from 10,686 to 17,569; Economics Ministry of Baden-Württemberg 1977, 1986). Thus considerable evidence suggests that state aid has a measurable and positive impact on the process of firm formation—an especially critical process for sustaining decentralized production.

As indicated above, technology programs expanded dramatically during the 1980s. From 1978 to 1983, 398 R&D projects in individual firms were supported with DM 91.5 million (Economics Ministry of Baden-Württemberg 1982, 1986). At this point in time, the government estimated that 3.4 percent of Baden-Württemberg's manufacturing firms with more than 20 employees had received such support (Euba 1985, 316). From 1984 (the first year of the new technology program) to 1986, 1,799 technology projects were supported in 1,441 firms (669 were manufacturing firms with more than 20 employees). I calculate that nearly 10 percent of all industrial manufacturing firms in the region received support from the Land government under its technology programs in these three years. In individual sectors, this percentage is much higher: in the machine tool sector, some 20 to 30 percent of firms with more than 20 employees received support; in the electronics sector, 15 to 20 percent of firms received support. These two sectors combined accounted for 40 to 50 percent of the total funds distributed to individual firms for technology promotion in this period.[86] The actual value of technology subsidies generally ranged between 5 and 15 percent of the total investment for the firm's project.[87] Of all loans granted for the introduction of modern technologies, 55 percent were granted to firms for the purchase of numerically controlled machinery.[88] In craft firms, this percentage was even higher.

The question of whether this level of state support was necessary to modernize Baden-Württemberg industry, and the machine tool sector in particular, cannot be answered unequivocally. The government's technology transfer program is based on the assumption that state measures would support the introduction of new, untested technologies in firms. But a survey by the Land's Economics Ministry in 1982 showed that of the state's some 1,100 machine tool firms, 60 percent already employed numerically controlled machinery in their production, and half of those firms produced numerically controlled machine tools themselves (Landtag of Baden-Württemberg, 8/3523).[89] On the other hand, for the many supplier firms receiving these loans, the utilization of new microelectronics technology was their most important adjustment challenge in the 1980s. Hence, even though many of these firms were already adopting these technologies, it is likely that generous state support accelerated the rate of modernization by making further technology investments cheaper. By assuming part of the risk and through a demonstration effect, anecdotal evidence indicates that generous state support further encouraged banks in the region to support these technology investments.

CHAPTER 6

Banking on the East?

Today the bogeyman is the Treuhand, but the next one is already deter-mined—the banks.
—Director of the state development bank of Saxony, August 1993

For most of the postunification period, the question of whether the banks are fulfilling their social and political responsibility in the East has been hotly debated in Germany. Much of the public and many politicians believe the banks shirked their social responsibility by avoiding risky but under the conditions necessary investments in the East. The bankers think they have done more than enough—perhaps even too much. There is, of course, no definitive answer to this question. Nonetheless, the transformation of the East German economy provides an excellent case study to examine the finance capitalism perspective on the role of the banks. In many respects, the German universal banking system seemed like the best financial system model for transition economies (for example, see Lipton and Sachs 1990). If ownership of privatized state firms were widely dispersed, there would be little incentive for individual owners to monitor firm managers. The state could retain a large stake and fulfill this function, but this would run against the logic of privatization. From a theoretical and practical perspective, banks may be seen as the ideal monitor. The combination of bank ownership and debt financing of firms places banks in a strong position to monitor firm management and assure needed restructuring.

Thus, from the finance capitalism perspective, we would have expected the banks to (1) play a prominent—if not leading—role in the privatization and reorganization of firms in the East; (2) to finance extensively the privatized and newly established firms in the East; and (3) to play a prominent role in corporate governance, that is, to monitor management of a wide range of firms and use this influence to guide firms. Indeed, the West German government's basic economic strategy for the East—privatization followed by rationalization of

189

firms once in the private sector—was heavily predicated on the participation of the banks. Together with the major industrial firms of the West, the banks were expected to play a vanguard role in sectoral rationalization through the purchase and reorganization of significant eastern firms. Chancellor Kohl in particular repeatedly likened the reunification challenge to the postwar reconstruction challenge. In so doing, he evoked the image of that earlier era when firms and banks (presumably) laid all on the line in order to get the job done. But the willingness of western firms to play this role fell short of what many had hoped for. Ultimately, the Treuhand (the state agency charged with privatizing eastern German firms) ended up "buying" western investments in order to privatize many of its firms. The banks in particular disappointed many by their perceived cautiousness in the East. Their role has fallen considerably short of the finance capitalism predictions: banks have purchased directly or indirectly relatively few stakes in eastern firms, nor are they playing an especially prominent role in the development or execution of firm or sectoral rationalization plans.

This chapter argues that the lesser rather than greater role of the banks should, and could, have been anticipated from the outset. Instead of providing the opportunity to enhance bank influence over industry, the experience in the East verifies trends and changes in bank strategy and bank-industry relations already evident in the West prior to reunification. The banks are assuming an eastern role in industrial development and governance that is largely consistent with the role that has evolved in western Germany. As argued earlier, one consequence of these changes is that banks are increasingly finding ways to reduce their risk exposure to particular firms and sectors. In turn, this means that banks are less willing to place themselves in a position where they may have to bail out and restructure firms. Thus the main argument of the chapter is that the difference between East and West is not so much in bank strategy and willingness to assume risk as it is in the different market situation of eastern firms. The greater risks and uncertainties in the East significantly outstrip bank capacity to monitor and thus assume risk. The gap is being filled by the state. In particular, it is the state that is presently most crucial in setting the framework for long-term industrial finance. This framework is the result of the complex interplay of institutional factors, including laws, regulations, and public development banks. Without the heavy—and not so invisible—hand of the state, this long-term financial framework would be impossible, in either the West or especially the East.

In chapter 2 we analyzed the reconstruction of the eastern banking sector after reunification; thus this chapter analyzes the role of the banks in rationalizing nonfinancial sectors in eastern Germany. The chapter examines first the role of the banks in the privatization of Treuhand firms. Through the provision of consulting services to the Treuhand, as well as to investors purchasing firms from the Treuhand, the West German banks played an important advisory role in the privatization process. Contrary to theoretical and political expectations, however, the banks invested comparatively little of their own capital in eastern firms. With some exceptions, the banks have made it clear that the risks of corporate ownership in the East go well beyond what they are willing to assume. Where the banks have directly invested in firms, they largely view it as a financial investment without any commitment to assuming managerial responsibility. Banks have financed a high proportion of all firm investments in the East, but their role in developing rationalization plans, or even helping firms develop plans, has been surprisingly circumscribed. The willingness of the banks to guide the rationalization of privatized or new firms was tamed by their risk concerns. This cautiousness has also limited the role of banks in eastern regional economic policy networks. The last part of the chapter examines briefly banks and these networks in the East.

Banks and Privatization

Upon reunification, the primary focus of the transition from planned to market economy in eastern Germany was the privatization of state-owned firms. The Treuhand Agency (Treuhandanstalt), established to oversee this process, turned quickly to the banking sector. The initial role of the West German banks in this process was twofold: first, to provide short-term liquidity to Treuhand firms in order to sustain their operations until they could be privatized. Well into 1991, lending of this sort was dominated by the Deutsche and Dresdner Banks, largely by virtue of their contacts to East German firms acquired in their respective joint ventures with the old East German Staatsbank. Lacking the capacity itself, the Treuhand relied on the banks to dispense and monitor these loans. In exchange, the Treuhand guaranteed a comfortable interest margin on the loans and assumed all risk of default. The second role of the banks was to utilize their investment banking capacities and/or subsidiaries to facilitate the privatization of Treuhand firms. In this process, the banks played all sides of the table: they advised the Treuhand in the sale of properties, they advised buyers of Treuhand properties (primarily their West German corporate clients), and they advised the managers of Treuhand firms to be privatized. The banks also organized various presentation seminars and tours on behalf of the Treuhand— wooing investors in West Germany and abroad. In short, the market (and the fees) for investment and general management consulting exploded, and the

German universal banks with their Allfinanz subsidiaries were well poised to take advantage of it. A prime example of this is the Deutsche Bank: its Roland Berger consulting subsidiary advised in the privatization of over 900 Treuhand firms; its Morgan Grenfell investment banking subsidiary advised the Treuhand extensively in sales to British firms (Krupp 1993).

However, this was not a market limited to German banks. In the first year after economic and monetary union, the Treuhand had already given contracts to 36 different investment banks to privatize 133 of its firms (Treuhandanstalt 1991). Press reports suggest that many of the biggest privatization deals were in fact done by non-German investment banks. The Treuhand also drew heavily on management consulting and accounting firms to assist in the privatization process. In other words, the West German banks—above all the major commercial banks—clearly played an *advising* role in the privatization process, but they were far from the central actors. Because there were so many ways to break up the combines and use their assets, the privatization process was, in essence, one of "making" new firms out of old pieces that would be attractive to outside investors. German banks did some of this, but overall they simply did not have the same kind of mergers and acquisitions experience as the leading international investment banks, nor did they have the sectoral knowledge of consulting and industrial firms. Thus intermediaries with stronger industrial knowledge and/or contacts to western (especially non-German) investors were more prominent in the privatization process (Griffin 1994). Later, as the stock of relatively easily privatized firms dwindled, the Treuhand was forced to turn to experimental privatization models that embodied cooperation among investors, firm managers, and often local and Länder political representatives. In most cases, West German banks were called upon to participate in these models, but they typically resisted their incorporation whenever possible.

More importantly, the West German banks were expected to become heavy equity investors themselves in eastern firms, and, at least initially, they were eager to fulfill this expectation. Already in 1990, many of the major western banks (from West Germany and abroad) established new equity participation funds or directed existing subsidiaries to begin scouring the East for investment opportunities. Within a short time, several hundred million marks were sitting in various eastern-focused equity participation corporations (*Kapitalbeteiligungsgesellschaften,* or KBGs). The banks and their fund managers invested heavily in examining hundreds of eastern firms for potential takeover or a partial shareholding. But very few opportunities in the East could meet their expectations. By the end of 1991, merely 10 percent of the more than DM 300 million available in eastern participation corporations had actually been spent; only one in

10 eastern firms interested in a western equity participation had actually secured one (Institut der deutschen Wirtschaft 1992). By the end of 1992, the amount invested in eastern firms reached DM 300 million, but this encompassed only 80 firms.[1] By the end of 1993, when the vast majority of Treuhand firms had already been privatized, all KBGs had invested just over DM 500 million in 343 firms, though much of this growth during 1993 is attributable to public, non-profit KBGs.[2] When compared to the glacial development of the equity partic-ipation (venture capital) market in West Germany over the 1970s and 1980s, the growth of this market in the East seems rapid. But when these numbers are compared to the tens of billions spent for the purchase of over 10,000 Treuhand firms in the same period, they are very modest indeed.

Probably the biggest single bank investor in the East is the Deutsche Bank. Yet even the Deutsche Bank could find little more than 40 acceptable eastern firms as of mid-1993.[3] With the exception of the Deutsche Bank's subsidiary, the Deutsche Industrie Holding (DIH), which purchased firms outright, the vast majority of bank participations in the East are minority stakes. The banks view them as financial investments and have no intent of pursuing an active man-agement role. Privately controlled KBGs are generally looking for annual re-turns in the range of 25 percent.[4] Thus, given the management and product mar-ket problems of most eastern firms, it is not surprising that participation funds invested comparatively little. Where the banks and their equity companies in-vested is primarily in construction and related industries. The postunification construction boom made this one of the leading growth sectors in the East. One leading manager of the Deutsche Bank expressly stated the bank's criteria for investing in eastern firms: they must be firms that will profit from public funds (either construction or public procurement contracts), are likely to have above-average profits, operate in local markets with competent managers, and do not need large rationalization investments (Nölting 1992). Obviously excluded from such a strategy are the industrial and other firms on which an eastern ex-port economy—indispensable to self-sustaining growth—must be built.

Available evidence indicates that most of the participations by equity com-panies took the form of minority participations in firms being purchased through a management buyout (MBO) or management buy-in (MBI) deal.[5] The banks, in fact, found the MBO/MBI phenomenon to be one of the more lucra-tive market segments in the East. Prior to reunification, MBOs were compara-tively uncommon in West Germany. The market was expanding during the 1980s, but the cumulative total of MBO deals was barely 150 by 1990. Banks were generally wary of MBOs, though in the late 1980s their desire to expand fee business, combined with the above-average returns realized by previous

MBOs, was beginning to stimulate their interest in advising, financing, and even investing in MBO deals (Leimbach 1991). Reunification thus sent the MBO market soaring: by mid-1993 more than 2,000 MBO/MBI deals—nearly one in five privatizations—had been done in eastern Germany alone, and banks were at the forefront.[6] The Deutsche Bank alone claims that a quarter of the eastern MBO/MBI privatizations involved its customers ("Noch grosszügigere Kreditvergabe ist in Ostdeutschland nicht zu verantworten," *Handelsblatt,* 21 June 1993).[7] One primary reason for bank interest in MBOs was the opportunity to combine the services of Allfinanz units: the bank or its consulting subsidiary could advise the buyers, the bank could finance the deal with loans, and the bank or its equity participation subsidiary could invest equity (or subordinated debt) in the deal.[8] The East in general, and MBOs in particular, proved to be the perfect opportunity for banks to realize the synergies of Allfinanz—something they have largely failed to do in the West.

Since small, direct bank equity investments in firms are not necessarily public information, it is impossible to determine the exact amount of equity that banks have actually invested in eastern firms. Thus the number of bank investments in the East may be larger than that indicated by the numbers of their equity participation companies alone. However, given the difficulties of equity participation companies in finding suitable investments in the East, it is likely that the banks have focused more heavily on consulting and financing than equity investment. Moreover, reports from bankers in the East indicate that most MBOs were done with comparatively little equity and a very high degree of external debt. In many cases a significant percentage of equity is actually composed of long-term state loans to the investing managers (Fromman 1991).[9]

The Bank Billion

Given this history, it was remarkable when banking community leaders agreed in early 1993 to invest another one billion marks of equity in eastern firms. The so-called bank billion was to be the banks' contribution to the Solidarity Pact, a broad political pact that called upon governments and major social groups to make specific and expanded financial commitments to financing the eastern transition (on the pact, see Sally and Webber 1994). With western industrial firms increasingly hesitant to invest in the East, the Treuhand and the Kohl government saw banks and their equity participation companies as the best hope to privatize remaining Treuhand firms. However, this public and political commitment made by a handful of banking association executives was not widely shared in the banking community. The savings and cooperative banks in particular balked at the request that they contribute DM 400 million and DM 200 million respectively. Aside from some equity investments by a few Landesbanks, these two banking groups had not previously sought to purchase holdings in eastern firms. Even within the commercial banking sector, there was great reluctance to invest more money when the money already committed to eastern investment funds could hardly be spent ("Martini on the Rocks" 1993).

The fact that the money was supposed to aid in the privatization of remaining Treuhand firms made the project even more harrowing, as most of these firms were viewed by investors as no longer viable. Unabashed, the Treuhand set a goal at the beginning of 1993 to privatize an additional 400 to 500 small- and medium-sized firms with the bank billion (Pahlen 1993; see also Friedhoff 1993). The Treuhand used public and political pressure to compel the banks to carry through on their commitment. With reluctance, the western commercial banks (about 200 banks altogether) finally established a new equity fund (Beteiligungsgesellschaft neuer Länder, or BNL) in June 1993 with the objective of purchasing Treuhand firms. In order to ease the privatization of these firms for the banks, the Treuhand reportedly agreed to provide greater than normal investment assistance and possibly to share in future losses (Krupp 1993). The first privatization under the bank billion occurred in late July 1993 when the Deutsche Industrie Holding purchased 13 firms from the Treuhand ("Treuhand verkauft 13 Portfolio-Unternehmen," *Frankfurter Allgemeine Zeitung,* 31 July 1993). By mid-1995 the banks claimed that they had virtually satisfied the bank billion deal. At this time the BNL had invested DM 340 million in 13 firms. Banks from the savings bank sector (Landesbanks) purchased stakes in 25 eastern firms totaling DM 412 million.[10] These latest efforts notwithstanding, the banks did not significantly change their cautious investment policies for the East. More likely, the banks viewed the bank billion as the price for stemming public criticism. Despite a widespread public image to the contrary, many West German bankers argued that they assumed an inordinate amount of risk in the East, some claiming they would probably not have purchased stakes in *any* firms if it were not for their social and political responsibility to do so (Nölting 1992).

So why have the banks invested comparatively little equity in eastern firms? An answer to this question can begin with broader structural factors and then move to narrower barriers to bank investment. First, the task of restructuring the East was enormous. To suggest that three, six, or even 20 big banks could collectively lead the transition was unrealistic. Second, the old firm debts of eastern firms were carved out of the banking system and lumped into the new, government-owned Deutsche Kreditbank. Thus the structural pressure that led banks in other East European countries to get heavily involved in firm restructuring was absent in eastern Germany: German banks were not forced to help firm restructuring in order to save their loans, a common reason for bank-led restructuring in the West (Carlin and Richthofen 1995, 3). The banks could choose their customers from a position of complete independence.

These structural factors aside, the banks could still have chosen to be more involved in firm restructuring than they did. The banks cite several reasons for their reluctance. First, they claimed they must accept lower rates of return in the East and expect a longer wait for profits to be realized—all while having to invest two to three times more consulting time in each firm ("Markt in neuen Ländern dürfte expansiv bleiben," *Handelsblatt,* 5 July 1993). Second, many bankers claimed that their ability to invest in firms is restricted by, among other things, the German law for limited liability companies (GmbH Gesetz). According to this law, a bank's loans to firms in which it also has an equity stake will be treated like equity in the case of bankruptcy ("Unternehmenskäufe durch Manager bergen im Osten hohe Risiken," *Frankfurter Allgemeine Zeitung,* 17 October 1992; also Hummel 1995). This factor raises the probability that banks will either call in loans as soon as there are signs of trouble or will refuse to both lend to and invest equity in the same firm. Third, difficulties in evaluating firm assets, unclarified property rights, and slow, sometimes testy negotiations with public authorities all hindered bank equity participations (and also bank lending).[11] While the problem of unclarified property rights was probably overstated, the difficulty in assessing firm assets (and prospects) was surely not (on the property rights problem, see Griffin 1994, 409–10).

Furthermore, whether one argues that the banks invested too little or too much equity in eastern firms, the banks are no more capable of playing a managerial role in eastern Germany than they are in western Germany. For more than a decade, the major West German private commercial banks have generally followed a more risk-averse policy regarding equity stakes in nonfinancial firms. In this period they tendentiously reduced their equity holdings (especially large holdings in individual firms), citing, among other things, their inability to assume, or even monitor, managerial functions (for a banker's view on this, see Krupp 1993). Given the greater uncertainties and managerial challenges in the East, the banks are even less in a position to become industrial entrepreneurs. Despite long-held beliefs to the contrary, the banks, if anything, had too little information gathering and processing capabilities in the East and relied heavily on third parties—for example, their own and other consulting firms—to help them assess the prospects and risks of various firm equity (and loan) investments. Thus, "instead of the financial institutions facilitating an efficient sale of [Treuhand] assets, the sale of assets actually facilitates the efficient participation of the financial institutions [in financing firms]" (Griffin 1994, 410).

Finally, the banks have long been criticized in West Germany for having excessive power over industry. Thus, for the banks, the great irony of reunification is that prominent national and local political leaders were calling on them to assume just such a role in the East, while at the very same time other politicians were demanding tight legal restrictions on bank involvement in industry! The banks were damned if they did and damned if they didn't. The banks chose the latter: despite demands to get more involved, the banks probably knew all too well that the more they were drawn into responsibility for restructuring eastern firms, the more likely they would be criticized—and criticized more heavily—for the problems of eastern firms. In such a situation, it is probably preferable to be criticized for doing too little, rather than be criticized later for layoffs or other problems resulting from restructuring (and lose more money in the process). In other words, the strategy of minimizing financial risk was also the strategy of minimizing reputational risk. For banks, their reputation as competent and reliable partners is extremely important. Thus, if they could not make credible commitments to supporting clients over the long term, it was better not to make any commitment to begin with. Widespread failure among a bank's clients would be very damaging to its reputation.

Accordingly, the banks have no known direct stakes in large firms in the East. However, this is largely a moot point, since there are very few large, independent companies left in the East. The banks have acquired a fairly significant number of stakes in eastern Mittelstand firms. But, as already noted, these are generally minority positions taken in safe sectors and viewed as financial investments. In other words, banks have generally taken equity positions in firms needing relatively little restructuring or where managerial expertise was being supplied by a third party. Banks purchased very few firms from the Treuhand. Thus the Treuhand carried the burden of privatization largely on its own.

Banks and Firm Rationalization

While privatization was the initial focus of market-building efforts, as each Treuhand firm was sold, the primary challenge became increasingly that of rationalizing firms. Since the banks have largely avoided a direct managerial role in firms, the remaining critical function for the banks is their capacity and willingness to finance the massive rationalization investments needed in the East.[12] While the banks have lent a considerable amount of money to firms in the East, a closer examination of investment finance patterns reveals that the long-term finance necessary for rationalization measures has come heavily from the state. And where banks have lent long-term, the terms and rates of lending have been heavily influenced by the state. While the commercial banks dominated loan markets early on, beginning in 1992 a dramatic shift in commercial lending from the private commercial banks to the cooperative and public savings banks indicates that the latter are becoming the central banking groups for the rationalization of eastern firms.

Rationalization in the "Treuhand Sector"

In the early stages of market building, when most firms belonged to the Treuhand, new corporate lending in the East was primarily oriented toward the short-term liquidity needs of Treuhand firms. These funds were provided overwhelmingly by a handful of West German commercial banks, especially the Deutsche and Dresdner Banks. At the end of 1990, 75 percent of the business loans made by the nine largest West German commercial banks in the East went to Treuhand firms (loans to Treuhand firms totaled DM 13.6 billion); 94 percent of these loans were fully guaranteed by the Treuhand (Federal Association of German Banks 1994). As Treuhand firms got new DM balance sheets and developed restructuring plans, the Treuhand pressed their managers to start seeking other sources of funds, including nonguaranteed commercial loans, to finance these plans (Breuel 1992). While the commercial banks had lent generously in the early going when their loans were guaranteed, they were extremely hesitant to lend funds to Treuhand firms at their own risk. At the end of 1992, for example, loans to Treuhand firms by the nine largest commercial banks had grown to DM 18.7 billion, but 88 percent of these remained fully guaranteed by the Treuhand.[13] A survey of firms in the summer of 1992 indicated that Treuhand firms had significantly greater difficulty than other categories of firms in the East in securing adequate investment finance (Deutsches Institut für Wirtschaftsforschung 1993). Consequently, Treuhand firms were generally not able to invest at rates comparable to private sector firms.[14] Thus the great bulk of funds provided to Treuhand firms had to come from the Treuhand itself. By the end of 1992, the Treuhand had invested roughly DM 120 billion, primarily in what it termed the "passive" financial rationalization of its firms—the assumption of old debts, injection of new equity, and guarantees for liquidity and investment credits (Ursula Weidenfeld and Martin Kessler, "Wir kaufen nur Zeit," *Wirtschaftswoche,* 1 January 1993).

While bankers sat on the supervisory boards of many Treuhand firms, there is no indication that they played a prominent role in developing restructuring plans for these firms. As they themselves would readily acknowledge, bankers could offer relatively little of the industry-specific knowledge that these firms needed.[15] Treuhand firms would have to find this knowledge from western investors or other investment banks and management consultants. Moreover, having close ties to the banks in this form, contrary to the predictions of the finance capitalism model, obviously did not lead to more generous bank lending to Treuhand firms.[16] In sum, the Treuhand could not pass the burden—or even a significant chunk of it—of firm rationalization on to the banks. Among other factors, this surely kept the pressure on the Treuhand to privatize firms as rapidly as possible.

Though privatization proceeded at a relatively brisk pace, by late 1991 the Treuhand was largely holding firms that were difficult to privatize and in desperate need of much more than passive financial rationalization. Public and political pressure on the Treuhand to become more active in rationalizing its firms was immense, and slowly the Treuhand undertook several initiatives in this direction. Yet the Treuhand's president, Birgit Breuel, was strongly criticized for doing too little in this regard, as she resisted with great ideological conviction any measures that would transform the Treuhand (or a successor agency) into a state industrial holding company involving long-term subsidization of weak firms. Instead she pushed forward on privatization and liquidation. To get the job done, the Treuhand began to experiment with various privatization models—such as its management holding companies model (Management KG)—and continued to call on the banks (Martin Kessler, "Jemand von oben," *Wirtschaftswoche,* 7 May 1993). By the time the Treuhand officially closed shop at the end of 1994, it had privatized more than 15,000 firms. It left its successor organizations, the BVS (Bundesanstalt für vereinigungsbedingte Sonderaufgaben), with a few dozen firms yet to sell and the job of monitoring the thousands of privatization contracts. In sum, aside from the Treuhand's extensive financial rationalization of its firms, the organizational and technical restructuring of firms in the East occurred after privatization. The banks' role in privatizing, financing, and restructuring Treuhand firms was surprisingly modest (Carlin and Mayer 1992, 1995). They systematically avoided at-risk lending to Treuhand firms and the assumption of managerial responsibility.

Rationalization in the Private Sector

As privatization proceeded, firm lending by banks shifted rapidly to privatized and reprivatized firms and new business start-ups. Various surveys of private sector firm managers in the East throughout the first two years after reunification suggest that securing investment finance was frequently a problem, but not necessarily the primary one. This underscores the widespread public observation that lending institutions were willing to take significant risks in 1990 and 1991. Despite the general lack of collateral and myriad other factors that enhanced credit risk, press reports and interviews with bankers all suggest that in the early going the bankers—above all commercial bankers—were willing to suppress their inbred instinct for risk aversion in order to gain market share.[17]

Ironically, it was the same banks that were most severely criticized for becoming too restrictive in their lending practices when the German economy headed into recession in 1992. Whether banks operating in the East became *excessively* risk-averse is, again, a speculative question not easily answered. However, few bankers would deny that after an initial phase of generous lending, they are now using the same credit assessment (and collateral) criteria in the East as in the West. Given the more difficult market conditions in the East, such a policy must ipso facto lead to a more restricted credit policy. While commercial banks continued to increase the volume of their lending in the East, they rapidly lost market share after the eastern credit cooperatives and savings banks completed their internal reorganizations and began to compete more aggressively for loan business. By late 1992, the eastern savings banks had already achieved a market share in loan markets greater than that of their counterparts in the West (see table 9). The eastern cooperative banks were also quickly approaching the market share of western cooperatives. In loans to enterprises, the same trend is apparent. By the end of 1993, the commercial banks had paid out a cumulative total of DM 56.9 billion in business loans in the East. The savings banks and Landesbanks, starting from a virtually insignificant base of business loans, managed to pay out DM 51.7 billion in loans to eastern firms in the same period.[18] At the end of 1995, commercial banks had a 39.6 percent market share in loans to businesses and self-employed individuals in the East; the savings bank sector had 30.4 percent; and the cooperative sector had 13.0 percent ("Bankenmarkt Ost auf Wachstumskurs" 1996).

Several reasons for this dramatic shift in market share can be identified. First, such a shift was to a considerable degree the inevitable outcome of a market-based economy. The initial high market share in lending of commercial banks was an artificial construction—a legacy of the GDR (German Democratic Republic) system. Under conditions of market competition, it was extremely unlikely, and probably undesirable even from the viewpoint of commercial banks, that their market share in the East should remain so high. In short, because the commercial banks were in the market first, the limits of their risk exposure were probably reached well before those of the savings and cooperative banks. Second, as privatization proceeded, there were fewer and fewer large firms in the East. The eastern German economy is today essentially a Mittelstand economy, and the savings and cooperative banks have traditionally dominated this market. But these explanations are less than wholly satisfactory given the fact that the eastern savings and cooperative banks surpassed the market shares in business lending of their western counterparts (Carlin and Richthofen 1995, 20a). One possible interpretation is that the commercial banks are more risk-averse in their lending practices than the cooperative and especially the savings banks. Stated conversely, the cooperative and savings banks may have a higher risk tolerance than private commercial banks.

Two potential explanations for a higher risk tolerance seem plausible. First, the savings and cooperative banks may be less concerned with profit maximization and have lower costs of capital. The cooperative banks are member-owned and legally obligated to serve the needs of their membership. In practice this obligation requires cooperatives to be profitable for their survival, but it also allows for the possibility that the members will collectively assume higher risks and accept lower rates of return than a purely commercial bank might. The savings banks also have a formal-legal obligation to serve the financial needs of the public. While the real meaning of the public mission

TABLE 9. Market Share for Loans to Domestic Firms and Individuals in the Five New States by Type of Bank (figures are percentage of total by banks)

	Short-Term	Medium-Term	Long-Term	Total Loans
Commercial banks				
1990	85.6	55.2	79.4	81.7
1991	85.8	14.3	78.1	73.9
1992	64.7	51.7	29.6	46.3
Savings banks				
1990	1.4	29.6	10.0	6.5
1991	6.9	10.6	15.0	11.5
1992	18.9	32.8	46.8	34.0
Credit cooperatives				
1990	4.0	12.9	4.7	4.6
1991	3.8	3.2	6.1	4.8
1992	8.4	10.3	19.8	13.4
Other				
1990	9.0	2.3	5.9	7.2
1991	3.5	71.9	0.8	9.8
1992	8.0	5.2	3.8	6.3

Source: Deutsche Bundesbank, "Regionalergebnisse," *Statistische Beihefte zu den Monatsberichten der Deutschen Bundesbank*, series 1, *Bankenstatistik nach Bankengruppen* (February 1991, September 1993); table 6.
Note: 1992 figures are for September; other figures are for end of year. "Other" bank category includes the Girozentrale, the cooperative central bank (including the DG Bank), mortgage banks, and special purpose banks.

(*öffentlicher Auftrag*) of the savings banks is frequently debated, they are communal institutions whose assets and liabilities are publicly guaranteed. Communal oversight and the public guarantee are probably enabling eastern savings banks to assume higher risks than commercial banks in the East. Given the intense public pressure on local politicians to "do something," it seems quite plausible that these politicians who sit on the boards of savings banks are encouraging the banks to push the limits of tolerable risks. This difference in profit orientation is probably reinforced by the differing costs of capital for the major banking groups. The savings banks dominate the eastern savings deposits markets and thus have relatively cheap capital.[19] The commercial banks have imported from the West much of the capital they have lent in the East.[20] This capital is probably more costly, and its use in the East has to be weighed against the opportunity costs of investing it in the West. Since savings and cooperative banks are also traditionally more willing than commercial banks to lend their funds long-term, the striking shift in business loan maturity structure from short- to long-term probably facilitated further the expanding market share of the savings and cooperative banks.[21]

The second plausible explanation is that cooperative and savings banks may have informational advantages over commercial banks. Most savings and cooperative banks in the East are being managed (or at least comanaged) by previous managers, who are likely to be more familiar with local market conditions and firm clients.[22] These banks may be in a better position to assess and monitor credit risks. The information advantage of these banks is reinforced by structural imperatives. Cooperatives and savings banks are highly dependent on their local market, since it is essentially their only market. Prosperity for these banks therefore depends much more directly on their ability to transform local savings into successful local investment. Eastern cooperatives and savings banks have few, if any, established relations to western firms investing in the East and are thus further compelled to focus on lending to local firms. If the western experience applies to the East, savings and cooperative banks are also more likely to seek the business of firm start-ups and smaller firms that many commercial banks consider too small to be profitable.

Western commercial banks operating in the East may in fact minimize credit monitoring demands (and risks) by focusing their lending on financing the investments made by western firms in the East. Such loans are probably fully secured by the western firm, which would also be managing its newly acquired operations in the East or, at a minimum, would closely monitor the management of its eastern business partner. The Deutsche Bank, the leading lender among commercial banks in the East, indicated that 60–70 percent of its loans

for investments by small- and medium-sized firms in the East are actually going to West German firms ("Noch grosszügigere Kreditvergabe ist in Ostdeutschland nicht zu verantworten," *Handelsblatt,* 21 June 1993).[23] Since well
over half of all business investment made in the East since reunification came
from West German or foreign firms, this market segment probably provides the
commercial banks ample opportunity for credit growth in the East (Neumann
1995). Various surveys of firm managers and investors in the East indicate that
large firms and smaller firms belonging to a (western) concern have the least
difficulty securing finance (Deutsches Institut für Wirtschaftsforschung 1993;
Carlin and Mayer 1995).

In general, then, the evidence indicates that the major commercial banks
focused their at-risk lending for rationalization investments on Treuhand firms
after they had been privatized and come under the control of a western partner.
These banks also lent considerable sums to start-ups in the East, but small firms
appear to be increasingly the province of the savings and cooperative banks.
The role of the banks in corporate governance is minimal. There are relatively
few large firms that might be influenced by bank representatives sitting on their
supervisory boards. Only a handful of eastern AGs are publicly traded on the
stock exchange.[24] Banks are assuming some managerial responsibility only in
a few dozen Mittelstand firms where they have equity investments. Nearly all
of the larger firms in the East, especially in industry, are privatized Treuhand
firms. But among such firms, ownership and managerial control is highly concentrated in the hands of West German nonfinancial firms, thus re-creating the
dominant pattern of ownership in West Germany. These western firms provided
most of the finance, managerial skills, technology, and access to markets needed for the rationalization of privatized eastern firms.[25]

Thus the role of the banks in the eastern transformation process is largely
limited to a traditional business lending function. And they have lent considerable sums to firms in the East. But even in this function, it is clear that, whether
lending to privatized Treuhand firms or business start-ups, banks and their firm
clients relied immensely on the same economic promotion system (*Fördersys-
tem*) that had been developed and firmly established in West Germany. Without
this promotion system, the banks would have lent virtually nothing in eastern
Germany.

The Strong Arm of the State

At the heart of the state's financial promotion system is close cooperation between public special purpose banks at both the federal and Land level on the

one hand, and commercial, savings, and cooperative banks on the other. In this bank-based system, the house bank assumes the responsibility of submitting applications for state loans on behalf of its firm clients and normally assumes the full risk of the loan (and thus is responsible for monitoring the loans). The special purpose banks provide long-term, fixed-rate loans that are generally set at some level below the market rate.[26] The most important special purpose banks, the KfW (Kreditanstalt für Wiederaufbau) and the DtA (Deutsche Ausgleichsbank), began work in the East in early 1990. By mid-1991 the transfer of the western federal and state level institutions of economic promotion was largely completed in the East (Seidel 1992).

State loans and loan guarantees were vital to the process of building a credit market in the East. In terms of volume alone, state funds account for a considerable share of all lending in the East. The impact of state loans is amplified through their demonstrated and significant leveraging effect on at-risk lending by other banks. The financial advantages of state funds for firms and their house banks are considerable. First, there is usually some level of subsidy involved that enhances the equity position of the firm. Second, state funds generally eliminate interest rate risk, as they have fixed rates on very long terms (up to 20 years). Because many state loans do not require repayment of principal for an initial period of two to five years (some do not even require interest payments in this period), these loans also greatly enhance the liquidity position of firms. Third, while in the West the house bank typically carries the full credit risk of state loans, in the East the public special purpose banks have been considerably more willing to carry part of the loan risk themselves; for example, 40 percent of the liability for ERP (European Recovery Program) Fund loans up to DM 1 million is carried by the fund itself. Finally, because the state is providing much of the finance for long-term rationalization investments, the house bank can focus on less risky short-term lending. Each of the three major banking groups has played an important role in passing through state loans, though the commercial and savings bank sectors together account for the large majority.[27]

As the Treuhand sector of the eastern economy shrank and was replaced by a revived private sector, state support for firm investment flowed increasingly through state-owned special purpose banks (as well as through tax credits). The Bundesbank estimated that in 1991, the first full year after reunification, "more than one-half of lending by banks [to the enterprise sector] is probably accounted for by interest-subsidized loans. But the other part, too, includes sizeable subsidy elements [because of the Treuhand]."[28] From mid-1990 to the end of 1994, state loans and investment tax credits for eastern investment totaled DM 170 billion—equal to 30 percent of gross investment expenditures in the East. If one adds in the total rationalization expenditures of the Treuhand, this sum reaches DM 295 billion (Deutsche Bundesbank 1995a). While not directly comparable statistically, the overwhelming role of state funds in the East becomes even more apparent when compared to the fact that total investment for capital equipment and commercial buildings from 1991 to the end of 1994 equaled DM 300 billion (Deutsches Institut für Wirtschaftsforschung 1995a). By the end of 1993, total loans made by the KfW and the DtA to support firm investment in the East equaled nearly DM 60 billion (Kreditanstalt für Wiederaufbau 1993; Deutsche Ausgleichsbank 1993). By comparison, all banks in the commercial and savings bank sectors in the East together lent about DM 100 million in the same period (Federal Association of German Banks 1994; German Savings Bank and Giro Association 1995).[29] The KfW estimated that it has supported three-quarters of all industrial Mittelstand firms in the East.[30] Both banks continue to channel a disproportionately high percentage of their loans to the East and in absolute terms continue to provide high levels of credits.[31]

Aside from the direct provision of credits, state loans stimulated the expansion of credit through their leveraging or multiplier effect. While in many cases the majority of a particular investment (or even the entire sum!) in the East was financed by state funds, in most cases state funds made up for less than half of the investment's cost.[32] In numerous interviews and articles, many bankers readily acknowledge that state loans and guarantees made many investments possible in the first place (for one banker's discussion of the importance of state loans, see Schmitt 1993). Thus state loans and loan guarantees made a considerable, if not easily estimated, contribution toward opening access to the credit market for thousands of firms in the East.[33] In short, it is the heavy presence of the state in credit markets that made it possible for other banks to engage in significant levels of lending in the East.

State loans also heavily condition the terms of credit, especially for long-term loans. In 1992, the Bundesbank concluded that the combined effect of all state loans and subsidies was to virtually insulate the eastern credit market from interest rate effects. The allocational effects of the state's presence in credit markets are also significant, if not easily measured. There can be little doubt that individual promotion programs have consciously (and politically) determined allocational objectives. In this respect it seems fully justified to speak of considerable state *dirigisme* in the East achieved through credit allocation effects. Without attempting to fully and systematically analyze these effects, it is clear that among the primary goals of state intervention is the creation of a significant small- and medium-sized business sector. To this end, considerable funds have been expended for the support of business start-ups and rationalization investments by Mittelstand firms.[34] It also seems clear that the state moved during 1992 to a policy of preventing further deindustrialization in the East. Thus, despite the dim prospects of many large firms, considerable amounts of money are being invested in them in the hope of maintaining "industrial cores" (*industrielle Kerne*).

Five Years of Market Building

At the end of 1994, the Treuhand closed its doors.[35] The agency had completed more than 15,000 privatizations, with just a handful left to its successor organization. The Treuhand and the federal government proclaimed this a rousing success, despite the massive loss of industrial capacity and employment that accompanied the process. Optimists pointed to the high levels of investment, rising productivity, rapid growth rate in output (7.5 percent per annum on average between the second half of 1990 and 1994), and declining unemployment (13.5 percent in mid-1995) as evidence of the successful turnaround in the East.[36] In mid-1995, the Kohl government even dared to speak of "blooming landscapes" in the East. The number of voices calling for a reduction in eastern subsidies began to grow. It was argued, particularly by the Bundesbank, that the East was on its way to self-sustaining growth and that subsidies should be curbed before firms became too dependent on them (Deutsche Bundesbank 1995a, 39).

It was not long, however, before this brief period of optimism was largely quashed by the onset of stagnation and, in some respects, regression in eastern economic development. It has become painfully obvious that the eastern German economy is still fragile and a long way from catching up to even the poorest western Länder. Since late 1995, the growth rate of output in eastern Germany has declined dramatically. The productivity growth rate has also slowed dramatically, and eastern labor productivity is still less than 60 percent of West German, leaving unit wage labor costs in the East still nearly a third higher than in the West. As in West Germany, but worse, unemployment began to rise again in the East, hitting 15.5 percent at the end of 1996 and still rising. Adding in early pensioners and people in retraining or make-work programs brought total un- and underemployment to nearly 24 percent (Brautzsch 1997). Only in 1994 did the East begin to increase (slowly) its exports again.[37] Most importantly, the all-important industrial sector of the East has shrunk to a dangerously small level. This sector is critical because of the production-oriented service sectors that it supports and the fact that industrial exports are the best chance for the East to reduce its dependence on western transfers and achieve self-sustaining growth.[38] Moreover, despite high levels of overall investment, the gross capital assets per capita ratio barely improved, remaining under 40 percent of that of western Germany. The capital assets ratio of the eastern manufacturing sector was even lower, equaling one-third that of the West (Deutsches Institut für Wirtschaftsforschung 1995a). Finally, the firm insolvency rate started accelerating rapidly in the East in 1993 and has continued to rise dramatically.[39] In short, the eastern economy is not self-sustaining and will be heavily dependent on financial transfers well into the future.[40]

Thus, despite growing public fiscal problems, political pressure on the federal government to continue subsidy programs, and even to increase them, remains quite high. Eastern Länder governments argue that the early high overall growth rate was deceptive and that the East is still critically dependent on subsidy programs and capital transfers ("Absage an schnelle Kürzung der Fördermittel," *Handelsblatt,* 29 August 1995).[41] Firms continue to complain to the government that their financial situation is poor and deteriorating. Many have blamed the banks for excessive risk aversion or excessive collateral demands.[42] Thus, despite early optimism regarding the East, in late 1994 and during 1995 the federal government decided to extend for several more years various subsidy programs that were scheduled to end (and introduced some new ones; Deutsche Bundesbank 1995a, 55–56).

In particular, many economists and politicians agreed that one of the key problems for eastern firms was their low level of equity capital. By 1994, the equity base of many eastern firms was so low they could no longer secure external funding for their investments, to carry them through cash-short periods, or even to qualify for state loan programs (Institut der deutschen Wirtschaft 1995d)![43] Thus, in 1995, the federal government agreed to several measures to stimulate equity capital investment in eastern Mittelstand firms, including a new government-backed fund administered by the KfW that would make DM 1.5 billion available from 1995 to 1998 for equity investments in Mittelstand firms. But, given the difficulties with promoting equity participations in the past, the likely effect of such measures is questionable.[44] Moreover, the federal government is starting to reduce its overall subsidies to the East, in good part because of its desire to meet the deficit criteria for European currency union. Nonetheless, the continued extension of still high levels of subsidies guarantees that the state will remain the critical backbone of eastern investment for many more years. And the precarious situation of a large number of eastern firms and sectors means that securing external resources, including finance, will be a central question of survival. Increasingly, these firms are turning to regional policy networks for these resources.

Banks and Regional Economic Policy Networks in the East

As the Treuhand sold off firms, the primary burden of firm rationalization and sectoral restructuring devolved to regional and local actors in both the public and private sectors. While the federal government continues to provide the bulk of financial aid to the East, it is essentially the eastern Länder that now carry primary responsibility for dealing with faltering firms and securing the basis for self-sustaining growth. To help them fulfill this responsibility, the eastern Länder have developed and utilized regional economic policy networks.

After reunification, all of the new Länder established many of the same organizations that are important elements of regional networks in the old Länder, such as equity participation corporations, special development banks, credit guarantee cooperatives, and technology agencies. All of these organizations were essentially transferred from the West.[45] As in the West, eastern Länder governments looked frequently to the banks to assist them in their industrial policy efforts. Yet the banks resisted their inclusion in the firm privatization or rationalization efforts of the Länder unless much of the risk was shared with government or other parties.

As in western Germany, financial institutions are important organizations in eastern regional policy networks, since one of the chief activities of networks is financial promotion of firms. First, all of the Länder have their own economic development banks, though these are operated by western public banking partners. These development banks mostly implement standardized promotion programs imported from the West: programs for business start-ups, firm expansion or rationalization, liquidity assistance loans, or technology promotion loans. Second, the eastern Länder established nonprofit equity participation corporations and loan guarantee banks as part of their regional policy networks. In volume terms, these financial institutions have generally been quite successful in the East, granting a considerable number of loan guarantees and making a substantial percentage of all Mittelstand equity investments by KBGs.[46] Given the equity capital problems of eastern Mittelstand firms and the inability of bank-owned equity corporations to provide needed capital, several eastern Länder also began in 1995 to initiate their own programs for providing equity capital.[47]

Third, all of the eastern Länder have a Landesbank, but only in the case of Saxony was a new Landesbank established.[48] Thuringia bought into the Landesbank of Hessen, which now functions as the Landesbank for both Länder. The remaining three eastern Länder have agreements with other western Landesbanks to fulfill typical Landesbank functions.[49] While these Landesbanks are fulfilling their house bank functions for eastern Land governments and central banking functions for savings banks, they have generally provided little of the industrial policy support common in several western Länder. The Saxon Landesbank is small and lacks experience and therefore has not been in a position to support regional industrial policy through equity ownership in firms or by leading financial restructuring.[50] Other Landesbanks only began to take equity investment in the East under pressure of the bank billion obligation, and Landesbank investments amount to only two dozen firms in the entire East.[51] Thus even the Landesbanks, which take central institutional positions in several western regional economic policy networks, have so far kept their involvement in eastern policy networks to a minimum.

All banks in the East participate in the financial promotion efforts of the eastern Länder, primarily through their role in disbursing and monitoring state loans. They also support the nonprofit equity corporations and loan guarantee banks through equity contributions to such corporations. Thus the banks have participated fully in the standard financial promotion efforts of the Länder, but most of these involve relatively small sums of money or go to safer investments. When larger firms have had serious financial difficulty, Länder governments have generally had to provide substantial loan guarantees in order to secure continued bank lending. It seems that virtually every financial rescue of larger firms in the East has only been possible when significant state loan guarantees are present. By the end of 1994, each of the five eastern Länder had granted between DM 400 and DM 750 million in loan guarantees (Birgit Marschall and Antje Sirleschtov, "Industriepolitik: Kritische Grenze," *Wirtschaftswoche,* 19 January 1995).

Such guarantees usually go to larger firms that Land governments consider to be of great economic (i.e., political) significance.[52] These guarantees tend to be disbursed in an ad hoc manner to stave off impending collapse of particular firms, rather than according to a coherent industrial policy, that is, an attempt to retain and develop strategic sectors and/or technologies. Indeed, loan guarantees have arguably become the most popular policy instrument for cash-short Land governments to manage regional crises. Guarantees are widely preferred over direct equity stakes since they allow the Land government to respond to political and economic pressures, while stopping short of the costs and future financial and political liabilities associated with direct equity stakes—something the banks have also diligently avoided.[53] While it may be reasonable for the risks of larger troubled firms to be shared between private investors (including banks) and the state, these cases all speak against the finance capitalism view of the banks, in which they are expected to lead firm reorganizations, not follow the lead of the state.

In West Germany during the 1980s, technology promotion took on increasing political and budgetary significance at both the federal and Land levels. The western policies and institutions in this area have also been largely transferred to the East, though for a long time after reunification research promotion was not given high priority by policymakers. Such was the case even though the loss of R&D personnel and capacity in the East was probably even more dramatic than the general loss of jobs and capacity. In growing recognition of the negative long-term implications of this trend, technology policy efforts have been gaining strength. On the federal level, the Federal Research Ministry and the Federal Economics Ministry established several programs for small- and medium-sized eastern firms that were mostly based on similar programs in the West: programs for technology-oriented start-ups, support for hiring of R&D personnel, support for contract research, support to research institutes, and grants for specific innovation projects.[54] In 1995 the federal government spent nearly DM 500 million for these programs, but in 1996 it already began to reduce its allocation.

The Länder have also sought to contribute to the revitalization of research in the East, partly in response to a flagging federal commitment. Most of the programs have been relatively modest and have concentrated on providing support to research institutes and cooperative undertakings, as opposed to direct financial support for firms. Technology centers are quickly becoming popular in the East, just as they did in the West in the 1980s. These centers are being established on the western model of semipublic organizations involving cooperation among Land and local governments, local banks, chambers, firms, and business associations. The eastern Länder together (minus Brandenburg) allocated DM 408 million in 1995 and DM 439 million in 1996 to technology programs (Holst 1996).

A couple of Länder, notably Thuringia and Saxony, have pursued regional and structural policies with a strong technology dimension to them. Thuringia started down this road in 1991 when it purchased a controlling share of the Carl-Zeiss Combine, a large maker of optical instruments. The government has since invested DM 1.2 billion in the company in an effort to make it the center of a high-technology growth region in Thuringia. It took the next step in 1993 by establishing the Thuringia Technology Foundation to provide financial support to innovative firms. Saxony has achieved some success in turning its capital city, Dresden, into a center for microelectronics technology. While there were several remnant electronics firms from the GDR era in the city, the real turning point was the decision of Siemens to build a semiconductor plant in the city—a DM 2.7 billion investment greased with DM 1.1 billion in subsidies (DM 800 million from the Land government).[55] Despite these federal and Länder efforts, the numbers on R&D activity in the East have not been very encouraging.[56] For too many firms, the long-term payoffs of R&D cannot be sustained in light of severe short-term financial problems. It is likely that banks are underfunding R&D investments by firms since they are intangible investments with unknown payoffs (Carlin and Richthofen 1995). Regional economic policy networks in the East have only just begun to fill this financing gap.

A final set of institutions common to western regional policy networks are those that center around providing firms information and helping them make contacts with customers and production partners. Most of these institutions—chambers, the RKW, and economic promotion corporations—are also found in eastern policy networks. Virtually all of these function in the East as they do in the West, and many of them have become important institutions within eastern regional policy networks. Many of the services provided by these organizations parallel or complement those of banks' Allfinanz services. These organizations therefore sometimes compete with banks. More often, though, the provision of these services involves cooperation between banks and these organizations within the context of the regional policy network.

In sum, the organizations and policies of eastern regional economic policy networks closely mimic those prevalent in the West, and banks have assumed most of their ordinary (low-risk) roles in such networks. However, regional policy networks in the East face severe economic crisis and extraordinary challenges unknown in the West. Ordinary promotion programs and ordinary bank participation are insufficient. In the first two years after reunification, the economic policies of the new Länder were shaped heavily by the federal government, Treuhand, and the western Länder acting as partners to the new Länder. With time, however, the eastern Länder grew frustrated with their economic progress and the economic policies imposed on them by the West.

Thus, during 1991, a debate began over whether the Treuhand was pursuing too vigorously its privatization strategy at the cost of excessive job and productive capacity loss. The alternative approach advanced by critics of the Treuhand was to invest significantly more resources in the reorganization of firms before privatization. The focal concept of the debate became the notion of preserving "industrial cores" (*industrielle Kerne*). In time, there was widespread agreement that industrial cores must be sustained in the East, though the understandings of what the term meant varied greatly. The more conservative interpretation, represented among others by Treuhand chief Birgit Breuel, was essentially to continue current privatization efforts. Some modifications in Treuhand policy were made, but the overriding commitment to the values of private ownership and market efficiency remained intact. The more expansive interpretation, advocated most strongly by regional politicians, unions, and many firm managers in the East concerned with jobs, was that selected firms, industries, and economic regions must be sustained, even if this meant a much more prominent role for the state and the placement of political criteria alongside (or over) criteria of economic efficiency.

Länder Interventionism

In the course of 1992, the new Länder negotiated an agreement with the federal government and the Treuhand to rationalize more firms through cooperative Treuhand-Land efforts, thus preserving industrial cores in the East for reindustrialization. Each new Länder and its regional policy network developed its own plan in which the Land government would target and coordinate financial and technical assistance from a variety of sources for selected firms (Nolte 1993a). The Länder called on the banks to assist them in this effort, but they generally found the banks no more willing to assume risk than the Treuhand had. Rather than banks' alleviating the pressure on the state to get involved in the affairs of industry, as the finance and organized capitalism models propound, the state (including the Länder) felt the need to pressure the banks to get involved in industry!

One of the most visible Länder initiatives to save industrial cores was Saxony's ATLAS program (Ausgesuchte Treuhandunternehmen vom Land angemeldet zur Sanierung). ATLAS was one of the more innovative and potentially radical policy directions to grow out of the general frustration in the East with the results of the transformation process (for a description of ATLAS, see Nolte 1993b; Saxon State Ministry for Economics and Labor 1993). In April 1992, Breuel and Kajo Schommer, economics minister of Saxony, agreed to the following deal: The Land government of Saxony—using a group of management experts and parliamentary, union, and business representatives—would identify Treuhand firms considered to be of significant regional economic importance. If the Treuhand agreed that an identified firm had a reasonable chance to become competitive and had a viable plan to do so, then both the Treuhand and the Land government would provide a new package of financial assistance to the firm and secure competent managers to carry out the plan. The ultimate goal was to prepare these firms for successful privatization—not to end up with state-owned firms—and the Treuhand reserved the right to privatize any "ATLAS firm" at any time. Should the firm not achieve a successful turnaround, then the Land government and the Treuhand would agree together when liquidation was the next step. The ATLAS program became a model that other eastern Länder emulated in some form, though none was more ambitious than ATLAS (for a review of eastern Länder initiatives to retain industrial cores, see Nolte 1993a).

At this time there was considerable political support in Saxony behind the principle of greater state intervention. Economics Minister Schommer and the minister-president of Saxony, Kurt Biedenkopf, made clear their belief that some form of greater state action was necessary, but they were not advocating state ownership of industry (interview with Biedenkopf, in "'Das Glas ist halbvoll'" 1993; Saxon State Ministry for Economics and Labor 1993, 8–13). The ruling party in Saxony, the CDU, also committed itself publicly to a policy of using limited-term state subsidies to promote industrial cores in Saxony; this included a willingness to target specific regions and industries such as machine tools, electronics, and textiles ("CDU-Visionen für Sachsen im Jahr 2000," *Freie Presse*, 14 July 1993). Not surprisingly, the unions and leftist opposition parties in Saxony pushed for an even more expansive interpretation of the industrial cores concept than the Land government ("Zeit für Privatisierung drängt," *Freie Presse*, 10–11 July 1993; "Haushaltsdebatte 1993," *Landtagskurier Freistaat Sachsen*, March 1993). While less enamored with statist solutions, even the state association of industry supported a policy of a stronger state (Treuhand) role in reorganizing firms in order to prevent further deindustrialization ("'Dem Niedergang der ostdeutschen Industrie entgegenwirken'," *Frankfurter Allgemeine Zeitung*, 31 October 1992).

In practice, however, there were considerable differences within Saxony's regional economic policy network over how far ATLAS should go toward an activist industrial strategy. Key leaders in the economics and finance ministries, as well as the Land's development bank, envisioned ATLAS as a more minimalist policy innovation in which the Land government would create opportunities for more firms to be saved, without committing the government to an open-ended financial and political responsibility for the future of these firms. This coalition remained committed to market principles and the belief that—in the long run—jobs are best secured through private firms and markets. A more maximalist concept of ATLAS was advocated by the unions, as well as some representatives of regional economic organizations, firm managers, and local governments. This coalition's policy vision would have committed the Land government to an active industrial policy guided by a strategic vision of regional and sectoral development.

In the end, the Land government left open the exact definition of ATLAS's responsibilities and placed control over it in the hands of representatives from both the minimalist and the maximalist camps. Thus ATLAS was hamstrung by two competing visions, resulting in a relatively slow decision-making process. Identifying firms for reorganization was not particularly difficult; by August 1993, nearly 200 firms (60 of which had already been privatized) had been identified as regionally significant.[57] But the slow pace of actually agreeing on which firms were to be reorganized—and how—seems to have resulted primarily from a growing hesitation by the Treuhand and the Land government to make explicit long-term commitments to assume hard-to-measure risks (interview with Treuhand officials in Dresden, August 1993; see also Kern and Sabel 1994). Even the union IG Metall, which played a central role in bringing about ATLAS, was reluctant to push its maximalist vision for fear of becoming the scapegoat for ill-conceived intervention (Jacoby 1994, 16). By mid-1994, the Land government began to wind down the ATLAS program, arguing that it had successfully contributed to the privatization of many regionally significant firms. The evidence indicates that ATLAS ultimately followed the minimalist vision, leading to more support for firms identified as too important to fail (especially those providing jobs in the economically weakest parts of the Land), but it did not develop into a strategic industrial policy.[58]

However, this did not mean the demise of the coalition advocating more active state-led industrial policy. As ATLAS was winding down, the Land government began to toy once again with the idea of creating an industrial holding company for regional firms.[59] Since reunification, Saxony has floated various proposals for a regionally based public-private industrial holding company—with extensive bank participation ("Die ostdeutschen Länder sammeln wieder Beteiligungen," *Frankfurter Allgemeine Zeitung,* 22 July 1994). In the first couple of years after reunification, such holdings were supposed to facilitate privatization. In subsequent years, such holdings were supposed to help out struggling firms. But these proposals never got off the ground—the banks had no interest, and the federal government discouraged the idea of state ownership. Accordingly, the Saxon government has frequently criticized the banks for their risk aversion and has often felt compelled to try to fill the gap, at least partly, through various industrial policy initiatives (not least of which was ATLAS) (Frank Matthias Drost, "Schommer mahnt bei Banken mehr Mut zum Risiko an," *Handelsblatt,* 18 January 1995). Thus, when the Treuhand formally closed its doors at the end of 1994, Saxony established a new fund (capitalized with DM 50 million) to provide liquidity assistance to troubled firms.[60]

Thuringia may well have gone furthest down the road toward an active industrial policy strategy. In early 1993, under pressure from regional unions, opposition parties, employer associations, and local governments, the Thuringian government took several steps in this direction. First, like other Länder, it developed a plan to promote industrial cores in Thuringia. The Thuringian plan was designed to promote particular regions within the Land primarily through infrastructure projects, promoting firm start-ups, and inducing firms to relocate in Thuringia. The Land government sought to avoid direct involvement in rationalizing firms (Nolte, Sitte, and Wagner 1993). But later in that year, under continuing political pressure and a deteriorating industrial base, the Land government adopted more radical measures. The centerpiece of the new policy was an industrial participation corporation (Thüringer Industriebeteiligungs-GmbH, or TIB) with DM 200 million capital. The TIB was expected to cooperate with the Land's development bank (Thüringer Aufbaubank) in financially supporting troubled firms that are nonetheless judged to have a good chance to become competitive. Since its establishment, the TIB has taken equity stakes in several regional manufacturing firms and is planning on more. The Land government hoped that private banks would contribute capital to the TIB, but, consistent with their previous behavior, the banks were not forthcoming ("Die ostdeutschen Länder sammeln wieder Beteiligungen," *Frankfurter Allgemeine Zeitung,* 22 July 1994; Birgit Marschall and Antje Sirleschtov, "Industriepolitik: Kritische Grenze," *Wirtschaftswoche,* 19 January 1995). With these latest policy initiatives, Thuringia moved to a strategy of de facto government ownership and active long-term involvement in reorganizing regional firms, placing the goals of job and firm retention over economic efficiency.

The other eastern Länder are pursuing generally more conservative strategies, emphasizing economic renewal primarily through building up the Mittelstand and technology promotion. These more modest strategies are probably due in part to their weaker financial and administrative capacities, but they are probably also due to the fact they have had less to lose than Thuringia and Saxony from deindustrialization, because the latter (along with Saxony-Anhalt) were more heavily industrialized.

Thus, despite relatively high dependency on the federal government, regional policy networks in the East are gaining more—though still limited—policy-making capacity and autonomy. Despite the participation of banks in a wide range of economic policy efforts, the eastern Länder have not been able to utilize them, or achieve their cooperation, extensively within regional economic policy networks. If anything, the Länder believe they have been forced to compensate for the banks' extreme risk aversion through large-scale government financial promotion of firms, and even direct industrial intervention.[61]

The Future of Bank-Firm Relations in the East

Many politicians and social observers likened the situation in eastern Germany after reunification to that of early postwar West Germany. But the East in the 1990s is, at least in hindsight, clearly not the same as the West in the 1950s. One important difference is the market context in which banks operate. The strategies of the different banking groups in the East—especially the commercial banks—are influenced considerably by the fact that it is only one part of their market. Banks cannot let excess risk assumption in the East jeopardize their ability to compete in western markets (with each other and with foreign banks) and their global market activities. Assuming high risks under long-term time horizons may have been possible in the comparatively isolated and segmented domestic market of 1950s Germany, but the realities of 1990s competition preclude banks from adopting similar policies. For this and related reasons, the state has been obliged to contribute a significantly greater amount of public funds and public power to restructuring the eastern economy than initially planned. This occurred through extensive federal initiatives and, increasingly, through the initiatives of regional economic policy networks in the East.

Whether they use state funds, bank funds, or both, firms in the East are highly leveraged. High levels of debt combined with generally low levels of equity place the banks (and state) at considerable credit risk. Because of their own credit exposure and their responsibility for administering most state loans, the banks have no choice but to closely monitor eastern firms. Moreover, because state loans are generally long-term, they effectively force the banks to develop long-term relations with firm clients (though the substance of these relations is in no way preordained). This raises questions as to whether banks have sufficient capacity to collect and analyze the information necessary for successful monitoring of firm management, as well as the question of what capacities the banks have to influence and aid firm management. Initial answers to these questions can distinguish between firms with a western investment partner and those without a western partner.

For firms without a western partner—mostly Mittelstand firms—banks will probably rely heavily on direct monitoring of management. Heavy debt and the recurrent need for additional funds are forcing managers of eastern firms to provide their bankers with frequent reports on internal developments.[62] The bankers, in turn, can use this information to frequently reassess their risk position vis-à-vis that firm. The banks may also use firm and their own information to negotiate with firm management over the firm's managerial decisions. To this end, the internal and external (nonfinancial) management consulting capacities that banks created in the 1980s have already been, and in the future will likely be even more, intensely utilized. In short, if they choose, banks in the East are in a position to develop very close relations with Mittelstand firms. The East affords a prime opportunity to adapt further the house bank tradition through extending Allfinanz. Quite possibly, an even more intense form of bank-firm cooperation might develop in the East (for further exposition, see Sabel, Griffin, and Deeg 1993). As argued in chapters 2 and 3, the savings and cooperative banks especially have a powerful market incentive to promote local economic development, and there are signs that they are increasingly willing to take greater risks in doing this in the East (Voigt 1997).

But it is not entirely clear to what extent banks will choose this sort of relationship. Market share trends and interviews suggest that minimizing risk might increasingly take precedent over establishing long-term bank-firm relationships in which both seek to maximize the growth prospects of the firm. Thus it is plausible that there will be adequate long-term finance available in the East (mostly because of the state) and banks will have long-term relations to firms, yet banks may still underfinance the critical investment in intangibles, such as R&D or marketing, essential to the successful expansion of firms (and to a self-sustaining eastern economy). Thus the framework for long-term financing may not adequately fund high-risk investments. Some evidence supporting this possibility is found in the fact that eastern firms continue to invest comparatively little in R&D and have barely used the R&D promotion funds made available to them through the KfW.[63] Also, a recent survey by the BDI of eastern firms indicated that banks place considerable emphasis on backing loans with collateral, precisely because of information deficiencies about the firms (cited in Carlin and Richthofen 1995, 20).

For firms with a western partner—which includes many Mittelstand and most larger firms—it appears that the banks have tried to minimize exposure and monitoring requirements by allowing the western business partner of eastern firms to carry much of these burdens.[64] While bankers do sit on the supervisory boards of many eastern AGs, there is no indication that they have extensively used these positions to influence firm management. More likely, they are using board seats for information gathering purposes and allowing other western managers on the board to guide strategic investment planning. Because many eastern firms with a western investment partner are being integrated into the western firm's interfirm production network, the kind of indirect monitoring (of a firm's reputation) common in western Germany is made possible for the banks. This helps us understand further why eastern firms with western partners have a much easier time getting investment financing from banks.

On the whole, one of the major challenges facing eastern firms is becoming a part of (national and international) interfirm production networks. The old communist-era networks that have collapsed are only slowly being replaced by the creation of new networks (for further discussion, see Albach 1993; Deutsches Institut für Wirtschaftsforschung 1995b). For banks, this means that the general conditions necessary for indirect monitoring are only weakly present, as many firms do not have sufficiently developed relations with other firms to generate information on a firm's reputation. To a certain extent, the banks do attempt to assist firms in building such across-company networks through various matchmaking services, but the ability of banks to do this is limited. For firms, this means that unless they are economically and technically strong, they will not be an especially attractive production partner in German-style diversified quality production. This suggests they will have to raise their investments in intangibles such as R&D, a difficult challenge even under normal conditions, let alone in eastern Germany.

The heavy role of the state in assuring long-term finance has, at least for the next few years, established the institutional framework of long-term finance necessary for DQP in eastern Germany—though this hardly guarantees success. Moreover, as state funding for long-term finance recedes, the regular banking sector may not provide sufficient long-term funds. Nonetheless, in the East, as in the West, the banks are a central component of the institutional "exoskeleton" that makes the industrial strategy of DQP possible. Through their role in Germany's long-term financial framework and their Allfinanz strategy, banks are helping to make DQP a potential strategy for eastern firms. While a framework for long-term finance is not the only—nor perhaps the central—institutional precondition for DQP, without this it seems inevitable that firms will be more susceptible to the short-termism that undermines DQP.[65] Thus, despite their failure to fulfill expectations derived from the finance capitalism perspective, the banks are still very much needed for the long-term success of the eastern economy.

Conclusion: Finance Capitalism
into the Twenty-First Century

At the beginning of this book, I set out to examine institutional change and adaptation in the German model of capitalism, with a particular focus on the financial system. It was argued that the financial system is one of the key institutions of the national institutional framework that helps create the particular patterns of industrial organization and adjustment that characterize the German economy. The traditional view of the German economy has long held that these patterns involve a high degree of interfirm coordination and a high capacity for collective action by business. Thus different sectors are characterized by institutionalized patterns of cooperation and, to a significant extent, adapt to changed market conditions through negotiated collective responses. The large commercial banks are presumably at the center of this system of organized capitalism. Through their control of shares in firms, their control of seats on supervisory boards, and their control of proxy votes, the banks are in a unique position to influence the major decisions of many of Germany's largest firms. Given their extensive power and overview of the German economy, the banks are ostensibly in a position to take a long-term perspective on industrial developments and mobilize resources and coordinate the actions of firms in line with the long-term needs of the economy. The role of the state in the economy is held to be largely subsidiary, supporting the system of privately coordinated capitalism through conducive regulation and occasional financial assistance. This view of the German economy and the role of the banks in shaping industry remains widely accepted in the comparative political economy literature.

While there is still a good deal of truth in this model, to depict Germany as a "system of coordination by banker," as Shonfield did, is inaccurate. Since the late 1960s, the ability of the banks to intervene in the affairs of industry has slowly but markedly weakened. While large banks continue to have significant

holdings in large firms and are often in a position to influence corporate decisions in particular firms, the disincentives and barriers to such intervention are
growing. Bank intervention in firms must be more clearly understood as the exception and not the rule. Moreover, the evidence examined in the preceding
chapters suggests that the capacity of banks to coordinate collective action
across a set of firms has weakened.

Decline of Bank Power

One of the presumed sources of bank influence in Germany is the dependence
of the firm on the bank for capital.[1] Accordingly, the critical structural conditions regarding bank influence are the supply of capital, the demand for capital, and the degree of concentration and coordination among suppliers of capital. Over the last two and a half decades, all of these conditions changed in favor
of greater firm independence, especially for large firms. One of the most important factors that produced this change was the growth of competition among
banks. The growing market orientation of the savings and cooperative banks,
especially since the market liberalization measures of the 1960s, greatly intensified business loan competition among banks. The associational (and federalist) form of these two banking groups enabled them to compete very effectively
with the often much larger commercial banks. This was true of both large-firm
and Mittelstand loan markets. Reflecting this heightened competition, since the
late 1960s market share in business lending shifted substantially from the commercial banking sector to the savings and cooperative sectors.

Furthermore, it was argued that state actors were crucial to the creation of
the three banking groups that form the basis for group competition in the industry. Without the establishment and state sanctioning of the associational organization of the savings and cooperative banks, it is highly unlikely that they
would have been able to compete with the commercial banks as successfully as
they have. Periodic and cumulative procompetition regulatory and tax policy
changes by the federal and Länder governments in the postwar period pushed
the three groups to greater direct competition with each other. This, in turn, facilitated the decline of the banks' finance capitalism role in industry and the rise
of their Allfinanz role. Bank competition in Germany is "bounded competition"
in that market competition has been structured in a manner that promotes long-
term finance and bank-firm relations while avoiding the possible pernicious effects of excessive competition. The promotion of financial market integration
by the European Union adds external impetus to what has been, since the late
1960s, already a domestic trend toward greater bank competition. Thus the

group nature of competition in German banking appears consistent with European efforts to stimulate market competition.

Not only did greater competition help raise the supply of capital, it also yielded a certain amount of deconcentration among suppliers of capital, since the number of financial institutions that a typical firm—be it large or small—could readily obtain capital from grew substantially.[2] The larger the number of competitors, the more difficult it becomes for the banks, especially the large banks in their dealings with large firms, to develop a joint strategy and pursue collective action vis-à-vis an individual firm or a set of firms. The inability of the major commercial banks to force a rationalization plan on the German steel industry in the early 1980s, discussed in chapter 4, illustrates the increasing difficulty of both bank coordination of firms and coordination among banks themselves.

The final key determinant of firm dependence on the banks, and therefore of bank influence, is the extent to which firms are dependent on the capital resources that banks supply. Since the 1970s, large firms have been able to finance their investments increasingly from their own financial reserves and from international loan and securities markets. Large firms have broken the boundaries of the German financial system and utilize domestic or foreign markets according to their own needs. Thus the demand by large firms for bank capital declined—and with it bank influence. As traditional bank business with large firms declined, investment banking activities (especially securities trading) became increasingly important sources of bank revenue. This helps explain why both the large banks and firms in Germany have been eager to develop German securities markets and an equity culture through their Finanzplatz Deutschland campaign. Mittelstand firms continue to rely heavily on bank loans, but here, too, intense competition among banks limits bank influence.

Financial dependence, however, is not the only potential source of bank power in the German system. Thus I also reviewed evidence regarding the ability of the banks to use board seats, voting shares in firms, and proxy votes as sources of influence. Here, too, there is ample evidence to support the argument that it has become more difficult for banks to use these as mechanisms of influence. First, faced with the growing autonomy of large firms and the opening of new financial market opportunities and risks, the banks have tendentiously reduced their shareholdings in industry, and individual shareholdings are becoming smaller. This means that the ability of a bank to intervene in a firm in which it holds shares is increasingly dependent on its ability to gain the support of several other shareholders, be they banks or other nonfinancial firms. Second, bank use of proxy votes to influence firms that otherwise have no major (nonbank) shareholder requires coordination among competing banks. But growing competition among the banks for loans, underwriting business, share ownership, and supervisory board seats mitigates such coordination in most instances. Third, banks occupy fewer and fewer supervisory board chairs—by far the most important seat on such boards. Thus, while the banks continue to have shareholdings in industry, the influence in corporate management (governance) that the banks derive from their nonmarket relations to firms is weakening. What all of this suggests is that the banks should not be seen as capable of anything more than periodic coordination or control of economic actors, and when this occurs, it usually involves a single firm. The systemic asymmetry of power presumed in the finance capitalism model is not evident.

Preserving a Bank-Based Financial System

Over the last two decades, several of the institutions that helped create and sustain the bank-based financial system have changed. Bank influence over large firms and bank capacity to coordinate firm actions declined. There has been a rapid development or introduction of modern financial products and securities market structure and regulation. In these terms (though not in depth of securities markets), Germany had largely caught up with Britain and the United States by the mid-1990s. Nevertheless, the core logic of a bank-based system has so far been preserved. This logic is characterized chiefly by the capacities of business for developing and pursuing long-term investment strategies and for regionally or sectorally coordinated responses to economic adjustment challenges. This logic has been preserved in large part because ownership among large firms in Germany continues to be highly concentrated. The typical large firm has a handful of major, long-term shareholders who together control the majority of the firm's shares or at least a blocking minority. This stability of ownership facilitates long-term investment and interfirm collaboration (interfirm coordination also continues to occur within industry associations), which are key elements of Germany's dominant production regime of diversified quality production. Banks are frequently among such major shareholders, but the overwhelming majority of these shareholders are families and other nonfinancial firms. This suggests that, in fact, the long-term logic of the bank-based system rested not in bank ownership (or proxy voting) and influence per se, but in concentrated ownership patterns.[3] Thus the decline of bank influence in large firms has not undermined, and will not in itself undermine, the bank-based logic. As I will discuss below, this concentrated ownership pattern appears to be the single most important feature that continues to distinguish the "bank-based" systems of Germany, France, and Japan from the market-based systems of Britain and the United States.

The declining importance of traditional large-firm business for banks also encourages them to promote securities markets in Germany and the further international integration of German financial markets. Continued efforts of this kind will sustain pressure on German firms to adopt many of the practices associated with market-based financial systems. This can already be seen in the current debates among large German firms and policymakers over the introduction of international standards in balance sheet reporting, corporate information disclosure requirements, Anglo-Saxon notions of maximizing shareholder value and cultivating investor relations, and the like. The more such institutions are adopted into the German system, the closer Germany inches toward the logic of the market-based financial system. Indeed, I have argued that the German financial system is increasingly bifurcated; in effect, two independent though closely intertwined models of industrial finance are discernable. The large-firm model retains the core institution of concentrated ownership but combines this with corporate financial patterns and practices of market-based systems. In the case of the Mittelstand financial model, the institutions and the logic of a bank-based system have been adapted and extended.

Despite repeated efforts to encourage Mittelstand firms to go public, they continue to resist their incorporation into a market-based system. Instead, they rely heavily on bank funds for investment financing and continue to enjoy access to long-term and competitively priced capital. These developments were explained by three variables. First, the federal organization of the banking industry and group competition facilitate strong and growing competition for the business of Mittelstand firms, especially by the savings and cooperative banks, which rely so heavily on this market segment (chap. 2). Second, group competition and federalist banking also facilitate the continual upgrading and modernization of the bank groups' capacities to meet the new demands of Mittelstand firms, notably expanded information and consulting services for Mittelstand firms (chap. 3). Third, a variety of state actions that promoted competition among the banks for Mittelstand firms and facilitated the continued provision of long-term funds by the banks to such firms were essential to extending the bank-based model (chaps. 2–6). This is consistent with the state's historical role in promoting the savings and cooperative banks (and thus group competition) in order to preserve a strong Mittelstand and counter economic concentration. Given the strength of this bank-based, long-term finance system that caters so well to the needs of most small- and medium-sized firms, it is little surprise that they have shown little interest in following the path of large German firms.

Banks and Economic Adjustment

In the first chapter of the book, it was posited that the financial system was one of the key institutions that collectively compose the German national institutional framework. It was argued that, as part of this framework, the financial system shaped firm behavior, the organization of production, and patterns of industrial adjustment. It was also argued that many of the institutions and the logic of the bank-based financial system have been adapted and therefore preserved. Thus adjustment by firms to changed market conditions still involves significant negotiation and coordination with other economic actors. Much of this coordination takes place on a sectoral level—for example, through trade and employer associations or through cooperative research institutions. Social partnership with unions and codetermination have come under various strains in the last decade as a result of international economic integration and reunification but continue to operate as central principles in the German political economy. The regional case studies in the book (chaps. 4, 5, and 6) analyzed in greater detail the collective responses by public and private actors on a regional level to new economic challenges. On this level, internationalization has arguably precipitated greater, not lesser, efforts to manage economic adjustment collectively.

Banks continue to contribute to coordination through their ongoing, albeit significantly reduced, role in networks of interlocking shareholdings. In chapter 3, I called these obligational networks. On top of such obligational networks are even broader monitoring networks constituted by overlapping multiple board memberships of a relatively small group of economic elites. At a minimum, these networks serve to keep managers of the largest German firms relatively well informed about conditions in other firms and sectors. They also serve corporate managers' mutual interest in stable, long-term shareholdership. However, the evidence clearly indicates that the banks are not at the center of these networks in the sense of occupying the pinnacle in a hierarchy of corporate decision-making power.

Collective business action in the form of sectoral promotional networks, however, seems increasingly harder to achieve, especially through bank coordination. The pattern of adjustment in the steel industry (chap. 4) and sectoral restructuring in eastern Germany (chap. 6) are cases in point. The decline of bank influence and coordinating capacity does, therefore, have significant consequences for the German model; namely, it raises the pressure on the state to intervene in the economy. Partly for this reason, the state and other, semipublic organizations, at both the national and regional level, have become increasingly important in promoting economic adjustment and facilitating collective action by business. This is visible first in growing direct state intervention or aid to firms via grants, tax deductions, and direct lending for firm modernization, research and development, training, and other processes of adjustment. Indirect intervention was also significant. In the banking arena, for example, we found considerable state efforts to preserve three banking groups and the basis of competition among them, to promote the adjustment of savings banks to changed market conditions, and to promote bank competition and regional adjustment through bank mergers and the market activities of government-controlled banks. The state also created and expanded a range of national, regional, and local institutions—from equity participation companies to technology transfer organizations—that promote firm and sectoral adjustment through resource provision to firms. The case of North Rhine–Westphalia and the case of restructuring the eastern German economy are the most powerful evidence of this outcome. Even in Baden-Württemberg (chap. 5), with its highly successful regional economy, we saw a substantial increase in the role of the Land government and regional institutions.

The provision of resources by the state and these other organizations to firms relies heavily on cooperation with the banking system. Thus banks became increasingly important for promoting firm and sectoral adjustment through their role in *regional* promotional or economic policy networks. Through their Allfinanz strategy, banks also provide resources to firms that complement those provided by such regional networks. For these reasons, it was argued that the state and banks must be seen as increasingly complementary (and institutionally entwined), rather than alternative, mechanisms for promoting firm coordination and adjustment.[4] It was argued further that increased state promotion via regional policy networks and the bank pursuit of Allfinanz promoted the pursuit of a diversified quality production strategy by German firms. Mittelstand firms are particularly dependent on external organizations—be it the state, semipublic organizations, or banks—for the resources and long-term financing needed for them to pursue DQP. The Allfinanz strategy of banks and extended resource provision through regional networks also benefit many larger firms, particularly those that are decentralizing production and therefore rely more heavily on Mittelstand firms for production inputs, but also for product development.

To summarize, the German model of capitalism is still a negotiated or coordinated one that rests importantly on a bank-based financial system. In this sense the system has been broadly stable. Within this stability, however, I have identified and elaborated upon three important institutional changes, or sets of changes, that affect how the model operates and influence the likely direction of future institutional development of the system. The first change is the declining influence of banks in large firms and thus bank capacity for steering economic adjustment. Associated with this is the emergence of a new large-firm financial model and the refinement of a Mittelstand finance model. Second, the German model has come to rely more heavily on various forms of direct and indirect state intervention. The expansion of market mechanisms does not appear to displace the state but in fact requires new (and even permits expanded) forms of state intervention that emphasize promotion of nonmobile forms of capital (for similar arguments see Levy 1997). And third, the German model of capitalism has become more decentralized in the sense that local and regional public and private organizations have come to play a greater role in shaping firm behavior and broader patterns of economic adjustment. Regional governments and institutions (including local and regional banks) have become more important within the German national institutional framework. The regional cases examined in the book show that regional institutions are not purely derivative of national institutions, since there were significant, regionally endogenous sources of institutional origination and change.

Comparative Lessons

One comparative lesson of these findings is that, even in a world of transnational capital and supranational integration, subnational institutions may become increasingly important for economic adjustment and states may still have substantial capacity to influence economic actors through provision of essential (and less mobile) resources. The enhanced role of subnational regions can be attributed in large measure to growing competition among such regions for investment capital and the fact that many of the still feasible (supply-side) economic policies are just as easily implemented by regional actors as they are by national ones. In fact, many such policies are better done at the subnational level, where they can be more responsive to regionally specific needs of firms (these points are elaborated in Deeg 1996; see also Allen 1989 and Scharpf 1994, 156–66).

The regional case studies examined in this book also suggest that there remain important regional differences in the organization of production in Germany (differences sustained, in part, through the industrial finance role of savings and cooperative banks). Baden-Württemberg thrives on a relatively decentralized model of industrial organization, while North Rhine–Westphalia's struggle to promote industrial adjustment remains hampered by the institutional legacies of centralized organized capitalism. Kitschelt has suggested that diversification of regional institutions, strategies, and production organization within nations may in fact promote overall national competitiveness, since the institutional preconditions for international success vary across sectors. Too powerful *national* institutions within the national institutional framework will therefore hinder a nation's ability to become competitive in sectors whose institutional needs vary from this predominant national pattern. Seen in this light, institutional convergence within and across national institutional frameworks would be expected to reduce net national and global economic welfare, since diversity in institutional arrangements facilitates different kinds of technical innovation (Kitschelt 1991, 493). This also suggests that the scope for institutional innovation and diversification in eastern Germany should be expanded, rather than pressed into the old West German mold.

A second comparative lesson is that there is probably a good deal of institutional flexibility and redundancy within national institutional frameworks. Thus the erosion of certain institutions associated with a bank-based financial system did not upset the institutional congruence, or controvert the logic, of the German national framework. For example, declining bank coordination capacity and the adoption of Anglo-Saxon style securities market structures and regulations have not undermined the system's logic because other institutions, most importantly concentrated ownership, appear sufficiently capable of sustaining it on their own. Moreover, new institutions more consistent with current conditions (e.g., European regulatory liberalization) may sustain traditional functions fulfilled by weakened or defunct institutions.

Convergence or Parallel Adjustment?

One of the questions raised in the beginning of this book was, in fact, whether such convergence in national institutional frameworks was occurring, and whether this was inevitable. While this book focused on the transformation of one model, the pattern and process of institutional change in the German model still provide us with useful insights on the convergence question. Let us look briefly at some comparative evidence and the debate regarding convergence in financial systems.

Broadly speaking, all advanced industrial nations' financial systems face a similar set of adjustment pressures and challenges. These include increased price and product competition within and across national financial sectors, increased concentration pressures, securitization of debt, and desegmentation of financial markets (this is directly associated with universalization of financial institutions). These changes in financial market structures were accompanied—

indeed, they were largely made possible—by a reconstruction of domestic financial regulation. Despite the rhetoric of deregulation, the evidence suggests that financial markets are still heavily regulated. What has changed, however, is the process and structure through which regulation is made and implemented, as well as the content of financial regulation.

Convergence in Regulation

Moran, examining securities market regulation in the United States, the United Kingdom, Germany, and Japan, argues that the old, more informal self-regulatory systems in all four countries have been reorganized into a more formalized meso-corporatism (Moran 1991, 1992).[5] Regulation is characterized by the increased codification of rules (more elaborate and written), the increased institutionalization of regulation and supervision (state-sanctioned regulatory organizations are becoming more important and equipped with greater resources), and increased juridification (rules embedded in statute and disputes adjudicated in court). Among other factors, the movement to a more formalized corporatism is driven on the one hand by the continuing desire of financial markets to regulate themselves, and on the other hand by the need to democratically legitimate self-regulation by subjecting it to formalized rules. It was also driven by U.S. pressure on other countries to adopt regulatory structures more similar to its own and ones that, because of their formalization, were more transparent to outsiders.[6] Thus there appears to be significant convergence among leading financial markets in the process or structure of financial regulation, though more for securities than banking markets.

To facilitate the further integration of financial markets and harmonize essential regulations, that is, to create a "level playing field," supranational and international regulatory regimes also emerged. Clearly, for Germany and the rest of Europe the market integration and regulatory harmonization measures of the European Union are the most important and are quite substantial. Best known among international regimes is the Basel Committee. In late 1988, driven by the desire to ensure international financial stability and fair competition for their domestic financial service industries, the committee produced an accord that established minimum capital adequacy standards for all banks in the member countries.[7] Similar to the banking industry, in the securities industry there has been a convergence among leading industrial countries in their approach to regulation and the emergence of a nascent international governance or regulatory system.[8] Nevertheless, for both the banking and securities industries, national regulatory regimes remain by far the most important.

This returns our focus to domestic financial regulation, where, in addition to structural convergence in the regulatory process, there is also substantial convergence among industrial nations in the content of regulation. First, promoted by the Basel Committee (and the EU), there has been significant convergence on capital adequacy standards. Second, there has been convergence toward a policy of open access of domestic financial markets for foreign competitors. This convergence greatly facilitated the institutional interpenetration of financial markets (Pauly 1988).Third, there is general convergence around the norm and policy of liberalization, that is, reducing barriers to competition and financial innovation. Finally, there is substantial convergence on the regulation of securities markets intended to facilitate their rapid expansion.

Several explanations for convergence in the mode and content of financial regulation have been advanced. One explanation is that convergence is the product of international negotiation, primarily within fixed regimes (Underhill 1992). A second explanation focuses on the intensifying competitive struggle among national financial sectors and their regulators to gain global market share. This competition induces regulators to adopt regulations favored by international financial institutions. Indeed, Moran has argued that this competition-driven convergence has been facilitated by cross-national alliances among internationally oriented financial institutions and their home country regulators (Moran 1991, 121–31; 1994).[9] A third explanation for convergence downplays the role of international negotiations and instead highlights how common norms and rules emerged across national financial regulatory authorities. The coordinating norms of liberalization, reciprocity, and competitive efficiency led states to individually adopt common regulatory standards (Pauly 1988). As is usually the case, each of these approaches helps us understand different aspects of regulatory change and convergence.

Convergence in Market Structures?

If we return to our two-system model, the bank-based and market-based financial systems could be depicted as endpoints on a continuum of financial system models. In principle, financial systems could converge, more or less, toward either one of the two ideal types. However, comparative studies already make clear that both models have undergone significant change and therefore convergence is toward a mixed model, incorporating features of both bank- and market-based models. The remaining question, though, is whether each system is just shifting some along the continuum, adapting to common challenges while retaining crucial distinctions, or whether each is moving inexorably toward a more or less single convergence point/model. Obviously, a speculative question such as this cannot be definitively answered. Nevertheless, we can hypothesize about the probability of various outcomes based on what has already occurred and what is already understood about processes of institutional change.

First, convergence to a single financial system model appears very unlikely. While there is a clear common trend toward universalization in banking, the organization of domestic banking industries and bank-firm relations, for example, continue to vary widely across national economies. In France, Germany, and Japan, equity market financing has grown substantially since the 1970s, especially for larger firms. Yet in all three cases, banks play an institutional role in the economy not yet found in Britain or the United States. In these three countries, banks are significant holders of equity in nonfinancial firms and help sustain systems of concentrated ownership. As in the German case, in France and Japan the systems of cross-shareholdings appear intact, despite financial liberalization. Indeed, in France the system of cross-shareholdings was expanded and deepened in the 1980s as a compensatory strategy to financial liberalization (Loriaux 1997). The French state made a deliberate and thoroughgoing effort to "Germanicize" its banking system, with particular emphasis on building large universal banks with significant direct holdings in industry (Loriaux 1997; Schmidt 1996, 369–92).[10] The fiasco of Crédit Lyonnais notwithstanding, this new bank-industry nexus continues in France. In all three countries, the concentrated ownership system is motivated significantly by the desire of large firms (and the state in France, and perhaps Japan) to prevent hostile takeovers and is not (at least yet) seen as inconsistent with promoting the development of securities markets. In the United States and the United Kingdom, the merging of commercial and investment banking activities has also occurred, though the United States still lags considerably behind. Moreover, even with universalization we do not find the same kinds of universal banks in the United States and the United Kingdom, where holding companies predominate as a means for linking the two, as we find in Germany or France, where we find integrated universal banks (Coleman 1996, 229).

Moving in the direction of the United States and the United Kingdom, in Germany, Japan, and France large firms have become substantially less dependent on bank finance, and bank capacity to monitor and influence firm management has declined (in France such capacity was never there).[11] Yet here, too, there are differences. Campbell and Hamao (1994) find that Japanese firms with strong main bank ties at the beginning of the 1980s still had strong bank ties (and high bank indebtedness) at the beginning of the 1990s, though they also found that firms without strong main bank ties at the beginning of the 1980s substantially reduced bank debt and exploited much more the opportunities for equity market finance at home and abroad. Similar to what I argued in the case of Germany, Yoshitomi (1997) argues that the reduced financial dependence of large firms on main banks has significantly reduced the monitoring role of the banks. In both countries, shareholders have begun to ask for more return on their investment, and corporate management has become more sensitive to these demands. Yet in both countries the stakeholder approach to corporate governance is still strong, as company employees continue to have significant influence over management (though the institutional basis of employee influence varies between the two). France, though it has constructed a bank-industry relationship similar to that of Germany, has a weak form of shareholder value in corporate governance—weak because neither employees nor shareholders have a great deal of influence on management, though shareholders arguably have more than employees (Schmidt 1996). In the United States and the United Kingdom, the traditional emphasis on shareholder value remains intact, and relatively little change in corporate governance systems has been undertaken.

One final distinction among the five countries discussed here that deserves note is the approach to small-firm finance. Only Germany (and possibly Japan) appears to have such a well-developed system for providing long-term finance to such firms combined with extensive service provision. This difference may rest in good part on the fact that only Germany has a banking system with three distinct banking types that are comparably strong politically and economically and in which two of the three are strongly oriented to small-firm finance (compare Vitols 1998; Deeg 1998). It also appears to be the only country among these five in which banking unions or associations so effectively unite a large number of relatively small (and some larger) banks into major competitive forces.

Financial regulation also remains a primarily national affair and serves a variety of politically determined goals, and it is therefore heavily shaped by domestic political structures and political coalitions. For example, Coleman finds substantial difference in banking policy-making networks, with Germany and France exhibiting strong corporatist characteristics while Canada, the United States, and the United Kingdom are more pluralist (Coleman 1996, 230–34). It therefore seems most persuasive to argue that all financial systems are moving away from the two endpoints or ideal types. Each is adopting institutional elements from the other. U.S. financial regulators, for example, have permitted creeping universalization of the United States' largest banks.[12] The Germans (and the EU generally) are adopting securities market regulations and practices characteristic of market-based systems. Yet, with the possible exception of France, each system seems to preserve enough established institutions that its traditional logic remains intact. The driving force of the U.S. and U.K. financial systems remains securities markets and the rapid reallocation of capital resources they facilitate. The German, French, and Japanese systems retain important institutionally intermediated (by financial firms) capital allocation mechanisms and long-term commitment of capital resources.

Convergence in Adjustment Patterns?

Zysman's (1983) postulation of three broad adjustment patterns in advanced industrial states—state-led, market- or company-led, and negotiated—has profoundly influenced scholarly work in comparative political economy since the early 1980s. The analysis of Germany presented in this book and the brief comparative discussion above suggest that the changes in financial systems have indeed significantly affected patterns of economic adjustment. In the five countries discussed here, market forces and individual company strategy have become much more important in shaping adjustment processes. France and Japan have clearly lost much of the credit allocation mechanisms upon which their statist patterns of intervention rested (Loriaux 1997; Calder 1997). I have argued that Germany remains a negotiated system, though one in which both markets and the state have actually become more important in shaping adjustment. As many others have argued, the era of financial liberalization and integration has not meant the end of state intervention. In France and Japan, the state continues to have significant tools of influence over the economy. Even in Britain under Thatcher, the state intervened heavily into firm affairs (Marklew 1995). Even as markets become more important, states at a minimum still play a crucial role in structuring their financial systems and in so doing can influence the kinds and costs of financing for their firms. All this suggests that Zysman's three patterns still exist but individual countries fit even less well into a single category. Each country's distinctiveness lies more in its particular (and changing) combination of these three patterns. As suggested by the regional case studies in the book, these combinations also vary sectorally and regionally.

Scenarios for the Future

Based on the evidence and arguments presented in this book, two future scenarios for the German model appear most likely. The first is that the current situation more or less holds well into the future, thus representing a new institutional equilibrium. This model would embody a continuation of the bank-based system for Mittelstand firms as was characterized in the book. Large firms would continue to have high financial autonomy but also concentrated ownership, thus enabling them to avoid the short-term logic of market-based systems. This equilibrium model is most likely to obtain if German securities markets continue to remain comparatively underdeveloped, despite European and international market integration—that is, as long as German firms continue to hold large blocks of shares in each other and small, private domestic investors continue to prefer strongly financial investments other than company shares. This equilibrium model suggests that the bank-based system can successfully adjust to changed conditions without losing its logic. The likelihood of this scenario is most heavily contingent on two related factors: first, whether the institutions that sustain concentrated ownership are sustainable; and second, whether the interests behind maintaining concentrated ownership remain greater than those behind promoting the further advancement of Finanzplatz Deutschland.

This leads us to the second likely scenario, which entails even greater bifurcation of the German financial system. Mittelstand firms continue to be rooted in a slowly evolving bank-based system. This system is likely to hold because Mittelstand firms remain hesitant to use securities markets for financing. Because of their high dependence on and success in traditional Mittelstand business, the savings and cooperative banks will continue to promote (as will the state, especially at the Land level) a bank-based system for the Mittelstand. Finally, even in a fully integrated financial market it will be very difficult for foreign (European) banks to penetrate (and potentially undermine) the bank-based system, because bank-firm relations in this segment are based heavily on long-term trust relationships.

Large firms, in contrast, will find themselves in an ever more strongly internationally integrated financial system operating on a market-based logic. This outcome is likely if many other institutions (including regulations) that sustained the bank-based system for large firms are transformed, including domestically concentrated ownership of large firms.[13] Certainly some of these institutions will change, though large German firms show no signs of drastically reducing their large shareholdings in the near future. This brings us back to the contradiction between sustaining concentrated ownership and developing the German securities industry: achieving the objective of deeper and more liquid equity markets, for example, requires that more firms be publicly listed and their shares be more widely held and actively traded. Thus this scenario will only be realized if the Finanzplatz Deutschland goal is consequently pursued and can override the interests behind concentrated ownership. In other words, the future hinges on both the perception by major market and political actors (especially large banks and firms) as to which of these two objectives will yield the greatest benefits for them and the struggle among them to realize one of these objectives. This is not a decision to be decided at once and forever. Rather, it will be repeatedly reevaluated and fought over as market and political conditions change. This second scenario does not represent a new institutional equilibrium, but continued evolution toward a significantly different future. This is a future, however, that will arrive after a long period of transformation.

Institutional Change and Stability

Institutional theory can add another dimension to these empirically driven arguments on institutional persistence in the German model. Over the twentieth century, the German financial system has proven surprisingly stable despite several highly disruptive national crises—most notably two world wars, hyperinflation, and a collapse of the banking system in 1931. The punctuated equilibrium model of institutional change, which essentially explains institutional change as the result of institutional breakdown, does not work well in the German case (Krasner 1984). Universal banking, the bank-based character of the financial system, and the group structure of banking have proven highly resilient. The institutionalist literature has identified many sources of institutional persistence or inertia. Three common sources are sunk costs, uncertainty, and political conflict (my discussion of these three factors draws on Genschel 1995). Institutions embody sunk costs because their creation and operation require actors to learn specific rules, gain certain skills, and establish relations with actors in other institutions. All of this represents a form of capital that is often institution-specific and therefore a sunk cost. Many of these skills, etc., cannot be transferred to other institutions. Thus it may be rational to retain old institutions even as potentially more efficient ones become available (Scharpf 1987). Uncertainty leads to institutional persistence because limited knowledge about institutional alternatives makes the costs and benefits of their adoption uncertain. Thus actors may prefer to stick to old institutions because their distributive costs and benefits are known, even if the alternative promises superior advantages. This distributive bias makes salient the third source of institutional inertia, political conflict. Actors have vested interests in current institutional arrangements. A switchover to new institutions is therefore associated with political conflict since beneficiaries of the status quo are likely to resist change, while advocates must invest in building a winning political coalition (Schepsle 1986, 1989).

Certainly we can find all these sources of institutional inertia at work in the German system. For example, in chapter 2 we saw how the federalist character of the banking system and group competition are importantly the result of the federal nature of the German state. Thus intergovernmental struggles for resources and power significantly shaped the evolution of the financial system. Changes in regulation of the banking industry therefore often involved intense political conflict among industry and state actors. Because subnational governments are dependent on the savings banks (and have high sunk costs in them), they are highly adverse to changes that might lead to an erosion of their traditional functions such as might occur through privatization. The struggle over stock exchange reform, long hindered by resistance of the Länder, is another example. In this sense it could also be argued that the strong social embeddedness of the German banking system raises further the costs of changing to a market-based financial system. The promotion of securities markets also requires tremendous investment in new skills and infrastructure by banks. Many of the skills and resources developed for doing long-term bank lending to firms are not needed in market-based finance.[14] All German banks, but especially the savings and cooperative banks, have huge sunk costs in these skills and are struggling to develop the resources needed for success in securities markets. It is also clear that Mittelstand firms harbor a great deal of uncertainty about market-based finance mechanisms and thus prefer strongly traditional bank finance. These factors add further to our understanding of why more radical institutional change in the German financial system has not occurred.

However, as was argued throughout the book, these sources of institutional inertia did not mean a failure to adapt successfully the institutions of the financial system. The German financial system demonstrated significant capacity for nondisruptive or incremental institutional change. Generally, there have been two sources of institutional dynamism in the financial system. First, during various periods, changes exogenous to the financial system led to shifts in the strategies and objectives of actors within the financial system. The pursuit of these new goals/strategies within the existing institutions gave them new functions and ultimately led to significant changes in the broader financial system. The institutional *transposition* of the Landesbanks from limited regional banking institutions into national (or even international) universal banks is a prime example. A second important form of institutional adaptation is *patching up*, that is, sustaining existing institutions and their functions by supplementing them with new institutions (I draw these two concepts from Genschel 1995). The creation of public and private equity participation companies, loan guarantee banks, and other public or quasi-public institutions involving risk sharing between banks and other actors helped sustain the traditional bank-based system for Mittelstand firms. This institutional patch-up lowers the incentives for Mittelstand firms to go public and raises the incentives to continue relying on banks for external finance.

The origins and evolution of the institutions of the German financial system also suggest that the theoretical differences between historical institutionalism and rational choice institutionalism may not be as great as many theorists argue.[15] Historical institutionalism emphasizes how institutions shape the objectives of political actors (i.e., the self-definition of their interests) and the distribution of power among them in the political system. The historical institutional approach assumes preferences are endogenously determined—the objectives and strategies of actors are shaped by their immediate institutional context. Preferences are socially and politically constructed. These assumptions lead to the claim that ideas, leadership, or cultural norms shape the formation of political coalitions, policy outcomes, and institutional development. Institutional rational choice theories assume actor preferences are exogenously determined and fixed, and that individual behavior is regularly goal-oriented and based on strategic calculation. From this theoretical perspective, institutions matter insofar as they shape actors' assessment of the costs and benefits of alternative choices. What is compatible with both perspectives is the assumption that actors' calculation of alternative choices is contextually dependent, that is, strategic behavior is not specifiable a priori because (1) the rational solution depends on a particular social (or institutional) context, and (2) there is frequently more than one rational or strategic solution. Thus, explaining the origination and evolution of institutions requires an examination of both contextually shaped strategic or purposive behavior as well as ideas, norms, and leadership.

For example, the emergence of the association structure for savings and cooperative banks was a construct of rational behavior insofar as it efficiently solved collective action problems and thus improved the market position of member banks. But the associational form was not the only plausibly efficient solution, nor was it necessarily the most efficient solution. Thus its emergence was also the result of historical circumstance and the formation of successful political coalitions guided by particular norms and ideas about the preferred social and political order. For the cooperatives, the ideas of self-help and individual economic autonomy defined their identity and guided their actions; for savings banks, the public mission of serving the Mittelstand and competing with the commercial banks in order to fight economic concentration constitutes their identity. Power relations among various social groups were essential in shaping the emergence of banking associations, and the institutional character of the financial system in general. Moreover, the association structure was solidified over a long period of time. It evolved to a significant extent through an iterative process in which one set of decisions—not always reducible to rational calculus—led to unforeseen consequences requiring subsequent responses. The association structure was therefore a combined result of strategic, goal-oriented behavior and the pursuit by actors of objectives shaped by cultural and social values.

Into the Euro-Future

Looking forward, one of the most significant events of the new century is likely to be a single European currency. At this point, forecasting the impact of this event would still be speculative—though some of the most far-reaching potential implications of the euro are already discernable. While many banks are concerned about the high costs associated with transferring accounts and computer systems to a new currency, this is not the interesting story. The interesting story of the future is the potentially huge global market power of the currency. Chances are, the euro will become a (if not the) major international reserve currency. This alone would have tremendous ramifications for nearly every aspect of market economies, including financial markets. The major German banks see in the euro a potential mechanism to catapult Europe and themselves into the forefront of international finance ("Kopper will die Euro-Währung für die Rolle als Global Player nützen," *Handelsblatt,* 27 November 1995). It could do much to help the major German (and European) banks become leading international investment banks. This suggests that the goal of making Frankfurt a leading international financial center will remain in the forefront of German politics. So far, financial liberalization and integration have produced only one merger among major German commercial banks (between the Bayerische Vereinsbank and the Bayerische Hypotheken- und Wechsel-Bank). But the advance of the euro might well precipitate a wave of major bank mergers in Germany and Europe. Since the major banks in Germany are already fairly large, such mergers could have profound effects on banking in Germany (and perhaps the rest of Europe). In short, in the near future we are likely to witness many highly consequential political decisions in Europe. Thus, perhaps the only thing we can say with some certainty about the future is that portentous institutional change will remain a constant.

Notes

Chapter 1

1. Frieden (1991) and Garrett and Lange (1991) argue that supply-side or sectoral policies appear less subject to convergence pressures.

2. See contributions by Dore, Kester, Streeten, and Kosai in Berger and Dore (1996).

3. Here I follow Zysman's (1994, 246–47) definition of market logic:

> Market logic, specific to a particular national institutional structure, drives corporate choice shaping the particular character of strategy, product development and production processes in a national system. A specific market logic (and political logic) then induces distinct patterns of corporate strategy (and government policy) and therefore encourages internal features of companies (and the government) that are unique to that country. There are typical strategies, routine approaches to problems and shared-decision rules that create predictable patterns in the way governments and companies go about their business in a particular political economy. Those institutions, routines and logics represent specific capacities and weaknesses within each system.

4. Governance is defined as "the totality of institutional arrangements—including rules and rule-making agents—that regulate transactions inside and across the boundaries of an economic system" (Hollingsworth, Schmitter, and Streeck 1994, 5). Kitschelt (1991) advances the argument that technology is one of the key determinants of industrial governance structures.

5. See Kitschelt (1991) for a theoretical synthesis of national and sectoral institutions. Other recent studies exploring the links between national and regional or sectoral institutions include Locke (1995) and Herrigel (1996).

6. This factor has been particularly important in the United States (Dale 1992, 61–67).

7. Japan is a good example (Hall 1993, 95–100).

8. On Japan, see Rosenbluth (1989); on Germany, see Moran (1992, 137–57).

9. Coleman (1994b) has argued that the international governance regime for securities markets regulation most closely approximates the principles of the market-based model of the United States and the United Kingdom.

239

10. See Coleman and Underhill (1995) and Kapstein (1994, 149–54). Thus the EU is an excellent case for learning how the two types of financial system models will interact within a fully integrated market. Dale (1992, 193) writes, "In short, the robustness of the universal banking model has yet to be tested in conditions of intense competition."

11. Commercial banks are defined as a group primarily by their common legal foundation, not because of interbank cooperation as is found in the savings or cooperative banking groups. Commercial banks compete individually against other commercial banks and the two other banking groups.

12. In the case of the commercial banks, this characterization applies not to the group, but to the large banks themselves, which are internally organized along federalist lines.

13. In this regard I follow Zysman's (1983) argument that the ability to allocate credit is the key instrument for state industrial policy, because it is a more effective means to control or influence specific business decisions than regulatory or administrative rules.

14. For a more detailed argument along these lines, see Frieden (1991).

15. In this respect I argue against Zysman's utilization of the financial system as an independent variable determining the pattern of state intervention and economic adjustment. It is not a priori clear whether the structure of the financial system is a determinant or outcome of the nature of state economic intervention; Zysman (1983, 94–95) himself acknowledged this as the potential Achilles' heel of his argument. For an argument similar to mine, see Cox (1986).

Chapter 2

1. For an extended theoretical treatment of this, see Sabel (1988).

2. Bavaria is somewhat of an exception. In this state, two private regional banks came to be the driving force of the regional banking industry.

3. Public savings banks were not legally independent entities but a department under the jurisdiction of local governments (Wysocki 1983, 152).

4. The 1838 savings bank regulations issued by the Prussian government represented the first state efforts to provide a legal basis for the homogenization and expansion of the savings bank sector (M. Pohl 1982; Wysocki 1985, 37–38).

5. In 1836 there were 280 savings banks in the German states; between 1840 and 1860, over 800 banks were established (Pohl 1986, 37–47; also H. Pohl 1982, 98).

6. However, by mobilizing a tremendous amount of savings and channeling these into regional and national capital markets, the banks played an indirect but indispensable role (Wysocki 1983).

7. In a parallel manner, Friedrich Wilhelm Raiffeisen led the rural cooperative movement (Pohl 1976, 40).

8. This self-enclosed money system also made it possible to lend at lower interest rates (Faust 1977, 584).

9. Though several important national and regional joint-stock banks had been created in the 1850s, banking markets at the time of unification were still dominated by private bankers and some 30 state note-issuing banks (M. Pohl 1982, 296–320). Altogether, some 100 joint-stock banks were established between 1870 and 1873 (Pohl 1986, 33–35; see also Tilly 1967).

10. The house bank is the firm's chief financial partner, defined practically by a current account connection (demand deposit accounts with a line of credit attached).

11. Among its many provisions, the 1889 law also required the cooperatives to establish supervisory boards and issue formal shares to members (Pohl 1986, 77; see also Kluthe 1985, 82–87).

12. In practice, the bank subsidized these groups by holding deposits from the Verbandskassen of the regional cooperative associations, for which it paid higher-than-market interest rates, and refinancing their loans at below-market rates (Faust 1977, 542–53; Kluthe 1985, 87).

13. In a giro payments system, a payer issues an instruction to his/her bank to transfer funds directly to another account. The predominant form of transfer payment in Germany is giro.

14. On the eve of World War I, the other banking groups were becoming increasingly worried about the savings banks' getting into short-term lending activities via giro (Dieckmann 1981, 49, 55–57; Klüpfel 1984, 117–18).

15. Attesting to this, a growing capital scarcity at the turn of the century was most severe outside the major urban centers (H. Pohl 1982, 23–27; Henze 1972, 56).

16. Since the savings banks were regulated by the Länder, the Länder had to promulgate detailed legislation before their savings banks could actually take up a giro system (Wysocki 1983, 186; Wysocki 1985, 37).

17. The giro associations were set up as parallel and formally independent structures to the preexisting savings bank association in each region. But close personal and organizational ties between the savings bank and giro association in each region meant that they were practically the same organization. Within a short time, the savings banks as a group completed their three-tier associational structure: in 1924 the national association of savings banks (Deutscher Sparkassenverband) joined with the central giro association (Deutscher Zentralgiroverband) to create the Deutscher Sparkassen- und Giroverband (DSGV), today's national association of the savings banks. The DSGV quickly became an important organizational force for the savings banks, particularly regarding the provision of collective goods such as advertising and management training.

18. Funds to recapitalize the banks and for special credit programs for craft firms and farmers flowed from the Reichsbank through the Preussenkasse (and were guaranteed by the Imperial Finance Ministry). The Preussenkasse also aided cooperative banks by pursuing a countercyclical interest rate policy, that is, it attempted to maintain low and constant interest rates on cooperative bank deposits and loans (Faust 1977, 552–60).

19. In 1927 rising loan defaults in agriculture forced yet another reorganization (and recapitalization) of the Preussenkasse. This time, however, the authority of the Preussenkasse to directly supervise cooperative banks was increased, much to the dismay of the cooperative sector (Born 1983, 92–93; Kluthe 1985, 109–13; Faust 1977, 569, 578–80).

20. By 1930 approximately one-quarter of all urban Mittelstand firms were cooperative members. Over 50 percent of all farmers were cooperative members (Kluthe 1985, 101). Even though the number of commercial cooperative banks declined from a peak of 1,549 in 1913 to 1,349 in 1925, in the second half of the decade the remaining banks steadily expanded their balance sheets (Deutsche Bundesbank 1976, 122).

21. In 1920 the two competing associations of the commercial cooperative banks

managed to unite and form the German Cooperative Association (Deutscher Genossen-schaftsverband). Born argues the fusion initiative stemmed from regional Crafts Chambers, which sought a more effective banking system for craft firms (1983, 92). Faust (1977, 282) adds that potential nationalization in social democratic Weimar Germany drove the competing associations to put aside their differences in order to provide a unified front.

22. The general thrust of these revisions was to make the internal decision-making process for large cooperatives easier through the introduction of member representative assemblies. They also allowed cooperatives to purchase holdings in other cooperative-related firms, such as the new cooperative insurance companies (Kluthe 1985, 104–5).

23. The Deutsche Bank went from just six branches in 1900 to 173 by 1926; the Dresdner Bank took over 16 banks between 1914 and 1924, attaining 86 branches by 1926; and the Commerz- und Discontobank went from eight branches in 1913 to 246 by 1924. The five other Berlin banks underwent equally impressive expansion in this period. In 1918 there were 120 private commercial banks in Germany, but by early 1927 this number had shrunk to 65 (Pohl 1986, 62–69, 85–88).

24. From a peak of about 3,100 in 1913, their numbers had declined to 2,622 in 1925. Inflation and communal reorganization accounted for the bulk of the fusions and liquidations (Deutsche Bundesbank 1976, 67, 122). From nine Girozentrale in 1909, there were 32 by 1930 (Pohl 1986, 90).

25. The balance sheets and equity base of the big Berlin banks deteriorated under the weight of inflation and their recent expansion. Increased competition from domestic and foreign banks and rising operating costs severely constrained big-bank profits (Balderston 1991, 554–605).

26. Though it also represented the Mittelstand, the Reichsverband was dominated by large firms that were more closely associated with the major commercial banks (Dieckmann 1981, 69).

27. In the banking sector, many large special and general purpose banks were created outside the savings bank sector by the central and Länder governments. The Reichs-kreditgesellschaft, for example, was created for a special purpose during the war, but by the mid-1920s it had grown to the proportions of the Berlin banks and began to compete with them (Born 1983, 87–90).

28. This view of the savings banks' role found resonance within the central government, as indicated in a 1931 essay by Müller-Armack (389–435), a high official in the Imperial Economics Ministry and a key champion of the social market economy in the postwar Federal Republic.

29. The signatories also established regional courts to adjudicate any violations of the agreement (Dieckmann 1981, 71).

30. In 1925, for example, the chemical giant IG Farben was formed, followed by the fusion of several major steel firms into the Vereinigte Stahlwerke in 1926 (Pohl 1986, 86–89; also Balderston 1991, 592).

31. The central government, in combination with the central bank, held over 90 percent of the equity of the Dresdner Bank; nearly 70 percent of the Commerzbank; and some 35 percent of the Deutsche Bank. The Deutsche managed to avoid majority control by the government through the infusion of equity capital from several of its "friends" in industry (Eglau 1989, 31).

32. Until 1931, regulation and legislation regarding the savings banks had been an exclusive affair of the individual Länder. The widespread liquidity and payments problems of hundreds of savings banks, however, prompted the central government to intervene. The decree required the separation of savings bank administrative boards from communal administrations. The banks were also required to increase their liquidity reserves and adopt more restrictive credit policies (Mura 1987b, 50–60).

33. The question of separating commercial from investment banking activities was raised but not given serious consideration (Born 1967, 158).

34. For example, in 1932 the government channeled RM 200 million through the bank to support the recovery of small- and medium-sized industry (Faust 1977, 575–76).

35. According to Günther Wysocki (1983, 185), informal interest rate cartels had existed since 1913.

36. The Deutsche Bank alone had representatives on 380 supervisory boards of firms—including key arms producers—and controlled 30 percent of the stock transactions of large industry in 1942 (Wysocki 1983, 177). After 1933 the government allowed the banks to buy back their shares such that by 1936 they were essentially reprivatized (Born 1967, 176–77).

37. From 1932 to 1939, the combined share of the Berlin big banks of all banking business declined from 15 percent to 10 percent (Wandel 1983, 184–86).

38. Through their holdings and subsidiaries in other financial institutions, especially mortgage banks, the three major banking groups combined control directly or indirectly about 90 percent of the banking industry's total business volume (Hahn 1986, 434).

39. The exceptions to this were the Saarland and Baden-Württemberg, where the Girozentrale remained solely in the hands of their respective regional savings bank associations; and Hamburg, where the Girozentrale was wholly owned by the government.

40. While most Länder passed new savings bank laws in the 1950s, several did not pass new laws until well into the 1960s (Mura 1987a, 53–56).

41. The commitment of the Länder to promoting the cooperative system was explicitly stated in seven postwar Länder constitutions. In the course of the 1960s, the share of public ownership in the DG Kasse dropped from nearly 50 percent to under 10 percent, reflecting the desire of the cooperative sector to reduce state support (Kluthe 1985, 166).

42. The DG Kasse was formed under public law yet controlled by the private cooperative sector. The chair and majority of the bank's administrative board seats were held by the cooperative banks; three were held by the federal government; three by representatives of the Länder governments; and one each by the Bundesbank and the Loan Corporation for Reconstruction (Kreditanstalt für Wiederaufbau) (Faust 1977, 583–86).

43. The first important step was taken in 1957 when the federal government, over the opposition of the other bank groups, permitted the DG Kasse to issue bank bonds, giving it direct access to the capital markets (Faust 1977, 591).

44. Prior to this measure, the establishment of a new bank or branch was possible only if the authorities determined a need for it. The court's decision was part of a general effort to bring down competition-restricting practices in several sectors (Ellgering 1987, 61–62).

45. The savings bank sector, however, would continue to be chartered by the Länder and subject to supplemental regulation by them (Dieckmann 1981, 167–68).

46. The Bundesbank's approval of interest rate deregulation—required by the KWG—may have been influenced by pressure from Schiller, but in any case it was also based on the Bundesbank's belief that it would be able to sufficiently influence interest rates through its discount, reserve, and open market policies (Dieckmann 1981, 175).

47. The savings banks, which expected to be the prime beneficiary of liberalization because of their dominance in the deposit-taking markets (they held 62 percent of all savings deposits in 1962), actually favored gradual deregulation (Dieckmann 1981, 173–78).

48. Strong economic growth, combined with state subsidies for saving and automatic wage deposits, made mass consumer banking the driving force behind the expansion of the banking sector (Büschgen 1983, 150–56).

49. Stützel (1964), for example, concluded that the savings banks—and to a lesser extent the cooperative banks—did enjoy competitive advantages due to their tax privileges.

50. Instead of the 40 percent rate that the federal government sought, the savings banks would be taxed at a rate of 35 percent. The commercial banks were taxed at a rate of 51 percent; the cooperatives at 32 percent (Henze 1972, 122).

51. Moreover, the report defended the right of communal and Länder governments to have their own house bank, especially because private banks were not always able or willing to carry out this function in a satisfactory manner (Meyer-Könster 1979, 179).

52. Most of the Landesbanks also carry the official designation of *Girozentrale;* the former refers to their function as a state bank, the latter to their central bank function for their region's savings banks.

53. Legislators generally viewed this as a rationalization measure with few partisan ramifications (Poullain 1979, 69–80).

54. As Poullain noted, however, this was a deceptive fact, since the major commercial banks had far more subsidiaries whose assets did not show up on their balance sheets. Moreover, within a few years the Deutsche and Dresdner Banks passed the WestLB in total assets (Poullain 1979, 70).

55. The Bavarian government also made a failed attempt to gain a stake in the other major private regional bank in Bavaria—the Bayerische Hypotheken- und Wechselbank, or Hypobank (Girke and Kopplin 1977; Pohl 1986, 115).

56. Because the savings banks were attached to communal governments, widespread communal reorganization and consolidations in the 1970s forced many savings banks to merge. From 880 savings banks in 1950, only 589 remained by 1986 (Mura 1987a, 27).

57. Poullain emphasized the need for modernization through technology, the elimination of civil service status for bank managers and more professional training, and carefully considered fusions between weaker savings banks. He also stressed that greater cooperation within the association was essential to future success (Poullain 1969; 1979, 48–63).

58. Schiller himself had served four years on the administrative board of a savings bank and nine years in a Landesbank/Girozentrale (Schiller 1969).

59. Poullain (1979, 80) writes that the big banks practiced informal cartels in large securities issues and consortial loans. The three banks resisted the inclusion of the WestLB for a year or so after its creation, but, once accepted, the WestLB was regularly granted its share.

60. This occurred in conjunction with the merger of the more comprehensive agri-

cultural and commercial cooperative associations, which produced a sole peak association (Deutscher Genossenschafts- und Raiffeisenverband, or DGRV) for the entire cooperative sector (Schramm 1985, 427–36).

61. For example, cooperative banks are not allowed to own shares in enterprises outside the cooperative sector, though their regional and central banks can (Zimmerman 1984, 31; Kluthe 1985, 166–67).

62. While the general assembly responsible for all major decisions is elected by the cooperative banks, revisions in the charter of the DG Bank still require government approval (Faust 1977, 623).

63. Ironically, the greatest impact of the new regulations was probably on the small cooperative banks. After 1976 the Bundesbank required every bank to have at least two directors, and since the vast majority of cooperative banks had only one, compliance was frequently met through mergers. The result was more concentration and more pressure to universalize further in order to cover higher costs.

64. For example, in the early 1970s the NordLB bailed out the ailing camera manufacturer Rollei under political pressure from the Land government. A few years later the firm went bankrupt anyway, costing the bank DM 700 million ("Unter Druck: Dauerstreit um Fusionen der Landesbanken" 1987, 2).

65. Poullain was eventually cleared of the charges.

66. Many savings banks demanded that their Landesbanks refocus their activities on their regions, since the former were liable for much of the losses of the latter. The ability of Land governments to both manage and regulate their Landesbanks responsibly was also seriously questioned (Hans E. Büschgen, "Klare Trennung zwischen Staatsaufsicht und Verwaltungsratmandat bei Landesbanken nötig," *Handelsblatt,* 21–22 April 1978; and Knemeyer 1986).

67. In 1978, Federal Chancellor Schmidt defended the Landesbanks and explicitly cited their indispensable role in local and regional restructuring efforts (Sinnwell 1978, 163–76).

68. In contrast, the Federal Tax Office and Federal Constitutional Court had both issued rulings in the mid-1970s that held the tax privileges of the savings banks to be justified by the limitations placed on their business practices. Key limitations on savings banks (which generally did not apply to Landesbanks) included tighter credit restrictions for commercial loans; and bans on shareholding in nonfinancial institutions, on currency and securities trading for their own accounts, and on the issuance of their own bank bonds (Gorniak 1981).

69. In a speech before the Bundesrat in early 1982, its president, Hans Koschnik (1982), made this very argument.

70. See statement by Bavarian minister Schmidhuber from the Bundesrat meeting on June 6, 1981, as quoted in Koschnik (1982, 176).

71. In fact, the original Banking Law of 1934 already empowered the supervisory authorities to grant the savings banks such a privilege (Koschnik 1982, 171, 194).

72. For a summary of the SPD's position, see "MdB Lenartz: 'Die KWG-Reform muss in dieser Legislaturperiode abgeschlossen werden'" (1982). The CDU preferred the elimination of the liability surcharge for the cooperatives but was willing to grant one to the savings banks in order to put the banks on a more equal footing ("Dr. Sprung: 'Die KWG-Novellierung muss jetzt kommen.'" 1982).

73. Alfred Herrhausen (1983, 13–20), head of the Deutsche Bank, argued that such a surcharge would permit "fictional capital" to generate an additional DM 100 billion of credit capacity by an already too large and competitive savings banks sector.

74. For a review of banking regulation history and changes in the definition of liable capital, see Krümmel (1983).

75. Geiger (1985) attributed their failure to obtain a liability surcharge to the political strength of the cooperatives, the anti–public ownership sentiment of the ruling coalition in Bonn, the lack of commitment to the proposal by the regulatory agencies, and insufficient political will in some Länder to adequately defend their own interests vis-à-vis the federal government.

76. The *Genussschein* is a hybrid debt-equity instrument. It provides risk-sharing, subordinated capital to the bank but is paid back over a fixed number of years at a fixed interest rate. The savings banks were unsatisfied with the settlement, arguing that the new provisions for equity capital were insufficient to meet their needs, and continued to demand a liability surcharge ("Bundesrat für Anerkennung des Haftungszuschlages für Sparkassen" 1987; Zügel 1985; Beber 1988).

77. The compromise was closest to the recommendations of the Gessler Commission and federal regulatory officials who preferred that all banks be backed as much as possible by paid-in capital (Schroeter 1985).

78. Two of every three citizens and three of every four firms ave a savings bank account ("Stark gefährdet. Falsche Produkte, falsche Kunden: Deutschlands Sparkassen und Landesbanken gehen harten Zeiten entgegen," *Der Spiegel,* 28 August 1989; "Sparkassenorganisation fast vor Zerreissprobe," *Süddeutsche Zeitung,* 31 August 1989).

79. For example, many savings banks would like to have local business representatives on their boards, like the cooperatives. Instead, they usually have political appointees chosen on the basis of their partisan association (Mura 1987a, 100–129).

80. One of the most vocal proponents of partial privatization for savings banks is Walter Zügel, head of the Stuttgart savings banks (Zügel 1985). The 1984 KWG amendments removed obstacles in federal regulation to savings bank privatization, but privatization would require legislative action by the Länder.

81. Recent privatization proponents have focused primarily on the Landesbanks. For example, see Graf Lambsdorff (1993).

82. In asserting this position, the DSGV was partly following the recommendations of an outside consultant that argued the group should become more concernlike in its structure. In other words, the Landesbanks should fuse and be empowered with some direct control over local savings banks ("Sparkassenorganisation fast vor Zerreissprobe," *Süddeutsche Zeitung,* 31 August 1989).

83. In most Länder, the Landesbank administers and funds a significant share of the interest-subsidized lending made under Länder and federal development programs. Land governments also use them to support regional economic policy objectives, from loans to bailouts of local firms. For the views of one Land government leader, see Streibl (1985).

84. The Land government of Hesse also sold its ownership in the HELABA to its regional savings bank association in 1990.

85. The DGZ Bank is nominally the central bank for the entire western savings bank

sector, but in practice such functions have been largely eclipsed by the generally bigger and more aggressive Landesbanks.

86. Beginning already in 1995, however, the relationship between the WestLB and SüdwestLB began to cool as different strategic priorities became too difficult to reconcile. These Landesbank alliances are also not exclusive; that is, banks in one alliance are cooperating, or may cooperate, with Landesbanks in other groups in certain areas. For example, in 1996 the SüdwestLB chose to cooperate with the Bavarian and Hessen-Thuringia Landesbanks in creating a securities trading house rather than with the WestLB alliance partners ("Die Landesbank ist auch für das laufende Jahr zuversichtlich," *Handelsblatt,* 17 June 1996).

87. For insights into the perspective of Land governments on strategic alliances, see Meister (1993).

88. Rather than compete with each other in international lending as Landesbanks do, the DG Bank and regional cooperative banks pool their foreign loans and take profits according to a negotiated formula ("Genossenschaften: Grosses Zusammenrücken," *Wirtschaftswoche,* 18 February 1983).

89. In 1987 the DG Bank had already taken over the badly mismanaged Bavarian regional bank. In 1969 there were 16 regional banks in the sector (Faust 1977, 620).

90. The old East German central cooperative bank (Genossenschaftsbank Berlin, or GBB) was taken over by the DG Bank on October 1, 1990, retroactive to July 1, 1990. The DG Bank retained 14 branches of the GBB and turned control of its remaining 176 branches over to local cooperative banks in eastern Germany.

91. Eastern cooperative banks became members of existing western regional cooperative associations, with the exception of the Saxon banks, which established their own association. The integration of the eastern cooperatives was completed at the end of 1991 when they were brought into the deposit insurance scheme of the western cooperative banking association (Paul 1992).

92. The Commerzbank did not follow the other two major banks until the early 1980s, when the new head of the bank, Walter Seipp, sought to shake up the bank, which he saw as overcentralized and bureaucratic (Smith 1983, 222).

93. As the banks do not publish information on this, it is difficult to determine exactly how much this changed. However, interviews conducted with several local branch managers in 1989 and 1990 confirm this trend. The decentralization of lending authority in the Deutsche Bank was also confirmed in an interview with the director of the central division for branch offices (July 1990). Quack and Hildebrandt (1995) estimate that the head offices of the German big banks handle firms with more than DM 350 million turnover; firms below that level are handled in the regional and local branches (in France, by comparison, head offices handle firms with more than DM 150 million turnover).

94. Winning over the Mittelstand is increasingly vital to the commercial branch banks, as their lending patterns make clear: from 1972 to 1982, the share of credits to the Mittelstand in their total credits to firms increased from 28 percent to 37 percent. Credits are considered Mittelstand when the total credit engagement of a customer does not exceed DM 1 million at year end (Lubitz 1985).

95. However, as many analysts have noted, there are limits to the ability of the commercial banks to decentralize, as well as organizational problems associated with the now popular profit-center approach (Süchting 1984; Zapp 1975, 57–66; Mertin 1981).

96. For example, the central office of the Deutsche Bank assesses its local market share by customer group and product. Based on this information, the central office then offers local branches assistance in the form of group- or product-oriented sales promotion packages (Zapp, 1985).

97. Some other, primarily back office functions would be centralized, however ("Filialen erhalten mehr Kompetenz," *Handelsblatt,* 10 October 1994).

98. At the end of 1990, the Deutsche Kreditbank sold its share in the joint ventures to its partners, leaving the Deutsche and Dresdner Banks as the sole inheritors of the former Staatsbank and its virtual monopoly of the bank accounts of East German firms.

99. One comparative study of France and Germany concluded that the relatively decentralized nature of the German banking industry helped maintain more even levels of economic development among regions within the Federal Republic. Decentralization was defined by the presence of a large number of small banks and the internal decentralization of the major commercial banks in West Germany (Hartmann 1977).

Chapter 3

1. For my own review of the literature on the relation between German banks and industry before 1914, I am indebted to the brief but excellent review by Wellhöner (1989, 66–75).

2. For more recent essays on the concept and history of organized capitalism, see Winkler (1974).

3. For example, compare with Henderson (1975) and Tilly (1980). For sociological analyses of German industrialization, see Dahrendorf (1967) and Veblen ([1939] 1984). In contrast to Hilferding, Dahrendorf sees economic concentration as a manifestation of Germany's general failure to adequately develop liberal social and political values (31–45).

4. For an excellent English-language synthesis of these critical views, see Edwards and Ogilvie (1996).

5. Following Stearns (1990, 180), I assume firm financial dependence on financial institutions to be primarily a function of the availability of capital, which is determined both by demand for it and by its supply, and the degree of concentration and coordination among financial institutions.

6. Their study covered the period from 1970 to 1994.

7. This pattern still held in the mid-1990s as the chemical, mechanical engineering, and vehicle manufacturing sectors all exhibit below-average bank borrowing (Deutsche Bundesbank 1996a, 56).

8. Similar results can also be found in Mayer and Alexander (1990).

9. This includes a trend among large firms and holding companies to borrow funds in foreign bond markets through their own financial subsidiaries and pass these on to firms in the group (Deutsche Bundesbank 1996b, 42). See also Massfeller (1993) and Welzmüller (1991).

10. For example, see an interview with Ronaldo Schmitz, a director of the Deutsche Bank, in Ulrich and Wilhelm (1991).

11. At the end of 1995, though, loans from foreign banks to domestic firms represented only about 5 percent of outstanding loans from domestic and foreign banks to firms (Deutsche Bundesbank 1996a, 54).

12. In 1974 the governing Social-Liberal coalition in Bonn, interested in expanding the pool of retirement funds for workers, changed the tax laws to favor the expansion of voluntary reserves by firms. In 1986 a new federal Balance Sheet Law, passed over the opposition of the unions and interest groups representing small shareholders, made it even easier for firms to build reserves (Welzk 1986, 44–56, 74–75).

13. A study by the Hessen branch of the Bundesbank confirms the strong role of foreign banks in such markets. Foreign banks account for half the members of the Frankfurt stock exchange and account for one-third of turnover; foreign banks account for one-half of turnover on the German futures exchange (Landeszentralbank in Hessen 1995).

14. For a proliberalization statement by the German Federation of Industry, see Kudiss (1991).

15. The Bundesbank long opposed money market funds, but its opposition weakened as changed market conditions alleviated many of its objections ("New Funds on the Block," *The Economist,* 14 May 1994; Wolfgang Köhler, "Mehr Zinsen für Bares," *Die Zeit,* 27 May 1994).

16. The declining market dominance of the Deutsche Bank can also be discerned over a longer period: 43 of the 85 IPOs (51 percent of the total) from 1977 to 1986 were underwritten by Deutsche; in the subsequent six years, only 35 of 111 (32 percent) were underwritten by Deutsche (Schuber 1993; also "Going Public 1995: Jahr der Rekorde" 1996).

17. The European Savings Bank Association, for example, is promoting cross-border cooperation in payments system, product development, and business with Mittelstand firms (Köhler 1996).

18. For example, in 1991 the Deutsche Bank combined units from its asset management with those from Morgan Grenfell to create an independent asset management unit—Deutsche Bank Trust Group (Steinig 1991).

19. In line with this objective, the first of several discount stock brokerages was introduced in 1994 by a large Bavarian bank, and all the major banks have since followed.

20. Roughly 70 percent of trading in German federal bonds occurs in London; likewise, London's share of DM-dollar currency trading expanded during the 1990s (Landeszentralbank in Hessen 1995).

21. See Lütz (1998) for an extensive analysis of the reorganization of German securities market regulation.

22. These particular arguments are drawn from a Dresdner Bank study; see Hellmann and Unterberg (1991).

23. Passage of the law was briefly delayed over a conflict between the Länder and the federal government over the financing of the exchange supervision undertaken by the Länder ("Vermittlungsverfahren soll vermieden werden," *Handelsblatt,* 30 June 1994; "Deutsche Position wird gestärkt," *Handelsblatt,* 11 July 1994). The contents of the law corresponded to a high degree with the demands of the industry (Jütten 1994; von Rosen 1995).

24. The Deutsche Bank was so eager to change the image of German capital markets that in April 1992 it already voluntarily adopted many of the investor protection rules that would come later in the 1994 finance law (Weiss 1993; "Bei Insider-Handel künftig fünf Jahre Gefängnis," *Frankfurter Allgemeine Zeitung,* 18 June 1994).

25. The BAWe will also be responsible for overseeing the rules of conduct for securities trading that must be adopted into German law as provided in an EC directive.

26. It remains to be seen what the new information culture in Germany will consider relevant—a change that will be importantly shaped by how the new BAWe defines in practice what is relevant information ("Die neue Publizitätspflicht verunsichert Aktiengesellschaften," *Frankfurter Allgemeine Zeitung*, 23 June 1994).

27. For example, capital investment companies (mutual funds) gained expanded investment opportunities. In line with international standards, the joint-stock law was amended to lower the minimum par value of stocks from DM 50 to DM 5 to stimulate demand for stocks. The new law also laid down a legal basis for money market funds to further institutionalize this new market.

28. This section draws importantly from Deeg (1993).

29. The 1984 KWG revisions required the banks to report all holdings greater than 10 percent, placed upper limits on the total value of nonbank shares that the banks may hold, and reduced tax privileges associated with holdings of 25 percent or more in firms. In most cases a holding of 10 percent became the optimal size for the banks ("Abspecken und Ausgliedern," *Wirtschaftswoche*, 21 June 1985).

30. These banks combined held 4.5 percent of the nominal capital of all publicly traded firms in 1976, but only 3.2 percent in 1986 (Cammann and Arnold 1987).

31. A blocking minority (*Sperrminorität*) is constituted by a holding of 25 percent plus one vote and generally allows the holder to block a variety of important corporate decisions.

32. These are Daimler-Benz and Karstadt, a major retailer. Of the 500 largest firms, the private banks hold more than 25 percent in 13 cases (Arndt 1986).

33. Nearly half (43 percent) of the reductions were accounted for by the big three banks, but they were also much more likely to merely reduce, rather than eliminate entirely, their holdings (Roggenbuck 1992, 173–74).

34. In fact, many of the old and largest industry holdings of the major commercial banks were acquired in the 1920s and 1930s to save their loans in failing firms (Eglau 1989, 63).

35. A leading Deutsche Bank official indicated that the total value of its shareholdings had remained roughly constant since the early 1980s, while the total number of holdings had declined (interviewed April 1993).

36. See interview with Hilmar Kopper, then head of the Deutsche Bank, in Hans Otto Eglau and Nikolaus Piper, "'Mehr selbstbewusste Bescheidenheit,'" *Die Zeit,* 6 May 1994.

37. Banks' equity interests as a percentage of their financial assets have remained relatively constant—at about 2.5 percent—since 1970 (Deutsche Bundesbank 1997, 39).

38. These numbers apply to the 10 largest private banks in Germany. Adding the public banking sector is unlikely to significantly change this picture. These data on changes in bank shareholdings are from "Die Macht der Banken—Anhörung im Bundestag" 1994.

39. The Second Financial Market Promotion Law of 1994 lowered this threshold to 5 percent.

40. For detailed analyses of bank shareholdings, supervisory board seats held, and proxy voting, see Böhm (1992) and Roggenbuck (1992).

41. Eglau (1989, 167, 182–87) argues that proxy votes are more important to the banks because the underwriting quota of each bank for new share issues is partly determined by its share of proxy votes (see also Wenger 1992).

42. Collectively, the three big banks and two large Bavarian regional banks control the majority of votes in all of their shareholder meetings (Baums and Fraune 1995, 106).

43. Since 1976, codetermination laws require that worker representatives control half the seats on the supervisory boards of firms with more than 2,000 employees.

44. Overall, Deutsche Bank directors occupied around 80 supervisory board seats in various firms at the end of 1993; directors of the Dresdner Bank occupied around 70 seats (including five supervisory board chairs); the Commerzbank directors occupied around 50 board seats (including seven board chairs); and the Bayerische Hypotheken- und Wechsel-Bank occupied 77 seats (including 10 chairs) ("Bisweilen eine Gesellschaft mit beschränktem Wissen," *Frankfurt Allgemeine Zeitung,* 18 February 1994).

45. Both Böhm (1992) and Roggenbuck (1992) also argue that the main reason banks acquire shareholdings is to secure other banking business with that firm.

46. The other major commercial banks and several of the Landesbanks, in contrast, are still willing to acquire shareholdings for these riskier purposes (Ringel 1992).

47. Study by the U.S. consulting firm Greenwich Associates, cited in Eglau (1989, 173–75).

48. In 1975 only one-third of corporations with loans in arrears were rescued by the banks (Edwards and Fischer 1991, 14).

49. Interview with a senior Deutsche Bank official, April 1993.

50. Grant, Paterson, and Whitston (1988, 118–19), however, argue that in the chemical industry banks have nothing to offer firms in terms of technical or market information. Given the growing complexity of technology and markets in general, this is likely to be true in other sectors as well.

51. Chirinko and Elston (1997) find that for firms with close bank ties there are no significant effects on firm profitability, nor are there lower finance costs. Another much-debated study by Perlitz and Seeger (1994) found that close bank ties reduced profitability.

52. These analytical concepts are drawn from Lindberg, Campbell, and Hollingsworth (1991).

53. Eglau (1989, 188–95, 241–46) makes these very same points and cites several cases where the Deutsche Bank used such a network to mobilize bank-external experts to the aid of a particular industrial firm.

54. These firms included Daimler, VW, Siemens, VEBA, BASF, Bayer, Hoechst, RWE, Thyssen, BMW, Mannesmann, and MAN. The big three banks held 34 of these seats (Eglau 1989, 241–43).

55. A study by Ziegler, Bender, and Biehler of interlocking directorates and financial interlocks among more than 250 German firms concluded, "Though banks were important in determining the global structure of the network [of interlocking directorates] and its coherence, they did not seem to have been very strongly tied to any specific combine or group of enterprises" (1985, 97). The study further concluded that the densely connected "core" of the German "network" consisted of some 30 firms and that 15 of these "were especially important as meetings points for internal communication" (98).

56. In many cases, large firms in which the banks own shares also frequently own shares in, and sit on the boards of, the major banks. Cases in which the banks own shares in firms but remain at arm's length, that is, do not become involved in firm management through the supervisory board or other means, are considered market relationships in this framework.

57. Completing the circle, the Dresdner also controls substantial holdings in these very same firms, including Allianz. Allianz also holds substantial shares in other banks, including 10 percent of the Deutsche Bank (Hans Otto Eglau, "Vermachtet und Verschachtelt: Gegenseitige Beteiligungen der Konzerne machen die deutsche Wirtschaft unkontrollierbar," *Die Zeit,* 23 August 1991).

58. For an excellent review of this debate, see Griffin (1995).

59. Many academics and politicians critical of German corporate governance, however, believe that such a market in Germany would enhance economic efficiency (Gröner 1992).

60. Many large German concerns are also planning on having shares in their subsidiaries publicly listed (Karsch 1993; Schmitz 1993).

61. This problem was also confirmed in interviews with representatives of the Deutsche Bank and its investment banking subsidiary, Morgan Grenfell (April 1993).

62. The Mittelstand sector (defined as firms with fewer than 500 employees and less than DM 100 million in revenues) accounts for more than 99 percent of all firms, 44 percent of gross investment, about two-thirds of total employment, and just under 50 percent of GDP, and it trains more than 80 percent of all apprentices. In the mining and manufacturing industries, the Mittelstand accounts for roughly 30 percent of investment and 40 percent of employment (Irsch 1986, 4). Medium-sized firms (between 100 and 500 employees) are especially important in Germany, accounting for 25 percent of manufacturing employment; by comparison, in the United Kingdom medium-sized firms account for 14.4 percent and in the United States for 13.7 percent (Acs 1996).

63. In 1970, 53.4 percent of employment was in firms with more than 500 employees; in 1993 this figure was down to 50.4 percent (OECD 1996, 105). For contributions on the economic role of Mittelstand firms in Germany, see Acs (1996) and Bade (1986).

64. This discussion of the banks and the Mittelstand parallels that in Deeg (1998, 1997).

65. The most intense competition (and the group for which the Allfinanz strategy is primarily targeted) is for the business of the "elevated Mittelstand"—the some 8,000 medium-sized firms with between DM 50 million and DM 250 million annual turnover (Wieandt 1994; Boening 1993).

66. The introduction of such services was a response to Mittelstand demands, as well as an attempt by banks to create new markets (Juncker 1985; Lauer 1990).

67. In reflection of the expanded role of the lending officer for the firm, the German banks no longer call them firm "advisors" (*Firmenkundenberater*), but "caretakers" (*Firmenkundenbetreuer*). See Landrock (1990).

68. This assessment is based on numerous interviews in local banks and branches conducted by the author between 1987 and 1993, as well as educational material and statements published for firm clients by all three bank groups.

69. More than 40 percent of Germany's foreign trade is accounted for by Mittelstand firms (Bickers 1992; Rohrmeier 1987).

70. Case studies conducted in the early 1980s show that between 18 and 27 percent of Mittelstand firms cooperate in some way with another firm. The vast majority of firms that did not cooperate with another claimed they did not because of an information deficit about potential partners (Lubitz 1984, 233–34).

71. In 1989, 57.1 percent of bank loans (excluding housing loans) to domestic non-bank firms and self-employed individuals were long-term (more than four years' original maturity). In 1970, this figure stood at 45.3 percent (Edwards and Fischer 1994, 132).

Another comparative study also inferred from 1970s data that German small firms received proportionately far more loans than did their British counterparts, even after allowing for GNP and population differences (Economists' Advisory Group 1981, 245).

72. The federal and Länder governments also provide extensive support to Mittelstand firms through grants and tax credits for certain kinds of investment. As discussed more in chapters 4, 5, and 6, the state also provides extensive support for R&D in individual firms and cooperative R&D by industry, as well as subsidies for business consulting to Mittelstand firms.

73. Both of these banks were founded in the early postwar years to implement various reconstruction programs. After these objectives were achieved, both banks shifted their primary focus to long-term lending to the Mittelstand. The Industriekreditbank (IKB) is another special development bank (with a public-private ownership structure) that plays a major role in providing long-term capital, primarily to Mittelstand manufacturing firms, as well as consulting, export finance, and corporate finance services.

74. In 1970 the KfW granted a total of DM 838 million in domestic loans; in 1986 the KfW granted a total of DM 9.8 billion in domestic loans, of which DM 6.2 billion went to the Mittelstand. In 1991, loans for domestic investment peaked at nearly DM 32 billion (over half went to the eastern Länder); DM 17.7 billion went to Mittelstand firms. In 1973 the DtA granted DM 33 million in loans for business start-ups; by 1983 such loans amounted to just over DM 1.4 billion and in 1996 reached nearly DM 8.2 billion (KfW 1986, 1993; DtA 1983, 1996).

75. This only includes manufacturing firms with more than 20 employees.

76. In 1987 the KfW lent DM 7.4 billion, a sum that would more than double if loans from other federal and Länder state banks are added; in 1987 the LKB (Landeskreditbank) of Baden-Württemberg, the LfA (Bayerische Landesanstalt für Aufbaufinanzierung) of Bavaria, the Investitions-Bank of North Rhine–Westphalia, and the DtA together granted approximately DM 7.5 billion of state-subsidized loans. See their respective annual reports. There are many other smaller state banks whose loans would also have to be included in a complete account of state lending. For a complete accounting of all the bank holdings of the Länder and their functions, see Dickertmann (1985).

77. The growth in eastern subsidies was financed in good part through a reduction in firm subsidies and loans in western Germany.

78. Vitols's study (1994, 6) confirms that differences in cost of capital between small and large firms in Germany are significantly less than the differences in the United Kingdom and United States.

79. An earlier study by the Economists' Advisory Group (1981) reached similar conclusions. They found that in 1979 state loans equaled roughly 4 percent of all loans to the Mittelstand. Though this may seem small, the authors were convinced that the pres-

ence of savings and cooperative banks, "as well as state efforts to stimulate bank lending, have played a major role in channeling more resources into small firms in Germany than in the UK, though other factors are undoubtedly at work" (267).

80. For example, the 33 KBGs within the savings bank sector together had 363 investments in firms worth DM 900 million at the end of 1996 (Land 1997).

81. One study by the savings bank association showed that only 3 percent of savings banks' small- and medium-sized business customers use their savings bank for their export or import transactions (Poweleit and Ulrich 1988).

82. In the area of export finance, for example, most local savings banks conduct their clients' business through a larger regional Landesbank. This cooperation is also functioning in the provision of management consulting services.

83. Many Mittelstand firms do have advisory boards, and many invite their house bank to participate in order to bring their valuable knowledge into the firm. Recent statistics on the number of firms with an advisory board are not available, though by one estimate in 1969, one in seven limited liability firms (GmbH), the typical legal form of Mittelstand firms, had such a board (Westhoff 1984).

Chapter 4

1. Zysman (1983, 251–65) suggests precisely the opposite: that the West German state is neoliberal in its economic policies because the big banks manage the affairs of industry.

2. These networks are characterized by stable, interorganizational relationships. This discussion of "exchange-based" interorganizational cooperation draws on Scharpf (1978) and Parri (1989).

3. Cobbled together from the Prussian provinces of the Rhine and Westphalia in 1946, the new Land of North Rhine–Westphalia became the largest in Germany. For an excellent historical account of the early postwar period in North Rhine–Westphalia, see Steininger (1990).

4. A broader codetermination law was passed in 1951 that applied to firms with more than 1,000 employees in the iron, coal, and steel industries (Schaaf 1978, 20–50).

5. Through the 1950s, the Land government remained comparatively circumscribed in its autonomy by local, federal, and supranational political bodies. The fragmentation of the regional party system further inhibited the emergence of a strong Land government role in the economy (Hüttenberger 1985).

6. By 1966 annual subsidies to Ruhr coal had swelled to DM 2.5 billion, but only 3 percent of this came from the Land government of North Rhine–Westphalia (Schaaf 1978, 65–69). Subsequent to its poor showing in the 1962 elections, the Land government implored the federal government to give greater priority to maintaining higher levels of coal consumption but was unable to significantly alter Erhard's approach and unwilling to do more on its own (Kühr 1985).

7. The SPD received 49.5 percent of the vote; the CDU, 42.8 percent; the FDP (Free Democratic Party), 7.4 percent. In the Ruhr, traditionally dominated by the Communist and Center parties, the SPD garnered 59.2 percent of the vote, while the CDU sank to 34.5 percent—a gap of nearly 25 percent (Bick 1985, 203–8).

8. The previous owners received RAG stock in proportion to the assets they con-

tributed. Roughly 60 percent of RAG's capital was held by steel firms and another 30 percent by electric utilities (Schaaf 1978, 316–20).

9. The coal talks also produced 20-year delivery contracts between RAG and the steel and electric utility industries. So that the coal buyers would only have to pay world prices, the state subsidized RAG's production (Brosch 1987, 281). From 1966 to 1986, the Land government channeled DM 14 billion out of its budget to the coal industry; the federal government provided an additional DM 28 billion in subsidies (DM 20 billion of this came directly from heating oil taxes; Landtag of North Rhine–Westphalia, protocol, 10 July 1987, 4598–99; also Petzina 1988, 506).

10. Since the federal government owned roughly 44 percent of VEBA, an electric utility that owned 27 percent of RAG, the federal government was indirectly a major shareholder (Schaaf 1978, 316–20).

11. This included electricity production, chemicals, and waste management. By the mid-1990s, less than half of RAG's revenue was from coal mining operations (Liedtke 1994, 381–87).

12. The state acquired 76 percent of Saarstahl; the remainder was acquired by the Luxembourg steelmaker Arbed, which also manages Saarstahl (Howell et al. 1988, 180–83).

13. From 1980 to 1985, direct state financial aid to the steel industry jumped from DM 144 million to DM 498 million; tax breaks jumped from DM 119 million to DM 996 million. At the peak of the crisis in the early 1980s, state funds accounted for about 30 percent of total R&D spending in the steel sector (Vitols 1993a, 63).

14. The emergency plan and aid from the ECSC also facilitated rationalization (Vitols 1995, 35–36).

15. Because the Ruhr was divided among more than one dozen political units, and because the Land government ignored proposals to create a strong regional Ruhr authority, regional policies for the Ruhr were largely developed and operated by the Land government (Hüttenberger 1985, 67–68).

16. In response to political pressure from other regions of North Rhine–Westphalia, in 1970 the Ruhr program was transformed into a Land-wide program with a five-year plan. The 1968 Ruhr program had a budget of DM 3.7 billion; the 1970 North Rhine–Westphalia program had a budget of DM 31 billion—primarily from the Land government, though the federal government also made a substantial contribution (Schlieper 1986, 187–88).

17. Attesting to its growing interventionism, between 1967 and 1970 the Land government of North Rhine–Westphalia increased its share of state coal subsidies from 3 percent to just over 20 percent (Schaaf 1978, 67, 340).

18. Partisan conflict over the fusion was minimal, as suggested by the fact that the question debated most in parliament was the name of the new bank (Landtag of North Rhine–Westphalia, protocol, 22 October 1968).

19. The WestLB also purchased shares in banks outside of North Rhine–Westphalia so that it could more easily provide industrial finance outside its home market.

20. In the early 1970s, the bank also invested capital in Mittelstand-oriented organizations such as the Land's credit guarantee cooperative and economic development corporation—two other institutions of North Rhine–Westphalia's expanding regional policy network.

21. The Land's finance minister made this point in a speech to the Land parliament in 1974 (Landtag of North Rhine–Westphalia, protocol, 14 November 1974, 4900).

22. Several observers argued that Landesbanks became increasingly politicized after the mid-1970s and that conflicts of interest inherent in the structure of the banks came to hamper their effective operation. For example, Land governments, as regulators of their regional savings bank sector, were responsible for the long-term viability of the banks, but as owners they also used the banks to engage in risky business for economic policy reasons (Korbach 1986, 205–12).

23. While the Land government supported the international activities of the bank, it wanted to ensure that it would not be circumvented. There are two provincial associations (*Landschaftsverbände*) of communal governments in North Rhine–Westphalia that have a minor role in the Land's political-administrative system, though each held 16.7 percent of the WestLB's equity and was therefore represented in its decision-making organs.

24. Poullain claimed he was removed because he resisted the government's efforts to politicize the bank (Landtag of North Rhine–Westphalia, publication, 22 February 1979, 24).

25. Support of the government and parliament for the WestLB is also verified by their willingness throughout the 1970s and 1980s to repeatedly raise the equity capital of the bank using funds from the Land's budget.

26. This time the national banking establishment joined the ranks of protestors, claiming that capital accumulated in a tax-free institution should not be transferred to a bank engaged in market competition ("Banken gegen weitere Begünstigung der WestLB," *Frankfurter Allgemeine Zeitung*, 16 March 1991). The EU later investigated whether the transfer of the housing agency to the WestLB constituted an unjustified government subsidy and approved it ("Erster WestLB-Erfolg in Brüssel," *Frankfurter Allgemeine Zeitung*, 1 September 1994).

27. In 1984 the bank hired Manfred Lennings, for nine years head of Europe's largest investment goods producer (*Guttehoffnungshütte*), to advise the bank on its industrial policy.

28. The active support of the Land government for the LTU purchase was confirmed in an interview in the Finance Ministry of North Rhine–Westphalia in August 1990.

29. For example, in 1992 LTU and the WestLB together purchased the Thomas Cook travel agency (Raithel 1992). The WestLB also holds nearly 30 percent of a third major German travel company, TUI.

30. Deckel Maho was itself the product of a recent (and ineffective) merger between ailing firms facilitated by the Deutsche Bank. The merger with Gildemeister involved extensive negotiations among the firms' major creditors—WestLB, Deutsche Bank, and Bayerische Vereinsbank ("Gildemeister führt Werkzeugmaschinenhersteller Deckel Maho fort," *Frankfurter Allgemeine Zeitung*, 26 July 1994).

31. At the behest of another North Rhine–Westphalia machine tool maker, the EU began an investigation of the Land government's subsidies to Gildemeister (Dietmar Student, "In den Hintern," *Wirtschaftswoche,* 4 May 1995; "Der Kampf um Deckel Maho entzweit die Werkzeugmaschinenbauer," *Frankfurter Allgemeine Zeitung*, 6 July 1994).

32. WestLB representatives occupy a wide range of supervisory board seats in many of the region's largest firms, including Krupp (steel), Bayer (chemicals and pharmaceuticals), and Lufthansa (airline). WestLB's significant industrial holdings in North Rhine–Westphalia include VEW (10.6 percent), a major electric utility that also owns

30 percent of Ruhrkohle; LTU (34.3 percent); Gerresheimer Glas (10 percent); Hoesch-Krupp (7 percent); Deutsche Babcock (10 percent), a major supplier of energy utility equipment; and Horten (over 30 percent), a major retailer. In 1993 the market value of all of WestLB's holdings was just over DM 5 billion (Liedtke 1994, 501–7). The three big banks also have significant holdings in many of the large steel, energy (utility), and engineering firms in North Rhine–Westphalia.

33. The WestLB reportedly held 12 percent of Hoesch's stock.

34. Rightfully fearing job reductions, steelworkers in the two firms complained to North Rhine–Westphalia's minister-president, Johannes Rau. Rau claimed the Land government was not involved, but that is very unlikely given the Land government's position in the bank. Moreover, Rau sits on the board of the Krupp Foundation, which controls 75 percent of the Krupp concern, thus providing further evidence that Rau and top Land government officials were important abettors in the takeover ("'Eine feindliche Übernahme'," *Der Spiegel,* 14 October 1991). The WestLB controls some 30 percent of Preussag, which owns another one of Germany's major steel producers (Salzgitter).

35. The centrality of the WestLB to the Land's economic policy is underscored by the fact that the Land government adamantly refuses to privatize it (while at the same time selling other enterprises), even though there are widespread political pressures to do so in Germany and Europe ("Privatisierungspläne in Nordrhein-Westfalen," *Frankfurter Allgemeine Zeitung,* 26 August 1994).

36. North Rhine–Westphalia's share of total national turnover in these two sectors is 15 percent and 18.4 percent respectively (Lamberts 1988, 73).

37. This includes manufacturing craft firms with more than 20 employees. Total employment dropped from 2,168,396 to 1,895,867 (Albach 1987).

38. In 1990 turnkey plant construction accounted for 14 percent of revenues; machinery production accounted for 21 percent; and steel production for 50 percent ("Krupp scheint nach Generalüberholung wieder flott," *Frankfurter Allgemeine Zeitung,* 4 July 1991).

39. According to one estimate, by 1981 this industry already employed in the Ruhr some 60,000 workers directly and another 350,000 to 500,000 workers in supplier firms (Geer 1985, 83–97).

40. The CDU, with a strong base of political support in the Mittelstand, pushed for a Mittelstand promotion law like that being adopted in other Länder, but the Land government declined (Landtag of North Rhine–Westphalia, protocol, 16 June 1977, 2794–2820).

41. Several observers have argued that the massive flow of subsidies largely reinforced traditional attitudes and production strategies. On a per capita basis, the Ruhr region was among the highest nationally in the receipt of government subsidies (Petzina 1988, 508; Klemmer 1988, 527).

42. In a much tighter fiscal bind than Bavaria or Baden-Württemberg, the Land government of North Rhine–Westphalia spoke out against this ruinous competition as provincial and egoistic and called on the federal government to initiate cooperative federalism in technology promotion in order to minimize Länder competition (Landtag of North Rhine–Westphalia, protocol, 13 June 1984, 6037–43).

43. This regional disparity can be partly explained by the fact that R&D intensity is greater in firms in the south, especially among Mittelstand firms (Meyer-Kramer 1988).

44. In practice, this would mean that the government's decision on applications by firms for technology-related subsidies would consider the position of the unions or works council on the firm's plans.

45. Though the Ruhr remained the SPD's stronghold, the population of the Ruhr—and its potential electorate—was steadily declining. Meanwhile, the SPD's electoral support was growing faster outside the Ruhr. It is likely that the SPD realized that much could be gained in the electoral arena from providing more support to Mittelstand firms and their workers outside the Ruhr (Bick 1985, 208). The willingness of the unions to back this policy change was likely facilitated by their dissatisfaction with current policies that, in their view, helped keep large firms in the Ruhr afloat that were reinvesting their profits largely outside of North Rhine–Westphalia. The coal and steel firms in particular were not creating the new jobs that the unions thought they should and could (Landtag of North Rhine–Westphalia, publication, 5 August 1981).

46. At the end of 1992, there were 48 technology centers in North Rhine–Westphalia, employing some 6,000 workers in 850 firms ("Schnittstellen zwischen Forschung und Produktion," *Handelsblatt*, 7 April 1993).

47. The capital of ZENIT is held in one-third portions by the Land government, the WestLB, and over 70 Mittelstand firms.

48. From its initiation in 1978 through 1983, the TPW supported roughly 400 research projects with DM 350 million. But in the early 1980s, the Land government was still primarily funding R&D in large firms via its sectoral technology programs for coal and energy (introduced in 1974) and steel (introduced in 1980). Together, these two programs received approximately DM 250 million annually from the Land government (Landtag of North Rhine–Westphalia, protocol, 13 June 1984, 6032–34).

49. These include environmental technology, energy, microelectronics, measurement and control technology, information technology, biotechnology, materials, and humanization of technology.

50. Of the DM 12.5 billion spent on R&D in North Rhine–Westphalia in 1986, 20 percent came from the federal government and 17 percent from the Land government, and the rest from firms. Neuber calculates that in 1986 approximately 15 percent of firm investment (including housing construction and railways) in North Rhine–Westphalia (DM 95 billion) was financed by state subsidies (roughly one-third from the Land government; Neuber 1988, 238–39).

51. One of the key areas of Land support is subsidies for Mittelstand firms to receive private export consulting services. From 1980 through 1986, 960 firms received consulting subsidies (588 of these were industrial firms). Other measures include the usual subsidies for trade fair participation and trade delegation excursions; and export loan guarantees. Through universities and other schools, the Land government also offers extensive educational courses and training regarding export promotion, and it attempts to coordinate much of this with industry organizations and associations that do the same (Economics Ministry of North Rhine–Westphalia 1987).

52. Individual savings banks have also begun to establish cooperative arrangements with foreign banks intended to serve similar aims. For example, in 1990 the savings bank of Essen signed an agreement with a Barcelona bank in order to offer its Mittelstand clients cross-border services.

53. The savings bank of Cologne, one of the largest in the Federal Republic, established a program in 1986 to promote cooperation among Mittelstand firms to solve their export problems (Leuenberger and Küppers 1987).

54. Since 1985 the GA has permitted the promotion of economic infrastructure projects of local governments such as the preparation of industry parks, transportation and energy facilities, continuing education institutions, and technology centers.

55. The CDU, unions, and Chambers of Industry and Commerce welcomed decentralization but expressed varying objections and reservations about this new process. The CDU argued that ZIM created corporatistic local structural councils without sufficient democratic control. The chambers argued that the government was demanding consensus without working to build it, and that its efforts to tie technology promotion with social responsibility gave unions de facto veto rights (Adam 1988; Landtag of North Rhine–Westphalia, protocol, 26 January 1989, 9051–80).

56. These include loans to firms and self-employed individuals in 1992. Market shares for the cooperatives and savings banks do not include their regional or central banks. These market shares do not take account of loans originated outside of North Rhine–Westphalia but made to firms in the region. Regional market data are from the Landeszentralbank in North Rhine–Westphalia.

57. Examples in North Rhine–Westphalia include equity corporations established in Gelsenkirchen, Aachen, Siegen, the Bergische Region, Essen, Cologne, and Düsseldorf. By 1988 there were 26 equity participation corporations in the national savings bank sector. Ten of these KBGs were subsidiaries of Landesbanks, four were formed through the cooperation of several savings banks, and 12 were established by individual savings banks. Their combined total investment was DM 264 million in 220 firms (Gröschel 1987; German Savings Bank and Giro Association 1988).

58. Dortmund, Essen, and Oberhausen are notable examples of Ruhr cities that have developed similar economic development programs and cooperation.

59. The Land government proudly claimed that the number of Mittelstand industrial firms had grown faster since the late 1970s in North Rhine–Westphalia than anywhere else in the Federal Republic (Landtag of North Rhine–Westphalia, protocols, 26 January 1989, 9056–62; 15 December 1988, 8880–86).

Chapter 5

1. For an excellent discussion of regional economic differentiation in nineteenth-century Germany, see Fremdling and Tilly (1979); see also Tipton (1976) and Herrigel (1996). The neighboring state of Baden was one of the more prosperous regions in Germany before World War I. However, because of political tensions between France and Germany, government policy limited further industrial development in Baden during the interwar period.

2. If this was still insufficient, many firms put their employees on short workweeks in order to retain them for the imminent upturn. In the Depression, Württemberg had three times as many such workers as the national average (Winkel 1981, 27).

3. Handwork was used extensively, and thus the utilization of power-driven machinery in the region was low relative to the rest of the nation (Megerle 1982, 112).

4. In 1897 there were already 107 credit cooperatives in Württemberg; in Baden there were 116 in 1882. The first significant regional (joint-stock) banks emerged during the 1870s (Pohl 1992, 64, 147).

5. On the eve of World War I, for example, the Rheinische Creditbank controlled the supervisory board chair of 47 regional firms and had representatives on dozens more firms spanning all sectors. The Deutsche Bank had already had significant influence (through equity stakes) in both banks for more than 30 years (Pohl 1992, 96–237).

6. For additional material on industrialization in southwest Germany, see Fischer (1962) and Kiesewetter (1985).

7. Early technology transfer was supported in numerous ways, including sending young technicians and managers abroad to learn new technologies (Gottlieb Daimler, cofounder of Daimler-Benz, was one prominent beneficiary of this practice) and creating an exhibit hall in Württemberg to demonstrate modern machinery from abroad to local entrepreneurs (Christmann 1970).

8. From 1877 to 1911, more than half of the state's expenditures on economic promotion went to education (Kullen 1983, 239–40). For example, the Fachhochschule in Reutlingen traces its lineage back to 1855. Today this polytechnic is a leader in the design of advanced textile technology. The Centralstelle also later became the State Commerce Office (Landesgewerbeamt, or LGA), which continues through the present as a state economic promotion agency.

9. These three sectors together provided 51 percent of industrial employment, 49 percent of turnover, and 64 percent of the state's industrial exports in 1986. Of every 1,000 inhabitants in Baden-Württemberg, 153 are employed in manufacturing (one-half of the state's workforce); the national average is 112 (Statistics Office of Baden-Württemberg 1987).

10. The quota for the Federal Republic was 30 percent. In 1986 the state accounted for 27.2 percent of all of West Germany's machinery exports; 22.3 percent of electrical products; and 26.7 percent of its automobile exports (Statistics Office of Baden-Württemberg 1987). Unless otherwise specified, all data in this chapter are taken from this source.

11. In Baden-Württemberg, 50.7 percent of industrial employment is in Mittelstand firms; the national average is 47.1 percent (figures for 1986; Körber-Weik 1989, 202).

12. In 1986 the Land's per capita expenditures on science and research were nearly 14 percent higher than the national average.

13. On a per capita basis, Baden-Württemberg had over 20 percent more craft (traditionally skilled) workers than the national average in 1986. From 1970 to 1986, the percentage of skilled workers among all industrial workers rose from 34.3 to 45.6. In 1986 the ratio of scientists and engineers to total workforce engaged in the manufacturing sector was 6.5 percent higher than the national average.

14. In the 1974–75 and 1981–82 recessions, the state of Baden-Württemberg had an above-average percentage of workers on short weeks (Meisel 1983).

15. In the late 1970s and early 1980s, Baden-Württemberg had approximately 11 percent of the nation's unemployed workers, but over 18 percent of the nation's unemployed participating in reeducation or continuing education courses (Meisel 1983, 69).

16. In the postwar period, the chambers of Baden-Württemberg began expanding their firm advising capacities. In 1963, the RKW also began building an advising ser-

vice with the help of state funds. The RKW is the Rationalisierungskuratorium der deutschen Wirtschaft, a private-industry service organization with largely independent operating units in each Land (Winkel 1981, 597–603).

17. In the reconstruction period, a severe shortage of capital induced the federal and Länder governments to become more directly involved in the finance of industry. Thus it was in the postwar period that Baden-Württemberg began continuous, systematized financial promotion (Goldschmidt 1985). However, in 1972 the Land government's direct financial support to firms—DM 27 million—was lowest of all Länder (including funds disbursed under the regional GA program); North Rhine–Westphalia's was DM 154 million, Bavaria's was DM 152 million, and Lower Saxony's was DM 149 million. Even in relation to population, workforce, or tax revenues, Baden-Württemberg was still last (Landtag of Baden-Württemberg, 30 January 1973).

18. Though Baden-Württemberg was governed by a Grand Coalition from 1966 to 1972, the presence of the SPD in government did not lead to a significant alteration of the basic tenets of business-government relations in the region.

19. The impetus for the Beteiligungsgesellschaft came largely from the federal government when it made funds available in 1970 for their creation. The formation of such corporations followed quickly in most Länder.

20. The federal and Land governments provide long-term, low-interest loans that act as equity for the Surety Bank, as well as providing counter-guarantees for 70 percent of the bank's liabilities (thus the bank is at risk for only 30 percent of its guaranteed loan volume). The MBG refinances its participations from other local banks, and since it was founded at the same time by many of the same partners and had a complementary mission, its operation was turned over to the Surety Bank.

21. Since the fusion of public banks was largely seen as a matter of raising the efficiency of the public banking sector and public administration, there was widespread support among political parties and the savings bank sector. The national savings bank association (DSGV) also considered it desirable for Baden-Württemberg to have one Girozentrale (Biehal 1984; Reiff 1985, 174–75).

22. In 1975 nearly one-half of the LKB's DM 507 million in loans to firms were for liquidity assistance (Landtag of Baden-Württemberg, 5 March 1975).

23. The law also created a permanent statewide committee of representatives from government, the crafts, industry, finance, and unions to advise the Economics Ministry on all Mittelstand programs.

24. The government also expanded its funding to the Steinbeis Foundation and the Surety Bank.

25. Prior to this, the Economics Ministry periodically granted guarantees on a case-by-case basis. For example, in 1975 and 1976, the Ministry granted 17 loan guarantees worth DM 70 million. (Economics Ministry of Baden Württemberg 1977, 46).

26. The government itself participated in the formation of an export cooperative involving over 200 firms in the investment goods industry. Despite strong support from the government and business community, the cooperative failed within a few years for various organizational reasons (Landtag of Baden-Württemberg, 10 March 1975; Economics Ministry of Baden-Württemberg 1977, 39).

27. Beginning in 1975, a program for free short-term business consultations for Mittelstand firms was created through cooperation between the regional chambers and the

RKW and with financial support from the Land government (Landtag of Baden-Württemberg, 9 August 1974; Economics Ministry of Baden-Württemberg 1977, 33–35).

28. Alongside grants from the Economics Ministry for research projects, the LGA introduced conditionally repayable grants for the development of new products or processes. The LKB, in turn, would augment the development grants with subsidized loans for the equipment necessary to produce a new product (Landtag of Baden-Württemberg, 7/4421).

29. The Steinbeis Foundation now operated technical advising offices at 14 Fachhochschulen. The Land government and Industry Chambers established four more innovation offices at various chambers by 1979. Rounding out the network of technical advising offices were the universities and basic research institutes, though these organizations are oriented far more toward cooperation with large industry. The government also supported the technical advising of Mittelstand firms through its support for several cooperative industrial research institutes, including five textile research organizations and one each in clocks and fine instruments, precious metals and alloys, and paints. The government also supports the research efforts of the Frauenhofer Institutes, which conduct R&D projects under contract from private firms, as well as offering advisory services. In 1977 the society founded a Technology Development Corporation to help the Mittelstand gain greater access to their research findings. In 1977 the RKW in Baden-Württemberg also established such an office with support from the Federal Ministry for Technology.

30. Land government expenditures for indirect (or "suprafirm") measures rose from DM 22.4 million in 1975 to DM 68.7 million by 1979. In this same period, the subsidy value of loans and grants made directly to firms (from all Land agencies, including the LKB) increased from DM 36 million to DM 146 million (Economics Ministry of Baden-Württemberg 1977, 1982).

31. Moreover, the majority of government loans were for business start-ups, a critical activity to the regeneration of the Mittelstand and an economic process where many believed that governments had a valuable promotional role to play.

32. The increase was from DM 28.5 million in 1970 to DM 298.9 million in 1979 (Economics Ministry of Baden-Württemberg 1977, 1982).

33. The cooperative banks had an 18.7 percent market share of Baden-Württemberg's total banking volume; nationally, the cooperative banks had 9.3 percent. Likewise, the savings banks in Baden-Württemberg had 27.8 percent (nationally, they had 22.1 percent)—not including their Girozentrale, which had an additional 22 percent. Thus the savings and cooperative sectors together had 68.5 percent of regional banking business versus a 53 percent national market share (Landtag of Baden-Württemberg, 6/8052).

34. Herrigel (1993a) has more recently argued that the large firms created their own production system largely autonomous from that of the regional Mittelstand, and that only since the early 1980s have the two systems begun to interpenetrate in a significant way.

35. In 1983 nearly 800 professors, technicians, and students were involved in conducting 1,700 R&D contracts from industry and close to 2,000 consulting sessions (Steinbeis Foundation 1986).

36. From just over 600 consultancies and research projects in 1972, this number expanded to nearly 10,000 in 1986. Revenues from consulting and contracts rose from DM

190,000 to DM 22 million in this period. Subsidies from the Land government for limited consultancies for small firms provided an additional DM 5 million in revenue (Steinbeis Foundation 1986).

37. The initiative, planning, and operation of such centers were done through local coalitions, typically involving a university or polytechnic, chambers, local governments, and banks. The success of such parks in achieving their stated goals has been mixed. For a broader analysis of technology parks in the 1980s, see Dose and Drexler (1988).

38. In 1983 the federal government started a similar program for technology-oriented firm start-ups, thus providing yet another source of funds.

39. There were some concrete outcomes, however. Through the initiative of the Land government, an industrial park was established in Japan for German Mittelstand firms (nine of the first 22 firms were from Baden-Württemberg), and another one was established in Baden-Württemberg for Japanese firms (Takashi Masuko, "German State Woos Small, Mid-sized Japan Firms," *The Japan Economic Journal,* 20 May 1989).

40. From a low of DM 179 million in 1982, government subsidies in the Mittelstand program alone rose 66 percent in three years, to DM 299 million in 1985 (Landeskreditbank Baden-Württemberg 1987).

41. On the spread of collaborative contracting and large-firm decentralization, see Sabel et al. (1989) and Herrigel (1993a, 1993b).

42. By 1991 there were over 150 technology transfer centers. Revenues generated from consulting and R&D contracts rose from DM 22.2 million in 1986 to DM 75 million in 1991 (Steinbeis Foundation 1986, 1991).

43. Criticism of the Land government's subsidy policies also came from the European Community (EC), which forced the government to alter or curtail some of its programs. For example, after 1984 liquidity assistance loans by the LKB could no longer be made at subsidized interest rates.

44. The textiles and clothing industry in Baden-Württemberg (which accounts for 30 percent of total sectoral employment in Germany) also faced intensified competitive pressures and is seeking, as in the past, to move more labor-intensive production abroad ("Ungewohnte Sorgen im Musterländle," *Frankfurter Allgemeine Zeitung,* 5 May 1993).

45. Iwer (1994, 80) argues further that these restructuring consequences of the large firms might well undermine the horizontal collaborative networks that help bring stability to the regional economy.

46. Mercedes also moved production abroad with the construction of plants in the United States and France ("Mercedes investiert 750 Millionen DM in Lothringen," *Frankfurter Allgemeine Zeitung,* 21 December 1994).

47. From 1991 to 1993, total employment in the sector dropped from 240,093 to 206,936. The total number of firms in the sector also dropped 3 percent in 1992 and 8 percent in 1993 (Iwer 1994, 15, 23).

48. In 1993, turnover in the machinery sector dropped 9 percent over the previous year; exports dropped 4.1 percent. Total employment in the sector dropped 3.4 percent in 1992 and 6.9 percent in 1993, though with 264,000 workers the regional machinery sector remained the largest sector in terms of employment. The number of machinery firms with more than 20 employees hardly changed in this period (Iwer 1994, 13, 23).

49. Mettler-Toledo, a Baden-Württemberg producer of scales, is a prime example of successful reorganization under the key principles of lean production ("'Menschen,

nicht Werkzeuge bestimmen die Qualität der Produkte'," *Frankfurter Allgemeine Zeitung,* 5 July 1994).

50. Participants in the auto group initiative included the economics minister, the head of Mercedes-Benz, a representative from Bosch, and leaders from various associations representing auto supplier firms (Economics Ministry of Baden-Württemberg, "Gemeinschaftsinitiative Wirtschaft und Politik: 'Automobilzulieferindustrie'," press report, 30 October 1992).

51. This function was explicitly evident when, in July 1993, representatives from the auto manufacturers and suppliers met again in the Economics Ministry. The meeting was called by the suppliers because they were being squeezed by manufacturers to reduce prices. The meeting produced an agreement between suppliers and manufacturers to seek cooperative ways to achieve, and more equitably share the burden of, cost reductions ("Autoindustrie setzt jetzt auf Partnerschaft," *Frankfurter Allgemeine Zeitung,* 9 July 1993).

52. In 1994, firms were expected to receive more than DM 400 million in liquidity assistance loans ("L-Bank erzielt einen Rekordgewinn," *Frankfurter Allgemeine Zeitung,* 7 February 1994).

53. Loan guarantees of less than DM 1 million are made by the Surety Bank; guarantees from DM 1–5 million are made by the L-Bank; and guarantees over DM 5 million are made by the Economics Ministry. Loan guarantee applications at the Surety Bank rose 24 percent from 1992 to 1993 (totaling DM 305 million), while losses on guarantees doubled in 1993 ("Rezession hinterlässt deutliche Spuren," *Frankfurter Allgemeine Zeitung,* 10 May 1994).

54. These included information, biogenetic, new materials, energy, environmental, and aerospace technologies (State Ministry of Baden-Württemberg 1993). The commission also called for a number of initiatives to help firms increase their flexibility and reduce costs (Iwer 1994, 83–89).

55. The Land government called on regional firms and banks to participate in many of these projects, but it intended to use much of the DM 1 billion revenue generated from the privatization of its commercial fire insurance company to support these projects ("Stuttgart will Einnahmen nicht 'verbraten'," *Frankfurter Allgemeine Zeitung,* 18 January 1994).

56. The first center was expected to open in 1995 in Singapore (with further centers planned primarily for other emerging markets, such as China), financed primarily by the WestLB and the SüdwestLB with additional backing by the governments of Baden-Württemberg and Bavaria ("Baden-Württemberg plant Zentren im Ausland," *Frankfurter Allgemeine Zeitung,* 21 July 1993).

57. Also, roughly 80 percent of the loan guarantees made by the Surety Bank go through savings and cooperative banks (Surety Bank of Baden-Württemberg 1994, 31).

58. This was apparently most true in regard to foreign and domestic banks that had tried to break into the regional banking market during the heady days of the 1980s (interview with director of L-Bank liquidity assistance program, 28 July 1993).

59. Based on his experience with hundreds of Mittelstand firms in the region, the long-time director of the L-Bank's liquidity assistance program (interviewed 28 July 1993) believes that the savings and cooperative banks (and other regionally based banks) are

most loyal to their firms during difficult times. The big banks are equally loyal to bigger Mittelstand firms if they are the main house bank; in other cases this commitment is apparently weaker.

60. The savings and cooperative banks of Baden-Württemberg have expanded their in-house consulting capacities but have not established significant independent consulting and equity participation corporations. This is largely because they utilize extensively the organizations of the regional policy network that offer many of the resources and services that are part of Allfinanz.

61. Of these major electronics firms, only Alcatel-SEL has any German bank representatives on its German supervisory board ("Das Werk Mannheim von Alcatel-SEL wird doch nicht geschlossen," *Frankfurter Allgemeine Zeitung,* 15 December 1994).

62. Ironically, the diversification strategy pursued by Reuter since the mid-1980s was strongly promoted by Alfred Herrhausen, head of the Deutsche Bank until late 1989. In 1993, Hilmar Kopper, head of the Deutsche Bank, announced his intention to vacate the supervisory board chair of Daimler in favor of a manager from industry. However, Kopper later changed his mind, most likely in order to ensure that Reuter's successor would adopt a more preferable business strategy.

63. In 1993 Daimler became the first German concern to sell shares on the New York Stock Exchange. In conjunction with this new listing, the Deutsche Bank reduced its stake in Daimler from over 28 percent. In 1991, Daimler also began to issue deutschmark-denominated commercial paper in Germany as a new source of capital market finance.

64. Porsche's other house banks include the Commerzbank and Deutsche Bank.

65. Walther Zügel, head of the Landesgirokasse, sits on Trumpf's Advisory Council (Verwaltungsrat).

66. The firm's key house banks include the Landesgirokasse Stuttgart, the Deutsche Bank, and the Dresdner Bank ("Werkzeugmaschinenbauer Traub entschuldet," *Frankfurter Allgemeine Zeitung,* 24 September 1993).

67. Even as the major banks intensified their efforts to win more consumer and Mittelstand business during the 1970s and 1980s, the savings bank sector managed to maintain its near 50 percent share of Baden-Württemberg's total banking business ("Württemberg's grösste Finanzgruppe nimmt Mass," *Schwäbische Zeitung,* 8 November 1988). Meanwhile, the cooperative sector increased its share of the region's market from just under 20 percent in 1974 to 30 percent in 1988 (Egon Gushurst, "Mehr Leistung durch Konzentration und Kooperation," *Börsen-Zeitung,* 30 November 1988).

68. These were the Girokasse Stuttgart, the savings bank of the capital city, and the Württembergische Landessparkasse, a savings bank that, for unique historical reasons, operated branches throughout the former state of Württemberg.

69. Opponents tried to block the fusion by citing it as a violation of the savings bank association's regional principle, since the fusion would allow the Stuttgart savings bank (Girokasse) to operate beyond its assigned region (Landtag of Baden-Württemberg, 6/3642, 6/6657, 6/6662).

70. While the parliament and Land government considered a Girozentrale fusion primarily an affair of the savings banks, it justified this ultimatum by arguing that fusion would further the integration of the two previously independent states and promote

needed concentration in the public banking sector (Biehal 1984; Landtag of Baden-Württemberg, 6/6999; Waldemar Schäfer, "Trotz vieler Bemühungen ist keine Ba-Wü-Laba in Sicht," *Handelsblatt,* 19 October 1977).

71. The first two were the former note-issuing banks of Baden and Württemberg. All three were threatened with closure or takeover by the big Berlin banks in the late 1920s and 1930s. However, both governments wanted to avoid greater dependence on the Berlin banks and through state intervention ensured that these banks remained independent (Pohl 1992, 215–30).

72. By one estimate, the savings banks of Baden-Württemberg financed only 6 percent of the region's exports, while the Deutsche Bank alone financed some 60 percent ("Südwest-Bankenfusion," *Wirtschaftswoche,* 30 August 1985).

73. The BW-Bank, a natural candidate for the fusion given its majority ownership (54 percent) by the Land, could not be considered because the four other major shareholders, especially Bosch and the Deutsche Bank, opposed it (Felix Spiess, "Schwierigkeiten mit einer neuen Bank," *Süddeutsche Zeitung,* 21 December 1985).

74. To assuage the objections of the local savings banks, the Landesgirokasse would have to shed one-third of its branches. To assuage the cooperative and commercial banks, the state lending programs administered by the LKB—which represented two-thirds of its balance sheet—would not be brought into the Landesbank (Dieter Ferber, "Landesgirokasse soll Badens Widerstand brechen," *Stuttgarter Zeitung,* 30 March 1985).

75. But with half the shares of the LGK in the government's hands, Zügel could do little in this regard without the blessing of the Land government (Jörg Bischoff and Gerhard Eigel, "Späth hat die Folterwerkzeuge parat gelegt," *Stuttgarter Zeitung,* 20 June 1986).

76. In Württemberg, for example, the highly successful savings banks are considerably larger than the average savings bank in Germany, yet they are still too small to carry out the international financial activities that Mittelstand firms increasingly demand. This is where the Girozentrale is supposed to play a leading role, but in Württemberg the Girozentrale was widely perceived by the savings banks as having too little to offer. At this time the DSGV was also zealously promoting mergers between Landesbanks, thereby adding further pressure on the Girozentrale to merge.

77. Even though relations between the two were strained after the 1986 Landesbank fiasco, in 1987 the government allowed the Landesgirokasse to become the first German savings bank to open an office in New York and the first one not located in Frankfurt to take a seat on the Frankfurt stock exchange ("Fusion der Girozentralen 'absolute Notwendigkeit'," *Handelsblatt,* 30 October 1987).

78. For legal reasons, this merger could only occur if the Landesgirokasse were first privatized (or the BW-Bank turned into a savings bank, which it refused). The politically powerful regional savings bank associations vehemently opposed privatization and pushed an alternative fusion involving the Landesgirokasse, SüdwestLB, and L-Bank. But the Landesgirokasse would only agree to a solution that would free it from the savings bank sector. The L-Bank would not agree to any solution that would bring it into the savings bank sector (Stefanie Burgmaier, "Fesseln Abstreichen," *Wirtschaftswoche,* 13 April 1995).

79. Indeed, during 1995 the Land government tried to get the L-Bank to buy a major

stake in a financially troubled regional firm, but the bank refused to do it (interview with L-Bank official, August 1995).

80. At this time the L-Bank and the Land government together controlled 36 percent of the BW Bank's shares. The L-Bank also acquired a 22 percent stake in Trinkaus & Burkhardt, a leading private bank with strong international business connections ("Banken in Südwesten rücken enger zusammen," *Frankfurter Allgemeine Zeitung,* 29 November 1994).

81. In an article written in the DSGV's journal, a board member of the DSGV condemned the Landesgirokasse's involvement in any bank mergers, because this would not only damage the basis of group competition within the banking sector—that is, successful cooperation within the association banking groups—it would also threaten the very structure of the West German state, with its principles of communal self-administration and decentralization (Tiedeken 1985).

82. From 1983 to 1986, the LKB granted a total of DM 884.1 million in start-up loans (between 3,500 and 4,000 loans each year); in this same period, the DtA granted DM 997.1 million in loans to start-ups in Baden-Württemberg (Economics Ministry of Baden-Württemberg 1977, 1982, 1986; Landeskreditbank Baden-Württemberg 1985, 1987).

83. While there were differences between economic sectors in these indicators, the conclusions hold with slightly greater or lesser validity for all (Economics Ministry of Baden-Württemberg 1986; Zahn et al.1985; Zahn 1981).

84. In another survey, approximately three-quarters of all firms sampled were familiar with the loan programs of the LKB and the DtA, and nearly all of these firms had applied for loans from these sources. Furthermore, 38 percent of firms indicated awareness of the Surety Bank; 15 percent, of the Mittelstand Participation Corporation (Zahn et al. 1985).

85. Sixty-four percent of the firms surveyed sought consultation from their tax advisor; 50 percent from their house bank; 20 percent consulted with an Industry Chamber; 30 percent with a Crafts Chamber; 17 percent with their trade association; and 11 percent with the LKB (multiple choices were possible) (Zahn 1981).

86. These calculations are based on statistics provided by the Frauenhofer Institut für Systemtechnik und Innovationsforschung in Karlsruhe at an October 1987 meeting in the Economics Ministry of Baden-Württemberg. Calculations are my own and are based on information from these sources and on two assumptions: (1) that there were 7,300 manufacturing firms with more than 20 employees in Baden-Württemberg in these three years (which is an overestimate, since there were 7,300 firms with more than *10* employees, according to official statistics); and (2) that no single firm received more than one grant or loan between 1984 and 1986 (though a small minority of firms do receive multiple subsidies).

87. For R&D projects, up to 50 percent of costs could be funded by state grants; the average grant per firm between 1984 and 1986 was DM 295,000. For technology transfer loans, which usually financed 50–70 percent of the total investment, the average loan was DM 415,000 (Frauenhofer Institut). Euba (1985) estimated that all state subsidies (Land and federal funds) to manufacturing firms in Baden-Württemberg between 1977 and 1982 represented 4 percent of total new investment in the region.

88. Of the loans craft firms received (29 percent of total L-Bank technology loan vol-

ume between 1984 and July 1987 went to craft firms), 77 percent was for the acquisition of CNC machines (unpublished data from Landeskreditbank).

89. In 1987 a preliminary study (unpublished study by the Frauenhofer Institut in Karlsruhe) of Baden-Württemberg's technology programs could not determine whether the state's policy had led to a significant increase in technology-oriented investments beyond that which would have occurred without state support.

Chapter 6

1. These figures include only members of the German Association for Equity Participation Companies (which account for over 90 percent of KBG equity investment). Most of these equity firms are controlled by West German banks, insurance companies, and other industrial firms ("Markt in neuen Ländern dürfte expansiv bleiben," *Handelsblatt*, 5 July 1993). Other estimates suggest that participations by all investment funds (including foreign-controlled) in eastern Germany totaled DM 450 million at the end of 1992 (Fromman 1993).

2. The rapid growth in the number of firms receiving participations is due largely to the establishment of public, non-profit KBGs during 1992 and 1993. In the East, the market share of public KBGs was 38 percent of equity volume; in the West they had a 15 percent share. In terms of invested equity volume, all KBG investments in the East still only represented 10 percent of their total (Hummel 1995).

3. The Deutsche Industrie Holding (DIH) had invested DM 46 million in nine firms; the Deutsche Beteiligungsgesellschaft (DBG), another subsidiary, had invested DM 100 million in 34 firms ("Noch grosszügigere Kreditvergabe ist in Ostdeutschland nicht zu verantworten," *Handelsblatt*, 21 June 1993).

4. KBGs owned by German public banks expect returns of 16.5 percent, and public, nonprofit KBGs expect returns of 8.5 percent. The lower expectations of the latter two groups are due partly to their public mission character and partly to the somewhat less risky form of equity participation they typically provide (Hummel 1995, 13).

5. One survey showed that through the end of 1991 over 75 percent of participations were part of an MBI by western managers (Institut der deutschen Wirtschaft 1992).

6. As of June 1, 1993, 2,339 Treuhand firms had been privatized via an MBO/MBI (of 12,360 total privatizations) (Federal Finance Ministry 1993).

7. The savings bank sector figures it supported more than 800 MBO/MBI projects with nearly DM 1 billion in financing (German Savings Bank and Giro Association 1995).

8. An example of this Allfinanz synergy can be taken from the Dresdner Bank: as of mid-1992, its Dresden Fund had invested DM 112 million in nine firms to which the bank also lent an additional DM 300 million (Nölting 1992; see also Fanselow and Stedler 1992).

9. This also suggests that many MBO deals would not have occurred without some state assistance.

10. The cooperative banks also claimed to have invested DM 150 million ("Die Bankenmilliarde geht zur Neige," *Handelsblatt*, 23 August 1995).

11. A final hindrance was the sales contract between the Treuhand and the buyers of a firm. Most contracts are laden with conditions and covenants that limit decision-mak-

ing room for management and might even require the already privatized firm to pay more to the Treuhand at a later point in time (e.g., if the firm realizes unanticipated profits such as through the sale of real estate) (Pahlen 1993).

12. The notable (but not the only) exception to this is the Deutsche Industrie Holding, which purchased some two dozen firms with the purpose of managing their rationalization. The DIH focused heavily on firms in the booming construction and related sectors. Twenty-five percent of the GDP of eastern states derives from public contracts; in the construction sector, the figure is 40 percent (Treuhandanstalt 1993). In essence, the DIH is building a construction-oriented holding company in the East that it hopes to sell in a few years, either on the stock market or to other industrial investors (Nölting 1992).

13. Overall, 38 percent of their paid-out commercial loans were state-guaranteed ("Banken und Aufbau Ost—das Konzept" 1993). These banks include the big three and the two biggest Bavarian commercial banks.

14. In support of this conclusion, one study showed that new manufacturing firms accounted for only 4 percent of employment in this sector, but 25 percent of its investment (reported in Ursula Weidenfeld and Martin Kessler, "Wir kaufen nur Zeit," *Wirtschaftswoche,* 1 January 1993).

15. The most important function of bank representatives was probably ensuring that eastern firms would not be exploited by their board members who were from competing firms in the West. See Carlin and Richthofen 1995, 3–4. In the early period, banks provided approximately one-quarter of board members in Treuhand firms (Carlin and Mayer 1992).

16. The Dresdner and Deutsche Banks, which took over the branches and personnel of the old Staatsbank, could have been expected most of all to play a major role in reorganizing the combines. These banks had the staff with long-term personal contacts to the combines (now in Treuhand possession), they administered the old loans to them, and they accounted for the bulk of new loans to them.

17. Some banks were also willing to reduce or eliminate fees to get market share (Köllhofer 1991).

18. At the end of 1990, the commercial banks had outstanding business loans totaling DM 18.3 billion (75 percent of which were to Treuhand firms); the savings banks and Landesbanks had less than DM 5 billion. These numbers do not include the billions of deutschmarks lent by western banks to western firms for eastern investments; for example, through the end of 1994, the savings banks lent some DM 27 billion for such investments (Federal Association of German Banks 1994; German Savings Bank and Giro Association 1995).

19. At the end of 1993, the savings banks had twice as much in savings deposits (DM 121 billion) as the commercial banks (DM 60 billion) in the East. Half of the savings banks' deposits were in the form of low-interest savings accounts (Federal Association of German Banks 1994; German Savings Bank and Giro Association 1995).

20. Roughly one-third of total commercial bank lending in the East was financed through capital transfers (the transferred sum equaled DM 37 billion at the end of 1993). The real transfer sum is even higher, since available statistics do not include the funds lent by western banks to western firms used for investments in the East (Federal Association of German Banks 1994).

21. Through the first quarter of 1992, short- and medium-term loans accounted for more than 80 percent of total loan volume in the East. By the end of 1993, short- and medium-term loans accounted for just over 50 percent; in West Germany long-term loans account for approximately 55 percent of total business loans (Carlin and Richthofen 1995, 20a).

22. Through the Staatsbank, the big banks had good contacts to the combines, but these were broken up, and thus the value of these contacts and the information they provided was greatly reduced. Moreover, since they controlled personal savings deposits and/or provided craft sector loans, it is the personnel of savings and cooperative banks that are more likely to know the individuals who took over small firms or established new businesses.

23. These figures are exclusive of loans for start-ups and small proprietors. In an interview conducted for this study, the director of a main regional office of another big bank also characterized the ideal eastern customer as one with a western partner (interviewed in Dresden, 9 August 1993).

24. Sachsenmilch AG was the first eastern firm to go public, and it did so at the end of 1991 under the guidance of the Deutsche Bank. In mid-1993, the Deutsche Bank was greatly embarrassed when Sachsenmilch became insolvent and had to be rescued through bank and government efforts.

25. In 72 percent of privatized Treuhand firms, there is a single majority shareholder, and the vast majority of these shareholders are West German nonfinancial firms and families (Carlin and Mayer 1995, 2–3, 10–12).

26. For example, the average subsidy on European Recovery Program (ERP) loans in 1992 was about 2.5 percent (Seidel 1992).

27. Each of these banking groups claims a 37 percent market share in state loans passed through. For the savings banks, state loans have been especially high relative to their total commercial loans: as of June 30, 1992, the eastern savings banks had lent a total of DM 12.2 billion to firms and passed through DM 6.7 billion in ERP loans (and another DM 4.7 billion in equity assistance loans from the DAB). The commercial banks passed through roughly comparable sums (Voigt 1992).

28. The Bundesbank concluded that "relative to the value of gross capital investment (including housing) in eastern Germany in the second half of 1990 and in 1991 as a whole, the average portion of official financing may be put at one-third. This share is even larger if the funds made available for investment by the Federal Railways, the Federal Post office and the Treuhandanstalt privatization agency are also taken into account" (Deutsche Bundesbank 1992a, 25).

29. The true amount of loans by banks for eastern investment is actually higher, since loans made by western banks to finance eastern investments are generally not included in official bank lending statistics.

30. At this point, a total of 48,000 firms had received a KfW loan. Nearly half of the KfW's loans went to industrial Mittelstand firms (Kreditanstalt für Wiederaufbau 1993). Two-thirds of KfW loans went to firms located in the east, the rest to western firms investing in the east (Seidel 1992). In early 1995, the KfW took over the Staatsbank Berlin, the last remnants of the former East German central bank. The takeover increased the equity capital of the KfW more than threefold, and thus its potential lending volume has dramatically increased.

31. Lending by the regular banking sector, however, has come to be more significant in time: in 1995 the commercial, savings, and cooperative banks lent DM 106 billion to firms and self-employed individuals in the East. The KfW and DtA together lent just over DM 20 billion in the East in that year ("Bankenmarkt Ost auf Wachstumskurs" 1996; Kreditanstalt für Wiederaufbau 1995; Deutsche Ausgleichsbank 1995).

32. In the case of start-ups, for example, up to 85 percent of the initial investment can be financed with state funds.

33. The Bundesbank (1992a) maintains that this effect of opening access should not be underestimated. Investment premiums, special depreciation allowances, and loan guarantees have similar effects. In 1991, one-sixth of long-term bank funds in the entire Federal Republic came from special credit banks and other public sources.

34. One survey of business start-ups in the East, for example, indicated that obtaining financing was one of these firms' least problems (Brandkamp 1993).

35. A successor agency was established to handle some remaining privatizations and monitor the implementation of privatization contracts.

36. During the second half of 1994, eastern productivity stood at 54 percent of that of the West (up from 26 percent four years earlier) (Deutsche Bundesbank 1995a, 44).

37. Eastern German exports collapsed from DM 41.1 billion in 1989 to DM 11.9 billion in 1993. In 1994 exports rose 1.7 percent (Institut der deutschen Wirtschaft 1995c).

38. In 1996, eastern manufacturing accounted for 14 percent of total value added in the East, compared to a 26 percent rate in the West. As could be expected, firms competing in international markets are having the greatest difficulty (Institut der deutschen Wirtschaft 1997a).

39. In 1994 there were 3,911 insolvencies; in 1993 there were 2,327 (Institut der deutschen Wirtschaft 1995a). From 1995 to 1996, the number of eastern insolvencies jumped 26 percent (versus 10 percent in the West) (Institut der deutschen Wirtschaft 1997b).

40. Net public transfers rose from DM 106 billion in 1991 (equal to 4 percent of West German GDP) to DM 155 billion in 1995 (equal to 5 percent of West German GDP and 40 percent of East German nominal value added) (Deutsche Bundesbank 1995a, 47).

41. The KfW also argued for sustaining investment promotion at present levels (Fritz Kral, "KfW: Investitionsförderung bleibt notwendig," *Handelsblatt,* 23 August 1995).

42. In 1994, one of the key business associations (Bundesverband der Deutschen Industrie, or BDI) reacted to the complaints of eastern firms by meeting with bank association representatives. Together, these associations sought ways (including requests to the federal government) to improve financing opportunities for eastern firms (internal memorandum of the BDI [AWW 20/94], 17 October 1994).

43. A Bundesbank study (1995b) showed that eastern firms had, on average, equity equal to 12.5 percent of assets (in the West the comparable figure is 17.5 percent). Manufacturing firms averaged only 10.5 percent.

44. An extensive survey of KBGs engaged in the East indicated that while they would welcome additional state measures to increase equity participations, the vast majority said none of the proposed changes would make any difference for their activities in the East because tax deductions (and other measures) cannot compensate for bad risks (Hummel 1995, 18).

45. In many cases this transfer process was greatly aided, if not actually done, by west-

ern Land governments and their agencies that signed on as partners for particular eastern Länder. In fact, there was nothing less than a competitive process among the major western Länder to see which agreements for institutional development they could get from the governments of eastern Länder. The pattern of eastern Länder emulating their western partner also encompassed the rebuilding of the entire public administrative apparatus (Goetz 1993).

46. At the end of 1993, public, nonprofit equity participation corporations accounted for 70 percent of all firms receiving equity investments by KBGs in the East, though because of the smaller average investment, public equity corporations accounted for only 38 percent of the total equity volume invested (Hummel 1995, 12). By the end of 1994, eastern loan guarantee banks had granted approximately DM 700 million in guarantees (German Savings Bank and Giro Association 1995, 13).

47. Both Saxony and Saxony-Anhalt planned such measures during 1995; Thuringia already had a Land-owned equity participation corporation ("Schucht: Beteiligungsfonds für kleinere Unternehmen geplant," *Frankfurter Allgemeine Zeitung,* 16 May 1995).

48. The SachsenLB is owned by the Saxon government, the Saxon savings banks, and the SüdwestLB (25.1 percent)—the Landesbank of Baden-Württemberg.

49. The Westdeutsche Landesbank (WestLB) is serving as the Landesbank of Brandenburg, and the Norddeutsche Landesbank (NordLB) is serving Mecklenburg–West Pomerania and Saxony-Anhalt.

50. The bank, though, apparently has some ambitions of this kind, noting that it would manage the Saxon government's planned risk equity investment (i.e., venture capital) fund ("SachsenLB will ein Handelszentrum werden," *Frankfurter Allgemeine Zeitung,* 1 June 1995).

51. For the example of the NordLB's equity investments, see Manfred Bodin, "Banken haben sich in neuen Ländern massiv engagiert," *Handelsblatt,* 23 May 1995.

52. Two forms of loan guarantees have been used in the East. The first is a federal loan guarantee in which the federal and Land governments together carry 80 percent of the risk (divided 60/40 respectively). The decision on these guarantees is made primarily by the Land government but requires the approval of federal officials if it exceeds DM 5 million. The second form of loan guarantee is that carried by Land governments alone. In Saxony, for example, most loan guarantees have been federal, since the cost is shared and the federal government has been fairly generous in supporting the Länder. But the willingness of the federal government to carry such risks is waning, and increasingly the pressure is on Land governments to carry the risks alone.

53. Examples of cases where firms could only be rescued through government guarantees are abundant. One recent example involves two Saxon textile makers that were part of a western textile group. When the western group became insolvent in late 1994, the two eastern firms (otherwise solvent) were affected. The house bank of one of the eastern firms, the Dresdner Bank, refused to grant further loans. The continuation of the two eastern firms was only made possible through the intervention of the Land government and the Treuhand successor organization (BVS) ("Sächsische Textilhersteller mit tausend Mitarbeitern in Not," *Frankfurter Allgemeine Zeitung,* 14 March 1995).

54. The administration of many of these programs has relied heavily on the Working Group of Industrial Research Associations (Arbeitsgruppe industrieller Forschungsver-

bände, or AiF) and the VDI/VDE Technology Center in Berlin—both are semipublic, trade association–operated organizations. With financial aid from the state, the AiF assumed responsibility for integrating eastern firms into the western system of cooperative industrial research (Institut der deutschen Wirtschaft 1993a).

55. In 1994, the American chip maker Advanced Micro Devices (AMD) also announced plans to build a factory in Dresden, using about DM 600 million in Land government subsidies. To build on this momentum, the Land government planned in 1995 to introduce a DM 35 million venture capital fund (some of which, if possible, was supposed to come from banks) to promote technology-oriented Mittelstand firms ("Zum Fliegen," *Wirtschaftswoche,* 16 February 1995).

56. In mid-1994 only 3 percent of industrial research was taking place in the new Länder ("Rexrodt will Hilfen für Ostdeutschland verlängern," *Frankfurter Allgemeine Zeitung,* 19 July 1994; see also Penzkofer 1992).

57. The Treuhand and the Land government were then negotiating over the reorganization of more than 40 of these firms; some two dozen had begun, or were about to begin, receiving financial aid to support their reorganization (Frank Matthias Drost, "Zukunft sanierungsfähiger Treuhand-Betriebe ist noch ungeklärt," *Handelsblatt,* 24–25 July 1993).

58. Interview with Sächsische Aufbaubank (SAB) director, July 1994. By this time, 207 firms had been identified for reorganization under ATLAS, and 135 of these had been privatized ("Treuhand-Betriebe in Management-KG," *Frankfurter Allgemeine Zeitung,* 23 June 1994).

59. The plan was to create a Management KG in which troubled regional firms and firms still owned by the Treuhand could be reorganized by a team of private managers and eventually privatized ("Freistaat plant Industrieholding," *Handelsblatt,* 11 July 1994). The Treuhand itself had already created five Management KGs in the East as a policy experiment for reorganizing firms.

60. At its closure, the Treuhand and the federal government set up an additional Consolidation Fund with DM 500 million to be distributed to the Länder for supporting privatized Treuhand firms.

61. In Saxony-Anhalt, for example, the Land government was so disappointed with the banks' lack of cooperation in its program to help troubled Mittelstand firms that it decided to bypass the banks and provide government assistance directly to firms ("Schucht kritisiert Kreditgewerbe," *Handelsblatt,* 5 December 1995).

62. Interviews conducted with eastern bankers for this study corroborate this argument.

63. Eastern firms are adopting new products and processes into their production at a fast rate, but these are typically adopted from outside, not developed in the firm. In 1993, German firms spent DM 58.4 billion on R&D, but only DM 1.6 billion (2.7 percent) was in the East (Institut der deutschen Wirtschaft 1995b). Of the DM 90.3 million dispensed by the KfW in 1993 for R&D project support or investment in technology-oriented firms, DM 10.1 million (11.2 percent) went to the East (Kreditanstalt für Wiederaufbau 1993, 28).

64. The BDI survey also found that eastern subsidiaries of West German firms generally only received credit when the parent firm assumed responsibility (Carlin and Richthofen 1995, 20).

65. For more explicit arguments regarding the role of banks in supporting DQP strategies, see Vitols (1993b).

Chapter 7

1. A resource dependence theory was implicit in my arguments about declining bank influence. The resource dependence perspective holds that firms or actors cooperate with each other in order to reduce uncertainty and secure scarce resources. When a firm seeks external resources, it opens the door to potential influence by the supplier of that resource. The resource dependence model is also commonly the basis of bank control theories (see Pfeffer and Salancik 1978).

2. In the late 1980s, West Germany had over 4,000 independent banks. Great Britain, France, and Italy all had fewer than 1,000 independent banks. In terms of asset concentration, Germany had the lowest in Europe after Luxembourg (Molyneux 1989).

3. Large-firm dependence on the banks was probably never as high as is commonly believed, and in this sense it may be somewhat misleading to characterize the German economy as bank-based. Nonetheless, given the generally high importance of the banking system in the German economy, it is still an accurate descriptive term.

4. Zysman (1983), Shonfield ([1965] 1980), and others argued that bank intervention preempted pressures for state intervention in the economy.

5. Similarly, in examining securities markets in the United States, Canada, and the United Kingdom, Coleman (1994a) finds a common development among regulatory regimes from pure industry self-regulation to negotiated self-regulation and finally to (government-) mandated self-regulation. In the case of banking regulation, however, he argues there has been relatively limited convergence in the structure of policymaking, primarily because of the weaker position of the United States in international banking markets.

6. Kapstein (1994, 55) adds that the formalization of regulation is also driven by the institutional interpenetration of financial markets. Major countries now host hundreds of foreign financial institutions, making informal supervision impractical and formal regulation imperative.

7. The Basle Committee is an intergovernmental body consisting of representatives of 10 leading industrial nations (the G-10) (Kapstein 1994, 44–53, 106–19).

8. Most important of these is IOSCO (International Organization of Securities Commissions) (Coleman and Underhill 1995).

9. Moran therefore prefers the notion of diffusion of regulatory policy (through these alliances and U.S. pressure) rather than convergence.

10. The Germanicization includes a monetary policy based on low inflation and a strong currency (and the attendant approach to bank regulation), increased incentives for long-term savings and lending, and encouraging banks to become active financial intermediaries for firms.

11. In the Japanese case, this line of development is less clear-cut. Sheard (1994), for example, argues the main banks still play a major role in corporate governance, while Yoshitomi (1997) suggests the traditional main bank role is virtually at an end.

12. An interesting discussion of such cross-national institutional learning can be found in Griffin (1995).

13. Some of the key institutions sustaining this concentrated ownership are a federal tax advantage for shareholdings greater than 10 percent, comparatively less stringent takeover rules, and relatively weak antitrust (competition policy) rules.

14. This helps explain why the major German banks, especially the Deutsche and Dresdner, have spent a lot of money buying investment banking talent in New York and London.

15. Both perspectives view institutions as the durable rules, norms, or procedures that guide or constrain human interaction over time. This section draws importantly on reviews of the institutionalism literature by Thelen and Steinmo (1992) and Hall and Taylor (1994).

References

Books and Articles

Abrahams, David. 1980. "Conflicts within German Industry and the Collapse of the Weimer Republic." *Past & Present* 88:88–128.

Acs, Zoltan J. 1996. "Small Firms and Economic Growth." In *Small Business in the Modern Economy,* ed. P. H. Admiraal. Oxford: Blackwell.

Adam, Hermann. 1988. "Konzeption der Wirtschaftspolitik in Nordrhein-Westfalen." In *Die Wirtschaft des Landes Nordrhein-Westfalen,* ed. Ludwig Bussmann. Cologne: W. Kohlhammer.

Albach, Horst. 1987. "In der Bundesrepublik Deutschland." In *Arbeitsmarkt und Mittelstand,* ed. Hans Pohl and Wilhelm Treue. Stuttgart: Steiner.

Albach, Horst. 1993. "The Transformation of Firms and Markets: A Network Approach to Economic Transformation Processes in East Germany." Wissenschaftszentrum Berlin, Discussion Paper FS IV 93-1.

Albert, Michel. 1993. *Capitalism against Capitalism.* London: Whurr.

Allen, Christopher S. 1989. "Corporatism and Regional Economic Policies in the Federal Republic of Germany: The 'Meso' Politics of Industrial Adjustment." *Publius: The Journal of Federalism* 19 (4): 147–64.

Allen, Franklin, and Douglas Gale. 1995. "A Welfare Comparison of Intermediaries and Financial Markets in Germany and the US." *European Economic Review* 39 (1): 179–209.

Andrews, David M. 1994. "Capital Mobility and State Autonomy: Toward a Structural Theory of International Monetary Relations." *International Studies Quarterly* 38 (2): 193–218.

Antrecht, Rolf, Thomas Luber, and Wolfgang Stiller. 1993. "Der zweite Mann." *Capital* (February).

Arndt, Franz-Josef. 1986. "'Macht der Banken' gegen Macht der Fakten—Anmerkungen zu einer DGB-Publikation." *Die Bank,* no. 2:641–43.

Bade, Franz-Josef. 1986. "The Economic Importance of Small and Medium-Sized Firms in the Federal Republic of Germany." In *New Firms and Regional Development in Europe,* ed. David Keeble and Egbert Wever. London: Croom Helm.

Bähre, Inge Lore. 1981. "Der Zusammenhang zwischen wirtschaftlicher Entwicklung und Bankenaufsicht von 1934 bis zur Gegenwart." *Bankhistorisches Archiv* 10: 23–33.

Balderston, Theo. 1991. "German Banking between the Wars: The Crisis of the Credit Banks." *Business History Review* 65:554–605.

Balzer, Arno. 1993. "Hoffnungswert." *Managermagazin* (July).

Balzer, Arno, and Winfried Wilhelm. 1997a. "Kredit für den Neuen." *Managermagazin* (June).

Balzer, Arno, and Winfried Wilhelm. 1997b. "Platzangst in Europa." *Managermagazin* (July).

Balzer, Arno, and Winfried Wilhelm. 1997c. "Machtspiele." *Managermagazin* (May).

"Bankenmarkt Ost auf Wachstumskurs." 1996. *Die Bank,* no. 10:634–36.

"Banken und Aufbau Ost—das Konzept." 1993. *Die Bank,* no. 4:244–47.

Baums, Theodor, and Christian Fraune. 1995. "Institutionelle Anleger und Publikumsgesellschaft: Eine empirische Untersuchung." *Die Aktiengesellschaft* 40 (3): 97–112.

Bayliss, B. T., and A. A. S. Butt Philip. 1980. *Capital Markets and Industrial Investment in Germany and France: Lessons for the U.K.* Farnborough: Saxon House.

Beber, Heike. 1988. *Wirkungen des bankaufsichtsrechtlichen Instrumentariums auf den Wettbewerb im Kreditgewerbe.* Göttingen: Vandenhoeck & Ruprecht.

Berger, Suzanne, and Ronald Dore. 1996. *National Diversity and Global Capitalism.* Ithaca: Cornell University Press.

Bick, Wolfgang. 1985. "Landtagswahlen in Nordrhein-Westfalen von 1947 bis 1985: Trends und Wendepunkte in der politischen Landschaft." In *Parteien und Wahlen in Nordrhein-Westfalen,* ed. Ulrich von Alemann. Cologne: W. Kohlhammer.

Bickers, Heinz-Josef. 1992. "Das Auslandsgeschäft—ein wichtiger Teil des Firmenkundengeschäftes." *Die Sparkasse* 109:432–34.

Biehal, Manfred. 1984. *Der Württembergischer Sparkassenverband, 1916–1982.* Berlin: Duncker & Humblot.

Boening, Dieter. 1993. "Konkurrenzlagen im (mittelständischen) Firmenkundengeschäft." *Bank und Markt* (June).

Böhm, Jürgen. 1992. *Der Einfluss der Banken auf Grossunternehmen.* Hamburg: S+W Steuer- und Wirtschaftsverlag.

Bohn, Jürgen. 1991. "Der Wandel in Ostdeutschland—Ansprüche an eine neue Wirtschafts- und Bankenstruktur." *Der Langfristige Kredit* 42 (24): 4–14.

Born, Karl Erich. 1967. *Die deutsche Bankenkrise 1931.* Munich: R. Piper & Co.

Born, Karl Erich. 1977. *Geld und Banken im 19. und 20. Jahrhundert.* Stuttgart: Kröner.

Born, Karl Erich. 1983. "Vom Beginn des Ersten Weltkrieges bis zum Ende der Weimar Republik (1914–1933)." In *Deutsche Bankengeschichte,* vol. 3. Frankfurt: Fritz Knapp.

Bössenecker, Hermann. 1972. *Bayern, Bosse, Bilanzen*. Munich: Kurt Desch.

Brandkamp, Michael. 1993. "Erfolgsaussichten von Unternehmensgründungen in den fünf neuen Bundesländern." *Zeitschrift für Betriebswirtschaft* 63:109–23.

Bräutigam, Jochen, and Johannes Bartz-Adrian. 1997. "Wirtschaftsförderung durch Gründerzentren in der Region Aachen." *Sparkasse* 114 (5): 234–37.

Brautzsch, Hans-Ulrich. 1997. "Arbeitsmarkt Ostdeutschland 1997: Beschäftigungsabbau setzt sich fort." *Wirtschaft im Wandel*, no. 3:3–5.

Bredemeier, Willi. 1992. "Banken als Informationsdienstleister." *Die Bank*, no. 10:592–98.

Breuel, Birgit. 1992. "Voraussetzung: Schnelle Privatisierung." *Bank Information und Genossenschaftsforum* (January).

Breuer, Rolf-E. 1997. "Venture Capital—besseres Umfeld ist notwendig." *Die Bank*, no. 6:324–29.

Brockhaus, Jürgen. 1984. "Wagnisfinanzierung aus der Sicht der Sparkassenaufsicht." *Sparkasse* 101 (9): 349–51.

Brosch, Karl-Ernst. 1987. "Die staatliche Kohlepolitik." In *Die Ruhrkohle AG: Sozialökonomische Unternehmensbiographie eines Konzerns*, ed. Lothar Neumann. Bochum: Germinal Verlag.

Bross, Holger F. L., Ivo G. Caytas, and Julian I. Mahori. 1991. *Consulting bei Mergers and Acquisitions in Deutschland: Internationale Kooperation und Konkurrenz*. Stuttgart: Schäfer Verlag.

"Bundesrat für Anerkennung des Haftungszuschlages für Sparkassen." 1987. *Sparkasse* 104:3–4.

Burdack, Heinrich. 1990. *Nordrhein-Westfalen in Zahlen*. Cologne: Deutscher Instituts-Verlag.

Büschgen, Hans E. 1983. *Die Grossbanken*. Frankfurt: Fritz Knapp.

Cable, John. 1985. "Capital Market Information and Industrial Performance: The Role of West German Banks." *Economic Journal* 3:118–32.

Calder, Kent E. 1997. "Assault on the Banker's Kingdom: Politics, Markets, and the Liberalization of Japanese Industrial Finance." In *Capital Ungoverned: Liberalizing Finance in Interventionist States*, ed. Michael Loriaux et al. Ithaca: Cornell University Press.

Cammann, Helmuth, and Wolfgang Arnold. 1987. "Anteilsbesitz der Banken: Die Fakten." *Die Bank*, no. 3:120–23.

Campbell, John L., J. Rogers Hollingsworth, and Leon N. Lindberg, eds. 1991. *Governance of the American Economy*. Cambridge: Cambridge University Press.

Campbell, John Y., and Yasushi Hamao. 1994. "Changing Patterns of Corporate Financing and the Main Bank System in Japan." In *The Japanese Main Bank System: Its Relevance for Developing and Transforming Economies*, ed. Masahiko Aoki and Hugh Patrick. Oxford: Oxford University Press.

Carlin, Wendy, and Colin Mayer. 1992. "Restructuring Enterprises in Eastern Europe." *Economic Policy* 15:312–52.

Carlin, Wendy, and Colin Mayer. 1995. "Structure and Ownership of East German Enterprises." Wissenschaftszentrum Berlin, Discussion Paper FS I 95-305.

Carlin, Wendy, and Peter Richthofen. 1995. "Finance, Economic Development and the
Transition: The East German Case." Wissenschaftszentrum Berlin, Discussion Paper FS I 95-301.

Cawson, Alan, ed. 1985. *Organized Interests and the State: Studies in Meso-Corporatism.* Beverly Hills: Sage.

Chamber of Commerce and Industry, Middle Neckar. 1984. *Mittlerer Neckar* (August).

Chirinko, Robert, and Julie Ann Elston. 1997. "Finance, Control, and Profitability: An
Evaluation of German Bank Influence." Economic Studies Working Paper No. 28,
American Institute for Contemporary German Studies. March.

Christmann, Helmut. 1970. *Ferdinand Steinbeis: Gewerbeförderer und Volkserzieher.*
Heidenheim/Br.: Heidenheimer.

Clement, Wolfgang. 1997. "Gründungs-Offensive 'Go!' zur Stärkung des Mittelstands."
Sparkasse 114 (5): 209–11.

Coleman, William D. 1994a. "Keeping the Shotgun behind the Door: Governing the Securities Industry in Canada, the United Kingdom, and the United States." In *Governing Capitalist Economies: Performance and Control of Economic Sectors,* ed.
J. Rogers Hollingsworth, Philippe C. Schmitter, and Wolfgang Streeck. New York:
Oxford University Press.

Coleman, William D. 1994b. "Policy Convergence in Banking: A Comparative Study."
Political Studies 42:274–92.

Coleman, William D. 1996. *Financial Services, Globalization, and Domestic Policy
Change.* New York: St. Martin's Press.

Coleman, William D., and Geoffrey R. D. Underhill. 1995. "Globalization, Regional-
ism and the Regulation of Securities Markets." *Journal of European Public Policy*
2:488–513.

Conze, Werner. 1973. "Möglichkeiten und Grenzen der liberalen Arbeiterbewegung in
Deutschland: Das Beispiel Schulze-Delitzsch." In *Interessenverbände in Deutschland,* ed. Heinz Josef Varain. Cologne: Kiepenheuer & Witsch.

Cooke, Philip, and Kevin Morgan. 1994. "Growth Regions under Duress: Renewal
Strategies in Baden-Württemberg and Emilia-Romagna." In *Globalization, Institutions, and Regional Development in Europe,* ed. Ash Amin and Nigel Thrift. Oxford: Oxford University Press.

Cox, Andrew. 1986. "State, Finance and Industry in Comparative Perspective." In *The
State, Finance and Industry,* ed. Andrew Cox. New York: St. Martin's Press.

Dahrendorf, Ralf. 1967. *Society and Democracy in Germany.* New York: W. W. Norton.

Dale, Richard. 1992. *International Banking Deregulation: The Great Banking Experiment.* Oxford: Blackwell.

" 'Das Glas ist halbvoll'." 1993. *Capital* (June).

Deeg, Richard. 1993. "The State, Banks, and Economic Governance in Germany." *German Politics* 2 (2): 149–76.

Deeg, Richard. 1996. "Economic Globalization and the Shifting Boundaries of German Federalism." *Publius: The Journal of Federalism* 26 (1): 27–52.

Deeg, Richard. 1997. "Banks and Industrial Finance in the 1990s." *Industry and Innovation* 4 (1): 53–73.

Deeg, Richard. 1998. "What Makes German Banks Different." *Small Business Economics* 10 (2): 93–101.

Deutsche Bundesbank. 1976. *Deutsches Geld- und Bankwesen in Zahlen, 1876–1975.* Frankfurt: Fritz Knapp.

Deutsche Bundesbank. 1992a. "Interest Subsidies and Other Financial Assistance in United Germany." *Monthly Report of the Deutsche Bundesbank* 44 (8): 21–28.

Deutsche Bundesbank. 1992b. "Longer-Term Trends in the Financing Patterns of West German Enterprises." *Monthly Report of the Deutsche Bundesbank* 44 (10): 25–39.

Deutsche Bundesbank. 1995a. "Fortschritte im Anpassungsprozess in Ostdeutschland und der Beitrag der Wirtschaftsförderung." *Deutsche Bundesbank Monatsbericht* 47 (7): 39–56.

Deutsche Bundesbank. 1995b. "Ertragslage und Finanzierungsverhältnisse ostdeutscher Unternehmen im Jahre 1993." *Deutsche Bundesbank Monatsbericht* 47 (7): 57–66.

Deutsche Bundesbank. 1996a. "Lending Trends, by Group of Borrowers and Category of Banks." *Monthly Report of the Deutsche Bundesbank* 48 (10): 47–59.

Deutsche Bundesbank. 1996b. "West German Enterprises' Profitability and Financing in 1995." *Monthly Report of the Deutsche Bundesbank* 48 (11): 33–45.

Deutsche Bundesbank. 1997. "Shares as Financing and Investment Instruments." *Monthly Report of the Deutsche Bundesbank* 49 (1): 27–40.

Deutsches Institut für Wirtschaftsforschung. 1993. "Industrieller Mittelstand in Ostdeutschland." *DIW Wochenbericht* 60:103–9.

Deutsches Institut für Wirtschaftsforschung. 1995a. "Nach wie vor grosse Defizite beim ostdeutschen Kapitalstock." *DIW Wochenbericht* 62:535–44.

Deutsches Institut für Wirtschaftsforschung. 1995b. "Unternehmerische Netzwerke in der ostdeutschen Industrie: Kooperation hilft überregionale Absatzmöglichkeiten erschliessen." *DIW Wochenbericht* 62:545–51.

Dickertmann, Dietrich. 1985. "Die Kreditinstitute der Länder." Parts 1 and 2. *Zeitschrift für öffentliche und gemeinwirtschaftliche Unternehmen* 8 (1, 2): 38–69, 164–86.

"Die Dealmaker auf der Pirsich." 1991. *Industriemagazin* (August).

"Die Macht der Banken—Anhörung im Bundestag." 1994. *Zeitschrift für Bankrecht und Bankwirtschaft* 6 (1): 74–76.

Dieckmann, Jens. 1981. *Der Einfluss der deutschen Sparkassen auf die staatliche Wirtschaftspolitik in der historischen Entwicklung.* Frankfurt: Rita K. Fischer.

"Dr. Sprung: 'Die KWG-Novellierung muss jetzt kommen.'" 1982. *Sparkasse* 99:41–43.

Dose, Nicolai, and Alexander Drexler, eds. 1988. *Technologieparks: Voraussetzungen, Bestandsaufnahme und Kritik.* Opladen: Westdeutscher Verlag.

Dyson, Kenneth. 1982. "The Politics of Economic Recession in West Germany." In *Politics, Policy, and the European Recession,* ed. Andrew Cox. London: Macmillan.

Dyson, Kenneth. 1983. "The Cultural, Ideological and Structural Context." In *Industrial Crisis: A Comparative Study of the State and Industry,* ed. Kenneth Dyson and Stephen Wilks. New York: St. Martin's Press.

Dyson, Kenneth. 1986. "The State, Banks and Industry: The West German Case." In *State, Finance, and Industry,* ed. Andrew Cox. New York: St. Martin's Press.

Economists' Advisory Group. 1981. *The British and German Banking System: A Comparative Study.* London: Anglo-German Foundation for the Study of Industrial Society.

Edwards, Jeremy, and Klaus Fischer. 1991. "An Overview of the German Financial System." Paper presented at the National Economic Development Office Conference on Capital Markets and Company Success, London, November.

Edwards, Jeremy, and Klaus Fischer. 1994. *Banks, Finance and Investment in Germany.* Cambridge: Cambridge University Press.

Edwards, Jeremy, and Sheilagh Ogilvie. 1996. "Universal Banks and German Industrialization: A Reappraisal." *Economic History Review* 49 (3): 427–46.

Eglau, Hans Otto. 1989. *Wie Gott in Frankfurt: Die Deutsche Bank und die deutsche Industrie.* Düsseldorf: ECON-Verlag.

Eistert, Ekkehard. 1970. *Die Beeinflussung des Wirtschaftswachstums in Deutschland von 1883 bis 1913 durch das Bankensystem.* Berlin: Duncker & Humblot.

Ellgering, Ingo. 1987. "Expansion und Strukturwandel der Sparkassen in der jüngeren Vergangenheit (ab 1958)." In *Entwicklungslinien der deutschen Sparkassengeschichte,* ed. Jürgen Mura. Stuttgart: Deutscher Sparkassenverlag.

Engel, Hans-Georg. 1991. "Der Finanzplatz Deutschland aus der Sicht der Auslandsbanken." *Zeitschrift für das gesamte Kreditwesen* 44 (2): 9–11.

Esser, Josef. 1990. "Bank Power in West Germany Revisited." *West European Politics* 13 (4): 17–32.

Esser, Josef, and Wolfgang Fach. 1989. "Crisis Management 'Made in Germany': The Steel Industry." In *Industry and Politics in West Germany,* ed. Peter J. Katzenstein. Ithaca: Cornell University Press.

Esser, Josef, and Wolfgang Fach with Kenneth Dyson. 1983. "'Social Market' and Modernization Policy: West Germany." In *Industrial Crisis: A Comparative Study of the State and Industry,* ed. Kenneth Dyson and Stephen Wilks. New York: St. Martin's Press.

Euba, Norbert. 1985. "Ziele und Wirksamkeit staatlicher Gewerbeförderung dargestellt am Beispiel Baden-Württemberg." In *Öffentliche Finanzen, Kredit und Kapital,* ed. Dieter Cansier and Dietmar Kath. Berlin: Duncker & Humblot.

Fahning, Hans. 1987. "Öffentliche und private Banken." *Der Langfristige Kredit* 38 (4): 100–102.

Faisst, Lothar, and Bruno Rühle. 1988. "Die Südwestdeutsche Landesbank Girozentrale." *Sparkasse* 105: 393–95.

Fanselow, Karl-Heinz, and Heinrich R. Stedler. 1992. "Management-Buy-Out und Mezzanine Money." *Die Bank,* no. 7:395–98.

Faust, Helmut. 1977. *Geschichte der Genossenschaftsbewegung.* Frankfurt: Fritz Knapp.

Feldenkirchen, Wilfried. 1979. "Banken und Stahlindustrie im Ruhrgebiet. Zur Entwicklung ihrer Beziehungen, 1873–1914." *Bankhistorisches Archiv* 2:27–52.

Fischer, Wolfram. 1962. *Der Staat und die Anfänge der Industrialisierung in Baden.* Berlin: Duncker & Humblot.

Fischer, Wolfram, ed. 1972. *Wirtschaft und Gesellschaft im Zeitalter der Industrialisierung.* Göttingen: Vandenhoeck & Ruprecht.

Franks, Julian, and Colin Mayer. 1990. "Corporate Ownership and Corporate Control: A Study of France, Germany and the UK." *Economic Policy* 10:189–232.

Franks, Julian, and Colin Mayer. 1994. "Ownership and Control." Paper presented at the International Workshop at the Kiel Institute, June.

Fremdling, Rainer, and Richard Tilly. 1976. "German Banks, German Growth, and Econometric History." *Journal of Economic History* 36:416–27.

Fremdling, Rainer, and Richard H. Tilly, eds. 1979. *Industrialisierung und Raum: Studien zur regionalen Differenzierung im Deutschland des 19. Jahrhunderts.* Stuttgart: Klett-Cotta.

Frieden, Jeffry A. 1991. "Invested Interests: The Politics of National Economic Policies in a World of Global Finance." *International Organization* 45 (4): 425–51.

Friedhoff, Paul K. 1993. "Das Kreditgewerbe als Partner." *Zeitschrift für das gesamte Kreditwesen* 46 (10): 24–26.

Fromman, Holger. 1991. "Die Rolle der Kapitalbeteiligungsgesellschaften in der Unternehmensfinanzierung." *Der Langfristige Kredit* 42 (22/23): 48–50.

Fromman, Holger. 1993. "Beteiligungskapital und Management-Buy-Out." *Zeitschrift für das gesamte Kreditwesen* 46 (10): 14–16.

Gaddum, Johann Wilhelm. 1993. "Der Finanzplatz Deutschland aus der Sicht der Deutschen Bundesbank." *Sparkasse* 110:150–52.

Garrett, Geoffrey, and Peter Lange. 1991. "Political Responses to Interdependence: What's 'Left' for the Left?" *International Organization* 45:539–64.

Geer, Thomas. 1985. "Internationaler Wettbewerb und regionale Entwicklung: Preisunempfindliche Branchen." In *Nordrhein-Westfalen in der Krise—Krise in Nordrhein-Westfalen?* ed. Willi Lamberts. Berlin: Duncker & Humblot.

Gehr, Martin. 1959. "Das Verhältnis zwischen Banken und Industrie in Deutschland seit der Mitte des 19. Jahrhunderts bis zur Bankenkrise 1931." Ph.D. diss., University of Tübingen.

Geiger, Helmut. 1981. "Wettbewerb erfordert keine Änderung der Besteuerung." *Sparkasse* 98:160–62.

Geiger, Helmut. 1985. "KWG-Reform: Zwiespältige Ergebnisse." *Sparkasse* 102:2–3.

Genschel, Philipp. 1995. "The Dynamics of Inertia: Institutional Persistence and Institutional Change in Telecommunications and Health Care." Max-Planck-Institut für Gesellschaftsforschung Discussion Paper 95/3.

Gerschenkron, Alexander. 1962. *Economic Backwardness in Historical Perspective.* Cambridge: Harvard University Press.

Gerschenkron, Alexander. 1966. *Bread and Democracy in Germany.* New York: H. Fertig.

Girke, Werner, and Bernd Kopplin. 1977. *Beteiligungspolitik deutscher Kreditinstitute: Am Beispiel der Bayerischen Hypotheken- und Wechselbank and der Westdeutschen Landesbank.* Berlin: Erich Schmidt Verlag.

Goetz, Klaus H. 1993. "Rebuilding Public Administration in the New German Länder: Transfer and Differentiation." *West European Politics* 16:447–69.

"Going Public 1995: Jahr der Rekorde." 1996. *Die Bank* (January).

Goldschmidt, Thomas. 1985. "Öffentliche Kredithilfe im Rahmen der Mittelstands und Regionalpolitik in Baden-Württemberg." Ph.D. diss., University of Hohenheim.

Gonzalez, Carlos Javier Moreiro. 1993. *Banking in Europe after 1992.* Brookfield, Vt.: Dartmouth Publishing.

Gorniak, Ulrich. 1981. "Gegen eine erneute Anhebung der Sparkassenbesteuerung." *Sparkasse* 98:4–8.

Götte, Gerhard. 1988. "Anmerkungen zur Effektivität von Investitions-förderungsprogrammen am Beispiel des KfWs." *Der Langfristige Kredit* 39 (21/22): 700–703.

Gottschalk, Arno. 1988. "Der Stimmrechtseinfluss der Banken in den Aktionärsversammlungen von Grossunternehmen." *WSI Mitteilungen* 41:294–304.

Grabher, Gernot. 1990. "Netzwerke statt Stahlwerke." *WZB-Mitteilungen* (March).

Grabher, Gernot, ed. 1993. *The Embedded Firm: On the Socioeconomics of Industrial Networks.* London: Routledge.

Graf Lambsdorff, Otto. 1993. "Soll der Staat Bankgeschäfte betreiben?" *Zeitschrift für das gesamte Kreditwesen* 46 (13): 602.

Grant, Wyn, William Paterson, and Colin Whitston. 1988. *Government and the Chemical Industry: A Comparative Study of Britain and West Germany.* Oxford: Clarendon.

Griffin, John R. 1994. "Investment and Ownership in a Volatile Economy: Big Banks and the Case of the East German Economic Transition." *Politics & Society* 22:389–420.

Griffin, John R. 1995. "Institutional Change as a Collective Learning Process? A U.S.-German Comparison of Corporate Governance Reform." Paper presented at the Annual Meeting of the American Political Science Association, Chicago, September.

Gröner, Helmut, ed. 1992. *Der Markt für Unternehmenskontrollen.* Berlin: Duncker & Humblot.

Gröschel, Ulrich. 1987. "Beteiligungsfinanzierung—Wettbewerbsfaktor im Firmenkundengeschäft." *Sparkasse* 104:380–83.

Gröschel, Ulrich. 1989. "Finanzdienstleistungen für wachsende Unternehmen." In *Corporate Finance,* ed. Hans J. Krümmel and Bernd Rudolph. Frankfurt: Fritz Knapp.

Gröschel, Ulrich. 1993. "Von der 4. zur 7. KWG-Novelle." *Sparkasse* 110:225–30.

Grunwald, Jörg-Günther. 1978. *Wettbewerb und Eigenkapital in der deutschen Wirtschaft.* Berlin: Duncker & Humblot.

Gundlach, Werner. 1985. "Gedanken zum Marketing-Konzept des genossenschaftlichen

Bankenverbundes." In *Aspekte bankwirtschaftlicher Forschung und Praxis,* ed. Helmut Guthardt et al. Frankfurt: Fritz Knapp.

Hage, Jerald. 1988. "The New Rules of Competition." In *Futures of Organizations,* ed. Jerald Hage. Lexington: Lexington Books.

Hahn, Oswald. 1977. *Die Führung des Bankbetriebes.* Stuttgart: W. Kohlhammer.

Hahn, Oswald. 1986. "Strukturwandlungen im Bankwesen der Bundesrepublik Deutschland." *Österreichsches Bankarchiv* 10:434.

Hall, Maximilian J. B. 1993. *Banking Regulation and Supervision: A Comparative Study of the UK, US and Japan.* Aldershot: Edward Elgar.

Hall, Peter. 1986. *Governing the Economy.* New York: Oxford University Press.

Hall, Peter. 1995. "The Political Economy of Europe in an Era of Interdependence." Paper presented at the Seminar on the State and Capitalism, Harvard.

Hall, Peter A., and Rosemary C. R. Taylor. 1994. "Political Science and the Four New Institutionalisms." Paper presented at the Annual Meeting of the American Political Science Association, New York.

Hamm, Rudiger, and Helmut Wienert. 1990. *Strukturelle Anpassung altindustrieller Regionen im internationalen Vergleich.* Berlin: Duncker & Humblot.

Hartmann, Manfred. 1977. *Raumwirtschaftliche Implikationen der Organization der Kreditwirtschaft.* Berlin: Duncker & Humblot.

Häuser, Karl. 1988. "Kreditinstitute und Wertpapiermärkte in Deutschland—Perioden ihrer Entwicklung." *Bankhistorisches Archiv* 14:11–38.

Heidenreich, Karl. 1993. "Anmerkungen zur Rolle der Landesbank als Geschäftsbank im universellen Umfeld." *Der Langfristige Kredit* 44 (5/6): 12–18.

Hellmann, Wolfgang, and Armin Unterberg. 1991. "Neue Chancen für den Finanzplatz Deutschland im Europa der Zukunft." *Die Bank,* no. 9:480–84.

Henderson, W. O. 1975. *The Rise of German Industrial Power.* London: Temple Smith.

Henze, Werner. 1972. *Grundriss für die Sparkassenarbeit: Grundzüge der Geschichte des Sparkassenwesens.* Stuttgart: Deutscher Sparkassenverlag.

Herrhausen, Alfred. 1983. *Wettbewerb und Regulierung in der Kreditwirtschaft.* Tübingen: J. C. B. Mohr.

Herrigel, Gary B. 1989. "Industrial Order and the Politics of Industrial Change: Mechanical Engineering." In *Industry and Politics in West Germany,* ed. Peter J. Katzenstein. Ithaca: Cornell University Press.

Herrigel, Gary B. 1993a. "Power and the Redefinition of Industrial Districts: The Case of Baden-Württemberg." In *The Embedded Firm: On the Socioeconomics of Industrial Networks,* ed. Gernot Grabher. London: Routledge.

Herrigel, Gary B. 1993b. "Large Firms, Small Firms, and the Governance of Flexible Specialization: The Case of Baden-Württemberg and Socialized Risk." In *Country Competitiveness: Technology and the Organization of Work,* ed. Bruce Kogut. Oxford: Oxford University Press.

Herrigel, Gary B. 1996. *Industrial Constructions: The Sources of German Industrial Power.* Cambridge: Cambridge University Press.

Heye, Bernd. 1985. "Die Steuerung der Inlandsfilialen einer Grossbank." *Die Bank,* no. 1:15–18.

Hilferding, Rudolf. [1910] 1981. *Finance Capital.* Ed. Tom Bottomore. London: Routledge & Kegan Paul.

Hirn, Wolfgang. 1993. "'Spätzle-Connection'." *Managermagazin* (July).

Hollingsworth, J. Rogers, and Wolfgang Streeck. 1994. "Countries and Sectors: Concluding Remarks on Performance, Convergence, and Competitiveness." In *Governing Capitalist Economies: Performance and Control of Economic Sectors,* ed. J. Rogers Hollingsworth, Philippe C. Schmitter, and Wolfgang Streeck. New York: Oxford University Press.

Hollingsworth, J. Rogers, Philippe C. Schmitter, and Wolfgang Streeck. 1994. *Governing Capitalist Economies: Performance and Control of Economic Sectors.* New York: Oxford University Press.

Holst, Klaus. 1996. "Strukturen und Perspektiven der ostdeutschen Technologiepolitik." *Wirtschaft im Wandel,* no. 3:3–7.

Howell, Thomas R., William A. Noellert, Jesse G. Kreier, and Alan Wm. Wolff. 1988. *Steel and the State: Government Intervention and Steel's Structural Crisis.* Boulder: Westview Press.

Huber, Ludwig. 1980. "Landesbanken—Herkunft und Aufgaben." In *Banken und Bankengruppen,* ed. Hugo J. Hahn. Baden-Baden: Nomos.

Hummel, Marlies. 1995. "Kapitalbeteiligungen in den neuen Bundesländern." *IFO Schnelldienst* 48 (13): 11–19.

Hüttenberger, Peter. 1985. "Grundprobleme der Geschichte Nordrhein-Westfalens zwischen 1945 und 1970." In *Parteien und Wahlen in Nordrhein-Westfalen,* ed. Ulrich von Alemann. Cologne: W. Kohlhammer.

Institut der deutschen Wirtschaft. 1992. "Mehr Geld als Know-how." *IWD: Informationsdienst des Instituts der deutschen Wirtschaft* 18 (18): 2.

Institut der deutschen Wirtschaft. 1993a. "Starthilfe für den Mittelstand." *IWD: Informationsdienst des Instituts der deutschen Wirtschaft* 19 (3): 6–7.

Institut der deutschen Wirtschaft. 1993b. "Die schlanke Produktion hält Einzug." *IWD: Informationsdienst des Instituts der deutschen Wirtschaft* 19 (30): 8.

Institut der deutschen Wirtschaft. 1995a. "Unternehmens-Insolvenzen: Nachwehen der Krise." *IWD: Informationsdienst des Instituts der deutschen Wirtschaft* 21 (15): 4–5.

Institut der deutschen Wirtschaft. 1995b. "Forschung und Entwicklung: Innovations-Schub im Osten." *IWD: Informationsdienst des Instituts der deutschen Wirtschaft* 21 (15): 6.

Institut der deutschen Wirtschaft. 1995c. "Ostdeutsche Exporte: Steile Talfahrt beendet." *IWD: Informationsdienst des Instituts der deutschen Wirtschaft* 21 (20): 7.

Institut der deutschen Wirtschaft. 1995d. "Ostdeutsche Unternehmen: Eigenkapital als Dreh- und Angelpunkt." *IWD: Informationsdienst des Instituts der deutschen Wirtschaft* 21 (2): 8.

Institut der deutschen Wirtschaft. 1995e. "Ost-Strukturwandel: Die Dienste hinken noch hinterher." *IWD: Informationsdienst des Instituts der deutschen Wirtschaft* 21 (8): 4.

Institut der deutschen Wirtschaft. 1997a. "Ostdeutsche Industrie: Mittel- und Grossbetrieben fehlen." *IWD: Informationsdienst des Instituts der deutschen Wirtschaft* 23 (10): 6.

Institut der deutschen Wirtschaft. 1997b. "Konkurswelle rollt." *IWD: Informationsdient des Instituts der deutschen Wirtschaft* 23 (24): 1.

Irsch, Norbert. 1986. *Small and Medium-Sized Enterprises and the Structural Change.* Frankfurt: Kreditanstalt für Wiederaufbau.

Iwer, Frank. 1994. "Industriestandort Stuttgart 1994—Beschäftigungspolitik in der Region." IMU-Institut für Medienforschung und Urbanistik. Typescript.

Jacoby, Wade. 1994. "Industrial Relations in Eastern Germany: The Politics of Imitation." Paper presented at the Annual Meeting of the American Political Science Association, New York, September.

Jeidels, Otto. 1905. "Das Verhältnis der deutschen Grossbanken zur Industrie mit besonderer Berücksichtigung der Eisenindustrie." *Staats- und sozialwissenschaftliche Forschung* 24:1–271.

Jenkinson, Tim, and Jenny Corbett. 1997. "How Is Investment Financed? A Study of Germany, Japan, UK, and US." Economic Studies Working Paper No. 16, American Institute for Contemporary German Studies. January.

Jens, Uwe. 1989. "Aktuelle Probleme der regionalen Strukturpolitik." *Wirtschaftsdienst* 69:459–64.

Jochimsen, Reimut. 1992. "The Regionalisation of Structural Policy: North Rhine–Westphalia in the Europe of the Regions." *German Politics* 1 (3): 82–101.

Juncker, Klaus. 1985. "Zielgruppe Mittelstand: Unternehmenservice der Banken ausgeweitet." *Bank und Markt* (November).

Juncker, Klaus. 1988. "Entwicklungstendenzen im Bereich der computergestützten Bankdienstleistungen." *Betriebswirtschaftliche Forschung und Praxis* 5:418–29.

Juncker, Klaus. 1992. "Perspektiven im Geschäft mit Konzernen." *Bank und Markt* (December).

Jütten, Herbert. 1994. "Finanzplatz Deutschland wird attraktiver." *Die Bank,* no. 1:34–39.

Kapstein, Ethan B. 1994. *Governing the Global Economy: International Finance and the State.* Cambridge: Harvard University Press.

Karsch, Werner. 1992. "Börsenneulinge: Renaissance der Aktie." *Die Bank,* no. 1:20–22.

Karsch, Werner. 1993. "Börsenkandidaten: Konzern-Töchter debütieren." *Die Bank,* no. 1:22–27.

Katzenstein, Peter, ed. 1989. *Industry and Politics in West Germany.* Ithaca: Cornell University Press.

Kaven, Jürgen-Peter. 1991. "Chancen und Strategien der Auslandsbanken in Deutschland." *Zeitschrift für das gesamte Kreditwesen* 44 (3): 7–9.

Keohane, Robert O., and Helen V. Milner, eds. 1996. *Internationalization and Domestic Politics.* Cambridge: Cambridge University Press.

Kern, Horst, and Charles Sabel. 1994. "Die Treuhandanstalt: Experimentierfeld zur Entwicklung neuer Unternehmensformen." In *Das Unmögliche Wagen,* ed. Wolfram Fischer, Herbert Hax, and Hans Karl Schneider. Berlin: Aufbau Verlag.

Kern, Horst, and Michael Schumann. 1989. "New Concepts of Production in West German Plants." In *Industry and Politics in West Germany,* ed. Peter J. Katzenstein. Ithaca: Cornell University Press.

Kiesewetter, Hubert. 1985. "Staat und regionale Industrialisierung: Württemberg und Sachsen im 19. Jahrhundert." In *Staat, Region und Industrialisierung,* ed. Hubert Kiesewetter and Rainer Fremdling. Ostfildern: Scripta Mercurae.

Kitschelt, Herbert. 1991. "Industrial Governance Structures, Innovation Strategies, and the Case of Japan: Sectoral or Cross-National Comparative Analysis?" *International Organization* 45:453–93.

Klagholz, Bernd. 1986. *Die Industrialisierung der Stadt Heilbronn von den Anfängen bis zum Jahr 1914.* Heilbronn: Stadtarchiv.

Klemmer, Paul. 1988. "Adaptation Problems of Old Industrial Areas: The Ruhr Area as an Example." In *Regional Structural Problems and Industrial Policy in International Perspective,* ed. Joachim Jens Hesse. Baden-Baden: Nomos.

Klüpfel, Wolfgang. 1984. "Entwicklungslinien im Sparkassenrecht." In *Standortbestimmung: Entwicklungslinien der deutschen Kreditwirtschaft,* ed. Günther Aschauer et al. Stuttgart: Deutscher Sparkassenverlag.

Kluthe, Klaus. 1985. *Genossenschaften und Staat in Deutschland.* Berlin: Duncker & Humblot.

Knemeyer, Franz-Ludwig. 1986. *Bankgeheimnis und parlamentarische Kontrolle bei Landesbanken.* Frankfurt: Fritz Knapp.

Kocka, Jürgen. 1978. "Entrepreneurs and Managers in German Industrialization." In *The Cambridge Economic History of Europe* 7 (1): 492–589.

Kocka, Jürgen. 1981. "Grossunternehmen und der Aufstieg des Managerkapitalismus im späten 19. und frühen 20. Jahrhundert: Deutschland im internationalen Vergleich." *Historische Zeitschrift* 232:39–60.

Köhler, Horst. 1996. "Globalisierung, sozialer Zusammenhalt und Demokratie-Renaissance der Sparkassenidee." *Sparkasse* 113:542–47.

Köllhofer, Dietrich. 1991. "Die Markt- und Wettbewerbssituation des Bankensektors in den neuen Bundesländern." In *Wirtschaftspolitische Probleme der Integration der ehemaligen DDR in die Bundesrepublik,* ed. Helmut Gröner et al. Berlin: Duncker & Humblot.

Korbach, Stefan. 1986. "Die Landesbanken/Girozentralen und die Interessen ihre Gewährträger." Ph.D. diss., University of Frankfurt.

Körber-Weik, Margot. 1989. "Die wirtschaftliche Stellung Baden-Württembergs." In *Baden-Württemberg under der Bund,* ed. Hartmut Klatt. Stuttgart: W. Kohlhammer.

Koschnik, Hans. 1982. "Die Eigenkapitaldiskussion—Dokumente für den Haftungszuschlag." *Sparkasse* 99:171–96.

Krasner, Stephen D. 1984. "Approaches to the State: Alternative Conceptions and Historical Dynamics." *Comparative Politics* 16:223–46.

Krümmel, Hans Jacob. 1983. *Bankenaufsichtsziele und Eigenkapitalbegriffe.* Frankfurt: Fritz Knapp.

Krupp, Georg. 1993. "Die Aufgaben der Banken." *Zeitschrift für das gesamte Kreditwesen* 46 (10): 8–10.

Kudiss, Reinhard. 1991. "DM Commercial Paper: Ein neues Finanzierungsinstrument für die Industrie." *Der Langfristige Kredit* 42 (22/23): 44–47.

Kühr, Herbert. 1985. "Die CDU in Nordrhein-Westfalen: Von der Unionsgründung zur modernen Mitgliedspartei." In *Parteien und Wahlen in Nordrhein-Westfalen,* ed. Ulrich von Alemann. Cologne: W. Kohlhammer.

Kullen, Siegfried. 1983. *Baden-Württemberg: Strukturen, Daten, und Entwicklungen.* Stuttgart: F. Klett.

Kurzer, Paulette. 1993. *Business and Banking: Political Change and Economic Integration in Western Europe.* Ithaca: Cornell University Press.

Lamberts, Willi. 1988. "Die gewerbliche Wirtschaft Nordrhein-Westfalens in der Bewährung." In *Die Wirtschaft des Landes Nordrhein-Westfalen,* ed. Ludwig Bussmann. Cologne: W. Kohlhammer.

Land, Günter. 1997. "Steigende Nachfrage nach Kapitalbeteiligungen der Sparkassen-Finanzgruppe." *Sparkasse* 114:241–44.

Landeszentralbank in Hessen. 1995. "Frankfurter Finanzmarkt-Bericht Nr. 22" (November).

Landrock, Rudolf. 1990. "Überlegungen zum Profil von Firmenkundenbetreuern." *Sparkasse* 107:212–13.

Landrock, Rudolf. 1997. "Schliessung der technischen Lücke bei der Kreditprüfung mit dem NTG." *Sparkasse* 114:222–26.

Lauer, Christoph. 1990. *Diversifizierung des Angebots und Wettbewerbsperspektiven im Bankensektor.* Stuttgart: Messidor.

Lehner, Franz, Birgit Geile, and Jürgen Nordhaus-Janz. 1987. "Wirtschaftsförderung als kommunale Aufgabe." In *Kommunale Selbstverwaltung und Kommunalpolitik in Nordrhein-Westfalen,* ed. Uwe Anderson. Cologne: W. Kohlhammer.

Lehner, Franz, et al. 1989. *Das Zukunftstechnologie-Programm des Landes Nordrhein-Westfalen: Eine Evaluationsstudie.* Bochum: Universitätsverlag Brockmeyer.

Leimbach, Andreas. 1991. "Unternehmensübernahmen im Wege des Management-Buy-Outs in der Bundesrepublik: Besonderheiten, Chancen und Risiken." *Zeitschrift für betriebswirtschaftliche Forschung* 43:450–64.

Lennertz, Achim. 1993. "Umstrukturierung durch M & A." *Zeitschrift für das gesamte kreditwesen* 46 (4): 12–16.

Leuenberger, Theodor, and Bernd Küppers. 1987. "Das Asia-Pacific-Center der Stadtsparkasse Köln." *Bank und Markt* (September).

Levy, Jonah D. 1997. "Globalization, liberalization, and national capitalisms." *Structural Change and Economic Dynamics* 8 (1): 87–98.

Liedtke, Rüdiger. 1994. *Wem gehört die Republik: Die Konzerne und ihre Verflechtung.* Frankfurt: Eichborn.

Lindberg, Leon N., John L. Campbell, and J. Rogers Hollingsworth. 1991. "Economic Governance and the Analysis of Structural Change in the American Economy." In *Governance of the American Economy,* ed. John L. Campbell, J. Rogers Hollingsworth, and Leon N. Lindberg. Cambridge: Cambridge University Press.

Lipton, David, and Jeffrey Sachs. 1990. "Privatization in Eastern Europe: The Case of Poland." *Brookings Papers on Economic Activity* 2:293–341.

Locke, Richard. 1995. *Remaking the Italian Economy.* Ithaca: Cornell University Press.

Loriaux, Michael. 1997. "Socialist Monetarism and Liberalization in France." In *Capital Ungoverned: Liberalizing Finance in Interventionist States,* ed. Michael Loriaux et al. Ithaca: Cornell University Press.

Lubitz, Karl-Joachim. 1984. *Bankmarketing gegenüber mittelständischen Betrieben.* Frankfurt: Fritz Knapp.

Lubitz, Karl-Joachim. 1985. "Bankmarketing gegenüber mittelständischen Unternehmen." *Bank und Markt* (September).

Lütz, Susanne. 1998. "The Revival of the Nation-State? Stock Exchange Regulation in an Era of Internationalized Financial Markets." *Journal of European Public Policy* 5 (1): 153–68.

Marklew, Victoria. 1995. *Cash, Crisis, and Corporate Governance.* Ann Arbor: University of Michigan Press.

Markovits, Andrei S., ed. 1982. *The Political Economy of West Germany.* New York: Praeger.

Marner, Bernd, and Felix Jaeger. 1991. "Kleine und mittlere Unternehmen von Beratern umworben." *Die Bank* (April).

"Martini on the Rocks." 1993. *Managermagazin* (April).

Massfeller, Norbert. 1993. "Strategie der Non Banks am Beispiel Volkswagen" *Die Bank* (May).

Mayer, Colin, and Ian Alexander. 1990. "Banks and Securities Markets: Corporate Financing in Germany and the UK." Centre for Economic Policy Research Discussion Paper No. 433.

"MdB Lenartz: 'Die KWG-Reform muss in dieser Legislaturperiode abgeschlossen werden'." 1982. *Sparkasse* 99:235–37.

Megerle, Klaus. 1982. *Württemberg im Industrialisierungsprozess.* Stuttgart: Klett-Cotta.

Meisel, Harry. 1983. "Arbeitsmarkt und Arbeitsmarktpolitik in der Bundesrepublik Deutschland und in Baden-Württemberg." In *Die Wirtschaft des Landes: Baden-Württemberg,* ed. Alfred E. Ott. Stuttgart: W. Kohlhammer.

Meister, Edgar. 1993. " 'Land ohne Bank'—braucht Rheinland-Pfalz keine Landesbank mehr?" *Der Langfristige Kredit* 44 (5/6): 8–11.

Mertin, Klaus. 1981. "Profit-Center-Steuerung in Universalbanken." In *Controlling in Banken und Sparkassen,* ed. Ludwig Mühlhaupt, Henner Schierenbeck, and Hans Wielens. Frankfurt: Fritz Knapp.

Meyer-Horn, Klaus. 1993. "Mindestreserven nur noch Ultima ratio?" *Sparkasse* 110:153.

Meyer-Könster, Jürgen. 1979. *Die Sonderstellung der Sparkassen im Wettbewerb.* Göttingen: Vandenhoeck & Ruprecht.

Meyer-Kramer, Friedel. 1988. "Industrielle Innovation und regionale Entwicklung in europäischen Ländern." *Vierteljahreshefte zur Wirtschaftsforschung* 1 (2): 5–14.

Michels, Ralf. 1993. "DM CP-Markt bleibt attraktiv." *Die Bank,* no. 2:87–90.

Molyneux, Philip. 1989. "1992 and Its Impact on Local and Regional Banking Markets." *Regional Studies* 23 (6): 523–33.

Moran, Michael. 1991. *The Politics of the Financial Services Revolution: The USA, UK and Japan.* New York: St. Martin's Press.

Moran, Michael. 1992. "Regulatory Change in German Financial Markets." In *The Politics of German Regulation,* ed. Kenneth Dyson. Aldershot: Edward Elgar.

Moran, Michael. 1994. "The State and the Financial Services Revolution: A Comparative Analysis." *West European Politics* 17 (3): 158–77.

Müller-Armack, Alfred. 1931. "Aufgaben und Organisationsprobleme der öffentlichen Unternehmung im Gebiete der Bankwirtschaft." *Schriften des Vereins für Sozialpolitik* 176:389–435.

Mura, Jürgen, ed. 1987a. *Entwicklungslinien der deutschen Sparkassengeschichte.* Stuttgart: Deutscher Sparkassenverlag.

Mura, Jürgen. 1987b. "Krisen und Kontinuität der Sparkassen (1908 bis 1931)." In *Die Entwicklung der Sparkassen zu Universalkreditinstituten,* ed. Jürgen Mura. Stuttgart: Deutscher Sparkassenverlag.

Musil, Susanne, and Michael Nippa. 1993. "Finanzmanagement-Angebote für Firmenkunden." *Die Bank,* no. 1:34–39.

Mussler, Claus-Peter. 1989. "Dieses Vorhaben verstösst gegen die Grundregeln eines gerechten Wettbewerbs." *Geldinstitute* (October).

Neubauer, Franz. 1997. "Der Streit um Gewährträgerhaftung und Anstaltslast—Wie sieht die Zukunft im Sparkassenverbund aus?" *Der Langfristige Kredit* 48 (6): 6–10.

Neuber, Friedel. 1988. "Die Kapitalversorgung und die Finanzierung des technischen Wandels in der privaten Wirtschaft Nordrhein-Westfalens." In *Die Wirtschaft des Landes Nordrhein-Westfalen,* ed. Ludwig Bussmann. Cologne: W. Kohlhammer.

Neuber, Friedel. 1993. "M&A aus Sicht einer Landesbank." *Zeitschrift für das gesamte Kreditwesen* 46 (4): 10–12.

Neuburger, Hugh, and Houston H. Stokes. 1974. "German Banks and German Growth, 1883–1913: An Empirical View." *Journal of Economic History* 34:710–31.

Neumann, Friedel. 1995. "Investitionen in den neuen Bundesländern: Dienstleistungsbereiche weiter expansiv, Industrieinvestitionen erhalten konjunkturelle Impulse." *IFO Schnelldienst* 48 (5): 3–10.

Nierhaus, Michael. 1985. "Sparkassen zwischen öffentlichem Auftrag und Wettbewerbsfunktion." *Sparkasse* 102:12–18.

Nolte, Dirk. 1993a. "Länderinitiativen zum Erhalt 'industrieller Kerne' in Ostdeutschland." *WSI Mitteilungen* 46:188–90.

Nolte, Dirk. 1993b. "Strukturpolitik in Sachsen—Sanierungskooperation zwischen dem Freistaat Sachsen und der Treuhandanstalt." *WSI Mitteilungen* 46:56–59

Nolte, Dirk, Ralf Sitte, and Alexandra Wagner. 1993. "Strukturpolitik in Thüringen— das Konzept 'Entwicklung industrieller Zentren'." *WSI Mitteilungen* 46:402–5.

Nölting, Andreas. 1992. "Nur eine milde Gabe." *Managermagazin* (October).

Notermans, Ton. 1993. "The Abdication of National Policy Autonomy." *Politics and Society* 21:133–67.

Oberbeck, Herbert, and Martin Baethge. 1989. "Computers and Pinstripes: Financial Institutions." In *Industry and Politics in West Germany,* ed. Peter J. Katzenstein. Ithaca: Cornell University Press.

OECD. 1996. *Economic Surveys—Germany.* Paris: OECD.

Pahlen, Dieter. 1993. "Probleme bei der Privatisierung und Finanzierung von Unternehmen in den neuen Bundesländern." *Zeitschrift für das gesamte Kreditwesen* 46 (10): 10–14.

Parnell, Martin F. 1994. *The German Tradition of Organized Capitalism: Self-Government in the Coal Industry.* New York: Oxford University Press.

Parri, Leonardo. 1989. "Territorial Political Exchange in Federal and Unitary Countries." *West European Politics* 12 (3): 197–219.

Paterson, William E., and Gordon Smith, eds. 1981. *The West German Model: Perspectives on a Stable State.* London: Cass.

Paul, Claudia. 1992. "Der Umbau der Bankgenossenschaften." *Zeitschrift für das gesamte Kreditwesen* 45 (4): 22–25.

Pauly, Louis W. 1988. *Opening Financial Markets: Banking Politics on the Pacific Rim.* Ithaca: Cornell University Press.

Penzkofer, Horst. 1992. "Innovationsaktivitäten in den neuen Bundesländern." *IFO-Schnelldienst* 45 (15): 3–9.

Perlitz, Manfred, and Frank Seeger. 1994. "Regarding the Particular Role of Universal Banks in German Corporate Governance." University of Mannheim. Typescript.

Petzina, Dietmar. 1988. "The Ruhr Area: Historical Development." In *Regional Structural Problems and Industrial Policy in International Perspective,* ed. Joachim Jens Hesse. Baden-Baden: Nomos.

Pfeffer, Jeffrey, and Gerald Salancik. 1978. *The External Control of Organizations: A Resource Dependence Perspective.* New York: Harper & Row.

Pfeiffer, Hermannus. 1989. "BASF und die Deutsche Bank—Eine Fallstudie zum Bankeneinfluss in der Wirtschaft." *WSI Mitteilungen* 42 (1): 9–16.

Piore, Michael J., and Charles F. Sabel. 1984. *The Second Industrial Divide.* New York: Basic Books.

Pleister, Christopher, and Eckart Hennigsen. 1991. "Das Spitzeninstitut der deutschen Genossenschaften und seine Tätigkeit in den neuen Bundesländern." *Zeitschrift für das gesamte Genossenschaftswesen* 41:101–10.

Pohl, Hans. 1982. "Das deutsche Bankwesen (1806–1848)." In *Deutsche Bankengeschichte,* vol. 2. Frankfurt: Fritz Knapp.

Pohl, Manfred. 1976. *Einführung in die deutsche Bankengeschichte.* Frankfurt: Fritz Knapp.

Pohl, Manfred. 1982. "Die Entwicklung des deutschen Bankwesens zwischen 1848 und 1870." In *Deutsche Bankengeschichte,* vol. 2. Frankfurt: Fritz Knapp.

Pohl, Manfred. 1986. *Entstehung und Entwicklung des Universalbankensystems.* Frankfurt: Fritz Knapp.

Pohl, Manfred. 1992. *Baden-Württembergische Bankengeschichte.* Stuttgart: W. Kohlhammer.

Porter, Michael. 1990. *The Competitive Advantage of Nations.* New York: Free Press.

Porter, Michael. 1992. "Capital Disadvantage: America's Failing Capital Investment System." *Harvard Business Review* (September–October).

Poullain, Ludwig. 1969. "Sparkassenpolitik für Morgen." *Sparkasse* 86:169–78.

Poullain, Ludwig. 1979. *Tätigkeitsbericht.* Stuttgart: Seewald Verlag.

Poweleit, Manfred, and Sigrid Ulrich. 1988. "Wenn der Groschen fehlt . . ." *Managermagazin* (November).

Prautzsch, Wolf-Albrecht. 1990. "Börseneinführungen—Chancen für den Verbund." *Sparkasse* 107:54–56.

Quack, Sigrid, and Swen Hildebrandt. 1995. "Hausbank or Fornisseur? Bank Services for Small and Medium Sized Enterprises in Germany and France." Wissenschaftszentrum Berlin, Discussion Paper FSI 95–102.

Raithel, Helmut. 1992. "Reisefieber." *Managermagazin* (July).

Reiff, Hermann. 1985. *Erlebtes Baden-Württemberg: Erinnerungen eines Ministerialbeamten.* Stuttgart: W. Kohlhammer.

Reimpell, Peter. 1990. "Strategien deutscher Banken im Investment Banking." *Die Bank,* no. 9:488–90.

Riesser, Jacob. 1911. *The Great German Banks and Their Concentration.* Washington, D.C.: U.S. Government Printing Office.

Ringel, Johannes. 1992. "Beteiligungen—ein wichtiges Geschäftsfeld auch für Landesbanken." *Sparkasse* 109:150–52.

Roggenbuck, Harald E. 1992. *Begrenzung des Anteilsbesitzes von Kreditinstituten an Nichtbanken: Gesetzliche Regelungen, empirischer Befund sowie anlage- und geschäftspolitische Bedeutung.* Frankfurt: Verlag Peter Lang.

Rohleder, Michael, and Gerald Schäfer. 1991. "Neues Finanzierungsinstrument im Inland: DM-Commercial Paper." *Die Bank,* no. 1:204–7.

Rohrmeier, Dieter. 1987. *Die Bedeutung der internationalisierung von kleinen und mittleren Betrieben für das Bankmarketing.* Munich: GBI-Verlag.

Rombeck-Jaschinski, Ursula. 1989. "Nordrhein-Westfalen im Nachkriegsdeutschland (1945–1958)." In *Nordrhein-Westfalen und der Bund,* ed. Hans Boldt. Cologne: W. Kohlhammer.

Rosen, Paul. 1990. "Förderung technologieorientierter innovativer Existenzgründer—Konzept und Erfahrungen." *Sparkasse* 107:122–26.

Rosenbluth, Francis McCall. 1989. *Financial Politics in Contemporary Japan.* Ithaca: Cornell University Press.

Sabel, Charles F. 1988. "The Re-emergence of Regional Economies." In *Reversing Industrial Decline,* ed. Paul Hirst and Jonathon Zeitlin. Oxford: Berg.

Sabel, Charles, John Griffin, and Richard Deeg. 1993. "Making Money Talk: Towards a New Debtor-Creditor Relation in German Banking." Paper presented at the Conference on Relational Investing, sponsored by Columbia University School of Law's Center for Law and Economic Studies, New York (May 6–7).

Sabel, Charles F., Gary B. Herrigel, Richard Deeg, and Richard Kazis. 1989. "Regional Prosperities Compared: Massachusetts and Baden-Württemberg in the 1980s." *Economy and Society* 18 (4): 374–405.

Sally, Razeen, and Douglas Webber. 1994. "The German Solidarity Pact: A Case Study in the Politics of the New Germany." *German Politics* 3 (1): 18–46.

Saunders, Anthony, and Ingo Walter. 1994. *Universal Banking in the United States.* New York: Oxford University Press.

Schaaf, Peter. 1978. *Ruhrbergbau und Sozialdemokratie: Die Energiepolitik der grossen Koalition, 1966–1969.* Marburg: Verlag Arbeiterbewegung und Gesellschaftswissenschaft.

Schäfer, Henry. 1993. "Banken als Unternehmensberater." *Die Bank,* no. 1:323–31.

Scharpf, Fritz W. 1978. "Interorganizational Policy Studies: Issues, Concepts and Perspectives." In *Interorganizational Policymaking: Limits to Coordination and Central Control,* ed. Kenneth Hanf and Fritz W. Scharpf. Beverly Hills: Sage.

Scharpf, Fritz W. 1987. "Grenzen der Institutionellen Reform." In *Jahrbuch zur Staats- und Verwaltungswissenschaft,* vol. 1, ed. Thomas Ellwein et al. Baden-Baden: Nomos.

Scharpf, Fritz W. 1994. *Optionen des Föderalismus in Deutschland und Europa.* Frankfurt: Campus.

Schatz, Heribert, and Michael Maas. 1988. "Die Bedeutung von Forschung und Entwicklung für die Wirtschaft Nordrhein-Westfalen." In *Die Wirtschaft des Landes Nordrhein-Westfalen,* ed. Ludwig Bussmann. Cologne: W. Kohlhammer.

Schepsle, Kenneth. 1986. "Institutional Equilibrium and Equilibrium Institutions." In *Political Science: The Science of Politics,* ed. Herbert F. Weisberg. New York: Agathon Press.

Schepsle, Kenneth. 1989. "Studying Institutions: Some Lessons from the Rational Choice Approach." *Journal of Theoretical Politics* 1:131–47.

Schildt, Werner. 1993. "NORD/LB—Mitteldeutsche Landesbank: Ein Jahr in Sachsen-Anhalt." *Sparkasse* 110:170–72.

Schiller, Karl. 1969. "Sparkassen in der Industriegesellschaft." *Sparkasse* 86:137–42.

Schlieper, Andreas. 1986. *150 Jahre Ruhrgebiet: Ein Kapitel deutscher Wirtschaftsgeschichte.* Düsseldorf: Schwann.

Schmid, Heiko Thorsten. 1989. *Regionale Wirtschaftsförderung—Schranke des "Modells Baden-Württemberg?"* Konstanz: Hartung-Gorre.

Schmidt, Vivien. 1996. *From State to Market: The Transformation of French Business and Government.* Cambridge: Cambridge University Press.

Schmitt, Hubert-Ralph. 1993. "ERP-Mittel—ein Zauberwort für die fünf neuen Bundesländer." *Zeitschrift für das gesamte Kreditwesen* 46 (7): 13–16.

Schmitz, Ronaldo H. 1993. "Going Public von Tochtergesellschaften deutscher Konzerne." *Zeitschrift für das gesamte Kreditwesen* 46 (18): 12–14.

Schramm, Bernhard. 1984. "Genossenschaftsbanken in Europa." *Zeitschrift für das gesamte Kreditwesen* 35 (10): 7–8.

Schramm, Bernhard. 1985. "Die Neuformierung der genossenschaftlichen Spitzenverbände zum Aufbau einer geschlossenen genossenschaftlichen Bankengruppe." In *Aspekte betriebswirtschaftlicher Forschung und Praxis,* ed. Helmut Guthardt et al. Frankfurt: Fritz Knapp.

Schroeter, Joachim. 1985. "Kreditwesengesetznovelle am 1. Januar 1985 in Kraft getreten." *Sparkasse* 102:49–51.

Schuber, Torsten. 1993. "Welche Bank den besten Riecher für neue Aktien hat." *Impulse* (April).

Schumann, Michael. 1997. "Die deutsche Automobilindustrie im Umbruch." *WSI Mitteilungen* 50 (4): 217–27.

Seidel, Petra. 1992. "Erfahrungen der Kreditanstalt für Wiederaufbau mit Investitionen in den neuen Bundesländern." *WSI Mitteilungen* 45 (9): 599–606.

Sheard, Paul. 1994. "Main Banks and the Governance of Financial Distress." In *The Japanese Main Bank System,* ed. Masahiko Aoki and Hugh Patrick. Oxford: Oxford University Press.

Shonfield, Andrew. [1965] 1980. *Modern Capitalism.* London: Oxford University Press.

Siepmann, Jürgen Dietrich. 1968. *Die Standortfrage bei Kreditinstituten.* Berlin: Duncker & Humblot.

Sinnwell, Erwin. 1978. "Geraten die Landesbanken in Misskredit?" *Zeitschrift für öffentliche und gemeinwirtschaftliche Unternehmen* 2 (2): 163–76.

Smith, Eric Owen. 1983. *The West German Economy.* London: Croom Helm.

Smyser, W. R. 1993. *The German Economy: Colossus at the Crossroads.* 2d ed. New York: St. Martin's Press.

Soskice, David. 1991. "The Institutional Infrastructure for International Competitiveness." In *The Economics of the New Europe,* ed. A. B. Atkinson and R. Brunetta. London: Macmillan.

Soskice, David. 1995. "Finer Varieties of Capitalism: Industry- versus Group-Based Coordination in Germany and Japan." Wissenschaftszentrum Berlin. Typescript.

Späth, Lothar. 1984. *Wende in die Zukunft.* Hamburg: Spiegel-Verlag.

Stearns, Linda Brewster. 1990. "Capital Market Effects on External Control of Corporations." In *Structures of Capital: The Social Organization of the Economy,* ed. Sharon Zukin and Paul Dimaggio. Cambridge: Cambridge University Press.

Stedler, Heinrich R. 1993. "Beteiligungskapital im bankbetrieblichen Leistungsangebot." *Die Bank,* no. 6:347–51.

Stein, Eckart. 1971. *Die Fusion der Girozentralen in Nordrhein-Westfalen.* Würzburg: Physica Verlag.

Steinig, Richard. 1991. "Das Konzept der Deutschen Bank im Asset Management." *Die Bank,* no. 10:552–57.

Steininger, Rolf. 1990. *Ein neues Land am Rhein und Ruhr.* Cologne: W. Kohlhammer.

Stolper, Gustav, Karl Häuser, and Knut Borchardt. 1967. *The German Economy: 1870 to the Present.* New York: Harcourt, Brace & World.

Streeck, Wolfgang. 1989. "Successful Adjustment to Turbulent Markets: The Automobile Industry." In *Industry and Politics in West Germany,* ed. Peter J. Katzenstein. Ithaca: Cornell University Press.

Streeck, Wolfgang. 1992. *Social Institutions and Economic Performance: Studies in the Industrial Relations in Advanced Capitalist Economies.* London: Sage.

Streeck, Wolfgang. 1996. "German Capitalism: Does It Exist? Can It Survive?" In *Modern Capitalism or Modern Capitalisms?* ed. Colin Crouch and Wolfgang Streeck. London: Francis Pinter.

Streeck, Wolfgang, and Philippe C. Schmitter. 1985. *Private Interest Government: Beyond Market and State.* London: Sage.

Streibl, Max. 1985. "Der Leistungsbeitrag der Landesbanken Girozentralen." *Sparkasse* 102:46–48.

Studienkommission "Grundsatzfragen der Kreditwirtschaft." 1979. *Bericht der Studienkommission 'Grundsatzfragen der Kreditwirtschaft.'* Bonn: Stollfuss Verlag.

Stützel, Wolfgang. 1964. *Bankpolitik Heute und Morgen.* Frankfurt: Fritz Knapp.

Süchting, Joachim. 1984. "Untermehmensführung in Banken und Sparkassen." In *Standortbestimmung: Entwicklungslinien der deutschen Kreditwirtschaft,* ed. Günther Aschauer et al. Stuttgart: Deutscher Sparkassenverlag.

Thelen, Kathleen, and Sven Steinmo. 1992. "Historical Institutionalism in Comparative Politics." In *Structuring Politics: Historical Institutionalism in Comparative Analysis,* ed. Sven Steinmo, Kathleen Thelen, and Frank Longstreth. New York: Cambridge University Press.

Thurow, Lester. 1992. *Head to Head: The Coming Battle among Japan, Europe and America.* New York: Morrow.

Tichy, Gunther. 1990. "Bestandsbedingungen und -probleme kleiner Unternehmungen." In *Kleinbetriebe im wirtschaftlichem Wandel,* ed. Johannes Berger et al. Frankfurt: Campus.

Tiedeken, Hans. 1985. "Sparkassen in Gefahr." *Sparkasse* 102 (8): 289–90.

Tilly, Richard H. 1966. *Financial Institutions and Industrialization in the Rhineland, 1815–1870.* Madison: University of Wisconsin Press.

Tilly, Richard H. 1967. "Germany: 1815–1870." In *Banking in the Early Stages of Industrialization,* ed. Rondo Cameron. New York: Oxford University Press.

Tilly, Richard H. 1980. *Kapital, Staat, und Sozialer Protest in der deutschen Industrialisierung.* Göttingen: Vandenhoeck & Ruprecht.

Tilly, Richard H. 1986. "German Banking, 1850–1914: Development Assistance for the Strong." *Journal of Economic History* 5:113–52.

Tipton, Frank Jr. 1976. *Regional Variations in the Economic Development of Germany during the Nineteenth Century.* Middletown, Conn.: Wesleyan University Press.

Trende, Adolf. 1957. *Geschichte der deutschen Sparkassen.* Stuttgart: Deutscher Sparkassenverlag.

Treuhandanstalt. 1991. "Treuhandanstalt schaltet Investmentbanken ein." *Treuhand Monatsinformationen* (September).

Treuhandanstalt. 1993. "Jeder vierte Auftrag durch die öffentliche Hand." *Treuhand Monatsinformationen* (March).

Ulrich, Sigrid, and Winfried Wilhelm. 1991. "Jeder braucht ein Freund." *Manager-magazin* (March).

Underhill, Geoffrey R. D. 1991. "Markets beyond Politics? The State and the Internationalisation of Financial Markets." *European Journal of Political Research* 19 (March/April): 197–225.

"Unter Druck: Dauerstreit um Fusionen der Landesbanken." 1987. *Capital* (October).

Veblen, Thorstein. [1939] 1984. *Imperial Germany and the Industrial Revolution.* Westport: Greenwood Press.

Vitols, Sigurt. 1993a. "Industrial Relations and Restructuring in the German Steel Industry." Wissenschaftszentrum Berlin, Discussion Paper FS I 93–320.

Vitols, Sigurt. 1993b. "National Institutions and the Restructuring of 'Old' Industrial Regions: Germany, Britain and the US." Paper presented at the International Conference on Production Regimes in an Integrating Europe, Berlin.

Vitols, Sigurt. 1994. "German Banks and the Modernization of the Small Firm Sector: Long-Term Finance in Comparative Perspective." Paper presented at the Ninth International Conference of Europeanists, Chicago.

Vitols, Sigurt. 1995. "Corporate Governance versus Economic Governance: Banks and Industrial Restructuring in the U.S. and Germany." Wissenschaftszentrum Berlin, Discussion Paper FS I 95-310.

Vitols, Sigurt. 1998. "Are German Banks Different?" *Small Business Economics* 10 (2): 79–91.

Voigt, Rainer. 1992. "Ostdeutsche Sparkassen weiter auf Erfolgskurs." *Zeitschrift für das gesamte Kreditwesen* 45 (18): 8–9.

Voigt, Rainer. 1997. "Aufbau Ost—Wirtschaftsentwicklung und der Beitrag der Sparkassen." *Sparkasse* 114:230–33.

Völling, Johannes. 1969. "Konzentration und Wettbewerb." *Sparkasse* 86:113–16.

von Rosen, Rüdiger. 1995. "Zweites Finanzmarktförderungsgesetz und Privatanleger." *Die Bank,* no. 1:9–14.

Wandel, Eckhard. 1983. "Das deutsche Bankwesen im Dritten Reich." In *Deutsche Bankengeschichte,* vol. 3. Frankfurt: Fritz Knapp.

Wauschkuhn, Friedrich-Franz. 1977. "Staatliche Gewerbepolitik und frühindustrielles

Unternehmertum in Württemberg von 1806 bis 1848." In *Zur Geschichte der Industrialisierung in den südwestdeutschen Staaten,* ed. Erich Maschke and Jürgen Sydow. Sigmaringen: Thorbecke.

Weinberger, Bruno. 1984. "Die Bedeutung der Sparkassen für die Entwicklung des kommunalen Raumes." In *Standortbestimmung: Entwicklungslinien der deutschen Kreditwirtschaft,* ed. Günther Aschauer. Stuttgart: Deutscher Sparkassenverlag.

Weiss, Ulrich. 1993. "Compliance-Funktion in einer deutschen Universalbank." *Die Bank,* no. 3:136–39.

Wellhöner, Volker. 1989. *Grossbanken und Grossindustrie im Kaiserreich.* Göttingen: Vandenhoeck & Ruprecht.

Welzk, Stefan. 1986. *Boom ohne Arbeitsplätze.* Cologne: Verlag Kiepenheuer & Witsch.

Welzmüller, Rudolf. 1991. "Siemens—Eine Unternehmensanalyse." *WSI Mitteilungen* 44 (10): 620–28.

Wenger, Ekkehard. 1992. "Universalbankensystem und Depotstimmrecht." In *Der Markt für Unternehmenskontrollen,* ed. Helmut Gröner. Berlin: Duncker & Humblot.

Westhoff, Norbert. 1984. *Bankenvertreter in den Beiräten mittelständischer Unternehmen.* Bonn: Stollfuss.

Whale, F. Barrett. [1930] 1968. *Joint-Stock Banking in Germany: A Study of the German Credit Banks before and after the War.* New York: A. M. Kelley.

Wieandt, Paul. 1994. "Wettbewerb im deutschen und europäischen Firmenkundengeschäft." *Bank und Markt* (May).

Wielens, Hans. 1977. *Fragen der Bankorganisation: Führt die verstärkte Marktorganisation der Universalbanken zur Divisionalisierung?* Frankfurt: Fritz Knapp.

Wilhelm, Winfried. 1991. "Manager unter Druck." *Managermagazin* (May).

Winkel, Harald. 1981. *Geschichte der Württembergischen IHKen: Heilbronn, Reutlingen, Stuttgart/Mittlerer Neckar, und Ulm, 1933–1980.* Stuttgart: W. Kohlhammer.

Winkler, Heinrich A. 1974. *Organisierter Kapitalismus.* Göttingen: Vandenhoeck & Ruprecht.

Wixforth, Harald. 1995. *Banken und Schwerindustrie in der Weimarer Republik.* Cologne: Böhlau.

Wurm, Franz F. 1969. *Wirtschaft und Gesellschaft in Deutschland, 1848–1948.* Opladen: Leske.

Wysocki, Günther. 1983. *Untersuchungen zur Wirtschafts- und Sozialgeschichte der Sparkassen im 19. Jahrhundert.* Stuttgart: Deutscher Sparkassenverlag.

Wysocki, Josef. 1985. "Der öffentliche Auftrag der Sparkassen im Zeitalter der Industrialisierung." In *Der öffentliche Auftrag der Sparkassen in der historischen Entwicklung,* ed. Jürgen Mura. Stuttgart: Deutscher Sparkassenverlag.

Wysocki, Josef. 1986. "Die bankmässige Entwicklung der Sparkassen (1908 bis 1931)." In *Die Entwicklung der Sparkassen zu Universalkreditinstituten,* ed. Jürgen Mura. Stuttgart: Deutscher Sparkassenverlag.

Yoshitomi, Masaru. 1997. "The Nature of New Challenges Impinging upon Uniquely Featured Corporate Governance and Board of Directors in Japan." Wharton School. Typescript.

Zahn, Erich. 1981. "Die Förderung von Existenzgründungen in Baden-Württemberg— Eine kritische Analyse der Massnahmen." Stuttgart: Betriebswirtschaftliches Institut der Universität Stuttgart.

Zahn, Erich, et al. 1985. "Erfolgskontrolle der finanziellen Existenzgründungsförderung des Landes Baden-Württemberg." Stuttgart: Betriebswirtschaftliches Institut der Universität Stuttgart.

Zapp, Herbert. 1975. "Zentrale and Dezentrale Planung in einer Grossbank." In *Controlling in Banken und Sparkassen,* ed. Ludwig Mühlhaupt, Henner Schierenbeck, and Hans Wielens. Frankfurt: Fritz Knapp.

Zapp, Herbert. 1985. "Der Kundenbetreuer im Rahmen des Firmenkunden-Marketings einer Grossbank." *Die Bank,* no. 1:10–14.

Ziegler, Rolf, Donald Bender, and Hermann Biehler. 1985. "Industry and Banking in the German Corporate Network." In *Networks of Corporate Power: A Corporate Analysis of Ten Countries,* ed. Frans N. Stokman, Rolf Ziegler, and John Scott. Cambridge: Polity Press.

Zimmermann, Wolf-Konrad. 1984. *Wettbewerbsverzerrungen im deutschen Bankensystem.* Göttingen: Vandenhoeck & Ruprecht.

Zügel, Walter. 1985. "Sparkassen zwischen Marktorientierung und öffentlichem Auftrag aus der Sicht der Praxis." *Sparkasse* 102:19–22.

Zysman, John. 1983. *Governments, Markets, and Growth: Financial Systems and the Politics of Industrial Change.* Ithaca: Cornell University Press.

Zysman, John. 1994. "How Institutions Create Historically Rooted Trajectories of Growth." *Industrial and Corporate Change* 4 (1): 243–83.

Government and Documents

Baden Savings Bank Association. 1994. Annual Report [in German]. Karlsruhe.

Bayerische Landesanstalt für Aufbaufinanzierung. 1987. Annual Report [in German]. Munich.

Bundesverband der Deutschen Industrie (Federal Association of German Industry). 1994. Internal Memorandum (AWW 20/94), 17 October.

Deutsche Ausgleichsbank. 1983. Annual Report [in German]. Bonn.

Deutsche Ausgleichsbank. 1987. Annual Report [in German]. Bonn.

Deutsche Ausgleichsbank. 1993. Annual Report [in German]. Bonn.

Deutsche Ausgleichsbank. 1995. Annual Report [in German]. Bonn.

Deutsche Ausgleichsbank. 1996. Annual Report [in German]. Bonn.

Economics Ministry of Baden-Württemberg. 1977. *Mittelstand Report of Baden-Württemberg.* Stuttgart.

Economics Ministry of Baden-Württemberg. 1982. *Mittelstand Report of Baden-Württemberg*. Stuttgart.

Economics Ministry of Baden-Württemberg. 1986. *Mittelstand Report of Baden-Württemberg*. Stuttgart.

Economics Ministry of Baden-Württemberg. 1992. "Gemeinschaftsinitiative Wirtschaft und Politik: 'Automobilzulieferindustrie'." Press release, 30 October.

Economics Ministry of North Rhine–Westphalia. 1987. *Aussenwirtschaftskonzept Nordrhein-Westfalen*. Düsseldorf.

Economics Ministry of North Rhine–Westphalia. 1988. *Technologieland NRW: 3 Jahre ZENIT*. Düsseldorf.

Economics Ministry of North Rhine–Westphalia. 1992. *Prozessuale Begleitforschung der Regionalisierung der Strukturpolitik in Nordrhein-Westfalen*. Düsseldorf.

Federal Association of German Banks (Bundesverband deutscher Banken). 1994. *Die privaten Banken in den neuen Bundesländern*. March.

Federal Finance Ministry. 1993. *Bundesministerium der Finanzen—Nachrichten*, no. 47 (5 June).

German Bundestag. 1988. Publication 11/3478 (24 November).

German Savings Bank and Giro Association. 1988. Annual Report [in German]. Bonn.

German Savings Bank and Giro Association. 1995. *Leistungen der Sparkassenorganisation in den neuen Bundesländern: Gesamtbilanz Ende 1994*. Bonn.

Investitions-Bank Nordrhein-Westfalen. 1987. Annual Report [in German] Düsseldorf.

Kreditanstalt für Wiederaufbau. 1986. Annual Report [in German]. Frankfurt.

Kreditanstalt für Wiederaufbau. 1987. Annual Report [in German]. Frankfurt.

Kreditanstalt für Wiederaufbau. 1993. Annual Report [in German]. Frankfurt.

Kreditanstalt für Wiederaufbau. 1995. Annual Report [in German]. Frankfurt.

Landeskreditbank Baden-Württemberg. 1982. Annual Report [in German]. Karlsruhe.

Landeskreditbank Baden-Württemberg. 1985. Annual Report [in German]. Karlsruhe.

Landeskreditbank Baden-Württemberg. 1987. Annual Report [in German]. Karlsruhe.

Landeszentralbank in Baden-Württemberg. 1994. Annual Report [in German]. Stuttgart.

Landtag of Baden-Württemberg. Publications: 6/1554 (30 January 1973); 6/3642; 6/5888 (9 August 1974); 6/6657; 6/6662; 6/6999; 6/7284 (5 March 1975); 6/7390 (10 March 1975); 6/8052; 7/1200 (10 February 1977); 7/4421; 8/3523.

Landtag of North Rhine–Westphalia. Plenary Protocols: 6/41 (22 October 1968); 7/117 (14 November 1974); 8/50 (16 June 1977); 8/116 (25 October 1979); 8/127 (8 February 1980); 8/132 (16 April 1980); 9/100 (13 June 1984); 10/54 (10 July 1987); 10/97 (15 December 1988); 10/99 (26 January 1989).

Landtag of North Rhine–Westphalia. Publications: 7/4061 (16 July 1974); 7/4068 (25 July 1974); 8/4557 (22 February 1979); 9/953 (5 August 1981); 10/3552.

Mittelstand Equity Participation Corporation of Baden-Württemberg. 1986. Annual Report [in German]. Stuttgart.

Mittelstand Equity Participation Corporation of Baden-Württemberg. 1994. Annual Report [in German]. Stuttgart.

Saxon State Ministry for Economics and Labor. 1993. *Wirtschaft und Arbeit in Sachsen: Bericht zur wirtschaftlichen Lage im Freistaat Sachsen.* Dresden.

State Ministry of Baden-Württemberg. 1993. *Bericht der Zukunftskommission Wirtschaft 2000.* Stuttgart.

Statistics Office of Baden-Württemberg. 1987. *Baden-Württemberg: Economic Facts and Figures.* Stuttgart.

Steinbeis Foundation. 1986. Annual Report [in German]. Stuttgart.

Steinbeis Foundation. 1991. Annual Report [in German]. Stuttgart.

Steinbeis Foundation. 1994. Annual Report [in German]. Stuttgart.

Surety Bank of Baden-Württemberg. 1986. Annual Report [in German]. Stuttgart.

Surety Bank of Baden-Württemberg. 1994. Annual Report [in German]. Stuttgart.

Württemberg Cooperative Association. 1985. Annual Report [in German]. Stuttgart.

Württemberg Cooperative Association. 1994. Annual Report [in German]. Stuttgart.

Württemberg Savings Bank Association. 1994. Annual Report [in German]. Stuttgart.

Index

Westdeutsche Landesbank (WestLB):
commercial expansion of, 140–41;
and the construction sector, 139; creation of, 52, 135; crises of, 56; export
promotion by, 150; government control of, 137–40, 141, 256n. 23; and
government industrial intervention,
127; influence in firms, 134; international expansion of, 53, 90, 94, 141;
and Landesbank mergers/alliances, 64;
and machine-tool sector, 143; and
mergers and acquisitions, 111; privatization of, 140, 257n. 35; in the regional policy network of NRW,
133–45; and the savings banks, 138,
141, 152–54; scandals involving,
139–40; shareholdings by, 136–37,
142–43, 256nn. 29, 30; and SMEs,
141, 147; and steel industry, 144; and
SüdwestLB, 183, 247n. 86; in supervisory boards, 256n. 32; and technology
policy, 149
Westphalian Girozentrale, 51
World Trade Organization (WTO), 14
Württembergische Bank, 180
Württembergische Vereinsbank, 159

Zügel, Walther, 178, 181, 246n. 80, 265n.
65
Zysman, John: definition of market
logic, 239n. 3; and industrial adjustment, 6–7, 232, 240nn. 13, 15,
254n. 1; and steel industry, 103,
131